NEW DIRECTIONS IN SCANDINAVIAN STUDIES
Christine Ingebritsen and Andy Nestingen, Series Editors

NEW DIRECTIONS IN SCANDINAVIAN STUDIES

This series offers interdisciplinary approaches to the study of the Nordic region of Scandinavia and the Baltic States and their cultural connections in North America. By redefining the boundaries of Scandinavian studies to include the Baltic States and Scandinavian America, the series presents books that focus on the study of the culture, history, literature, and politics of the North.

Small States in International Relations, edited by Christine Ingebritsen, Iver B. Neumann, Sieglinde Gstohl, and Jessica Beyer

Danish Cookbooks: Domesticity and National Identity, 1616–1901, by Carol Gold

Crime and Fantasy in Scandinavia: Fiction, Film, and Social Change, by Andrew Nestingen

Selected Plays of Marcus Thrane, translated and introduced by Terje I. Leiren

Munch's Ibsen: A Painter's Visions of a Playwright, by Joan Templeton

Knut Hamsun: The Dark Side of Literary Brilliance, by Monika Žagar

Nordic Exposures: Scandinavian Identities in Classical Hollywood Cinema, by Arne Lunde

Icons of Danish Modernity: Georg Brandes and Asta Nielsen, by Julie K. Allen

Danish Folktales, Legends, and Other Stories, edited and translated by Timothy R. Tangherlini

The Power of Song: Nonviolent National Culture in the Baltic Singing Revolution, by Guntis Šmidchens

Church Resistance to Nazism in Norway, 1940–1945, by Arne Hassing

Christian Krohg's Naturalism, by Øystein Sjåstad

Fascism and Modernist Literature in Norway, by Dean Krouk

Sacred to the Touch: Nordic and Baltic Religious Wood Carving, by Thomas A. DuBois

Christian Krohg's Naturalism

Øystein Sjåstad

UNIVERSITY OF WASHINGTON PRESS

Seattle and London

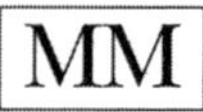

Publication of Christian Krohg's Naturalism *has been aided by a grant from the Millard Meiss Publication Fund of the College Art Association.*

Additional support was provided by the Research Council of Norway and the Department of Scandinavian Studies at the University of Washington.

Printed and bound in the United States of America
Composed in Adobe Caslon Pro, typeface designed by William Caslon
21 20 19 18 17 5 4 3 2 1

University of Washington Press
www.washington.edu/uwpress

Library of Congress Cataloging-in-Publication Data
Names: Sjåstad, Øystein, author.
Title: Christian Krohg's naturalism / Øystein Sjåstad.
Description: Seattle : University of Washington Press, 2017. | Series: New directions in Scandinavian studies | Includes bibliographical references and index. |
Identifiers: LCCN 2017017194 (print) | LCCN 2017019354 (ebook) | ISBN 9780295742076 (ebook) | ISBN 9780295742069 (hardcover : alk. paper)
Subjects: LCSH: Krohg, Christian, 1852–1925—Criticism and interpretation. | Naturalism in art—Europe. | Realism in art—Europe. | Europe—Intellectual life—19th century.
Classification: LCC ND773.K68 (ebook) | LCC ND773.K68 S59 2017 (print) | DDC 759.9481—dc23
LC record available at https://lccn.loc.gov/2017017194

Cover image: (front) *Detail.* Christian Krohg, *Albertine in the Police Doctor's Waiting Room* (1887). Oil on canvas, 211 × 326 cm. Photo: Jacques Lathion/The National Museum of Art, Architecture and Design, Oslo. (back) Christian Krohg, *Port Side!* (1879). Oil on canvas, 99 x 70 cm. Photo: Jacques Lathion / The National Museum of Art, Architecture and Design, Oslo.

The paper used in this publication is acid-free and meets the minimum requirements of American National Standard for Information Sciences—Permanence of Paper for Printed Library Materials, ANSI Z39.48–1984. ∞

For my mother, Asbjørg Sjåstad

Contents

Illustrations

Acknowledgments

> The modern method, which I strive to pursue, and which is beginning to be introduced in all the moral sciences, consists in considering human products, and particularly works of art, as facts and products of which it is essential to mark the characteristics and seek the causes, and nothing more. Thus understood, science neither proscribes nor pardons; it verifies and explains. It does not say to you, "Despise Dutch art because it is vulgar, and prize only Italian art." Nor does it say to you, "Despise Gothic art because it is vulgar, and prize only Greek art." It leaves everyone free to follow their own predilections, to prefer that which is germane to one's temperament, and to study with the greatest care that which best corresponds to the development of one's own mind.
>
> HIPPOLYTE TAINE

This book has been long in the making. My passion for Christian Krohg's art started when I flipped through a coffee-table book with Norwegian artwork at my local school library. I was instantly struck by Krohg's emotional way of painting people; I immediately connected with his figures. A few years later, when I was able to view for the first time an original Krohg canvas, I was struck by his wonderful sense of color and his playful brushwork. At the same time, I became more interested in Krohg's character and his important contributions to Norwegian art as a teacher, art critic, author, editor, journalist, and activist.

As time passed, I grew more involved with nineteenth-century French art, but a few years ago, I decided to return to Krohg and his work in a more dedicated manner and try to place his art in a European context. Could Krohg be understood as an original artist at work on the larger art scene, or was he strictly a local Norwegian hero? In 2011, I was granted a three-year postdoctoral scholarship from the Norwegian Research Council for my project "Christian Krohg's Naturalism: Painting in the Light of Émile Zola's *Méthode Expérimentale.*" This book is the result. With it, I hope to show that Krohg truly can be understood as one of the most original naturalist painters of late nineteenth-century Europe.

Many people have helped me on this journey with Krohg and his work. First, I must thank Øivind Storm Bjerke, who has followed my work closely for many years. His support has been of extreme importance. I must also give my thanks to Norman Bryson. During my stay at the University of California, San Diego, in 2007 and 2008, I wrote a paper on Krohg's naturalist art for Bryson's "Re-thinking Art History" course. Our conversations on this topic inspired me to return to this material after I had finished my book on French art, *A Theory of the* Tache *in Nineteenth-Century Painting* (2014). The observant reader will notice that the *Tache* book in a way is a *pendant* to the Krohg book. Both works evolved out of my understanding of Bryson's semiotic theory concerning the discursive and figural image. The *Tache* book was an exploration of what could be termed the semiotics of the figural sign, meaning signs without discursive meaning, or what I identify as the index in C. S. Peirce's philosophy: the brushmark as a trace. Can meaning arise from such "meaningless" signs? The present book, on the other hand, emerges from the other term referenced in Bryson's theory and is a discussion of the semiotics of the discursive image: an image filled with literary and political content, in which form often plays a secondary role. The discursive/figural model has proven fruitful in my study of naturalism in painting. These two books demonstrate how paintings created during the same period can produce meaning in different ways, based on different ideas about what is "real" and what is "life." Impressionism and the semiotics of the figural are concerned with an idea of the direct, unmediated relation between work and the world, while naturalism and the semiotics of the discursive are about experimentation and the testing of different sign categories in the search for a realistic image.

In 2012, I had the great pleasure to return to California, where I spent a year as a visiting scholar at the University of California, Berkeley. I was soon adopted by the welcoming environment in the Department of Scandinavian. I would like to offer my warmest thanks to the department's faculty, especially Linda H. Rugg, Mark Sandberg, and Karin Sanders, as well as the graduate students, for generously including me and letting me present my material at their university. I must also thank my academic home, the Department of Philosophy, Classics, and History of Art and Ideas at University of Oslo. It is such a good place to be. I also wish to thank the department for financial support for expenses related to images and imaging. I thank the Norwegian University Center in Paris for a travel grant to carry out research for this project in Paris during the 2011 fall semester. The project also received a publication grant from the Norwegian Research Council.

Where not otherwise noted, I am responsible for the translations from the Scandinavian languages, German, and French to English. My warmest gratitude goes to Nicholas Parkinson and Arlyne Moi for helping me with these translations. (A short note on translations of titles provided for artworks, novels, and other texts: All artwork titles are given in English. All Scandinavian titles of literary works are translated into English. If an English translation of French and German texts exists, I have used that; otherwise, I have retained the original titles). In addition, I thank former director Audun Eckhoff and the National Museum in Oslo as well as the former director at Lillehammer Art Museum, Svein Olav Hoff, for all their help and support with image rights. I also want to acknowledge the efficiency, patience, and professionalism of the University of Washington Press staff. The whole process in working with them has been a pleasure. I thank the peer reviewers for sharpening my final thoughts on Krohg, as their comments have certainly improved my book. I have presented papers on Krohg at numerous conferences and discussed my project with many individuals over the years. I will not try to list them all, lest I forget some, but I do want to mention one person: Patricia Gray Berman. Thanks, Pat, for all your help and support for my Krohg project.

I gratefully acknowledge the permissions granted by copyright holders and institutions to reproduce the images printed in this book. Every attempt has been made to obtain permission to reproduce copyrighted material. If any proper acknowledgment has been overlooked, copyright holders are invited to inform the author of the oversight.

CHRISTIAN KROHG'S NATURALISM

Introduction

In an article translated from *La revue des revues*, published in the Norwegian radical journal *Samtiden* in 1893 and titled "Er vi syge?" (Are we sick?), the Italian historian Guillermo Ferrero discussed the predominance of the theme of degeneration in nineteenth-century art and sciences: "The educated, poets, artists, everyone who thinks and creates, gathers inspiration and materials from the forms of degeneration."[1] He described how sickness, crime, madness, suicide, and prostitution had entirely overshadowed all other topics in science and art, and asked if the world had become an enormous hospital or, rather, a mental hospital. Ferrero sought to capture the zeitgeist of his era:

> They [artists and scientists] are brothers, and that is how one can explain the mutual admiration they nurture for each other, and that, to say the truth, is not without egoism: Taine's admiration for Lombroso; Lombroso's admiration for Zola, Ibsen, Flaubert, Dostoyevsky, Taine; Zola's admiration for Lombroso. Without knowing it, all of them have been working at the same task, which is to say, at raising the great memorial to the degeneration of this fin de siècle that historians of the nineteenth century will find to be one of its most remarkable phenomena.[2]

The Norwegian painter, novelist, critic, and journalist Christian Krohg (1852–1925) can be placed into this chain of admiration. His naturalist art of the 1880s was a symptom of "the degeneration of this fin de siècle" but also an original interpretation of it.

The latter half of the nineteenth century saw a growing interest in sociology and anthropology: the society was mapped out in detail and everything was accounted for through statistics. Norway and its capital, Kristiania (now Oslo), were studied by scientists who examined the escalation of diseases, death rates, prostitution, and poverty.[3] Naturalist art became the visualization of these subjects. In naturalist aesthetics we find both an admiration for scientific research and progress as well as a socialist critique of the modern age's admiration for positivism and materialism (and how this resulted in capitalism and class society). This double-edged attitude was present in Krohg's art and in the very nature of naturalism, the mode in which he painted and wrote.

On December 20, 1886, the Norwegian radical newspaper *Dagbladet* published a small ad on the front page advertising Christian Krohg's new book *Albertine* (1886), issued by the

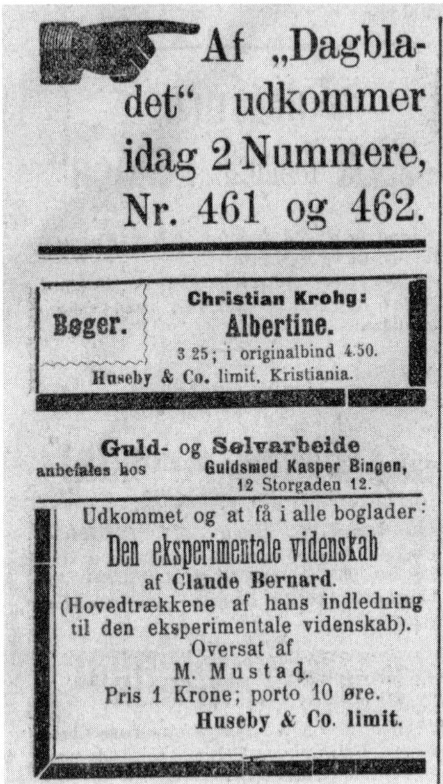
Af „Dagbladet“ udkommer idag 2 Nummere, Nr. 461 og 462.

Bøger. Christian Krohg: Albertine. 3 25; i originalbind 4.50. Huseby & Co. limit. Kristiania.

Guld- og Sølvarbeide anbefales hos Guldsmed Kasper Bingen, 12 Storgaden 12.

Udkommet og at få i alle boglader:
Den eksperimentale videnskab
af Claude Bernard.
(Hovedtrækkene af hans indledning til den eksperimentale videnskab).
Oversat af
M. Mustad.
Pris 1 Krone; porto 10 øre.
Huseby & Co. limit.

Figure I.1.

Advertisement for Christian Krohg's *Albertine* and Claude Bernard's *An Introduction to the Study of Experimental Medicine* in *Dagbladet*, December 20, 1886. Facsimile.

leftist publisher Huseby. The ad was removed the next day, as were all copies of the book from the city's bookstores. The police seized *Albertine* immediately after its publication for violating the good morals of the citizens with its descriptions of prostitution. That same day saw the promotion of another book by Huseby, right under the *Albertine* ad: the Norwegian translation of Claude Bernard's *An Introduction to the Study of Experimental Medicine* (1865, fig. I.1). It is an interesting coincidence that the two books were published simultaneously. They both exemplified the intellectual, aesthetic, and political climate in Kristiania in the 1880s, and Bernard plays an important part in my understanding of naturalism. The present book is, however, not primarily a study of direct influences. The ideas of Bernard, Taine, Zola, Darwin, and others are part of a shared cultural discourse in which Krohg also took part. He was in many instances directly influenced by Zola's writings, but often I discuss Krohg's art as an indirect response to or test of the ideas and attitudes of the time.[4] His art certainly reflects, in original ways, the gestalt of the Tainean and Zolaesque imagination.[5] In 1894 an anonymous critic in *The Art Critic* wrote:

> Zolaism in painting began with Courbet, a revolutionist who saw truth in everything which offended the Academy and conventional taste, and became an established fact in Manet, who beheld in nature combinations of colors never before seen on canvas. After these first endeavors to *étonner les imbeciles* and

embêter les bourgeois, naturalism became a natural language, unrestrained, mature, and simple in Millet and Bastien Lepage, and, perhaps, in old Troyon, though he is more bourgeois. They are naturalists by instinct, without any theoretical resolution, almost without any show of vanity.[6]

This study argues that Christian Krohg, in his 1880s works, was one of the most Zolaesque painters on the European art scene, producing true Zolaism in painting. The American art critic, collector, and curator Christian Brinton referred to Krohg in 1922 as "the epic apostle of Zolaism in paint."[7] I will elucidate these claims by looking at Zola's theories and their reception in Scandinavian intellectual circles, alongside Taine's aesthetics, and the ways Krohg interpreted Zola's aims and reacted, both directly and indirectly, to his methods. I hope that this contextualization (I could call it a "playful iconology") will reveal why Krohg's art was seen as radical in Scandinavia and show that he stood out as an original artist in a wider European context.

Another aim of this book is to examine Krohg's art as an extraordinary test case for the study of naturalism. Nineteenth-century naturalism entailed a complex relationship between literature and painting, text and image, discursivity and figurality. Naturalist painters struggled with literary content and the challenges of theatricality. Meanwhile naturalist novelists wanted literature to be as visually striking as painting. Naturalist literature and painting were entangled in each other's areas of specialty, yet it was also a period when the arts were trying to be self-critical and focus on their own materiality and distinctiveness. As both a prominent painter and a novelist, Krohg presents a particularly interesting example of this complicated connection.

THE NEW NORDIC SCHOOL OF PAINTING

Christian Brinton wrote the following positivist summary of Nordic art in his introduction to *Scandinavian Art Illustrated* (1922):

> While it may appear extraneous to apply to aesthetic considerations the rigid determinism exemplified by Hippolyte Taine, yet it is obvious that a knowledge of the land and its people is essential to a proper understanding of the art of a given country. . . . You will fail to grasp the spirit of Northern painting if you are not in some degree familiar with the conformation of the country and the composition of the light that slants obliquely upon a shimmering fjord or a sparse upland pasture. There can be no question concerning the fundamental differences between the art of the North and the art of the South. The one is septentrional, the other meridional, with all the distinctions this implies, and it should be apparent to any observant person that these divergences are in large part due to circumstances of race, clime, and climate.[8]

Almost forty years before, in conjunction with the Exposition Universelle des Beaux-Arts d'Anvers in 1885, similar stereotypical thoughts appeared about Scandinavian art. The commentator in *Courrier de l'art* wrote that Norway—this little corner of northern Europe—

finally has developed an art characteristic for its race and being, and that Paris now "sees rushing in from the vicinities of the North Pole, a swarm of those starved for 'plein air.' The impressionists, the naturalists, and even the impossibilists there have impassioned enthusiasts: the greatest audacities of Manet are timid efforts next to certain paintings by Mr. Krohg and Mr. Wentzel."[9] Krohg exhibited three canvases in Antwerp, including *Look Ahead* (1884, fig. 1.6) and *Portrait of Gerhard Munthe* (1885, fig. 1.9),[10] and it is clear that he was seen as one of the most talented representatives of the Norwegian school at this exhibition.

It is interesting to see how French critics wrote about Scandinavian art. When the French critic Louis Edmond Duranty described the Scandinavian section for *La gazette des beaux-arts*'s publication on the Universal Exhibition of 1878, he turned to a positivistic art-critical language with a focus on a land's meteorological (*les tendances météorologiques*) and geological conditions: "In these northern regions, we find ourselves faced with natural phenomena. Painting there often is somewhat metrological. Red mountains, green waterfalls, blue rocks, black suns—in a word, all manners of disordering, inverting, and disrupting things, constituting an anti-pictorial, disharmonious genre that is disturbing to the eyes and the spirit, although it may enrich a treatise on optics with curious phenomena."[11]

In the late 1870s a new and ambitious generation of Scandinavian artists started traveling to Paris rather than Rome or the German cities. An interesting question is whether this made the Scandinavian school more French or more Scandinavian—or something new, Franco-Scandinavian? When writing for the *Gazette des beaux-arts* about the Nordic exhibition in Copenhagen in 1888, Maurice Hamel stated that the Norwegian school was characterized by observation, and that painters such as Sven Jørgensen, Gustav Wentzel, and Krohg were truthful interpreters of modern life. Here he describes Krohg's *North Wind* (1887, fig. 1.12) and *Sunshine* (1886):

> M. Krohg is not an introvert but totally an extrovert in love with strength and action. He knows the sea and sailors, the struggle of man and the ocean's waves. His sections of boats, impudently truncated, with the helmsman who rises powerfully from the sea or against the sky, well launched in their movement, imply the wave, the pitch and the roll without actually depicting them. Extremely original in effect and boldly painted, this seaman's torso emerges from below deck to observe the threatening weather. The often coarse colors soften on the occasion of a charming young fisherwoman seen in the fresh light of spring. The brush of this impassionate artist can reveal a wonderful tenderness.[12]

Art critic André Michel wrote that this Copenhagen show clearly illustrated the new Nordic school of painting: "This little crowd forms in old Europe one of the most homogenous and most vital schools, and each group, the Norwegians, Swedes and Danes—and one can also add the Finnish people—preserves its independent physiognomy."[13] In many of the reviews, the Nordic painters were largely grouped into one school, although different countries were also discussed as individual regions with distinct traits and sensibilities. To Hamel, art is an expression of a people's dream of happiness, and it is determined by social life and natural environment. That is why naturalism in the North is different from art elsewhere, and also why the three Scandinavian countries have slightly different arts: "The naturalism familiar to the North takes on different aspects within three countries very close in origin, religion and language."[14]

Overall, the Nordic school was characterized, according to the critics, by clean air, sea breeze, and mountain air; its art was seen as primitive, healthy, and easy.[15] Georges Lafenestre, curator at the Louvre, professor of aesthetics and art history at the Collège de France, and member of the Académie des Beaux-Arts and of the jury of paintings and drawings at the 1889 Universal Exhibition, asserted that the Nordic school was poignantly original. The Nordic artists were, according to Lafenestre, freer from continental academic traditions, and because of their isolation and distance from the interruptions of audiences and critics, approached human beings and nature with a purer gaze: "Here is a whole group of really individual, convinced, interesting artists, who from their homelands bring with them an original and striking art."[16] As did so many other critics, Lafanestre drew an image of the crude, primitive, isolated, honest Nordic painter who paints landscapes, farmers, and fishermen. The Norwegians were, according to Lafanestre, less amenable to French assimilation than the Swedes.

The same year, the French critic Charles Ponsonailhe wrote in *Les artistes scandinaves à Paris* (1889), following the Universal Exhibition, that among the foreign school, the Scandinavians were closest to the French, robust and copious in their production: "Sweden, Norway and Denmark, free of pictorial traditions, peoples trembling with a beautiful and fertile youth, were quick to judge the inanity of academic education; without any hesitation, they adopted pleinairism, which was also in tune with their reason and temperament."[17] Scandinavian art was, to many, the perfect combination of French aesthetics and local exoticism. It seems that for Parisian observers *l'école norvégienne* was especially characterized by realistic and rough representations of the world. Ponsonailhe wrote that "Norway remains a self-sufficient people, having retained a distinctive character that is a littler coarse, but never trite."[18] When a number of Nordic artists exhibited at the Societé Nationale des Beaux-Arts's Paris Salon of 1902, Hamel repeated much of the same: "The Scandinavian school is more faithful to us, and indeed closely related to ours." He went on to say that art in Sweden, Denmark, and Norway had "a common character of sincerity, freshness, youthfulness, and vigorous ardor."[19] Krohg exhibited *Port Side!* (also called *Pilote*, 1879, fig. 1.1) at that show, prompting Hamel to add: "The Pilot by Krohg is powerfully realistic."[20]

It is interesting to note that Norway was often viewed as the most "naturalistic" in its artistic output, at least among the Nordic countries. In Brinton's words:

> The Norwegians espoused the gospel of naturalism in all sincerity, each pursuing his pathway with independence of spirit. That same tendency, which in Sweden initiated a school of synthetic landscape interpreters, and in Denmark fostered a genuine decorative renaissance, aroused in Norway a different set of reactions. In particular it gave birth to a group afflicted with social and pathological sympathies. In literature this coterie included Hans Jæger, Arne Garborg, Gunnar Heiberg, and Knut Hamsun, and in art it found its leading exponents in

> Christian Krohg and Edvard Munch. Robust and defiantly objective looms the massive form of Krohg, while in the shadowland of an acute subjectivity lingers the solitary, enigmatic apparition of Munch.[21]

A NEGOTIATED MODERNISM

In the history of art, Krohg can be said to represent what art historian Thor J. Mednick has called a "negotiated modernism." Mednick uses this term in discussing Krohg's Danish colleague Peder Severin Krøyer: "It is argued here that Krøyer was trying to create a visual style calibrated to be effective not only in Copenhagen but in Paris as well: a negotiated modernism that would be at once comfortingly familiar and intriguingly exotic to both audiences."[22] This "negotiated modernism" is common to all the different naturalisms around Europe in the 1880s; it represents a negotiation between Paris and the national art scenes. Nordic art is an interesting example of an art that moves between the local and the cosmopolitan.

The present study of Krohg situates him within a large and complex web of ideas and images. Traditionally his art has been examined exclusively in a Norwegian context, as a local version of the new Parisian trends of naturalism and impressionism. He is a minor figure in a European context, mostly known as Edvard Munch's early mentor. Sometimes his works are viewed in a Scandinavian or Nordic perspective. This study seeks to combine these three different but related contexts and examine Krohg at once as a Norwegian, Scandinavian/Nordic, and European artist (but my emphasis will be on the European context)—an approach that corresponds to his own experience. Nordic artists in the 1880s thought of themselves as European; they received their education in Germany and France, traveled to southern Europe on study trips, read German and French newspapers, journals, and books. They took an active part in European intellectual life, and at the same time many of them, including Krohg, were immersed in their homeland's art scene, exhibiting, writing, teaching, and participating in artists' organizations. At the same time, Nordic artists were identified, both locally and abroad, as members of the Scandinavian school. A number of Nordic exhibitions and Nordic art meetings were held in those years. In Paris there was an informal Scandinavian Society whose members assembled in each other's studios for discussions and parties, in which someone might give a lecture, play the piano, or sing. Krohg and his generation identified themselves as belonging together as a group, and they hung out together in Germany and France, rather than mixing with the locals or with artists from southern or eastern Europe or the United Kingdom. The Scandinavians in Paris can be seen, as art historian Brian Dudley Barrett puts it, as an "urban artists' colony."[23] (Nonetheless, the Swedish painter Eva Bonnier wrote from Paris on March 28, 1885, "The Norwegians are thus the only ones of the Scandinavians that try to hold together.")[24] One can see such a Scandinavian grouping in Hugo Birger's *Scandinavian Artists' Luncheon at Café Ledoyen, on Varnishing Day 1886* (1886), with recognizable depictions of painters Albert Edelfelt and Carl Larsson. Severin Segelcke's painting *Scandinavians at Café de la Régence* (1894) features, among others, the novelists Jonas Lie and Herman Bang, composer Edvard Grieg, and painter Frits Thaulow.

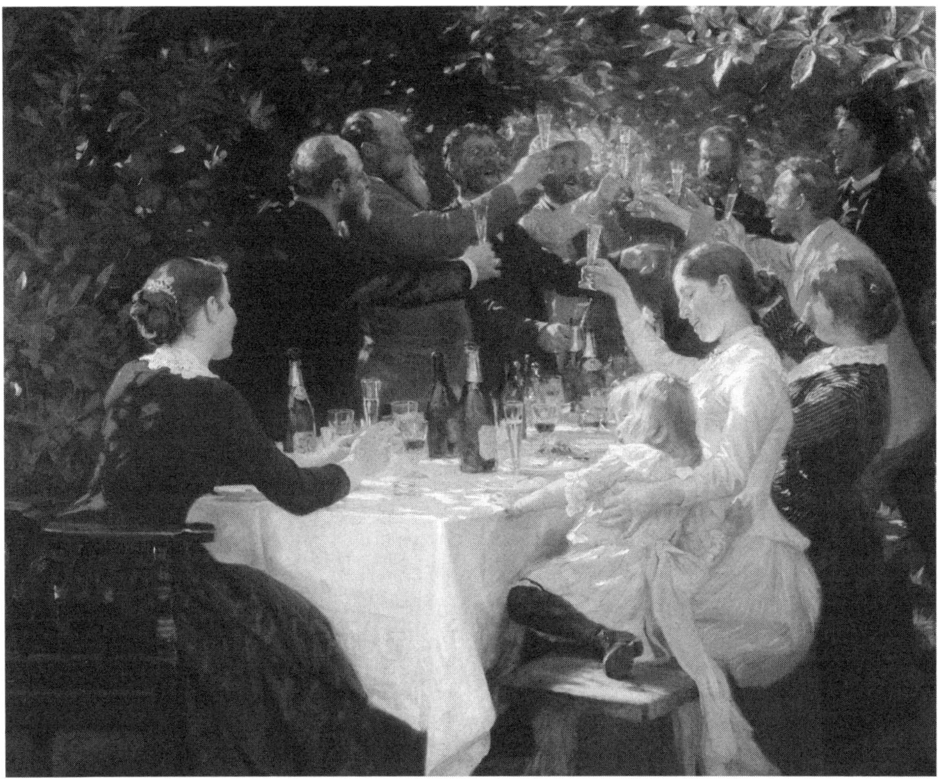

Figure I.2. Peder Severin Krøyer, *Hip, Hip, Hurrah!* (1888). Oil on canvas, 134.5 × 165.5 cm. Gothenburg Museum of Art, Sweden. © Photo: O. Væring Eftf. AS, Norway.

At the universal exhibitions or other large shows, and in the international art historical literature, these artists were often grouped together as members of the Scandinavian school of European art. Even today, for both academic and practical reasons, Scandinavian studies categorizes authors and artists as Scandinavian or Nordic rather than Norwegian, Swedish, Danish, Icelandic, or Finnish. As art historian Patricia G. Berman writes, "By the early 1990s, the notion of a pan-Nordic set of formal, aesthetic, and cultural issues shaping local painting became accepted."[25] The Skagen painters were a typical pan-Nordic group, and in *Hip, Hip, Hurrah!* (1888, fig. I.2) Krøyer has included Danish, Swedish, and Norwegian painters from that colony; Krohg, with his large golden beard and a glass of champagne, appears close to the center of the composition.

It has become usual to talk about Nordic modernism as a movement distinct from European modernism. Traditionally the Nordic countries have been seen, like many other places far from Paris, as outposts where authors and artists did their best to copy the French masters. But as the foreword to the anthology *European and Nordic Modernisms* (2004) states, "Nordic Modernism was not just a passive recipient of international trends. Rather, we encounter an intricate interplay of trends and ideas where Nordic authors also make significant contributions to European Modernism."[26] In Patricia G. Berman's words, "The history of Danish painting can be outlined as a series of subtle tensions between nationalism and internationalism, and as offering shifting affiliations with historical memory produced within a newly marginalized country on the edge of Europe."[27] The same can be said of Norwegian painting. I will not address nationalism or the national identity of young Norway in this book. Krohg thought of himself as a European and was not interested in creating a national art. Instead, I will focus on Krohg as a representative of European realism and naturalism with an awareness of the Norwegian and Nordic contexts (local cultural, political, social, and ideological powers). Nordic artists such as Krohg demonstrate that there existed in Europe not one modernism but many modernisms.

This last view is also the starting point for the literary historian Toril Moi as she examines Henrik Ibsen's overlooked modernity. Moi's study is relevant to this book because Ibsen was an intellectual hero for Krohg and his generation of radical artists, and because Moi demonstrates that realism and modernism were not opposites: "Realism . . . is not one; to cast something called 'realism' as modernism's negative other simply will not do."[28] In her view, as in mine, realism and naturalism are not formally naïve or historically passé. Part of this argument is that theatricality is by its nature not-modern, which is why nineteenth-century drama, including Ibsen's work, has not been perceived as belonging to modernism, unlike the formally self-reflexive novels or paintings of Flaubert and Manet.[29] Michael Fried defines modernism in painting as absorbed and antitheatrical. This kind of vocabulary formed part of the art discourse in the 1880s as well; Krohg was dissatisfied with his large painting *Albertine in the Police Doctor's Waiting Room* because it was too theatrical and not realistic enough. My claim is that theatricality in itself is not the opposite of modernity. Naturalist painting, such as Krohg's works in the 1880s and the art of French naturalists Jules Bastien-Lepage and Léon Lhermitte among others, have been excluded from the Great History of Art because of their theatricality, whereas Manet and the impressionists have been praised as the real modernists. Naturalism is *too* narrative, *too* easy, *too* figurative, *too* straightforward, *too* popular, *too* melodramatic, or *too* discursive. It has been considered, often rightly so, as the remains of academism. The influence of visual culture on art history has shown, however, that the art scene is more complex and varied; as art historian Hollis Clayson states in her discussion of Edgar Degas and Henri Gervex, "The modernist and the *pompier* modern life painter can be reincorporated into a shared sphere for social and sexual ideologies, even while considering the different kind of ideological work their images perform or are meant to perform."[30] This shared social sphere is what the present study of Krohg is about. I would also suggest that Krohg's art shows that there is no fundamental opposition between naturalism and sophisticated, formal, critical reflection.

A "LOST" GENERATION?

Krohg was born in 1852 and was a contemporary of Léon Lhermitte, Alfred Roll, Jules Bastien-Lepage, Gustave Caillebotte, Jean-François Raffaëlli, and Henri Gervex. He was part of the generation between impressionism and neo-impressionism, born some ten years after Claude Monet, twenty years after Édouard Manet, and about thirty years after Gustave Courbet. Georges Seurat was born a few years after him. Michael Fried describes the generation of around 1850 as "lost" and writes that it is hard to place a painter like Caillebotte, Krohg's close contemporary in the French art world.[31] Fried terms Caillebotte's art "material impressionism," as opposed to "idealist impressionism."[32] The latter is the original meaning of impressionism, referring to the ambition of its practitioners to paint sensations of things and not the things themselves. Material impressionism is a return to the realisms before impressionism but influenced by Monet's ocular impressionism. Caillebotte and Krohg were representatives of the kind of realism that evolved in Europe in the 1870s and 1880s, which does not fit into the dichotomy between avant-garde impressionism and reactionary academism, often termed naturalism. Their stylistic realism was creatively aware of older realisms, impressionism, and photography, and it operated as a sort of stylistic negotiation. Kirk Varnedoe describes this "special kind of realism": "This unstable strain of later Realism is the product of a peculiar conjunction of forces in a limited time period—often a stretching of the possibilities of Realist style at its last hour."[33] Fried calls Caillebotte "an intertextual painter par excellence, one who worked with a latecomer's knowledge of the entire modern realist tradition vividly present to his mind."[34] This is true of several ambitious artists born around 1850, including Krohg.

CHAPTER ONE

Christian Krohg, the Radical Naturalist

He [Krohg] had in a youthful way his mouth full of theories, and he sought after the most extreme views so that he could acknowledge them.

GEORG BRANDES DESCRIBING THE TWENTY-FIVE-YEAR OLD CHRISTIAN KROHG

His [Krohg's] cocksure resoluteness impressed me a lot. I have never met anyone who so honed and polished their meanings and their fanaticism out in the light as he did.

BJØRN BJØRNSON ON THE TWENTY-FIVE-YEAR-OLD KROHG

As an author—I mean even just as someone who writes about art—he is known as a fanatic, yes, a true zealot for Modernism, and it is a Modernism driven to such a thoughtless extreme that it can't walk ten steps down the road without stumbling over its own legs. He seems seriously to believe that mankind's development and work can develop to the point where the Now is perpetually detached from the Past and turns completely away from the recent past, thus sparkling in isolated splendors, only to be quickly snuffed out.

JULIUS LANGE, 1892

CHRISTIAN Krohg was by the mid-1880s a well-known name in Norwegian cultural life. He was part of the intellectual milieu later known as "les révoltés Scandinaves,"[1] and together with his good friend and fellow painter Frits Thaulow (1847–1906), he set out, in Thaulow's words in 1880, "to scare the good bourgeois," to irritate, and "to challenge good taste."[2] The most important Norwegian art historian, Lorentz Dietrichson (1834–1917), called Krohg "the leading power in our social radical extreme left wing,"[3] and the preeminent art critic Andreas Aubert (1851–1913) stated in 1884 that Krohg was Norway's most cosmopolitan artist.[4] To Aubert, Krohg was the most typical example of a Scandinavian artist following in Manet's tracks.[5] Krohg had studied in Karlsruhe and

Berlin in the 1870s under Hans Gude and Karl Gussow, had been to Paris several times, and was an important member of the Skagen painters. Michael Ancher wrote about Krohg's arrival in Skagen in 1879: "Krohg came right from Max Klinger's circle and was the most radical one in every field."[6]

Of Krohg's large exhibition in Kristiania in 1885, *Dagbladet*'s critic wrote that Krohg was an artist people could not agree upon. Many beholders thought there were too many drawing mistakes in his paintings and that he painted ugly subjects. The critic Olaf Hansson noted that Krohg had become over the last few years "bolder and bolder, both in choice of motifs and in the way he paints them."[7] Hansson reported that the audience found Krohg's paintings of the poor and suffering brutal and offensive, but that his images were hard to forget: "He has, with gradually increasing intensity and compassionate truth, represented the struggle for life through a series of high-quality artworks."[8] (Notice the Darwinist theme in this quote.) In 1925 the Swedish art historian Carl G. Laurin called Krohg "a Norwegian Courbet" and wrote that as a painter in the 1880s Krohg was "the one in the Nordic countries that most successfully gave us what the age wanted to say and that he in many ways in his over fifty years of work has made the greatest artistic contribution in Nordic art."[9] In Laurin's view Krohg was the most successful naturalist in the Nordic countries.[10] Painter Eilif Peterssen wrote in 1885: "Anyone who has paid interested attention to our art knows how isolated Krohg stands with his talent—perhaps more than any other."[11] In 1885 Krohg was the most radical painter in Scandinavia: he painted the most shocking and "ugly" motifs in the new French manner.

EDUCATION

Krohg came from a renowned and respected bourgeois family. His grandfather, also named Christian Krohg, was a politician and a law professor with a specialization in criminal law. He became a national hero for his work on Norway's independence in 1814. His son, Georg Anton Krohg, also held a law degree, but was more interested in arts and letters. He worked as a journalist and editor and knew many artists of his generation, including Adolph Tidemand and Hans Gude, his son's first professor. The Krohg family was conservative, although with liberal tendencies; they supported the right-wing party Høyre. The young Christian Krohg had to finish a four-year law degree before being allowed to pursue his art studies. Among his favorite artists at that time were Paul Delaroche, Gustave Doré, and Tidemand—rather conservative choices. This soon changed. Krohg's mother died when he was eight, and his father followed her in 1873, the year Christian completed his law degree. He was now free to follow his heart, and over the next ten years he developed into the most radical painter in Scandinavia; he even became, for a period, a close friend and working partner of the bohemian anarchist Hans Jæger (1854–1910), nicknamed "Zola of the North."[12]

Krohg first studied art under Hans Gude (1825–1903) in Karlsruhe; soon afterward, he became a disciple of Karl Gussow (1843–1907). When Gussow was appointed professor at the art academy in Berlin in 1875, Krohg followed him there. In Germany in the 1870s Gussow was seen as one of the most reputable representatives of the younger generation of artists and was known as a realist and a colorist.[13] The conservative German critic Adolf Rosenberg wrote in his history of modern painting (1889): "Never before in German painting had such a bold, ruthless Realist appeared who grappled with nature as energetically as Gussow."[14] Rosenberg added that Gussow did not shrink from that which was most ugly in his quest to come as close as possible to nature. Krohg called himself a Gussow student and wrote in a letter in 1875 that Gussow's pupils stood in opposition to everyone else and were naturalists of the purest water.[15] During his years in Berlin, Krohg had the opportunity to see work by the more influential German realists Adolf von Menzel and Max Lieberman. Menzel's masterpiece *The Iron Rolling Mill* (1875) was one of the stars at the opening of the Nationalgalerie in Berlin in 1876, and it is clear that Krohg was inspired by the German master.[16] While in Germany, Krohg also had a chance to see French art, including works by Courbet and Manet. From early on, he was a well-educated, curious, and informed art student.

Krohg's first large artistic project was a series of paintings executed in the Danish fishing village of Skagen. He painted almost forty pictures of the local Gaihede family between 1879 and 1888, producing studies of single individuals as well as paintings in which they were engaged in daily activities, documenting them as if he were a Tainean social anthropologist. His second naturalist project was the Zolaesque novel *Albertine* (1886) and paintings related to it: a series of works exploring prostitution. His last ambitious naturalist project was *The Struggle for Existence* (1889), a depiction of the poor with a Darwinist undertone.

PORT SIDE! (1879)

Krohg's first, and really only, international success was *Port Side!* (sometimes titled *Pilote* or *Bâbord!* [1879, fig. 1.1, plate 1]), which he began while studying in Berlin and finished at the artists' colony in Skagen. Krohg wanted to paint a pilot—a standard marine motif—and a fellow Skagen painter Michael Ancher directed him to the fisherman Niels Gaihede, who became the model for the painting. Karl Madsen, also a Skagen painter and an art historian, pointed out the surprisingly bold cropping of the painting and Krohg's precise brushwork.[17] Krohg has pulled the figure as close as possible to the picture frame to abolish the distance between image and beholder. The work has a striking snapshot aesthetic, and the use of different angles creates an effect of being at sea as well as making the painting more exciting. The work was well received by critics in Kristiania, and in 1882 it was shown at the Paris Salon. The newspaper *Verdens Gang* wrote: "His painting attracted much attention among artists and in the press and was considered to be among the best works at the Salon that year."[18] This report was probably slightly exaggerated: Krohg's two accepted paintings, *Calm Sea* (1881; today known only through photographs) and *Port Side!*, were among 2,722 paintings exhibited in the show, and he was not mentioned in even the most comprehensive accounts of the 1882 Salon. But *Courrier de l'art* did describe *Port Side!* as "by far one of the best paintings at the Salon,"[19] and among the plein-air works, *Port Side!* was one of nine to be mentioned by *La presse*.[20] It was also represented with a drawing in both *La presse* on May 9, 1882[21] (fig. 1.2) and *L'art: Revue hebdomadaire illustré* (fig. 1.3). Paul Leroi wrote kind words about the painting in *L'art: Revue hebdomadaire illustré*:

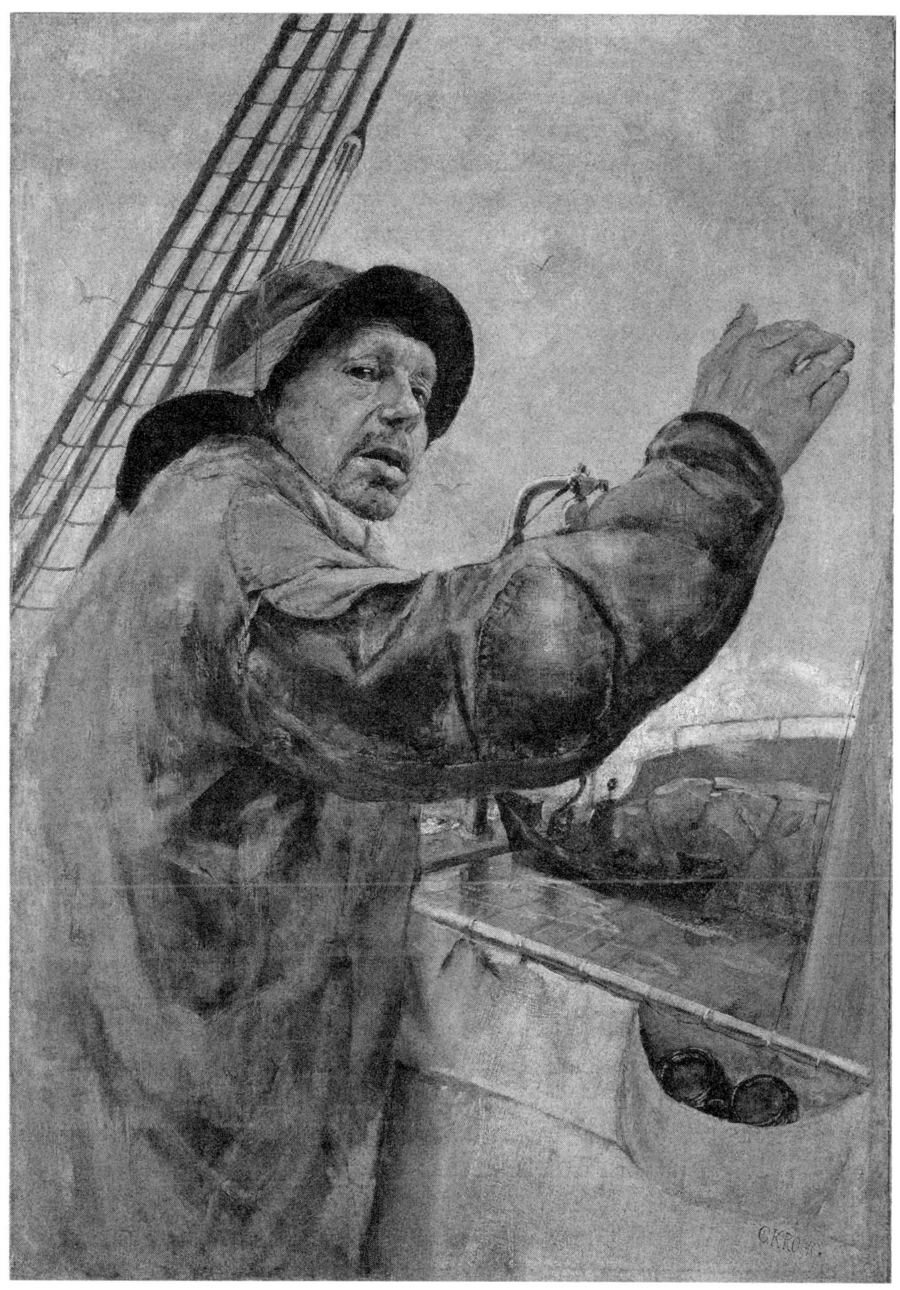

Figure 1.1 (Plate 1).Christian Krohg, *Port Side!* (1879). Oil on canvas, 99 × 70 cm. Photo: Jacques Lathion/The National Museum of Art, Architecture and Design, Oslo.

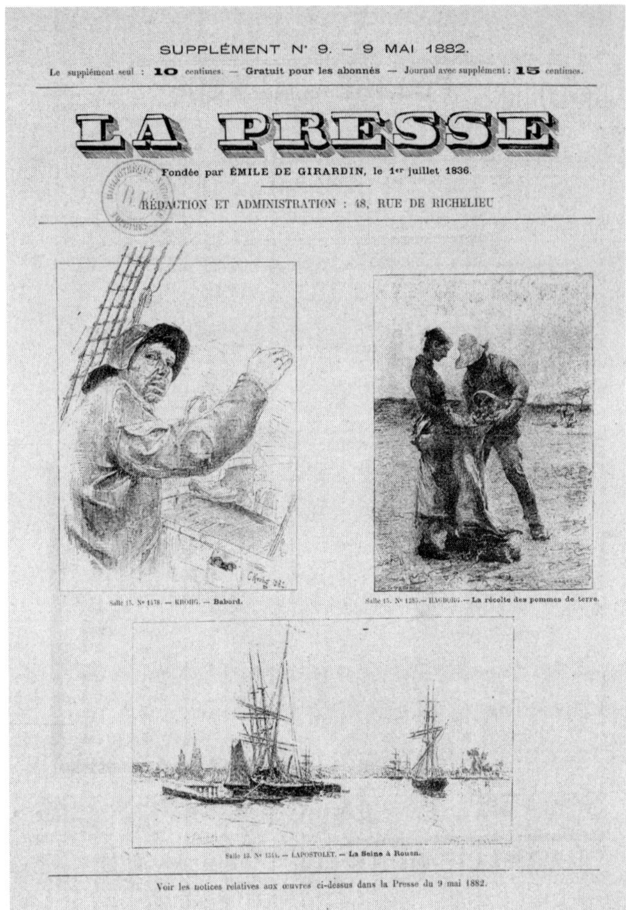

SUPPLÉMENT N° 9. — 9 MAI 1882.

Le supplément seul : **10** centimes. — **Gratuit pour les abonnés** — Journal avec supplément : **15** centimes.

LA PRESSE

Fondée par ÉMILE DE GIRARDIN, le 1er juillet 1836.

RÉDACTION ET ADMINISTRATION : 48, RUE DE RICHELIEU

Salle 15. N° 1378. — KROHG. — **Babord.**

Salle 15. N° 1285.— HAGBORG.— **La récolte des pommes de terre.**

Salle 13. N° 1514. — LAPOSTOLET. — **La Seine à Rouen.**

Voir les notices relatives aux œuvres ci-dessus dans la Presse du 9 mai 1882.

Figure 1.2.

Facsimile from *La presse* 9 (suppl.), May 9, 1882. Photo: Bibliothèque Nationale de France, Paris.

> Mr. Christian Krohg, born in Christiania, debuts at the Salon with a masterstroke. I am not referring to *Calm Sea,* an insignificant work that was wholly useless to send, but to *Bàbord!*, an excellent piece to lend without any restriction.
>
> The sea is terrible; one senses it more than one sees it; the captain, represented at mid-waist—life-size—leans in port side and commands the maneuver with a resolute gesture. The expression of the face, the truthfulness of the movement, the articulation of the drawing, and the harmony of the whole composed from an extremely delicate bouquet of gray within a blond scale of exquisite color, all of these together make the Norwegian painter's painting an elite work.
>
> *Bàbord!* is much more than a genre painting. It's a powerful page taken from the poem of the sea.[22]

Krohg showed *Sleeping Mother* (1883, fig. 1.4, plate 2) at the Paris Salon in 1884, but it did not get much notice in the French press.[23] *Port Side!* was exhibited once more at the 1902 Salon.[24] Clearly, Krohg himself considered it a very important painting.[25]

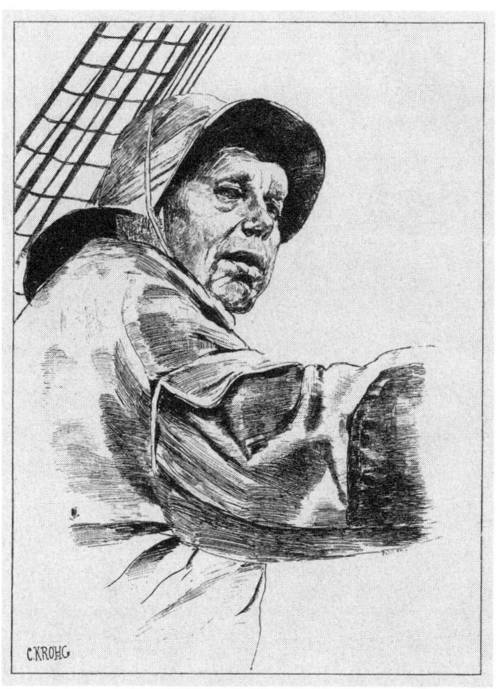

Figure 1.3.

Illustration of Christian Krohg's *Port Side!* in *L'art: Revue hebdomadaire illustré* 2 (1882). Facsimile.

THE IMPRESSIONIST EXHIBITION OF 1882

In 1881 Krohg finally got a chance to explore the art life of Paris, the city that would become his second home. His painter friend Erik Werenskiold (1855–1938) recounted that both of them saw all the art they could around the city, and that they were especially interested in Courbet, Manet, and the Impressionists.[26]

The year 1882 was a good one for the Nordic artists in Paris. Krohg and Werenskiold were in town, as were Christian Skredsvig, Hans Heyerdahl, Nicolai Ulfsten, Carl Larsson, Karl Nordström, Richard Bergh, and others. Many of them, like Krohg, had works at the Salon, and the French state bought Heyerdahl's *The Dying Child* (1881) and pieces by Albert Edelfelt and Hugo Salmson. At that year's Salon, Krohg got a chance to closely study Édouard Manet's *A Bar at the Folies-Bergères* (1881–82) and *Primavera* (1881). These paintings must have made a strong impression on him, as one can see the influence of Manet in many of Krohg's pictures, not least in the large *Albertine in the Police Doctor's Waiting Room* (1887), with its many women depicted in their impressive dresses and hats. Favorite painters such as Bastien-Lepage, Léon Lhermitte, and Alfred Roll were also represented. There was also a retrospective of Courbet's art at the École des Beaux-Arts that summer, and Krohg most likely went to see it. But the large 1882 impressionist exhibition was the year's highlight.

There Krohg found examples of both motifs and techniques that he would soon adopt and develop. He was especially influenced by Gustave Caillebotte and might also have visited Caillebotte's private art collection.[27] Werenskiold mentions Caillebotte's paintings at

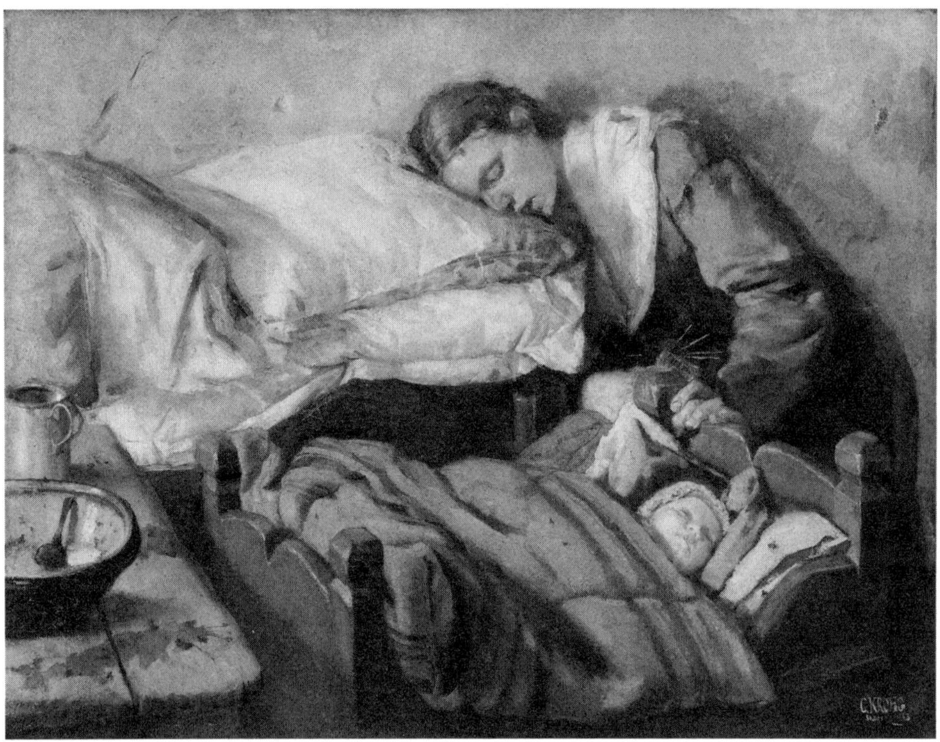

Figure 1.4 (Plate 2).Christian Krohg, *Sleeping Mother* (also known as *Sleeping Fisher Family*, 1883). Oil on canvas, 107.5 × 142 cm. Photo: Dag Fosse/KODE—Art Museums of Bergen, Rasmus Meyer Collection.

the 1882 exhibition and states that he showed "a number of images with a striking truth and effect."[28] In response to Caillebotte's art, Krohg refined his style, brushwork, and structure, as well as his composition, using surprising perspectives and scale jumps, asymmetry and broad empty spaces. Kirk Varnedoe writes that Krohg's Skagen paintings from 1879 already had "an odd perspective, involving greatly enlarged foreground forms and a peculiarly compressed spatial recession."[29] Krohg used a camera lucida in composing several of these paintings, and this resulted in dramatic close-up cropping of the images. His distinctive spatial vision became more advanced and sophisticated after seeing works by Caillebotte and other French masters, including Manet and Degas. One of Krohg's best paintings from this period is *Portrait of Karl Nordström* (1882, fig. 1.5), with its striking resemblances to Caillebotte's *The Man on the Balcony* (1880; exhibited at the 1882 show). Karl Nordström remembered many years later:

> Here in Grèz-sur-Loing, with its carefree and quiet spring days, did the small Krohg portrait of me come into being. We had both just studied Impressionism

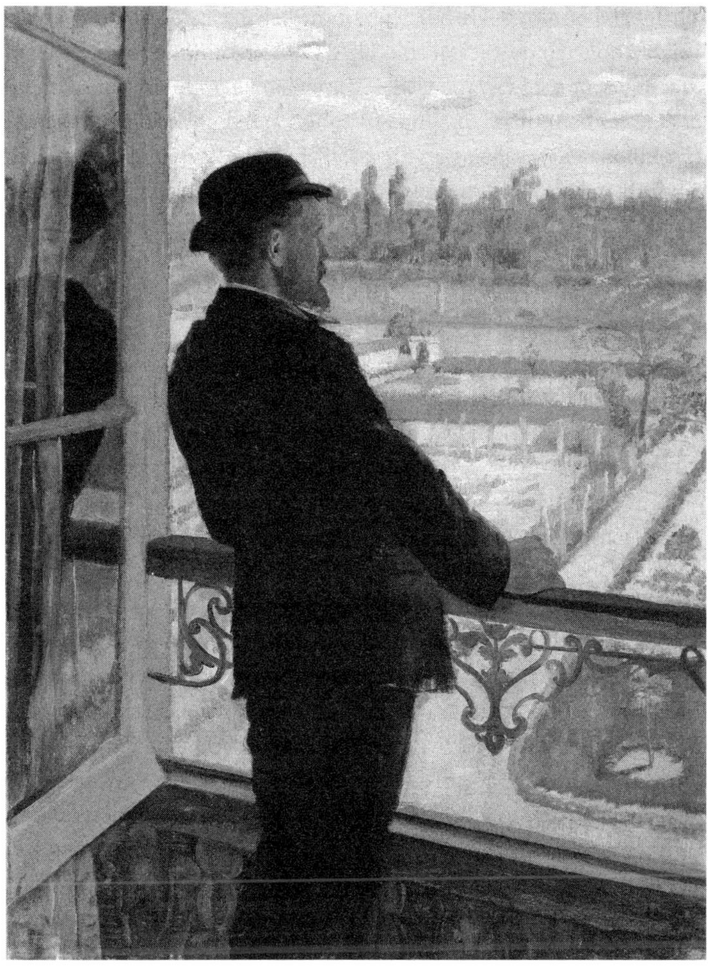

Figure 1.5. Christian Krohg, *Portrait of Karl Nordström* (1882). Oil on canvas, 61 × 46.5 cm. Photo: Jacques Lathion/The National Museum of Art, Architecture and Design, Oslo.

> at an exhibition in Paris and had our minds full of the new, strong visual impressions. Krohg then saw me one day standing there at the open window of my room, in the blue suit against the sunny garden on the outside. He eagerly asked me to stand still in my pose, ran after a canvas and the other tools, and a few moments later he was fully at work.[30]

Another painting that shows Krohg's interest in Caillebotte was *Look Ahead* (1884, fig. 1.6). It had similarities to Caillebotte's *Boaters Rowing on the Yerres* (ca. 1877) and *Rower in a Top Hat* (1877). Krohg's painting truly showcased his ability to derive impulses—motif, colors,

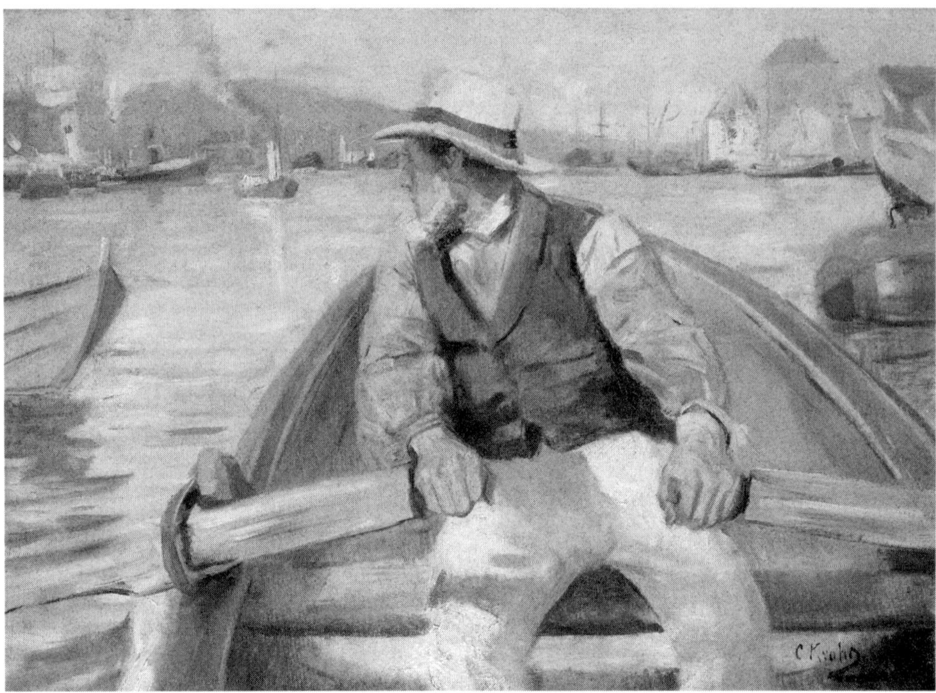

Figure 1.6. Christian Krohg, *Look Ahead* (1884). Oil on canvas, 62.5 × 86 cm. Photo: Jacques Lathion/The National Museum of Art, Architecture and Design, Oslo.

brushwork, composition—from other artists yet make them his own. He managed to paint with his own characteristic "rhythm" in the way he composed and cropped the images and in his varied brushwork.

THE MODERN BREAKTHROUGH: TRUTH, SERIOUSNESS, AND HONESTY

Krohg was part of the radical, modern generation that brought new ideas from Paris to Norway, which has been termed "the modern breakthrough" in Scandinavia. Painter and art historian Karl Madsen summarized in 1887 the goal of the modern breakthrough: "More truth! Greater seriousness! Deeper honesty!"[31] Literary historian Henrik Jæger (not to be confused with the anarchist Hans Jæger) wrote in 1890: "They [Norwegian artists] have in the past decade surpassed even the socialists when it comes to demonstrations and agitations."[32] He described the situation like this in 1896, when he wrote about Henrik Ibsen's *The Pillars of Society* (1877):

> Everything that had happened out there in the world over the last decade made an incredible impression here at home [Norway]. It has turned the temperature

> up; the Parisian Commune wrought havoc here as in other places, so that one became scared of everything new and unproven, everything that had appeared out in the great world. What contributed to making the fear more powerful was that many of the new ideas that began to show up here at home were braver and they appeared more often than any time before.[33]

Henrik Jæger—himself a radical academic who appears in Krohg's drawing *Outdoor Dining at Café Engebret* (ca. 1880) along with the famous actors Johannes Brun and Hjalmar Hammer—also points to the significance of Darwin, Mill, and Taine in Norwegian culture. Ibsen wrote his groundbreaking *A Doll's House* (1879) and *Ghosts* (1881); Darwin and Taine were translated into Danish in the 1870s; and in 1875 the biologist Georg Ossian Sars held the first biology lecture at the university in Christiania (Oslo) based on Darwin's theories.[34] The Norwegian author Alexander Kielland's favorite philosopher was John Stuart Mill, and he also enjoyed reading Herbert Spencer, Charles Darwin, Ernst Haeckel, Hippolyte Taine, and Jens Peter Jacobsen.[35] These Norwegian authors and their cultural heroes were part of the intellectual climate that shaped academic youth in the 1870s—a class of people, Christian Krohg among them, who would become radical authors and journalists in the 1880s.

Kristiania in that decade was characterized by many ideological and intellectual disputes between the right-wing party Høyre and the left-wing party Venstre. The city was becoming an urban center with all its challenges; the class issue was an underlying factor in many of the clashes. Many writers and artists, such as Bjørnstjerne Bjørnson and Ibsen, supported the liberal party, and political subjects became an important part of literature at that time. These intellectuals were also challenging the freedom of the press and speech.

Sexual discourse played an especially important role in both the politics and aesthetics of Scandinavia's "modern breakthrough."[36] Almost every one of the leading Scandinavian writers, including Ibsen and Strindberg, took part in the debates about sexuality, marriage, morality, and women's rights. Taboo issues prompted lively discussions in newspapers and journals and were explored in novels and plays. Krohg's originality lay in transferring much of this discourse to the art of painting and exploring it in both his pictures and writings.

Le Figaro published an article on January 11, 1888, titled "La polygamie en Scandinavie," written by Jacques St-Cère (a pseudonym for *Le Figaro*'s editor, Armand Rosenthal). It demonstrated that by then the idea that Scandinavian avant-garde art was concerned with sex was already current: "Polygamy, monogamy, the question of marriage, prostitution, all together have taken, in the political language of the Scandinavian countries, the name of the 'sexual question.'"[37] The writer claimed that this discourse began with Ibsen's *A Doll's House* and its protagonist Nora, and he included in his discussion works by Bjørnson, Strindberg, Hans Jæger, and Krohg. He referred to Krohg's as *Albertine, histoire d'une prostituée* and presented a short synopsis as well as information about its confiscation and the riots following its publication.

Christian Krohg and the litigious anarchist Hans Jæger coedited the journal *Impressionisten* (The impressionist) from 1886 to 1890. Most of the contributors where anonymous; it was risky to be associated with Jæger's anarchism and destructive bohemianism. The coeditors translated texts by French authors, such as Guy de Maupassant, and they included in their journal texts on aesthetics and politics. The journal's title, *Impressionisten*, shows that naturalism, modernism, bohemianism, and impressionism were overlapping ideas for Jæger and Krohg. In an essay in the first volume, an anonymous author, probably Jæger, wrote that the only way the youth can become a "working powerhouse in the machinery of development and thus manifest itself as 'modern'" is to "perform a naturalistic literature."[38] The point was to write about the life one knew: *art should be life*. This notion echoed Émile Zola's ideas from *Mon salon* (1866). The *Impressionisten* author stated that no Norwegian writers, including such figures as Alexander Kielland, achieved this goal:

> Why do I remember all of Zola's novels, from *Les Rougon* to *L'oeuvre*, why do I remember Guy de Maupassant's *Une vie* and *Belami* and a bunch of his short stories—but I've forgotten almost everything Kielland has written? Because *they* give life itself, the living pulsating life, while *he* gives us dreary Kiellandesque stories about life. Zola and Guy de Maupassant let me see and listen to the people they wrote about, they let me live these peoples' lives; they give me living flesh and blood, and not dead story-abstractions like Kielland. And that is why *they* have gripped me and he has not.[39]

Ordinary realism was to Jæger not true enough, as he stated in the foreword to his novel *Fra Kristiania-Bohemen* (From the Kristiania bohemians, 1885): "Naturalism is—briefly defined—deterministic writing."[40] In Jæger's view, nature was responsible for human actions, and a human being could therefore not be held responsible for his actions, even the so-called immoral ones. The artist's task was to show the world the whole *bête humaine*, especially the dark, ugly, and obscene sides of humanity. The goal was to attack and shock, through form and content, public opinion's moral tyranny.[41] Krohg challenged his own class background when he entered Jæger's circle, and the Kristiania bohemians sought to spread radical ideas, especially naturalism, emanating from Paris. Very few Norwegian painters, however, concerned themselves directly with political issues in their art. Krohg was quite extraordinary in that regard.

In 1880s Norway, naturalism was synonymous with Zola's theories, and his *Nana* (1880) epitomized the most shocking sexual literature. *Nana* and *L'assommoir* (1877) were Zola's most discussed books in the Norwegian press, seen as the greatest examples of the new radical literature coming out of France.[42] Intellectuals and artists who could not read French could enjoy Scandinavian translations of the many naturalist novels, whether as books or as installments in journals and newspapers. Zola's "Le carnet de dance" from *Contes à Ninon* (1864), for example, was published as "Balbogen" (The dance card) in *Romsdals Amtstidende* beginning on April 8, 1879; and *Germinal* (1885) appeared as a serial in *Verdens Gang* in 1886 under the title "Vaarbrudd" (Spring break). *The Masterpiece* (1886) was issued in both Swedish and Danish the year it was published in France. Erik Werenskiold read the Danish translation and wrote in a letter to Jonas Lie: "This is great art, it moves all the way to the bottom of human nature."[43] Painters such as Christian Skredsvig and Edvard Munch were also very interested in Zola; Skredsvig even had a picture of the French author on his desk.[44] Further translations of Zola's books included *L'assommoir* (1877), published in Swedish in 1879 and in Danish in 1882; *Une page d'amour* (1878), translated into Danish in 1880;

and *Pot-Luck* (1883), issued in 1882 (the book originally appeared as a serial in *Le Gaulois* in 1882). *The Joy of Life* (1883) was translated into Swedish in 1884, and many more Zola novels followed. Naturalist authors such as the Goncourts and Maupassant were also translated in the 1880s, but Zola remained the star. In addition to Scandinavian editions of his books, his theories were widely discussed by Scandinavian intellectuals, including Johan Vibe's *Nogle Bemærkninger i Anledning Naturalismen* (Some remarks about naturalism) from 1884, a relatively thoroughgoing presentation of Zola's experimental method—although Vibe spent most of his book criticizing it.

KROHG'S BREAKTHROUGH: 1884–85

Krohg's artistic breakthrough in Norway came with the Autumn Exhibition in 1884 and an exhibition at Fritzner's Pavilion in 1885, where his works were featured together with those of Erik Werenskiold. It was also in 1884 that Krohg showed *Sleeping Mother* at the Paris Salon. Andreas Aubert wrote a positive review of the painting, stating that Krohg's art was immediate and filled with nature (there is an immediate relationship between art and life), that his paintings drew their power from life and gave new blood to the anemic and weak Norwegian art. He then asked if we should call Krohg's art raw, and answered: "Not raw, but bold."[45] He complimented the realness of *Sleeping Mother*, how it represents tiredness after hard work: deep sleep, heavy bodies, the woman's open mouth, the dirty tray, and lazy flies. Krohg also demonstrated his artistic talent with paintings such as *Mother at Her Child's Bed* (1884, fig. 1.7, plate 3) and *Look Ahead* (1884), both painted in Skagen, as was *Sleeping Mother*. His intellectual ambitions became clear in two portraits of radicals: *Gerhard Gran* (1884, fig. 4.2) and *Ola Thommessen (Sitting)* (1884).

The exhibition at Fritzner's Pavilion in 1885 further revealed Krohg to be a searching and experimental artist as he explored new subjects painted in different styles. The show was a huge event that spurred debates about realism, naturalism, and impressionism on the Norwegian art scene.[46] Reportedly one thousand people saw the exhibition the first week, four hundred of them on the first Sunday. A new modern heating device was even installed in the gallery—Friedlender's air heating system—to keep the space warm in the cold March weather.[47] Henrik Jæger wrote in a review of the exhibition that Krohg had created a modern painting both in its execution and in its humanity and compassion toward his subjects. He commented that what made Krohg so original and interesting was that he "gives more of his personality in his images than anyone else."[48] His paintings were felt to be personal *statements* and not objective observations or representations of beautiful scenery. The review conveyed a feeling that Krohg painted real, lived life as experienced through his unique temperament.

Two of the most important paintings in the show were *Karl Johan Street* (*Impression*) (1883, fig. 1.8) and *Portrait of Gerhard Munthe* (1885, fig. 1.9). The first was a small picture in which Krohg tried to paint like Claude Monet, the second a large portrait inspired by Édouard Manet. It was no coincidence, since Monet and Manet were considered in Norway of the 1880s to be the most important of the impressionists. Hansson, the *Dagbladet* critic, wrote about Krohg's *Karl Johan Street* as if he were describing a Monet canvas: "'Karl Johan Street' is a bright little impression, as far as I know the first of this kind of picture by

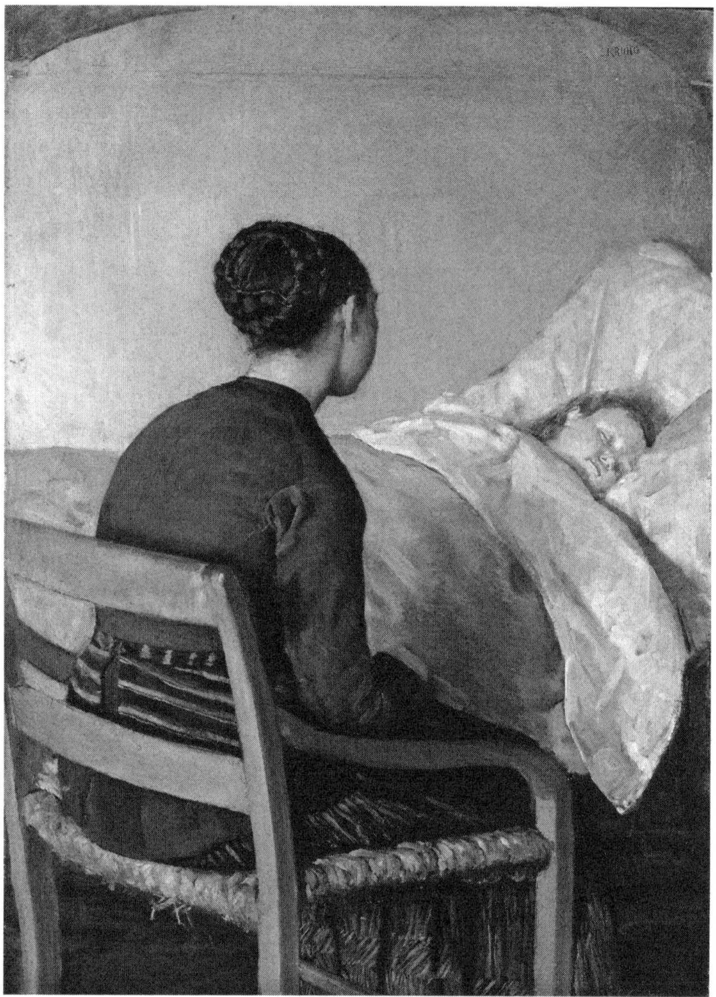

Figure 1.7 (Plate 3).Christian Krohg, *Mother at Her Child's Bed* (1884). Oil on canvas, 131 × 95 cm. Photo: Jacques Lathion/The National Museum of Art, Architecture and Design, Oslo.

a Norwegian artist that has been shown here in Norway. The street is decorated with flags and a large number of people are out walking. If you move close to the painting, it seems like an insane number of spots; but from a distance, the mass of people comes alive, the tram is moving fast, and the flags are fluttering in the wind."[49] The critic said more about what Krohg tried to do than about the quality of the work itself.

The portrait of Gerhard Munthe was a much more successful work. Krohg presented the bourgeois painter well dressed and groomed with his perfect mustache and hair, wearing a lorgnette, and smoking a cigarette. Munthe was the perfect subject for Krohg's Manet-

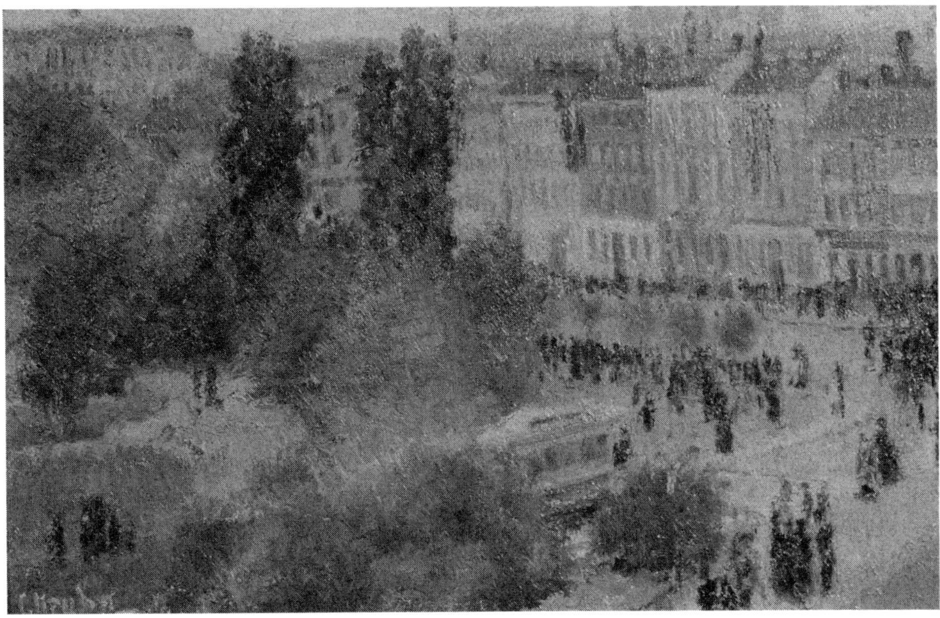

Figure 1.8. Christian Krohg, *Karl Johan Street (Impression)*, (1883). Oil on board, 25.5 × 40 cm. Private collection. © Photo: O. Væring Eftf. AS, Norway.

inspired portrait. Christian Skredsvig, a friend and colleague of both painters, described Munthe in their student days at Eckerberg's art school as an elegant "Frenchman": "There he stood in the morning, leaning against an easel. Dark, elegant, with parted hair and short mustache. Almost repulsive in his strangeness. His portrait would have been a joy in a photographer's exhibition cabinet."[50] Krohg captured these qualities in his portrait, depicting Munthe at the well-known Grand Café located on Karl Johan Street, an important meeting place for artists and intellectuals in Kristiania. Its most famous regular customer was Henrik Ibsen. The Grand Café was decorated in the 1870s style and was said to resemble Manet's Paris, with a modern Parisian feel and atmosphere.[51] In a guidebook to Kristiania, the Grand Café and Hotel were illustrated and described as elegant, popular, and "a splendid place for those who want to study the daily life of the Norwegian capital."[52]

In Krohg's painting the room is so full of smoke that it is hard to see anything, but we catch a glimpse of the painter Reinholdt Boll sitting in the background reading a newspaper. (Boll was a well-known Grand Café habitué, and it was said that he spent more time there than in his studio.)[53] Krohg's brushstrokes are bold but precise, and his command of colors—especially in the skin and the black coat—masterful. The portrait says as much about Krohg's artistic talent and ambitions as about his model. It is interesting that he depicted two painters (Munthe and Boll) associated with the more conservative elements of the art scene while using a radical impressionist style reminiscent of Manet. He may have done so with irony, a quality not unfamiliar in the art of Manet himself.

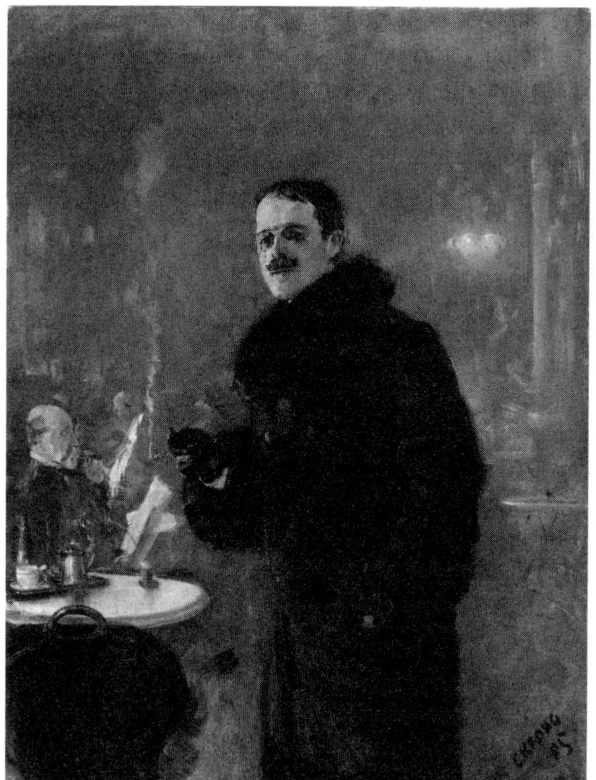

Figure 1.9.

Christian Krohg, *Portrait of Gerhard Munthe* (1885). Oil on canvas, 150 × 115 cm. Photo: Børre Høstland/The National Museum of Art, Architecture and Design, Oslo.

KARL JOHAN STREET

The most sophisticated street in the 1880s in Norway was Karl Johans Gate (Karl Johan Street) in the center of Kristiania.[54] It was considered an oasis for the bourgeoisie and bohemians in the small, gray, poor city. The street was named after King Karl Johan, the ruler of Sweden and Norway from 1818 until his death in 1844. At one end of it stood the Royal Castle, at the other the parliament building situated next to Egertorvet (Eger Square). The main street of Kristiania often served as scenery for Krohg and other painters in the 1880s. (As Henrik Jæger stated in his book about Kristiania in 1890: "From an artistic perspective Kristiania in the 1880s was as unexplored as inner Africa was from a geographical point of view before Livingstone and Stanley's expeditions.")[55] Here was located the Grand Café and the university, as well as many shops and the horse-drawn tram, as we can see in Krohg's *Karl Johan Street (Impression)*. Also found here was a building called "Pultosten," where Krohg from 1882 had his studio together with a group of other artists, including Thaulow and Edvard Munch.

Karl Johan Street was said to have its own rhythm from early morning till late at night, with people rushing up and down, a military band playing at one in the afternoon, and

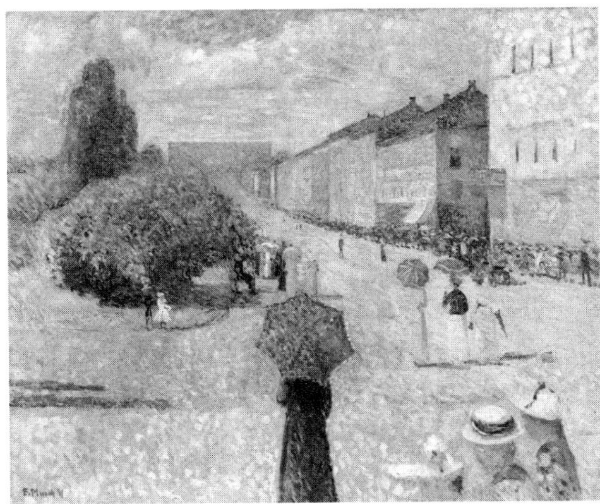

Figure 1.10.

Edvard Munch, *Spring Day on Karl Johan Street* (1891). Oil on canvas, 80 × 100 cm. Photo: Dag Fosse/KODE—Art Museums of Bergen, Norway.

strollers coming out for "the dinner promenade"—the flaneur's favorite time. In a Munch sketch called *Karl Johan Characters* (1883), we see the military band and Krohg surrounded by fellow painters Munthe and Thaulow. Krohg also described the marching band and the buzzing life of the street in his novel *Albertine* (1886), in a scene in which the heroine is sitting at her sewing machine and daydreaming:

> It was spring and lovely weather, and Karl Johan Street lay before her. In the student's grove under the bright green trees she heard the band playing the Cadet March—on the top of the hill she could see the large white castle. . . . Lots of people in the street, walking up and down—most fine people—it was daily life. She walked slowly up the street—on her head she had a brown lady's hat with pearls, in her arms she carried a red umbrella of the modern kind and a notebook inscribed *Music* in golden letters—because she was a fine young lady.[56]

Munch's *Spring Day on Karl Johan Street* (1891, fig. 1.10) recalls this description, showing a woman with a red umbrella enjoying a sunny spring day and gazing at the green trees, the big white Royal Castle, and strolling passersby. The street became a favorite subject for a number of Kristiania artists, and we can see how Krohg's depictions of it inspired the younger painters in the Pultosten group, including Munch, who also made the sketch *The Military Band: Christian Krohg and Hans Jæger on Karl Johan Street* (ca. 1885, fig. 1.11). Karl Johan Street was vital to Krohg's artistic vision. Modernism in painting often has to do with urbanity. The artists labeled as modernists, such as Manet and Caillebotte, were representing the new mythic city, a place signified by new spaces for leisure and entertainment, consumption and spectacle, different urban environments inhabited by different classes, and the masculine and feminine spheres. Krohg painted himself directly into this kind of modernism.

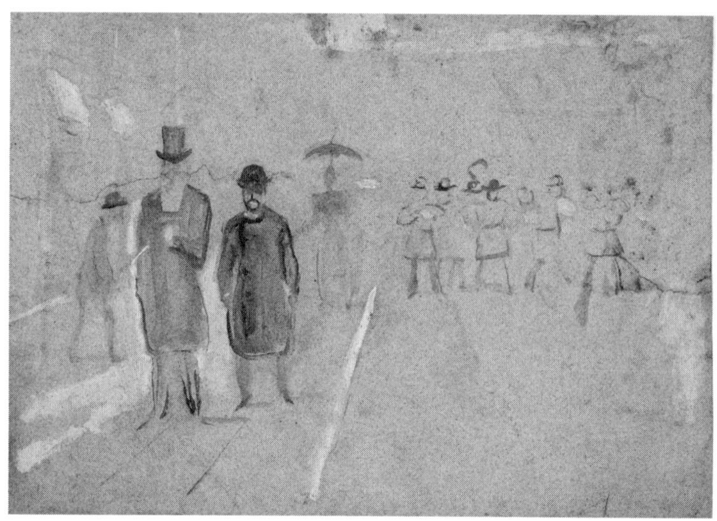

Figure 1.11. Edvard Munch, *The Military Band: Christian Krohg and Hans Jæger on Karl Johan Street* (ca. 1885). Gouache and possibly oil, 22.89 × 34.5 cm. Photo © Munch Museum, Oslo.

KROHG AND THE SCANDINAVIAN AVANT-GARDE

The leading art critic in Norway, Andreas Aubert, stated in an exhibition review in 1887 that "Krohg is at the moment without a doubt the greatest painter in Scandinavian art when it comes to the experimental study of light. Even in a French context he walks in the frontline. He makes his own contribution to the development."[57] This quote illustrates that Krohg was considered to be among the leading modernist painters in Scandinavia in the 1880s—even avant-garde, according to Aubert. In a review of Krohg's large *Albertine* painting, Rosenkrantz Johnsen wrote: "*Albertine* is a powerful work of art. Our country's modern art has with this painting made a huge step forward. And that is why one can say of Krohg that he has done what few are able to do: move borders."[58] Aubert asserted that through Krohg the younger painters in Norway got to know impressionism. Aubert wrote that Krohg showed "reckless bravery" in the way he composed pictures, cropped them, and adopted experimental methods.[59] He repeated the same assessment in his review of Krohg's large exhibition in 1889: "He dares more than most."[60] Krohg's painting *The North Wind* (1887, fig. 1.12), Aubert claimed, was the first impressionist painting in Norwegian art: "'The North Wind' by *Christian Krohg* shows a more reckless boldness in the application of the impressionist method's two main theorems than any previous work here in Norway. Never before has the instantaneous been more powerfully emphasized in the subject, or a more fierce color divisionism been used in the technique."[61] In 1890 he called this painting one of the greatest achievements in Norwegian art.[62]

Figure 1.12. Christian Krohg, *The North Wind* (1887). Oil on canvas, 102 × 125 cm. Photo: Anne Hansteen/The National Museum of Art, Architecture and Design, Oslo.

Krohg's most ambitious undertaking was the Albertine novel and paintings. Krohg started working on the Albertine novel in Belgium in 1885; it was published on December 20, 1886.[63] It was not a coincidence that he chose to write about prostitution—the most modern and shocking subject for a book in those years. It is likely that he envisioned *Albertine* as a Norwegian version of Huysmans's Marthe, Goncourt's Elisa, and Zola's Nana.

THE ALBERTINE AFFAIR

Pall Mall Gazette reported on January 6, 1887:

> All Norway is up in arms on account of the confiscation by the Liberal Ministry of a novel named *Albertine*, the first literary work of a painter named Christian Krogh [*sic*]. It gives the history of a young girl's gradual decline into profligacy, and is, in fact, a stern indictment of police-regulated prostitution. The leading critics of the day, and honorable women not a few, declare it to be profoundly moral

> in effect, and as delicate as it is skillful in handling; yet the Justice Department, encouraged by its success in suppressing Hans Jæger's *Kristiania-Bohème*, has confiscated the edition (or as many copies as it could lay its hands on), and instituted a prosecution against the author. The excitement in literary circles is intense. . . . The leaders of Norwegian literature—Ibsen, Bjørnson, and Kielland—are all at present abroad, and their utterances on the subject are awaited with the greatest interest.[64]

Albertine tells the story of how a poor young seamstress ends up as a prostitute. Early in the novel a young man of higher class is attracted to Albertine but does not dare get seriously involved with her because he has the opportunity to marry in his own class. Police officer Winther, the chief of the section controlling prostitution, notices Albertine with the young man and takes her for a prostitute. He seeks her out and summons her to a meeting at his private home. There he seduces her by serving her alcohol, and then rapes her. Albertine is ashamed and demoralized, and this is the beginning of her decline. After the rape, she tries to fight her destiny but without luck. Soon she is summoned for an official visit to the police doctor's clinic, where registered prostitutes are examined for venereal disease. There she is placed in the infamous inspection chair, and she feels so much shame when the speculum penetrates her that she loses all power to fight her lot. She begins to believe that she is meant to be a prostitute. The novel then jumps ahead two years, and in the last chapter Albertine is shown as a vulgar, noisy, experienced whore.

The day after its publication, the police seized the novel in an extensive raid, but got hold of only 439 of 1,600 copies. Some 850 books remained in circulation in Norway, 300 in Sweden and Denmark, and 50 in Paris. The Swedish painter Eva Bonnier recounted in a letter from Paris in March 1887 that the only book she had received from her homeland that year was Krohg's *Albertine* and it was circulating among her friends in Paris.[65]

The publication of *Albertine* unleashed an intellectual storm in Kristiania. Krohg's goal was to make prostitution illegal. It was tolerated by the government under strict police control, and Krohg sought to criticize this "official" prostitution through his art. This was a bold move for an artist. The case was discussed for weeks not only in Norway but all over Scandinavia. It became the subject of a fight between the liberals, who called the book moral and pure, and the conservative press, who looked on it as "immoral filth," nonsense, humbug, speculation, and unworthy of being called literature.[66] One critic called the naturalist style of Hans Jæger and Krohg "literary sulfuric acid" and stated that Krohg was abusing the writing instruction he had gained in school.[67] The conservative press decried the book as socialist propaganda. It was a highly charged subject.

Krohg was defended by a number of supporters: the authors Arne Garborg, Amalie Skram, and partly Bjørnstjerne Bjørnson; composer Edvard Grieg; and critic Georg Brandes. Brandes wrote in *Politiken* on December 27 that *Albertine* "without a doubt is one of the best composed and best conducted novels in contemporary Nordic literature. If Edmond de Goncourt could read this book, he would shake your hand."[68] He called the visitation scene great and unforgettable. The *Albertine* case was also strongly supported by the women's movement. Author Margrete Vullum wrote a long review of the book on December 21, 1886, in the newspaper *Verdens Gang*, arguing that "everyone should read this book. A cheap edition should be made available to the people."[69] It was even proposed to make the book into a confirmation present for girls.[70] To female commentators such as Vullum and Amalie Skram, one of the most important qualities of Krohg's book was the respect it showed for prostitutes and the acknowledgment that they were human beings rather than monsters.[71] *Albertine* became quite a phenomenon in the Kristiania press and satirical journals.

The Social Democratic Association (Socialdemokratisk Forening) arranged a discussion of the book in support of Krohg that was attended by hundreds of people, mostly workers. Ola Thommessen, a well-known liberal newspaper editor, arranged a meeting of the Kristiania Worker's Association (Kristiania Arbeidersamfund) on January 9, 1887, at which over one thousand people showed up. Thommessen read aloud from the book and, as one newspaper emphasized, did so in front of many women.[72] People shouted out, "Long live Christian Krohg and editor Ola Thommessen!" followed by cheers.[73] It was decided to organize a demonstration and parade through Kristiania, and on Sunday, January 16, 1887, thousands of people marched through the city chanting, "Respect for the constitution's paragraph 100," which guaranteed freedom of speech, and "Free Albertine."[74] The prime minister responded that the government would consider abolishing prostitution. The case thus came to involve two political issues: freedom of the press and the removal of official prostitution. The latter actually happened in February 1888. Arne Garborg wrote in *Dagbladet* on December 22, 1886: "We have an association for the abolition of prostitution; that association will not accomplish as much in ten years as Krohg has done in this one book."[75] The *Albertine* case was not the sole factor—many had worked on this issue for years—but it was a powerful demonstration that art could be political and that it could challenge the authorities.

Krohg was judged guilty in the Albertine affair on March 10, 1887, and had to pay a fine for writing an immoral book. Symbolically, on March 11, the large painting *Albertine in the Police Doctor's Waiting Room* (fig. 8.1, plate 12) was officially exhibited in Kristiania. Hung in a hall in a working-class district, it remained on view until April 3, 1887, without a doubt the most notorious painting in Norway, possibly in Scandinavia, in the 1880s. So many people wanted to see it that the exhibition had to be extended by one week. Many workers went because they felt that Krohg was their hero. *Dagbladet* specified that some of the ticket income went to the jobless and that the exhibition was visited by "both women and men from all layers of society."[76] The painting was illuminated between 6 and 9 p.m. so that those working long days could have the opportunity to see it in the evening. Up to 1,500 visitors came every day. The painting was then sent on a tour, spending the summer in Sweden, where it was shown in Stockholm, Malmö, and Gothenburg. Later in the year it came back to Norway and was exhibited in Kristiansand, Bergen, and Trondheim. The following summer it was sent to Copenhagen. It was debated in the newspapers wherever it was shown.

THE ART CRITIC

Krohg was not only an ambitious painter and novelist but also an influential art critic, publishing several texts on aesthetics and the mission of art. The two main ideas in his theoretical texts were, firstly, that painting is superior to literature (the paragone debate), and secondly, that art should have a political and moral mission and not just be produced and viewed for art's sake.[77] Krohg gave a lecture, "On the Visual Art's Role in the Cultural Movement," at the Liberal Students' Association (Den Frisindede Studenterforening) on March 22, 1886. The lecture was soon published. The large *Albertine* painting was, interestingly enough, shown at that event (a year before its official exhibition). The unfinished canvas was presented to a large audience, and Krohg used it as an example of how efficiently an image could tell the Albertine story, compared to the novel he was still working on at the time.

The title of the lecture, with its notion of "cultural movement" (kulturbevægelse), was a play on the title of Georg Brandes's widely read work *Main Currents* [Hovedstrømninger] *in Nineteenth Century Literature* (1872). The "cultural movement" must be understood as a collection of the cultural expressions of a given time: the different arts and sciences. The painter works alongside actors, scientists, and authors to create the image of his time. This idea comes very close to Taine's Hegelian aesthetics, for Krohg also thought of history in a collectivist way.[78] History is the development of large forces, which are represented by individuals—such as artists—in great works of art. Art therefore becomes a historical truth about a particular time and place. Modernist artists are those gripped by "the time's turmoil."[79] Krohg's claim was that of all the arts the visual ones most adequately represent their time. Hence painting is superior to literature. That is also why a painter needs to be of his own time and not try to copy works from the past. This explains the need to always move forward—the logic of the avant-garde. Krohg's arguments were not unlike those of Jean-François Raffaëlli, who expressed similar ideas in his essay on modern art in 1884, which Krohg probably knew. Like Raffaëlli, Krohg held that the image of the time is best represented by paintings of people.[80] As an example, he showed, surprisingly, Max Klinger's *Second Future* (1880). To Krohg, modern art had to be the result of anxiety and unrest coming from a wish to change society: "When we look around ourselves, we see a restless anxiety and dissatisfaction everywhere."[81] To be modern is to know one's own time and not try to paint as if one were living in a previous era. Krohg claimed that the time "is painting its own image" through modern artists.[82] This image is restless and anxious because it stems from such an environment. Klinger's etching presents a pessimistic vision of human future because an artist must show something so genuine, shocking, and "unpleasantly true" that it can change the thinking of his viewers.[83] Arne Garborg, a naturalist author and supporter of Krohg, expressed a similar idea in a lecture on naturalism in 1882: "Art has to be so true that it makes us think."[84] The same point was reiterated by Hans Jæger in 1886 in the first volume of *Impressionisten*, in which he wrote that literature should transform the heart and brain and "make us into new human beings and give us a new will."[85] Krohg believed that a novelist could better describe the inner life of his characters, but a painter could more efficiently depict the outer environment and do it in such a way that the beholder would never forget the image. The painting's mission was to emphasize the uncanny so as to shock the viewer into a change.[86] It was the artist's duty to "take the stubborn audience by the collar and make them stop and look at what you have to show them."[87] He claimed that the novelist could never make his work uncanny enough, which is why painting was the most important modern art.

Krohg argued that art should not be a luxury—a pretty object for the bourgeoisie to buy for their homes. He associated that practice with *l'art pour l'art*. Krohg wanted to make art for the masses—but not to entertain them, for that would be what we now call kitsch. Rather, art should be powerful and based on a true experience, making the beholders feel what the artist felt. The aim was to make the masses change society thanks to art, to put art in the service of democracy. Krohg believed that "the visual arts are absolutely necessary for any progress in the development of human beings."[88]

THE RADICAL NATURALIST

Krohg's art took part in the international naturalist movement, as described by Gabriel P. Weisberg in his groundbreaking work on the subject. Krohg was, in Weisberg's analysis, the most progressive of the Scandinavian naturalists and the one who most actively responded to Zola's theories. Weisberg labels Krohg a "radical naturalist." The most striking thing about his art was how he combined, or assimilated, ideas and trends from naturalist (Bastien-Lepage, Roll, Raffaëlli), impressionist, and avant-garde sources (Manet). In Weisberg's words, "With the work of Christian Krohg, the boundaries separating Scandinavian art, Naturalism, and Impressionism melt away."[89] This, together with its radical social aspect, makes Krohg's naturalism unique, not only in Scandinavia but in Europe at large. In Weisberg's estimation, Krohg "added a dimension of protest to the Naturalist movement that was not often evident in other countries."[90]

The rest of this book will focus on Krohg's naturalist projects, which answered Zola's and Taine's demands for a modern art to be based on the experimental method and to represent one's own time. Krohg knew Zola's work, and even if he did not call his naturalist method experimental, his Albertine projects might be the most Zolaesque artworks in Europe in terms of their ambition, size, and public effect. Krohg's naturalism is interesting because it fuses political naturalism with formal solutions learned from impressionist painters.

The paintings Krohg displayed at the annual Autumn Exhibitions in 1889 and 1890 show a shift in his art. The 1889 show focused on images of idyllic family life, such as *The Fishing Pier in Grimstad* (1890). His motifs were not shocking or especially political. *Morgenbladet's* critic wrote how surprising these paintings were and that many would not recognize Krohg as their author: "One will not here find the violent anarchist who laughs at everything that can be called authority or school."[91] These paintings were much more moderate and restrained in their form and color; the conservative *Morgenbladet* thought them nicer and more well done. Krohg was no longer a young, angry man, and with neo-romantic and symbolist art coming into vogue, naturalism was considered outdated. Munch was the new star. Krohg could not keep up with the new trends and did not paint much in the 1890s, focusing his career instead on journalism and moving between Kristiania, Copenhagen, and Berlin. In 1901 he went to Paris to work as a correspondent for several Norwegian newspapers and took on private art students, and in 1902 he become a professor at Académie Colarossi. He moved back to Kristiania for good in 1909, reinvented himself as an artist, and took a post as the first director and professor of painting at the newly established National Academy of Art, positions he retained until the end of his life in 1925.

CHAPTER TWO

Naturalism, the Dark Side of Realism

So it is not Realism we should fear, but Naturalism and Materialism.

AFTENPOSTEN, APRIL 12, 1879

Naturalism was a religion, and we were its fanatic confessors.

FRITS THAULOW

THE Danish philosopher Harald Høffding wrote in the first issue of the progressive Danish journal *Tilskueren* (The spectator) in 1884 that the word *realism* in art is seldom used with a clear awareness of what it really signifies, and that only time will tell what it was.[1] Now, more than 120 years later, it should be fairly easy to understand what realism (and naturalism) in art was, but it is still confusing, messy, slippery, and problematic—or "elastic and vague," in Ernst Fischer's words.[2] Time does not make a phenomenon clearer and easier to understand; we only end up with an archive of information that is somehow related.

As with most art historical terms, or "isms," naturalism is used in various, sometimes contradictory, ways. The literary critic Leo Berg sighs in the introduction to *Der Naturalismus* (1892): "'Naturalism,' 'Realism,' 'Impressionism,' 'Symbolism,' 'Verismo,' 'Decadence,' 'Fin de siècle'! Oh these foreign words!"[3] Even Christian Krohg offered a sarcastic hint to the art historian in an interview in 1920: "And all these words like impressionism and expressionism are only words and something that is made up just so that a few people have something to do."[4] *Naturalism* is a word that is used with different meanings at different times in art history, as well as in literary theory and philosophy. It also carries different connotations in different countries. If naturalism is to make sense and be a productive tool in art history, one has to be very clear about how the term is employed. In this chapter different meanings will be explored in order to better understand the art of Christian Krohg in the 1880s and the intellectual climate in which he operated. Krohg's naturalism circles, throughout this book, around Émile Zola's theory of naturalism. The French novelist and critic wrote that naturalism is the main movement of the nineteenth century. It was for him not a stylistic school but the "application of the experimental method to the study of nature and of man."[5]

Marxist literary theory commonly looks at naturalism as something that follows realism alongside formalism. In Terry Eagleton's words, "Realism, deprived of the historical conditions which gave it birth, splinters and declines into 'naturalism' on the one hand and 'formalism' on the other."[6] Georg Lukács describes "the pseudo-objectivism of the naturalist school and the mirage-subjectivism of the psychologist or abstract-formalist school."[7] Naturalism as represented by Zola is, according to Lukács, the result of the failure of the 1848 revolution. This event marked the freezing of the class struggle; the bourgeois class gave up its revolutionary ideals and, to quote Eagleton, "accepted society as a natural fact."[8] For Lukács, Balzac is the last writer who depicted a real class struggle. Naturalism is an impoverishment of literature. With Zola and naturalism, the writer became a passive observer: "The writer no longer participates in the great struggles of his time, but is reduced to a mere spectator and chronicler of public life."[9] The greatest example of this was the naturalist writers' use of extremely detailed description, as if they had a camera. They emphasized individual details instead of the typical; average life, psychology, and physiology became the determining forces in their narratives. To Lukács this is an alienated vision of reality, and the writer goes from being a realist—an active participant in society—to being a clinical observer, using naturalism as his method. Eagleton summarizes: "Lacking an understanding of the typical, naturalism can create no significant totality from its materials; the unified epic or dramatic actions launched by realism collapse into a set of purely private interests."[10] But Zola wanted naturalism to be a more democratic form of the realism of the 1850s, which he claimed was "exclusively bourgeois."[11] He wanted naturalist art to be about the *other* classes, as well as the classless. In my study the naturalist will be seen, in contrast to Lukács's view, as an active realist rather than a passive impressionist.

Raymond Williams calls the realism/naturalism distinction in late nineteenth-century literature and drama a "complication," and introduces the term "modern naturalism."[12] In Williams's narrative, it was Henrik Ibsen (1828–1906) who invented that decisive first bourgeois dissident form named naturalism, which later in Ibsen's oeuvre developed into symbolism and expressionism.[13] All these stages were supposed to shock the bourgeoisie, and the shock was an important part of modernist art, as was the case with many of Krohg's paintings. In Williams's words, "Hostile or indifferent or merely vulgar, the bourgeois was the mass which the creative artist must either ignore and circumvent, or now increasingly shock, deride and attack."[14] Ibsen's dramatic naturalism was, according to Williams, one of the first major manifestations of modernism, and Williams's definition of naturalism is as good as any: "At its center was the humanist and secular—and, in political terms, liberal and later socialist—proposition that human nature was not, or at least not decisively, unchanging and timeless, but was socially and culturally specific."[15] He adds that naturalism puts "emphasis on the evolutionary process, commonly seen as a struggle for existence, by which a new kind of life tried and as often failed to come through."[16] For Williams, symbolism and expressionism were further examination of "the unexplored dark areas of the bourgeois human order of its time."[17]

The dramatic and literary naturalism of Ibsen and his Norwegian contemporaries was important to Krohg's work. This was the national school of radical art he wrote and painted himself into—or, possibly, out of. That is why his art is so interesting as a negotiation between modern naturalism (Ibsen, Strindberg), as described by Williams, and French naturalism both in radical literature (Zola, the Goncourts) and naturalist painting (Bastien-Lepage, Roll, Raffaëlli). Krohg was in a unique intellectual position when he created his strongest canvases, such as the Albertine series. Ibsen was a great example to Krohg even though they never became friends. The generational gap between them seems to have been too large. Ibsen and Krohg were both well-known figures in Kristiania and regulars at Grand Café, and Krohg most likely considered himself a follower of Ibsen. In 1891 he made the drawing *From Grand Café*, in which Ibsen is shown standing outside on the pavement (fig. 2.1), and he painted *Henrik Ibsen by the Parliament Building* (1920s, fig. 2.2), posing the writer in almost the same spot as the one in which Krohg himself appeared in Oda Krohg's *Christian Krohg on Karl Johan Street* (1912, fig. 2.3). Both are shown on the stretch of Karl Johan Street where Grand Café was located. A further biographical link between Krohg and modern naturalism is his friendship with August Strindberg (1849–1912), whom he got to know in Berlin in the 1890s. In 1893 Krohg painted an expressive portrait of Strindberg (fig. 2.4), and this painting was bought by none other than Ibsen in 1895, and it was the most modern artwork in the latter's art collection. He hung it over the desk in his study and called it a "masterful picture" and "Insanity Emergent." Ibsen supposedly said that he worked better with Strindberg looking down at him with his demonic eyes: "He is my mortal enemy; he shall hang there and watch what I write."[18] It is important to remember this aspect of Krohg's biographical connection to modern literary naturalism. It made him more political and disobedient than many of his naturalist painter colleagues in Europe.

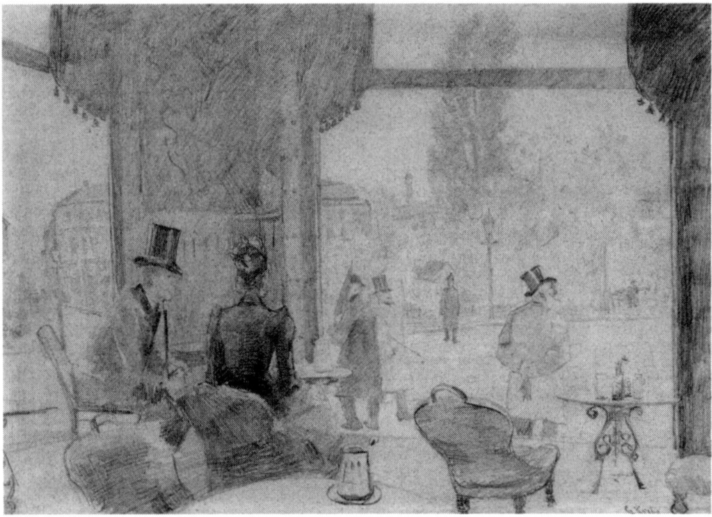

Figure 2.1. Christian Krohg, *From Grand Café (Henrik Ibsen on the Pavement Outside)*, (1891). Drawing, 29.4 × 42.7 cm. Private collection. © Photo: O. Væring Eftf. AS, Norway.

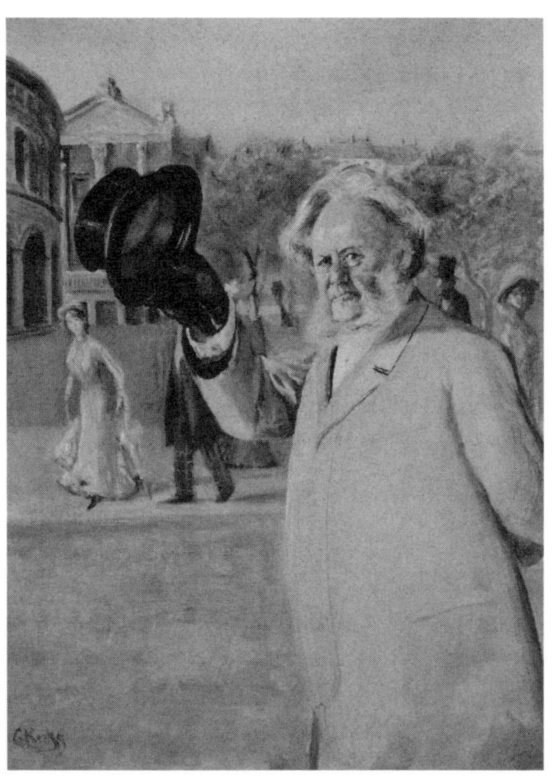

Figure 2.2.

Christian Krohg, *Henrik Ibsen by the Parliament Building* (1920s). Oil on canvas, 60 × 45 cm. Private collection. © Photo: O. Væring Eftf. AS, Norway.

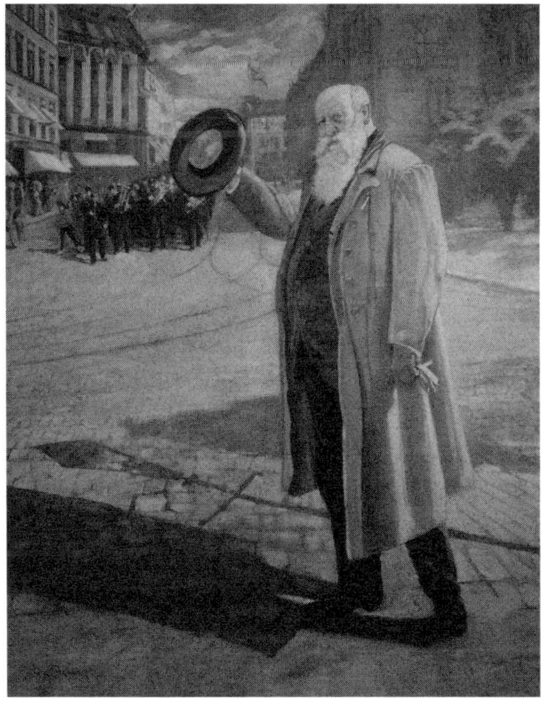

Figure 2.3.

Oda Krohg, *Christian Krohg on Karl Johan Street* (1912). Oslo City Museum. © Photo: O. Væring Eftf. AS, Norway.

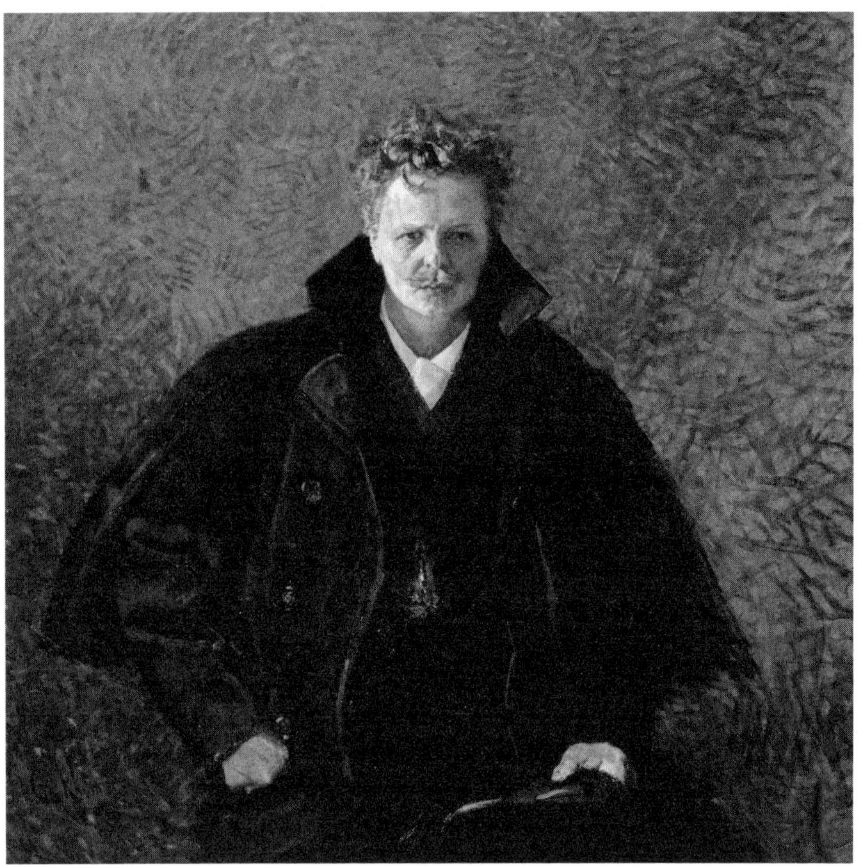

Figure 2.4. Christian Krohg, *August Strindberg* (1893). Oil on canvas, 126 × 128 cm. The Ibsen Museum, Oslo. © Photo: O. Væring Eftf. AS, Norway.

FROM REALISM TO NATURALISM

Realism in French art is often said to begin with the Salon of 1851. There was a new way of representing "truth" and it was done in a political way, with Courbet and Millet at the forefront. The realist school in the 1850s had, in T. J. Clark's words, "become more ambitious, taken its subjects from more modern and less picturesque sources, painted bigger, adopted a certain political stance."[19] A naturalism theory has, however, in art history, a considerably longer evolution than a realism theory,[20] a point Castagnary made in his Salon of 1868:

> The word *naturalism*, which I use to define current tendencies, is not new in the history of art, and this is one of the reasons that I prefer the word *realism*. Each

time we encounter within the world a nation, or within a nation a group of men, making the immediate object of painting the reproduction of surrounding life, and striving to visually reproduce the image of society seen within its natural setting, this art was, and this art is called naturalist. Naturalism is indeed what characterizes art in much of modern times.[21]

Castagnary defined naturalism in a review of the Salon as early as 1863: "The naturalists, young, ardent, committed, immune to blows, mount an assault from all sides; and already their daring heads appear at all the summits of art. . . . The naturalist school affirms that art is the expression of life in all of its forms and all of its degrees, and that its unique goal is to reproduce nature by bringing it to its maximum power and intensity: it is truth in equilibrium with science."[22] Note Castagnary's last sentence regarding art growing out of truth and science. Confusingly enough, in his review of the 1863 Salon, Castagnary also used the term *école naturaliste* for the group of independent artists who would later come to be known as the impressionists. For Castagnary, impressionism was a form of extreme naturalism with its emphasis on subjective sense experience.[23]

Thus, from second half of the nineteenth century, realism and naturalism have often been used as synonyms in art history, and it is not always clear how one distinguishes naturalism from realism.[24] This has created some "Verwirrung," to cite art historian Adolf J. Schmoll gen. Eisenwerth.[25] Traditionally, naturalism in the visual arts has been understood as an exceptionally faithful representation of nature based on thorough study: Albrecht Dürer, for example, made precise drawings based on careful observation of nature. In baroque painting it could mean a more "realistic" way of depicting religious scenes, as practiced by Caravaggio and the *naturalisti* of his school. The English landscape school, with Constable as its most important proponent, has also been named naturalist for depicting nature from direct studies.[26] Baroque naturalism could actually be seen as the main inspiration for the development of both nineteenth-century landscapes and realistic genre scenes.[27] Dutch seventeenth-century paintings, too, became models for many artists and critics in the nineteenth century, as will be further demonstrated in the chapter on Krohg's Skagen paintings.

Philosopher Anthony Savile tries to explain the difference between realism and naturalism: "It is sometimes said that naturalism in literature is no more than an extension or exaggeration of realism, or that it is nothing other than the transposition to literature of what realism is in art. But in the literary productions of the mid- and late-nineteenth century both sorts of narrative writings can be found and there are differences between them that need to be noted even if critical practice has not always kept them apart."[28] I will follow the last claim and say that there is a difference between realism and naturalism in painting as well, but I will examine naturalism as an extension of realism and an exaggeration of some of realism's aesthetic qualities. When the conservative German art historian Adolf Rosenberg wrote about the new radical art, such as that of Wilhelm Leibl, he stigmatized naturalism as "an outgrowth of the left wing of realism."[29] I will argue that naturalism is *one* aspect of realism—a development of realistic tendencies in art combined with a more scientific and matter-of-fact attitude toward life, often inspired by radical political ideas. Krohg's art is an example of this phenomenon.

ZOLA'S NATURALISM

Émile Zola (1840–1902) made naturalism a dictum, defining it as follows:

> Naturalism, that is, a return to nature; it is this operation which the savants performed on the day when they decided to set out from the study of bodies and phenomena, to build on experiment, and to proceed by analysis. Naturalism in letters is equally the return to nature and to man, direct observation, exact anatomy, the acceptance and depiction of what is. The task was the same for the writer as for the savant. One and the other replaced abstractions by realities, empirical formulas by rigorous analysis.[30]

Zola perceived naturalism as part of a longer literary tradition, and he looked to Diderot as the forefather of modern positivism. He also saw himself as writing in the tradition of Stendhal and especially Balzac. Zola explained his own experimental project to the Goncourts at a lunch in 1870: "He [Zola] spoke to me about a series of novels which he wants to write, an epic in ten volumes called *The Natural and Social History of a Family* which he wants to attempt, depicting temperaments, characters, vices, and virtues developed by various environments and as sharply distinguished as the sunny and shady parts of a garden."[31] Naturalism is supposed to be inspired by science and function as sociology.

It is not exactly clear what Zola meant by naturalism in painting when he wrote his review "Le naturalisme au Salon" in 1880. His art criticism over the years was not always consistent.[32] He often used *naturalism*, *impressionism*, *actualiste*, *positivism*, *materialism*, and *modernism* as synonyms, and applied the term *naturalism* for the first time to Hippolyte Taine in 1866.[33] Zola later labeled Manet a naturalist, then gave that label to the impressionists. He called Manet a naturalist in 1875: "Manet is a modern artist, a realist, a positivist. . . . Let me repeat, the public's incomprehension dissipates little by little, and Manet appears as he is in reality, the most original painter of our times, the only one since Courbet who has been distinguished by truly original traits announcing the naturalist school that I seek for the renewal of art and the expansion of human creation."[34] He also counted Henri Fantin-Latour as one of the painters "of the young naturalist school."[35] A year later, at the 1876 Salon, Zola penned one of his most quoted remarks about Manet: "This is a naturalist, an analyst. He knows neither how to sing nor how to philosophize. He knows how to paint, that is all, and it's a gift so rare that it has been sufficient to make Manet the most original artist of the last fifteen years."[36] In contrast, impressionism seemed to him a form of painting focused on the visual effects of light and color.

In 1880 it seemed that the generation of artists after the impressionists, caught somewhere between academism and impressionism, was potentially the true exponent of naturalism. Zola wrote that the impressionists (Monet, Renoir, Pissarro, Degas, Caillebotte, and Rouart), with their independent exhibitions, had influenced the paintings shown at the official Salon. The impressionists had been seen as outcasts but were now, almost in disguise, entering the official arena through the naturalist painters. Zola observed that in the almost twenty years since the Salon des Refusés in 1863, the mythological and classical motifs and dark romantic pictures had been gradually replaced by a contemporary mode inspired by mundane plein air subjects, scenes from Les Halles and the boulevards, and the intimate life: "It's a rising tide of modernity, irresistible, that little by little sweeps away the École des Beaux-Arts, the Institut, all prescriptions and all conventions. The motion begins, the movement continues, by a fatal force, without anyone being able to stop it; and this is not an agreement, this is simply the spirit of the passing century, which propels and unites individuals."[37] Naturalism in painting around 1880 was, for Zola, a kind of realistic academism influenced by impressionism. He had to admit that there were not many really good naturalists, but there was hope: "If none of the young painters are masters, all at least use the same formula, each with his different temperament."[38] He then discussed the successful naturalist paintings at the 1880 Salon. It is an interesting text because it shows what the Scandinavian painters who were in Paris at this time saw at that exhibition and tells us about the painters who were talked about in those years.

Zola began with Manet, whom he called a tireless naturalist and the single most interesting artist of his time. Zola observed how Manet had influenced the students of Gérôme and Cabanel, and argued that the impressionists were his true sons. He then turned to a group of newer artists whom he labeled naturalists, starting with the young Jules Bastien-Lepage (1848–1884). Zola wrote that this much-praised painter had won all the awards and medals possible. Bastien-Lepage's teacher, Alexandre Cabanel (1823–1889), perhaps most famous for his painting *Birth of Venus* (1863), had many students, including Eugène Carrière and Henri Gervex. Zola declared that it was not a crime to be Cabanel's student, for, interestingly enough, studios such as his provided naturalist recruits.[39] (The conservative critic Henri Houssaye even called painters like Bastien-Lepage and Gervex "deserters" from the École des Beaux-Arts).[40] Zola wrote: "Therefore, if we study the painter Mr. Bastien-Lepage, we will see that he owes much to the impressionists; he took their bright tones, their simplifications and also some of their reflections; but he took all this from them as would a student of Mr. Cabanel, with an extremely balanced skillfulness that delights the public. It's impressionism corrected, softened, placed within the reach of the crowd."[41] Here naturalism is a modified impressionism that pleases a wider audience. Zola noted that Bastien-Lepage was still very young, and that one should give him time to develop as a naturalist. Zola's critical remark came mainly because Bastien-Lepage's painting at that year's Salon was *Joan of Arc* (1880), a historical and mystical subject represented with Joan's hallucinations in the background and thus not following the naturalist formula. But Zola observed a modernist will in the painting and urged the audience to wait for the painter's next development.

Zola mentioned Henri Gervex (1852–1929) as the leader of the group of painters who broke away from the École to become naturalists.[42] Bastien-Lepage and Gervex were, for Zola, the future. Sadly, Bastien-Lepage died only four years later. Some of the other naturalist recruits (*recrues du naturalism*) discussed in Zola's review were Jean Charles Cazin, characterized by his mediocre *naturalisme mystique*, Jules Breton with his naturalism steeped in poetry, and Alfred Roll. Zola concluded: "Each year, at each Salon, one can see the evolution become more obvious. The painters of the academic tradition tire, producing works of greater and greater mediocrity, within an increasing isolation, while all of life, all strength is accorded to the painters of reality and modernity."[43]

It is interesting that Joris-Karl Huysmans in his Salon reviews almost always wrote about Bastien-Lepage and Gervex as a couple, as representatives of the same art. Guy de

Maupassant managed to include the names of these two most prominent naturalist painters in *Bel-Ami* (1885), but he regarded them as creators of art for a bourgeois taste and categorized them as representatives of academism.[44] There seemed to be a consensus that naturalism in French painting around 1880 was practiced by a group of painters associated with Bastien-Lepage and Gervex. This was the visual world Krohg and other Nordic painters encountered when they came to Paris.

NATURALISM AND IMPRESSIONISM

I argue that naturalism and impressionism were two contemporary but different ways of being a realist painter. Naturalism in painting came as a "period" after impressionism, and they developed in dialogue with each other. They were both empirical and concerned with observation, but, as Arnold Hauser writes, "the representations of impressionism are closer to sensual experience than those of naturalism in the narrower sense, and replace the object of theoretical knowledge by that of direct optical experience more completely than any earlier art. . . . But by detaching the optical elements of experience from the conceptual and elaborating the autonomy of the visual, impressionism departs from all art practiced hitherto, and thereby from naturalism as well."[45] Impressionism does not create mimetic illusions, as does naturalism, but both create—or aim to create—subjective representations of sensory experiences. Claude Monet's art is the great example of this aesthetic. From this follows that naturalism is a complex art, while impressionism is a simplified one. The naturalist canvas is trying to tell many things at the same time, while the impressionist one only wants to show a moment of time.

Literary historian Alfred Stoeckius talked about two attitudes in naturalism, one active, the other passive: "In the former [active] case the naturalist describes and analyzes common reality, as Zola does, for instance. In the latter case he yields to the influences of reality, he is impressed by it; here we get impressionism and 'Kleinmalerei,' which is the special character of German naturalism."[46] Naturalism was essentially active and impressionism passive. Impressionism and naturalism could also be linked to two attitudes in philosophical naturalism: sensationalism and experimentalism. As philosopher Ralph Barton Perry pointed out, these two are normally united "but owing to a characteristic difference of emphasis."[47] Sensationalism emphasizes how conceptions are made from sense impressions. Sense impressions are the only way we can know reality, and an external object that at first sight appears as a simple thing turns out to be a construct of sensible properties.[48]

Mathematician Karl Pearson wrote in *Grammar of Science* (1892) that experience of these external objects comes from "a combination of immediate with past or stored sense-impressions."[49] These "crude" sense impressions are regarded as truths in themselves. An experimentalist, on the other hand, claims that facts cannot be viewed as totally undefined, because that, in Perry's words, "would imply the deriving of physical nature wholly from subjective activity."[50] Mathematician Henri Poincaré stated in *Science and Hypothesis* (1904) that facts could be truths only if they took part in a method of experimentation: "Experiment is the sole source of truth. It alone can teach us anything new; it alone can give us certainty."[51] These positivist concepts can be useful in formulating the differences between impressionism and naturalism: impressionists often emphasized direct sense impressions and subjective experiences (sensationalism), while naturalists highlighted the context of whatever they were studying and made the motif or subject into a discourse (experimentalism).

Another way of analyzing the relationship between impressionism and naturalism is through the distinction between looking from without and looking from within. The American philosopher George S. Morris wrote: "By the one method we simply record the impressions which phenomena produce on the observer, together with the order in which they are seen to coexist or to follow each other. By the other we seek to enter into the nature of things, to comprehend the force which causes them, and which constitutes their true being." The pure impressionist becomes "any animal with failed logical powers, with well developed faculties of analysis and classification, but without the rational insight and emotion of man."[52] The naturalist wants to go farther, to look from within and to show a casus and its causes, not just a sight impression.

The difference between impressionism and naturalism can also be described using terms from Claude Bernard's well-known treatise *An Introduction to the Study of Experimental Medicine* (1865). One of Bernard's goals was to create a science that was not purely empirical; he drew a distinction between observation and experiment. This is also the distinction between impressionism and naturalism: the impressionist observes and the naturalist experiments. Observation displays; experiment instructs. But this does not mean that the naturalist is working in opposition to the impressionist, since the naturalist also needs to observe. It is a more active way of being a realist: one is allowed to take an active part in the creation of an artwork. The impressionist is, in theory, closer to an observing camera, just showing what he or she is recording, while the naturalist is instructing the beholder with his or her observations.

Zola was inspired by Bernard's book, paraphrased it, borrowed its vocabulary, and adopted Bernard's idea about the experimental method. Naturalism was, for Zola, the experimental method in art.[53] He presented his ideas, partly influenced by Bernard, in a series of columns in *Le messager de l'Europe* in 1879, later collected as *The Experimental Novel* (1880) and *From Naturalism in the Theatre* (1881). Inspired by the natural sciences, Zola wanted the artist to be an experimenter: someone who did not just observe but rather performed an experiment. He wrote in *The Experimental Novel*: "If the experimental novelist is still groping in the most obscure and complex of all the sciences, this does not prevent this science from existing. It is undeniable that the naturalistic novel, such as we understand it to-day, is a real experiment that a novelist makes on man with the help of observation."[54] Zola wrote:

> But see what splendid clearness breaks forth when this conception of the application of the experimental method to the novel is adequately grasped and is carried out with all the scientific rigor which the matter permits to-day. A contemptible reproach which they heap upon us naturalistic writers is the desire to be solely photographers. We have in vain declared that we admit the necessity of an artist's possessing an individual temperament and a personal expression; they continue to reply to us with these imbecile arguments, about the impossibility of being strictly true, about the necessity of arranging facts to produce a work of art of any kind. Well, with the application of the experimental method to the novel

> that quarrel dies out. The idea of experiment carries with it the idea of modification. We start, indeed, from the true facts, which are our indestructible basis; but to show the mechanism of these facts it is necessary for us to produce and direct the phenomena; this is our share of invention, here is the genius in the book. Thus without having recourse to the question of form and of style, which I shall examine later, I maintain even at this point that we must modify nature, without departing from nature, when we employ the experimental method in our novels. If we bear in mind this definition, that "observation indicates and experiment teaches," we can even now claim for our books this great lesson of experiment.[55]

This also makes the naturalist artwork political in a different way: the work is instructing beholders to react in a certain way to make a change. The goal of the experimental method in both science and art is to make the world a better place. This is the aim of many positivist writers: to combine objectivity with ethics or morality. The question is whether morality can be objective, for one can easily end up with a kind of quasi-science. This tension can be found in naturalist painting: morality is hidden under the veil of "science." Moreover, since naturalism can only be about "real" and definable things, naturalist art cannot concern itself with something as indefinable as beauty. Naturalist art has to be more than empirical and more than naïvely impressionist. For Krohg and the artists of his generation, being political was a natural choice, and it necessitated a connection between aesthetics and ethics.

One also needs to note an important difference when it came to subjects and class in impressionism versus naturalism. Impressionists *tended* to be more concerned with the bourgeoisie, while naturalists *tended* to focus on the proletariat, the peasants, and those who have fallen outside the class system: the poor, the beggars, the prostitutes. Impressionists and naturalists presented different images of class. Whenever impressionists painted prostitutes (as did Degas), farmers (Pissarro), or workers (Caillebotte's floor scrapers), they moved into the realm of naturalists.

ART AS POLITICS: SOCIALISM

Pierre-Joseph Proudhon, the "father" of anarchism, wanted economic revolution and the abolition of distinctions between a ruling class and a working class. His *Du principe de l'art et de sa destination sociale* (1865) was an important book for artists and critics concerned with social issues. Viewed through the lens of Proudhon's writings, art was certainly a political force in society. Artist and art critic Philip Gilbert Hamerton claimed that Proudhon "was the first to announce in print the relation between some modern art and the new Positive Philosophy. He fished up *that* murex, and deserves great credit for it."[56] In Proudhon's view, the artist should be a social moralist. For Proudhon, and for his friend Courbet, social and artistic truths were the same. Courbet stated in a letter in 1851: "I am not only a socialist but a democrat and a Republican as well—in a word, a partisan of all the revolution and above all a Realist . . ., for 'Realist' means a sincere lover of the honest truth."[57] In a review of the 1851 Salon, L. Enault wrote: "M. Courbet is the Proudhon of painting. M. Proudhon—M. Courbet, I should say—does democratic and social painting—God knows at what cost."[58] Another critic commented: "In M. Courbet art makes itself part of the people."[59] The principle of *l'art pour l'art* was repugnant to Proudhon: art had to have a political mission.[60] Théophile Thoré-Bürger might also be mentioned in this context. He applied revolutionary ideas to art in his treatise *Nouvelles tendances de l'art* (1830), where he argued that modern realist painting had to be about and for the living man: it had to be of one's own time.

Krohg was on several occasions linked to socialist ideas. His colleague, relative, and good friend Frits Thaulow wrote: "Krohg wanted to show the opposition between the rich and the poor. I even believe he meant that he painted in the service of socialism."[61] Erik Werenskiold wrote that among the Norwegians in Paris at the beginning of the 1880s, Krohg was mostly interested in Courbet, because they shared the same "society-reforming tendencies."[62] Andreas Aubert, in his comprehensive review of the large *Albertine* canvas in 1887, pointed out the "socialist tendencies" in Krohg's art,[63] and he wrote that Krohg was working in the tradition of Courbet's realistic program. Aubert also mentioned the large Raffaëlli exhibition in 1884 and quoted from Raffaëlli's "Étude des mouvements de l'art moderne et du beau caractériste," published in the exhibition catalog: "For a new society, a new art is required. For an egalitarian and democratic society, for the modern scientific man, an art in constant movement is required."[64] Aubert emphasized that Raffaëlli wanted to represent his times through portraits of different types, and that an important part of this endeavor was showing the lower classes of society, their beauty and misery.[65] The 1884 exhibition was shown at Avenue de l'Opéra and included over 150 works. Raffaëlli had many supporters at that time, including *Le Figaro* art critic Albert Wolff, who also championed Bastien-Lepage.[66] Aubert continued by saying that it was Krohg who had brought the ideas of Courbet, Rafaëlli, and Zola to Norway.[67]

When Henrik Jæger wrote about Krohg's breakthrough exhibition in 1885, he presented Krohg as the worker's painter, a chronicler of the worker's toil and fatigue: "[He] gives a definition of work which does not correlate with the old, common expression 'work is a blessing.' This expression can be true when it is applied to work that requires a special kind of talent and interest; but it is not true when it is about the bodily toil Krohg is representing. It looks more like an accident or an unfair punishment for someone who is innocent but has been condemned for life."[68] The reviewer wrote that Krohg, in an extraordinary way, showed sympathy with the worker, but without agitation and without easy and banal effects. He concluded that Krohg was becoming more and more honest and true in his representation of the workers. It is interesting to contrast this view with that expressed by a critic writing for the conservative newspaper *Aftenposten*, who in 1889 called Krohg's *Struggle for Existence* (1889, fig. 9.1, plate 16) "fruitless agitational activity" and a "meaningless gamboling among problems."[69] This kind of political message, the critic said, was not worthy of being addressed in serious and harmonious art. In 1888 Krohg painted *Socialists* (fig. 2.5). Here we see two men taking part in a demonstration; they have red ribbons on their jackets (a socialist symbol) and red signs on their hats saying "Live the social democracy."

Krohg's art views in the 1880s can be characterized as socialist, with Saint-Simonian tendencies. According to Saint-Simonism, all people in a society should work together to create the image of their time; this applies to intellectuals, engineers, businessmen, and

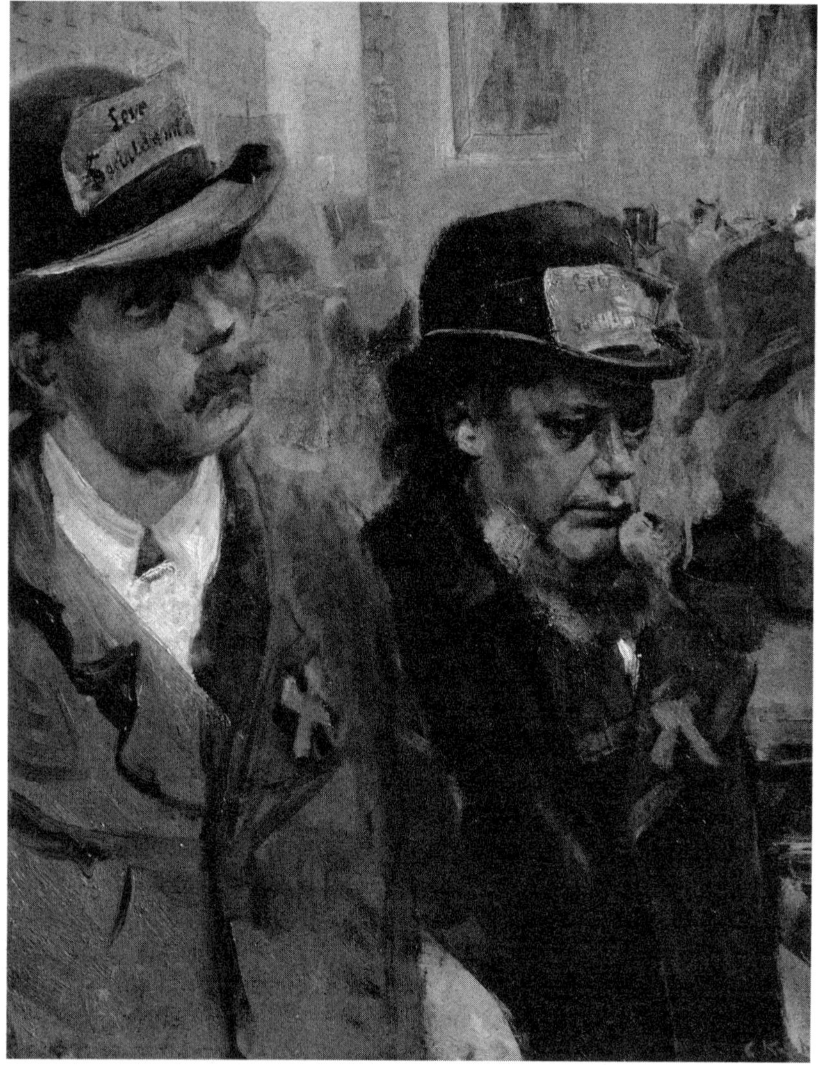

Figure 2.5. Christian Krohg, *Socialists* (1888). Oil on canvas, 67 × 55 cm. Private collection. © Photo: O. Væring Eftf. AS, Norway.

artists. Marxism envisioned similar goals for the working class. The Saint-Simonian journal *Le producteur* had as its purpose to "foster the union of scientists, industrialists, and artists, as the only means of rescuing society from its present state of crisis," and literature was especially important for the "development of moral energies."[70] Krohg, too, believed that art should have social usefulness and appeal to the people. He saw painting as the most powerful medium in this respect.

NATURALISM IN NORWAY

The term *naturalism* was much debated in Norway in the early 1880s, and Zola's work was well known among Norwegian artists, authors, and intellectuals. In 1879, the Danish critic Georg Brandes (1842–1927), who had discovered Zola's *Mes haines* in Paris in 1870, wrote a lengthy presentation of Zola's literary theory in the newspaper *Dagbladet*; it is one of the earliest introductions of Zola to Norwegian readers. Brandes offered Zola's main ideas as well as the slogan "an artwork [a sculpture, a painting, a book] is a corner of nature seen through a temperament."[71] Naturalism was for Brandes and his contemporaries the most avant-garde art and part of French contemporary philosophy and literary theory. The Student Association in Kristiania arranged two important panel discussions in 1882 at which the subject of discussion was whether naturalism represented progress or decline in literature. There were four participants in these panels: arguing against naturalism was the conservative professor of art history Lorentz Dietrichson and in defense were the radical author Arne Garborg (1851–1924), the literary historian and critic Henrik Jæger (1854–1895), and the professor of philosophy Georg Vilhelm Lyng (1827–1884).

To Dietrichson the naturalist school was the same as the modern school in art. He linked naturalism to Darwinism, Taine's theories, Schopenhauer's pessimism, socialism, and primarily to Zola's literary theory. Dietrichson based his understanding of naturalism on original texts by Zola and a review of naturalism in the conservative journal *Revue des deux mondes* from 1879, which he did not identify but was likely Charles Bigot's "L'esthétique naturaliste."[72] Dietrichson built his arguments around the polemic between Zola and Bigot.[73] Bigot defined naturalism as follows: "Two traits properly characterize naturalist literature. On one hand, it endeavors above all to paint a picture of vice, moral ugliness, the repugnant sickness of the body and the soul; on the other hand, it prefers to borrow the subjects of its paintings from the lower classes of society."[74] Dietrichson derived many of his arguments from Bigot's text and saw naturalism as going too far—compared to the more healthy realism—when it came to the depiction of the lower classes and the ambition of artists to paint the ugly aspects of life. He admitted that he admired naturalism for depicting such subjects as drinking dens, bordellos, and hospitals, and for the sympathy that naturalist artists showed toward people in difficult situations. But he criticized the naturalists for treating them "objectively," without comedy or tragedy. Dietrichson mentioned Jules Breton as an example of healthy realism and called him "the most real and true portraitist of the life of the people."[75] Dietrichson stated that objective art was an illusion. The naturalist's choices were subjective: "The naturalist's hobbyhorse seems to be the contemplation of the rotten and bad in human nature, and his senses seem to be graced with a special affinity for the hideous and the low."[76] He also attacked the quasi-scientific approach of naturalism and questioned its morality and its effects on the beholder. He criticized the naturalists for their scientism, or "scientific dilettantism," writing sarcastically that the naturalists "actually believe, in all seriousness, that the method suitable for scientific research also must be suitable for the poetic depiction." He continued: "It [naturalism] has apparently been seduced by the great results the natural sciences have won in our time; it wants to study pathology, make diagnoses, and practice therapy."[77] Instead of responsible people who exercise free will, naturalism showed "patients and animals."[78] He mentioned Fyodor Dostoyevsky's

Crime and Punishment (1866) as the most full-blooded and successful naturalist work and called it a pure hospital clinic, "not far from a veterinary clinic."[79] Dietrichson stated that naturalism was not making progress; rather, it only made one depressed.[80] To the art history professor, naturalism was an art that had misunderstood both aesthetics and sciences; it was thus a double failure.

Author Arne Garborg responded to Dietrichson that being of one's own time in 1882 meant being a naturalist. If naturalism was a sign of decay, then the society of that time was in decay. The naturalist's interest in the lower classes had, for Garborg, to do with the time's general interest in them (with parallel trends in fields like politics and sociology). Being a symptom of its times, naturalism could not be judged aesthetically. The naturalist could not solve the problems of society, but he or she could "through living images show us the truth in a way that makes us think."[81] Krohg made a similar point in his writings. The work of art needed to shock to have an effect.[82] Literary historian and critic Henrik Jæger similarly defended naturalism, but he called for a more strict use of the term. In his opinion, naturalism as a literary term referred strictly to Zola and his school; he adduced several quotes from the French author.[83]

Editor, journalist, and theater director Johan Vibe wrote a critical book about Zola's experimental method, *Nogle Bemærkninger i Anledning af Naturalismen* (Some remarks about naturalism), in 1884. He provided a thorough presentation of Zola's theories and even showed how Zola applied them in his novels. Vibe's main example was Zola's exploration of alcoholism in *L'assommoir* (1877). Vibe emphasized that Zola wanted the novelist to be nothing but a scientist. Vibe showed that he was quite familiar with Zola's writings, both his theories and his novels, as well as Taine's books, and spent most of his book attacking the positivist aesthetics and the quasi-scientific methods of these authors: "Even the poorest thesis of a skilled doctor at an insane institution will have more scientific value than the elaborate novel by a fiction writer."[84] The author could never compete with the scientist and make real scientific contributions, and a novel could never make a significant difference in the world. To Vibe the novel and art in general were pure luxuries. The need for luxury was a sign of a developed culture, and literature and art were the noblest forms of luxury.[85] Vibe stated: "In our day literature has fallen into the hands of sick people whose works are just as depressing as they are without imagination. It is mental patients writing about mental patients for mental patients. Every new story is a new miserable book, or a storage room for tiresome and banal psychological analysis."[86] Vibe was a proponent of *l'art pour l'art* aesthetics, in direct opposition to Krohg.

Looking at impressionism and naturalism as two attitudes, or modes, means that an artist such as Krohg could at the same time paint a painting with a "naturalist" attitude and an "impressionist" one. This was common for many European painters who came to Paris in the 1870s and 1880s. They were inspired by different kinds of painters and styles. The art scene was not as clear cut as later art history books often suggest. With so many schools and styles around, it was difficult to be original, and most painters ended up as mediocre and forgettable artists. Only a few succeeded in charting their own memorable path. The Nordic artists were exposed to romantic as well as academic painting, to *juste milieu*, realism, and impressionism. Christian Skredsvig wrote about his first stay in Paris in 1874–75: "In Paris, Corot and Millet were idolized."[87] When he returned to Paris in 1879, and naturalism and impressionism were the most important subjects in the art world, "names such as Manet, Monet, Bastien Lepage crackled like pennants in a storm."[88]

Bastien-Lepage, Breton, Caillebotte, Courbet, Manet, Millet, Monet, and Raffaëlli can all be characterized as realists. But they are at the same time extremely different: their paintings represent different ideological positions in French culture. In general, French naturalism in painting is a product of the new republic in 1870s France. It is a democratic art, concerned with the heroic people. It shows contemporary life—work, progress, enlightenment, and science—on canvases that are often large and focused on daily, prosaic, contemporary life.[89] Nordic painters who drew inspiration from these various sources did not necessarily "copy" their ideologies. Krohg's paintings that exhibit influences of Bastien-Lepage and Manet must not be looked at through the lens of the French artists and their positions, but rather in the context of Krohg and his own aims. The point here is that a French naturalist painting is different from a Scandinavian one. French naturalism is normally understood as a more conservative art form than impressionism or the realism of Courbet and Manet. More like *juste milieu*, it was often painted on behalf of the authorities and ended up in official buildings (where we can still find such paintings today). In the Nordic countries, naturalism was the most radical and avant-garde art on the scene. It was wildly discussed, and Krohg's paintings of prostitution were a shock to both their audiences and the authorities. In a text written in 1889, Krohg looked back at the preceding decade: "We who believed we were the most radical of the radical. We took it upon ourselves to paint the ugly—even the ugliest in nature."[90] He wrote that he and his generation "had a silent inner awareness that we were the avant-garde."[91]

There is thus no final definition of naturalism, neither in literature nor in painting; there are only its many, and sometimes conflicting, descriptions. I have argued that naturalism is an active and experimental art form, an art that is seen from within. Naturalism in painting has a social mission, is aimed at the masses, and represents daily motifs drawn from people's shared experiences. Art historian Richard Thomson writes that French naturalist painting is "descriptive, frank, direct" and calls it a "dynamic kind of art."[92] French naturalism was legible and easy to understand in comparison with impressionism and symbolism. Its effectiveness in communication also meant that it could be used to critique official ideas—and it was Krohg's naturalist project to use the legible language of naturalism to attack the political authorities and conventional art.

CHAPTER THREE

The Heroism of the Scientist

This literature is a giant clinic of the century's maladies.

GIACOMO BARZELLOTTI ON NATURALISM

THIS chapter takes a closer look at the philosophical ideas and zeitgeist that formed the aesthetics of naturalism and examines how science and the scientist inspired the arts. The French critic C. A. Sainte-Beuve's review of Gustave Flaubert's *Madame Bovary* (1856) serves as a useful illustration of the relationship between art and science: "For in many places, and in many different forms, I think I have recognized the signs of new literatures: science, the spirit of observation, maturity, strength, and a little hardiness. These are the characteristics that seem to affect the leaders of the new generations. Son and brother of distinguished doctors, Mr. Flaubert uses his pen like others would a scalpel. Anatomists and physiologists, I find you everywhere!"[1] The scientist was seen as a modern hero in the nineteenth century. He had the power to really make the world a better and more modern place, and his methods, techniques, and tools were modern—if not avant-garde. Henri de Saint-Simon stated: "Only the scientists are capable of exercising power for the benefit of all."[2] He also wrote, "A scientist, my friend, is a man who foresees; it is because science provides the means to predict that it is useful, and the scientists are superior to all other men."[3] Saint-Simon even claimed that the French Revolution "was secretly fomented by scientists and artists."[4] The anti-aristocratic and antireligious attitude of modern science spoke to avant-garde artists such as Zola and Krohg. Zola wrote in 1868 that "the modern method of universal inquiry . . . is the tool our age is using so enthusiastically to open up the future."[5] In Zola's *Le docteur Pascal* (1893) we read: "In sum, doctor Pascal had only one belief: a belief in life. Life was the sole divine manifestation. Life was God, the grand motor, the soul of the universe. And life had no other instrument than heredity, heredity made the world; therefore, if one could know heredity, capture it and command it, one could shape it to one's liking."[6]

Georg Brandes stated in his very first book, published in 1866: "The nineteenth century is the era of the natural sciences and the great discoveries."[7] The Norwegian literary historian Herman Jæger wrote in his 1917 book on Hippolyte Taine: "All those things one single generation succeeded in doing! And the extreme [scientific] differences are bound together by one thing: method. All fields have been developed with the help of the experiment. Let us mention some names — Pasteur, Cuvier and Geoffroy St. Hilaire, Berthelot."[8] It was thus not a far-fetched idea to compare art to medicine, as Zola, indeed, did: "Since medicine, which was an art, is becoming a science, why should not literature also become a science by means of the experimental method?"[9] Georg Brandes remarked in his book on Hippolyte Taine (1870): "The genius of the great Master [artist] consists of being a physiologist in the same way as the great authors are psychologists."[10] He added that "the purpose of literature is to record and store emotions, and the more important the emotions a book stores, the higher its historic status. It is similar to the excellent devices physicists use when they are examining and measuring the finest internal changes in a body."[11] Arne Garborg wrote about naturalism and science in 1882: "The scientific aspect of the naturalistic method consists simply of a poet using the basis of general scientific principles to build his depictions on *observations*, scientifically accurate observations, and relating to them in a scientifically sober way — objectively — in his depiction." Garborg continued, "He [the artist] builds upon observation but creates images; in other words, he is and remains an artist."[12]

Auguste Comte also resorted to medicine as an important example when he developed his notion of positivism. He used medicine as his main analogy and called the sociologist the doctor of society.[13] Saint-Simon claimed something similar and looked at social relations as physiological phenomena.[14] No wonder one of the major themes in art and literature in the latter half of the nineteenth century was the importance of objective sciences such as medicine. It is also interesting to see how the language of the sciences — physiognomy, criminology, and anthropology — gave art critics a new vocabulary,[15] especially for the description of impressionism, but also, as this study demonstrates, of naturalist painting. The Danish philosopher and sociologist Claudius Wilkens stated in the 1880s that modern aesthetics was about analysis as well as "experience and experiment."[16]

Many artists welcomed the scientific impulse, although others feared it and believed that art should be about the ideal — that it should perfect nature. Thomas Sergeant Perry, American literary critic, and husband of the impressionism-influenced painter Lilla Cabot Perry, wrote in 1883: "Certain lovers of letters are alarmed at the advance of science and seem to fear that, unless extraordinary precautions are taken, the imagination will expire like the Ptolemaic system of astronomy." He offered an accurate image of the situation:

> Still, it is possible to conceive of a time when the division between literature and science shall be less sharply drawn than it is at present. Now they are looked upon as two hostile camps, and skirmishing is warm at the outposts. Yet there may be peace in the future when the man of letters shall cease to amuse himself and others with picturing the man of science as an arrogant person whose sole occupation is pouring some unsavory decoction from one glass tube into another, and when the scientific man shall no more imagine the man of letters to be a somewhat contemptuous person who prefers alliterations to more solid good. After all, what surprises people who have ceased to quarrel is the extent to which they agree, and when we consider that every one of us is the product of both

scientific and literary training, we are conscious of no vast dissensions within ourselves. Possibly society may tolerate both literature and science.[17]

Art theorist Eugène Véron wrote in his *Æsthetics* (1879) about science's importance in general and to contemporary art in particular. Art turning itself to reality instead of metaphysics felt fresh and new. As Véron stated, "At present the public . . . is equally tired of the ideal abstractions of the academic schools, and of the artificial enthusiasms of the romanticists; it has returned to the search for truth and demands sincerity."[18] He continued, "Everywhere and in every pursuit, truth has become a *sine quâ non*. Painting, in obedience to this tendency, has entered more thoroughly than ever before, into the study of nature and reality; searching there for new and powerful means of expression, appropriate to the requirements of modern intellect."[19] The scientist became a role model for many artists and writers of the era, and especially for the avant-garde artist, always on the look for new impulses. Guy de Maupassant elegantly commented on this in his *Alien Hearts* (1890): "Georges de Maltry [philosopher] was telling Gaston de Lamarthe [novelist] about the latest and still-disputed discovery in microbiology. He elaborated on the subject endlessly, and the novelist responded with the enthusiasm with which men of letters welcome anything that strikes them as original and new."[20]

THE DOCTOR

The scientist received growing recognition and intellectual stature in the nineteenth century. He was a new type of intellectual with specific qualifications in a particular area of knowledge.[21] The doctor especially became an everyday representative of the sciences. In Michel Foucault's words, "We would find that, in the nineteenth century, medicine—specifically, the medical doctor—had become middle class. In the nineteenth century, the bourgeoisie found in the medical science, in the concern with body and health, a form of day-to-day rationalism. In that sense, we can say that medical rationalism was substituted for religious ethics."[22] A "clinical eye" or "medical perception" was developed, so that society was seen as a clinic and citizens as patients.[23] The doctor enjoyed the right and the privilege to intrude in people's private lives, and in so doing became a symbol of the observing artist. It is symptomatic that the scientist appeared as a figure in many literary and painterly works by artists associated with naturalism. Krohg's first ambitious naturalist painting was titled *Coming for the Doctor* (1880, fig. 3.1): it depicted a poorly dressed woman coming to the doctor's house and interrupting a fine dinner party. As the servant helps him on with his coat, the doctor looks at his pocket watch, signaling the importance and value of his time. In the background the festive party goes on. The doctor's wife gazes at him—perhaps displeased by the inappropriate disturbance. The scene is ambiguous. The doctor is a wealthy man, living in a bourgeois world, far from the realities of the poor woman. Yet his duty is to treat everyone, regardless of class. He has to leave his well-appointed house and enter the homes of the poor to help them, although he always gets back to his dinner and drinks. Krohg's painting shows the doctor as a person who moves between different worlds. Krohg himself was similar to the doctor: coming from a bourgeois world, yet engaging with the

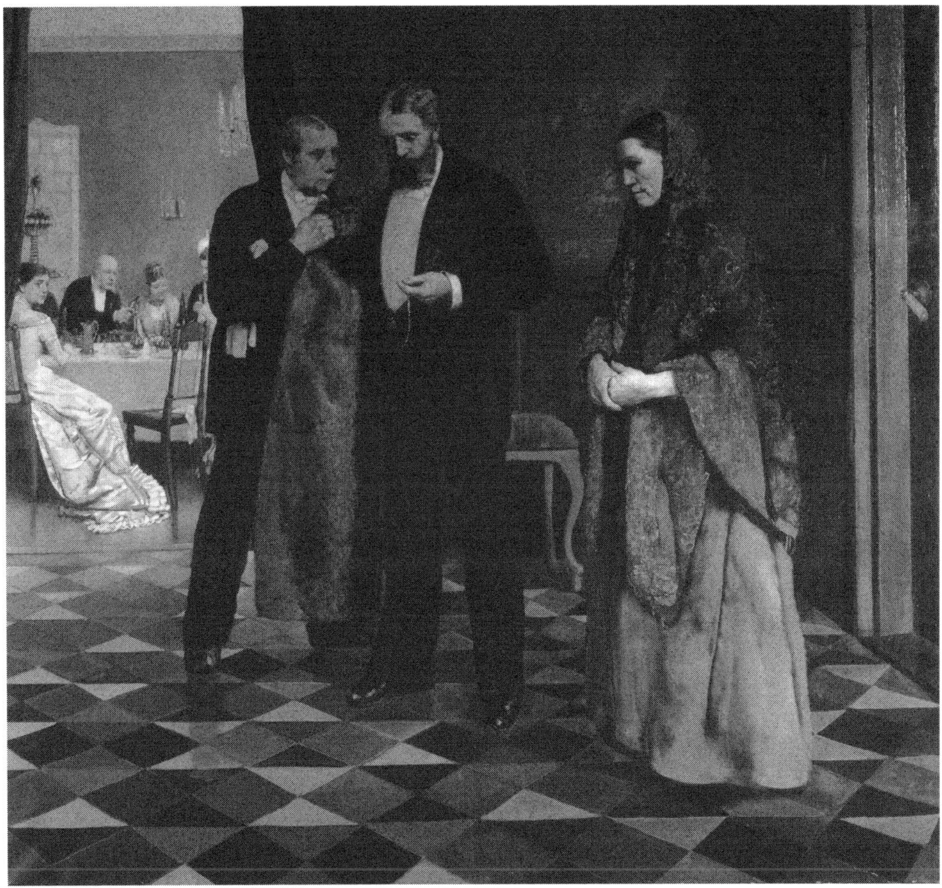

Figure 3.1. Christian Krohg, *Coming for the Doctor* (1880). Oil on canvas, 177 × 192.5 cm. Trondheim Kunstmuseum, Norway. © Photo: O. Væring Eftf. AS, Norway.

lower classes in his paintings with sympathy and care; observing their lives with a keen eye and seeking to better their lot with the tools at his disposal.

Many naturalist works at the time featured doctors: Richard Bergh's *Hypnotic Séance* (1887), Henri Gervex's *Before the Operation* (1887), and Léon Lhermitte's *Claude Bernard Performs an Experimental Vivisection* (1889, fig. 3.2).[24] Bergh's painting is noteworthy because it shows how the experimental sciences in the 1880s moved into experimental psychology (hysteria, psychosis, and the unconscious), providing a parallel to the movement from naturalism to symbolism in art. Gervex's work was one of the most popular paintings at the 1887 Salon. It depicted the famous surgeon Jules Émile Péan, who commissioned the painting, surrounded by colleagues and two nurses, just before cutting into a young

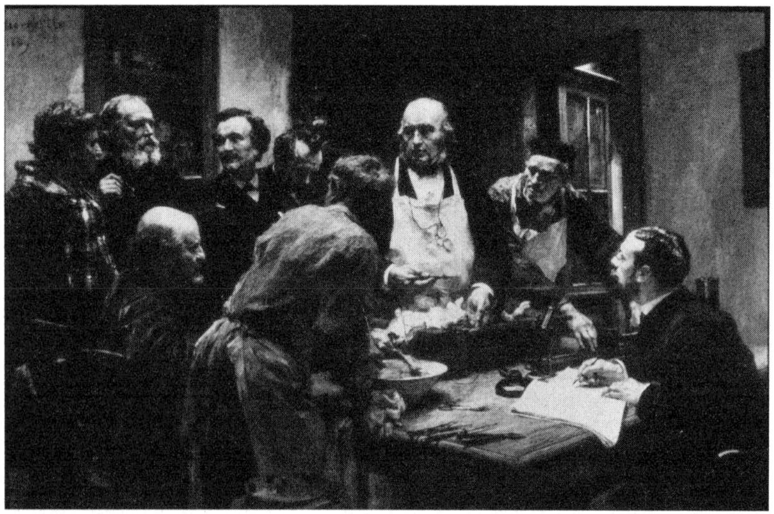

Figure 3.2. Léon Lhermitte, *Claude Bernard Performs an Experimental Vivisection* (1889). Oil on canvas, 46 × 61 cm. Photo © bpk.

woman.[25] In Lhermitte's painting, the famous physiologist Claude Bernard is engaged in a dissection as his students look on. The operation is a vivisection of a rabbit, and a number of tools are visible on the table, alongside a microscope. Lhermitte was a friend of Zola and one of the French painters most strongly associated with the naturalist movement.[26] He was well known for his large canvases of rural life, often exhibited at the Salon and bought by the state. His painting of Bernard's performance of a modern medical procedure was commissioned by the Sorbonne in 1886 and exhibited at the 1889 Salon.

THE POSITIVIST *ÉTAT D'ESPRIT*

How was naturalism in art related to contemporary philosophical naturalism? Even though the latter also belonged to the nineteenth century, its roots went back to mid-seventeenth-century philosophy and such thinkers as Spinoza and the late Hume. In metaphysics and general philosophy, naturalism stood in opposition to all that was supernatural and transcendental: mysticism, dualism, idealism, pantheism, teleology, and vitalism.[27] But the first *real* philosophical naturalism was related to the first wave of Darwinism in the nineteenth century, while a more mature naturalism developed in the twentieth century alongside "pragmatism, genetic psychology, behaviorism, electronic physics, social ethics, and epistemological realism," in the words of philosopher Roy Wood Sellars.[28]

Science's power and importance increased considerably during the nineteenth century, constituting a paradigmatic or epistemic shift. The Western world experienced a remarkable growth in scientific societies and educational institution.[29] Developments in chemistry, biology, and zoology were especially important for the positivist turn in French philosophy. Fields such as geology, paleontology, physics, and physiology; the human sciences of sociology, psychology, and anthropology; and more scientifically based history made significant contributions to this turn. As H. S. Williams wrote in his *History of Science* (1904), now the philosophical chemist looked at animal and plant organisms as "chemical laboratories in which conditions are peculiarly favorable for building up complex compounds of a few familiar elements, under the operation of universal chemical laws. The chimera of 'vital force' could no longer gain recognition in the domain of chemistry."[30] The experiments carried out in the laboratories and the search for new ways to systematize the world were shaking up old axioms, and it is not surprising that all of these scientific activities became part of the artistic imagination. French critic Ferdinand Brunetière commented on the late nineteenth-century "mania" for classification and systematization: "As to the power and, if I may say so, the virtue of classification, so many philosophers, so many scholars have spoken of it so well, that I hardly know whom I should here call to my aid, a Hæckel or an Agassiz, a Stuart Mill or an Auguste Comte. I could add also the Darwins and the Huxleys."[31] This is a good indication of how scientists influenced the literary world. One could now talk of a more coherent scientific society. The expansion of science was followed by the growth of an educated readership, and scientific texts sold as many copies as novels.[32]

One of the things that made naturalist sciences different from the work of scientists associated with the romantic movement and idealism was the naturalists' emphasis on the search for underlying laws of creation: knowledge of the world was based on the understanding of natural laws.[33] Each species had to be looked at as an individual case formed by local environment. The romantics and idealists tended to be more interested in the sublime powers of nature and believed in its underlying unity.[34] As Taine described it, positivism had to be understood as an alternative to spiritualism and its belief in vitalistic life powers. Positivism, with its belief in chemical reactions and physical action, was the domain of the scientist (*des savants*). Taine defined positivism as follows: "The positivists . . . declare they know nothing about the cause of life or on the cause of the universe. They simply note the sum and direction of chemical reactions and the physical actions that make up life, and group the experimental laws that summarize all observable facts in our universe."[35] In art the romantics were spiritualists, while the realists/naturalists were positivists, although the boundaries between them were often blurry.

"IL FAUT ÊTRE DE SON TEMPS"

The different branches of naturalism in the history of philosophy were united by a refusal to accept explanations based on supernatural or transcendental principles. One could recognize only what took place in time and space—in the natural world. Art historian Julius Lange wrote in 1884 that both the artist's and the scientist's work starts with observation, that both painting and science demand one thing: "To be in as immediate and incessant relation to their subject as possible."[36] Painting and writing about what you can see and touch here and now, and being in an immediate relationship with your subject, were necessary to realist and naturalist artists. This was the same as to be of one's own time—one of Taine's most important doctrines: the artist could only be of his own time, and thus should not try to repeat the ideals of other eras. The greatest artists were those who most reliably represented their times, because artists were witnesses.[37]

This motto of realism and naturalism, "Il faut être de son temps," was also one of the main points in Charles Baudelaire's *The Painter of Modern Life* (1863): "It is doubtless an excellent thing to study the old masters in order to learn how to paint; but it can be no more than a waste of labour if your aim is to understand the special nature of present-day beauty. . . . In short, for any 'modernity' to be worthy of one day taking its place as 'antiquity,' it is necessary for the mysterious beauty which human life accidentally puts into it to be distilled from it."[38] Being of one's own time becomes a definition of modernism.

The imperative "to be of one's own time," invoked in Baudelaire's "heroism of modern life," was repeated by many realist and naturalist artists.[39] An important example is Courbet's theory of realism, expressed in his letter of 1861: "Art, or talent, should be to an artist no more than the means of applying his personal faculties to the ideas and the events of the times in which he lives. . . . Every age should be represented only by its own artists, that is to say, by the artists who have lived in it. . . . Every age must have its artists, who give expression to it and reproduce it for the future."[40] Raffaëlli wrote in his essay on aesthetics that a new society requires a new art.[41] Eugène Véron declared in his aesthetic treatise: "Men whose lives belong to the same period are generally influenced by the same set of facts. The sources of inspiration afford but little variety. Sometimes a single idea or sentiment is impressed upon a whole generation. But each man interprets it after his own fashion, after the fulness of his own personal inspiration, and according to the measure of his own genius. . . . In fact, the artist is never more powerful or more inspired, than when he finds himself in perfect accord with the age in which he lives; and art is never greater than when it marches with the ideas and sentiments that influence a whole condition of society."[42] Krohg would agree. He wrote in 1886 that the modern artist's mission was to capture his time's characteristic properties, and claimed that "the image of the time is first and foremost an image of that time's people."[43] Two years later he wrote: "The same heartbeat that is common to the whole great life we call the contemporary must be felt in an artwork if it shall have importance for its time."[44] This is why he preferred realistic depictions of typical contemporary people in their daily surroundings, like seamstresses, workers, friends, and family. Together these images would, according to Krohg, make a relatively comprehensive image of that specific time in history. His views were close to those of Courbet, who wrote in his statement on realism: "To record the manners, ideas and aspect of the age as I myself saw them—to be a man as well as a painter, in short to create living art—that is my aim."[45]

BERNARD'S DOUBT

Claude Bernard (1813–1878) was one of the most influential thinkers of his age and the most important physiologist of his generation (physiology being defined the science of the laws of life). In the Norwegian newspaper *Aftenposten,* he was identified in 1861 as "the famous Claude Bernard."[46] He was the one who most fully developed the experimental method: the shift from passive empiricism to active experimentalism. His research was seen as part of psychology and nerve physiology, for he experimented with nerve stimulation; his studies were exceptionally important for the understanding of how the nervous system worked as a net of impulses.[47] He won fame through his many books—particularly the much-admired *An Introduction to the Study of Experimental Medicine* (1865)—and through his lectures at the Sorbonne. His *Introduction* was based on over twenty-five years of laboratory research and became the bedside book for Taine and his generation.[48] Bernard introduced a new style of scientific writing and drew examples from literature and philosophy. He offered not a philosophical system but rather a creative way of doing research based on doubt (as opposed to skepticism).[49] As he wrote at the end of his *Introduction*:

> When a man of science takes a philosophical system as his base in pursuing a scientific investigation, he goes astray in regions that are too far from reality, or else the system gives his mind a sort of false confidence and an inflexibility out of harmony with the freedom and suppleness that experimenters should always maintain in their researches. We must therefore carefully avoid every species of system, because systems are not found in nature, but only in the mind of man. Positivism, like philosophical systems that it rejects in the name of science, has the fault of being a system. Now, to find truth, men of science need only stand face to face with nature, and in following experimental medicine, question her with the help of more and more perfect means of investigation. In this case, I think that the best philosophical system consists in not having any.[50]

It was thus not a strict, rational, and logical scientific method, but rather included vagueness and inconsistency. The positivist aspect in Bernard's thinking was his belief in progress—that science was always getting better and that preexisting laws determined all phenomena.[51]

The play between observation and experimentation, and the rejection of a priori knowledge, were at the core of Bernard's philosophy. He claimed that knowledge was relative and provisional. A scientific fact was not the same as a mathematical truth: a scientific conclusion could change in the future. Scientific theories represented the present state of our knowledge. He described a truth-seeking method in which creativity played an important role: "The experimental method, the free thinker's method, seeks only scientific truth. Feeling, from which everything emanates, must keep its complete spontaneity and all its freedom for putting forth experimental ideas; reason also must preserve that freedom to doubt, which forces it always to submit ideas to the test of experiment."[52] He stated that all conclusions must remain doubtful, and that absolute truth only exists in mathematical principles. All other truths were relative.

Henri Bergson found in Bernard's writings a "happy combination of spontaneity and reflection, of science and philosophy."[53] Indeed, the experimental method was not just observing things in accordance with pure empiricism, but also testing them and reflecting on them; it was a collaboration of facts and ideas, a dialogue between nature and mind. In Bergson's words, "Nature rouses our curiosity; we ask it questions; its answers give an unexpected turn to the conversation, starting new questions to which nature replies by suggesting new ideas, and so on indefinitely."[54] Physiology could not, according to Bernard, answer metaphysical questions; it could only study material phenomena. But he did not deny the existence of the metaphysical.[55] Bernard wrote in a critique of Comte: "Never will metaphysics disappear. That is another error of the Positivist philosophy."[56] He argued that one is an idealist when one thinks but a materialist when one acts. He meant that all great philosophers had been both materialists and idealists, and wrote in one of his notebooks: "To understand, *think*, and believe one must be an idealist; for matter alone explains nothing. In other words, to *act* one must be an empiricist. To *understand*, one must be a theorist."[57]

BERNARD AND ART

Bernard's seemingly flexible theory could, to his own frustration, serve as a foundation for many philosophical and intellectual purposes, including naturalism in art. But it is important to remember that he had no intention of writing an aesthetic theory. He himself thought that art was not part of the sciences but rather their opposite. He was interested in both literature and art, and as a young man wanted to become a playwright and a poet. He knew well figures from literary and artistic circles, such as Edmond About, author of the novel *L'homme à l'oreille cassée* (1861), which was inspired by Bernard and the experimental method;[58] the romantic poet and playwright Emile Deschamps; and the artist Paul Chenavard. Bernard frequented Café Magny, a meeting place of the literary group led by Sainte-Beuve, and of intellectuals such as Taine and the Goncourts.[59]

Bernard wrote in his *Introduction* that art was personal and science impersonal, and quoted from an anonymous "poëte contemporain": "Art is myself; science is ourselves [l'art, c'est *moi*; la science, c'est *nous*]."[60] This contemporary poet was most likely Victor Hugo, whose *William Shakespeare* (1864) is full of similar one-liners, such as "Science is perfectible; Art is not," "Science is relative; Art definitive," and "Science makes discoveries; Art composes works."[61] Bernard shared Hugo's view on the relationship between art and science. To Hugo:

> Science is the asymptote of truth; it approaches unceasingly, and never touches. Nevertheless, it has every kind of greatness. It has will, precision, enthusiasm, profound attention, penetration, shrewdness, strength, patience in concatenation, permanent watchfulness of phenomena, the ardor of progress, and even fits of bravery. Witness La Pérouse; witness Pilastre des Rosiers; witness Sir John Franklin; witness Jacquemont; witness Livingstone; witness Mazet; witness, at this very hour, Nadar.
>
> But Science is series. It proceeds by proofs superposed one above the other, whose obscure stratification rises slowly to the level of Truth.
>
> Art has nothing like it. Art is not successive. All art is *ensemble*.[62]

Bernard wrote: "Literary and artistic productions never grow old, in this sense, they are expressions of feeling, changeless as human nature. . . . But science, which stands for what man has learned, is essentially mobile in expression; it varies and perfects itself in proportion to the increase of acquired knowledge."[63] It is therefore, somehow, a paradox that artists like Zola should have been so inspired by Bernard's theory.

Bernard's *Introduction* gave Zola the theoretical foundation he needed for his literary theory about the experimental novel. It is true that Zola only read Bernard's *Introduction* when he was finishing *The Experimental Novel* (1880), so many of his ideas were already formed.[64] But he had read Bernard's *Leçons de physiologie expérimentale appliquée à la médicine* (1855–56) in the course of his research for the Rougon-Macquart books in 1868–69. The principles derived from Bernard's later book are already present here.[65] Zola had all the right to claim in *The Experimental Novel*: "I intend on all points to entrench myself behind Claude Bernard."[66] So even if Zola got his philosophical ideas mainly from Taine, Bernard gave him the final framework and a proper vocabulary.[67] Perhaps he was inspired by the following instruction from Bernard's book: "Every science has its own kind of investigation and its equipment of special instruments and methods. This, after all, is plain enough, since every science is characterized by the nature of its problems and by the variety of the phenomena that it studies."[68] Zola just replaced the word *doctor* with *novelist* in his treatise.

Zola's naturalism was both an abstract concept and a concrete program describing preferred motifs and how they should be presented to the reader. Zola was specific about it in *From Naturalism in the Theatre* (1881). He lists several examples of desirable scenes: "Inside a factory, the interior of a mine, the gingerbread market, a railway station, flower stalls, a racetrack, and so on. All the activities of modern life can take place in them. . . . The environment must determine the character."[69] Taine wrote something similar in his advice to the historian, which can be easily transferred to the artist: "Leave aside the theory and the mechanism of constitutions, religions and their systems, and try to see men in their workshops, in their offices, in their fields, with their sky and soil, their houses, their dress, cultivations, meals, as you do when, landing in England or Italy, you [the historian] look at faces and motions, roads and inns, a citizen taking his walk, a workman drinking."[70] There were "rules" about which subjects could be characterized as naturalistic: all of Krohg's subjects were typical of naturalism, including seamstresses and prostitutes, poverty and sickness. Zola further described how characters should be attired, and how they should speak in their distinctive diction: "What I want to hear on the stage is the language as it is spoken every day."[71] Diction was also important in Krohg's book: his working class characters and the prostitute speak in a vivid colloquial language. With Bernard's scientific vocabulary, Zola was ready to create the experimental artwork: "Now that we possess the tool, the experimental method, our goal is very plain—to know the determinism of phenomena and to make ourselves masters of these phenomena."[72]

THE NATURALIST ARTWORK AS AN EXPERIMENT

As already hinted at, naturalism in the sciences marked a shift from passive to active observation. In the first half of the nineteenth century, scientific naturalism grew into an experimental science. Observation alone, which Bernard called *science passive*, was not enough; the scientist needed to carry out experiments on nature—*sciences expérimentales actives*. Bernard was a pioneer in developing this new scientific approach to, and active intervention in, nature.[73]

Zola wrote that each chapter of *Thérèse Raquin* "is a study of a curious physiological case."[74] Artworks should likewise be case studies: experiments in the study of man. Zola took this part of his writing very seriously, as his friend Paul Alexis described in his 1882 book about Zola. He recounted Zola's meticulous method, similar to that of a social historian: traveling to different sites and making notes on what he saw, using different documents to ensure the correctness of details in his novels.[75] Numerous dossiers with Zola's notes survive.[76] Krohg did something similar in his Albertine novel and paintings: he studied carefully the life of a woman like Albertine and tried to show how it was shaped—by specific details and incidents—into the tragedy of her decline.

Naturalistic artworks can be seen as controlled experiments that confirmed specific hypotheses. The artist described individuals who reacted in this or that way to their environment; the beholder or the reader was supposed to think that these individuals could hardly act in any other way under given circumstances. The artist should be both an observer and an experimentalist. Zola described it as follows: "The observer in him [the novelist] gives the facts as he has observed them, suggests the point of departure, displays the solid earth on which his characters are to tread and the phenomena to develop. Then the experimentalist appears and introduces an experiment, that is to say, sets his characters going in a certain story so as to show that the succession of facts will be such as the requirements of the determinism of the phenomena under examination call for."[77] In Bernard's words: "To be worthy of the name, an experimenter must be at once theorist and practitioner. . . . We cannot separate these two things: head and hand. An able hand, without a head to direct it, is a blind tool; the head is powerless without its executive hand."[78] He continued: "In the philosophical sense, observation shows [*montre*], and experiment teaches [*instruit*]."[79] Bernard was well aware of the problematic distinction between the two roles, and his description of the play between them could also function as a description of the naturalist artist's creative process:

> At first sight, and considering things in a general way, this distinction between the experimenter's activity and the observer's passivity seems plain and easy to establish. But as soon as we come down to experimental practice we find that, in many instances, the separation is very hard to make, and that it sometimes even involves obscurity. This comes, it seems to me, from confusing the art of investigation, which seeks and establishes facts, with the art of reasoning, which works them up logically in the search for truth. Now in investigation there may be activity, at once of the mind and of the senses, whether in making observations or in making experiments.[80]

Bernard argued that it was normal in the sciences to differentiate between passive observation and active experiment, yet this differentiation was questionable. Observation was also a form of activity. Observation and experiment, passivity and activity, happen at the same time. It is a play between states, and Bernard claimed that the scientist's mind always intervened between the two states. The experiment was, for Bernard, the mediator between the objective and the subjective. Much like the naturalist artist, the scientist shifted imperceptibly between being an empirical observer and positivist experimenter.[81] Krohg clearly both observed and sought to teach a moral lesson through his works: he selected and presented details that amounted to a social argument. This made his work sometimes moving and eloquent, and other times too didactic, which was the danger of this approach to creation.

The artist's experiment was controlled only by his or her own senses. This meant that the naturalistic artwork was a *thought experiment* rather than quasi-scientific research.[82] The role of the imagination was to give the artist the idea for the experiment. The experiment in art began with a feeling and ended with reasoning. J. G. Patterson, author of *A Zola Dictionary* (1912), wrote on this subject: "It is self-evident that the 'experiments' by the novelist cannot be made on subjects apart from himself, but are made by him and in him; so that they prove more regarding his own temperament than about what he professes to regard as the inevitable actions of his characters. The conclusion drawn by a writer from such actions must always be open to the retort that he invented the whole himself and that fiction is only fiction."[83]

THE OBJECTIVE SELF

It is useful at this point to refer to Lorraine Daston and Peter Galison's groundbreaking study *Objectivity* (2007). The authors claim that the idea of scientific objectivity emerged in the mid-nineteenth century as a new epistemic virtue. This story of objectivity is one of a historically located, objective self that evolved simultaneously with the idea of a subjective self. Their discussion of the negotiation between the objective and the subjective self offers a fruitful perspective on the work of naturalist artists, including Krohg. Daston and Galison write: "To embrace objectivity . . . was not only to practice a science but also to pattern a self."[84] To be objective became a performance—an act—that stood in opposition to the subjective self. This can explain how these two poles, applied to artistic creations, produced different aesthetic results—akin to the differences between impressionism and naturalism. The ultimate goal of the objective self was an objective view, in which anything that reminded one about the subjective self was a failure. The fear was that the subjective self would, even unconsciously, make things prettier than they were, idealize the results; that the scientists made the results fit their hypothesis, saw what they hoped to see. The scientific self was seen as the opposite of the traditional artistic self.[85] Hence "ugly" paintings were looked upon as more real. The contest between the scientific objective "truth" and the artist's subjective temperament is one of the most problematic and paradoxical issues in Zola's theory.

TEMPERAMENT

In an article on Zola's *Mes haines* in the Norwegian newspaper *Dagbladet* on August 23, 1879, Brandes presented one of Zola's mottos: "Zola's starting point is this: an artwork (a sculpture, a painting, a book) is a piece of nature seen through a temperament."[86] This would become a mantra for many Nordic novelists and artists in the 1880s. Critic Rosenkrantz Johnsen, for example, wrote of the large Albertine canvas in 1887: "One looks at this painting with a strong impression that the figures are moving freely, talking, breathing, living; and with a conviction that this is a 'piece of nature seen straight through a temperament.'"[87]

Temperament was a key idea in realism, naturalism, and impressionism; it was also used extensively by Taine, often in combination with race and environment. The term was a key component of Edmund Duranty's definition of realism in 1856: "A realist is completely independent of his neighbor; he renders sensations that his nature and temperament lead him to feel when he confronts something."[88] In his pamphlet *La nouvelle peinture* from 1876, he wrote: "With a back, we want to reveal a temperament, an age, a social status; with a pair of hands, we must express a magistrate or a merchant; with a gesture, a whole series of sentiments."[89] Zola introduced his slogan in *Mon salon* (1866): "Coin de la création vu à travers un tempérament"[90] and repeated it in "Naturalism on the Stage": "One thing is certain, that any piece of work will always be only a corner of nature seen through a certain temperament."[91] One could say that the word *temperament* replaced *imagination* when it came to the artist's subjective being in the art-making process. A person's vision of something depended on his or her psychological state and not a creative fantastic imagination. The visual impression of nature was filtered through the person's temperament before it ended on the canvas. The French author Émile Deschanel defined temperament in 1864: "[Temperament is the] particular state of the physical constitution of each person, caused by the diverse proportion of elements which enter into the composition of his body."[92] Champfleury, Courbet's friend and "king of Bohemia," wrote that "man is always borne along by his particular temperament . . . which makes him render nature according to the impression he receives of it."[93] This is similar to Charles Baudelaire's formulation in *The Painter of Modern Life* (1863): "In the most frivolous work of a sophisticated artist belonging to one of those ages which, in our vanity, we characterized as civilized, the duality is no less to be seen; at the same time the eternal parts of beauty will be veiled and expressed if not by fashion, at least by the particular temperament of the artist."[94] Joris-Karl Huysmans wrote in in *Le Salon de 1879*: "As it is, and above all as it will be, impressionist art demonstrates a very curious observation, a very particular and profound analysis of temperaments placed on stage."[95]

Temperament is the variable element of the body, and it has to do with both romantic and impressionist notions about originality and authenticity. For Baudelaire, temperament was an expression of the artist's individuality, his quality of naïveté and sincere expression; he stated in "The Salon of 1863": "An artist without temperament is not worthy of painting pictures."[96] Zola similarly commented: "I want us to make life; I want it to be living, newly created, beyond anything else, according to his own eyes and his own temperament. What I look for above all else in a painting is a man, not a painting."[97] A new painterly language had to grow out of an original, always-present subject. Zola never thought that the artist should or could be completely objective. A personal style and expression were important parts of the experimental artwork, which might not be so different from imagination after all. Huysmans emphasized the importance of temperament in artistic creations in *Against Nature* (1884). He describes the artistic creed of his character Des Esseintes: "And yet the point of view from which his ideas on art had sprung was a simple one: for him, literary schools did not exist; the only thing that mattered was the temperament of the artist; the only thing of interest was the way his brain worked, regardless of the subject he was treating."[98] Temperament was the subjective, original, creative power of the naturalist artist.

Temperament appears several times in Krohg's writings on art as a synonym for the artist's mind and personality. Nature becomes poetic when it goes through an artist's temperament.[99] In a text on symbolism and Edvard Munch, Krohg makes an interesting observation. He paraphrases Zola's saying "to see nature through a temperament" but remarks that for realists and naturalists, nature, the work's motif, is in reality more important than the artist's personal temperament. The temperament is just a glass through which the artist sees when he paints nature. It is more like a personal style than a part of the creation. In Krohg's view, Munch and the symbolists really painted their personal temperament, the subjects of their paintings being secondary. They used nature to make their temperament visible. Krohg wrote that the realist has only one glass to see through, but "Munch has many hundreds and constantly creates new ones. He makes them himself. Some enlarge, some make smaller, some distort, others break apart."[100] Here Krohg describes symbolism as proto-expressionism and Munch as a proto-expressionist. At the same time he shows how these more personal arts are improvements over naturalism.

THE ARTWORK AS A "DOCUMENT HUMAIN"

A scientist conducting a scientific experiment made notes on loose sheets of paper, which he later gathered in a final laboratory notebook, or *cahier*.[101] The journal was a helpful tool in the battle between the objective and the subjective.[102] It was a way to tidy up and organize the chaos of sense impressions and to find one's objective self. The journal made room for observation, experiments, and reflections—the "zig-zag between hypothesis and experimental test."[103] In Bernard's words, "Two oppositions must therefore be considered in any experiment. The first consists in premeditating and bringing to pass the conditions of the experiment; the second consists in noting [*constater*] the results of the experiment."[104] A little later he wrote that the "observer does not reason, he notes."[105] Noting is important at any stage of the process, and in the *cahier* different degrees of subjective writings can function side by side.

An awareness of the status of the naturalist artwork as a document was expressed by critic Roger Marx in 1884: "We want the realist to trace us in our own image and to prepare for the coming centuries documentation of the age in which we live."[106] In 1885 novelist and critic Paul Bourget called Edmond de Goncourt's *Chérie* (1884) a "protocol of a young girl's hours from her early childhood to her twentieth year."[107] The naturalist artwork was a collection of facts organized in an aesthetic way, and to look at artworks as documents was a common approach in the 1880s. The influential Danish art historian Emil Hannover said that reading the Goncourt brothers, Brandes, and Taine made his own method scientific; he shifted from looking at artworks as autonomous creations and began to treat them as "cultural-historical-scientificdocuments."[108] Herman Jæger wrote that Taine looked at artworks and novels as "psychological documents" in his historical writings.[109] Inspired by the same philosophical sources, the naturalist writer and artist consciously created cultural-historical-scientific documents instead of autonomous art for art's sake.

The naturalist writer was both an observer who collected the facts and an experimenter who conducted the actual experiments as described in this chapter. The naturalist novel became a report, a journal, a medical protocol, a cahier, a dossier, or a log of the process of creating such documents. Zola said that Balzac's *Cousin Bette* (1846) was "simply the report [*le procès-verbal*] of the experiment that the novelist conducts before the eyes of the public."[110] As early as 1866 he called Balzac an "anatomist of the soul and the flesh" in an address to a gathering of Congrès Scientifique de France.[111] Zola's view of the artwork as a document echoes Balzac writing in his foreword to *The Human Comedy* in 1842: "French society was going to be the historian, I only needed to be the secretary."[112] To Balzac the writer had to be an archeologist of society (*l'archéologue du mobilier social*), a cataloguer of professions (*le nomenclateur des professions*), and a registrar of good and evil (*l'enregistreur du bien et du mal*).[113] Zola also stated: "We novelists are the examining magistrates [*juges d'instruction*] of men and their passions."[114] Symptomatically, Bernard wrote: "I am the *secretary* of nature."[115]

Making notes was therefore important to the naturalist writer. The naturalist novelist made notes while researching his project (not unlike a journalist or historian). The Goncourt brothers were famous for basing their writings on firsthand notes and documents,[116] and Zola wrote in his preface to *La Fortune des Rougon* (1871): "For three years I had been collecting the documents I needed for this great project."[117] He wrote in his text about the experimental novel: "They [authors] base nearly all their works on profuse notes. When they have studied with scrupulous care the ground over which they are to walk, when they have gotten information from all the possible sources, and when they hold in their hands the manifold data of which they have need, only then do they decide to sit down and write."[118] The idea is that the novel is the sum of the notes (observations) put together in some kind of a system (experiment). The final product became, for Zola, a log: "Well! Our naturalistic novel is properly the product of the classification of the notes and of the intuition which completes them."[119]

Taking notes, working with sketches, and collecting information was also important to naturalist painters; Raffaëlli was especially known for this practice. An anonymous critic wrote in 1894: "With Raffaelli [*sic*] naturalism became a doctrine. He flirted with scientific research, always had his notebook on hand and his pockets full of documents, so that with their help he could prove, like Taine and Zola, the correctness of every line in the fingers of his absynth [*sic*] drinkers, every crease in the dress of his bending street sweepers."[120] Some years later, in 1904, the British painter Wynford Dewhurst wrote that Raffaëlli "is the historian of the 'banlieue' of Paris." He continued: "His street scenes are typical, life-like, and modern, and they will be treasured in future years as veritable documents of the daily existence of the great city."[121] Alfred Roll worked in a similar manner, and curator Léonce Bénédite compared Roll to the doctor who analyzed and dissected individuals and social milieus, and wrote that he used laboratory methods.[122]

THE ALBERTINE EXPERIMENT

Krohg's *Albertine* novel, together with his sketches, paintings, newspaper articles, pamphlets, and lecture manuscripts, became a collection of documents. The artistic originality and importance of the Albertine project lay in the *collection* of materials compiled over the course of several years. It is precisely in this way of working with material that Krohg demonstrated his experimental method.

A novel or a play offers more space for the collection of information and observations than a single painting. It is challenging to present an experiment in a single picture,[123]

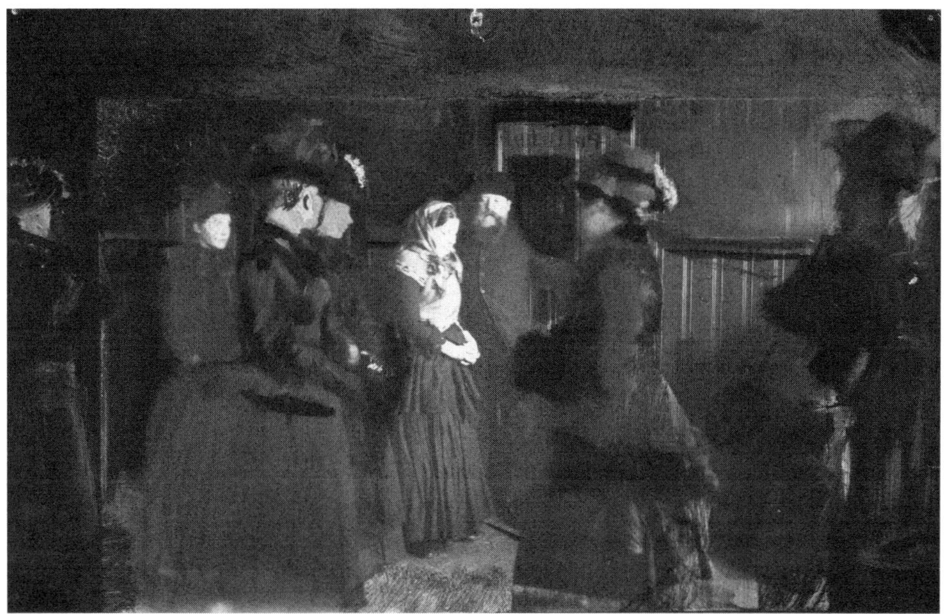

Figure 3.3. Christian Krohg, *Albertine in the Police Doctor's Waiting Room (study)* (probably 1884). Mixed media (photography, cardboard, and oil), 14 × 22 cm. Private collection. © Photo: O. Væring Eftf. AS, Norway.

and the most obvious and easiest way to show a developing story/experiment is to make a series of paintings. Krohg did that with his Albertine canvases (as well as with his Skagen paintings). He painted several images of Albertine, following her development. The seamstress paintings made between 1879 and 1885 were preliminary studies for the larger project/experiment. In the mid-1880s, Krohg painted a number of smaller Albertine canvases, as well as those showing Albertine's mother (1884) and her friend Jossa (1886). The novel itself was illustrated with six drawings, and he even used photographs when making the composition for the large Albertine painting (fig. 3.3).

An important part of the experimental method was an implied comparison of two conditions or a set of conditions. Bernard stated: "Science can be established only by the comparative method."[124] Zola wrote about *Thérèse Raquin*: "I simply applied to two living bodies the analytical method that surgeons apply to corpses."[125] The experiment was not a passive observation, then, but involved a disturbance to nature. The effects of this disturbance were then compared with the natural condition. A typical comparison in an experiment would be to place two animals in the same condition, but with one difference to see how they react to it and develop as a consequence. In his *Albertine* novel, Krohg tried to demonstrate how different girls reacted to their innate traits as well as to their environment: Albertine and her sister provided a comparative experiment, since they came from the same background, family roots, upbringing, and circumstances. They both entered the world of prostitution, but Albertine's older sister managed to get married and ended up a respectable woman, while Albertine did not. Much of the book was devoted to illuminating the differences between the two women.

Was the aesthetics of naturalism as described in this chapter really suited to art, and did it take the artwork's intrinsic qualities seriously? Ferdinand Brunetière wrote in *Revue des deux mondes* in 1880 about the experimental novel: "Descriptions and pictures do not prove that an author knows how to write: they only prove that he is a very sensitive individual."[126] He also questioned the way determinism was used as a model for art: "A man is born into a certain social condition, and he dies in it, but he does not always behave, and in all the deeds of his life, like the typical man of his condition."[127] Claudius Wilkens was also critical of Zola's theories, and especially of the low status accorded to imagination. He criticized Zola's "use" of scientific ways of speaking about the artwork and claimed that Zola misunderstood the experimental method, arguing that the scientific eye was different from an artistic one. For that reason, according to Wilkens, Zola misunderstood art. A police record could never be the same as literature for the Danish philosopher.[128] Lukács, in his turn, was skeptical about Zola's aesthetics and wrote that his experimental method reduced the writer to a simple spectator: the characters were mechanical and average, while epic situations and plots were replaced by descriptions. He called this a "social degradation of the writer."[129] Lukács actually stated that Zola's scientific method "spells the doom of great literature."[130] Zola's creative method has also been compared to journalism: George Moore called Zola a "prodigious journalist."[131] (Interestingly, and possibly symptomatically, Krohg supported himself financially for many years by working as a journalist for several leading Norwegian newspapers.) Regardless of whether one looks at the scientific impulse in naturalism as a success or a failure, it certainly made naturalism stand out from other contemporary art trends such as impressionism and symbolism—although the judgment of its efficacy clearly varied. It may be fitting to quote the Goncourt brothers' stark skepticism of Bernard's positivism:

> Claude Bernard . . . was reported to have announced that after a hundred years of physiological science, one would be able to make laws for organisms and carry out human creation in competition with the Creator Himself.
>
> We made no objection, but we do believe that when science has reached that point, the good Lord with white beard will arrive on earth with his key-chain and tell mankind, just as they do at the Art Show at five o'clock: "Gentlemen, it is closing time!"[132]

CHAPTER FOUR

Hippolyte Taine and the Modern Breakthrough in Scandinavia

> But it must be said, and if we have said it, it must be repeated, that since Hegel, perhaps nobody in Europe has thrown into circulation on the history of literature and art more novel, powerful, or profound ideas—and regardless of their veracity, in each case *suggestive* and provocative—than the author of *The Philosophy of Art*.
>
> FERDINAND BRUNETIÈRE

HIPPOLYTE Taine's ideas played a vital role in Scandinavian cultural life in the 1870s and 1880s, especially in the so-called modern breakthrough in Scandinavian literature. It would have been close to impossible for an intellectual artist like Krohg not to be influenced by Taine in one way or another. Krohg painted friendship portraits of two of Taine's most central disciples in Scandinavia: Georg Brandes in 1879 (fig. 4.1) and Gerhard Gran in 1884 (fig. 4.2) He had spent a great deal of time with these two intellectuals when he was developing his own aesthetics, and the ideas of Bernard, Taine, and Zola must have provoked lively discussions among them.

It is easy to forget how influential Hippolyte Taine (1828–1893) was in his own time. Today his name is typically mentioned only in passing in texts on nineteenth-century literature and art, and his books are seldom read. Many historians, theoreticians, and philosophers neglect him and regard him as an intellectual failure. This is peculiar, for as literary historian Albert Guérard wrote, Taine's positivism "was the *Zeitgeist* of Scientific Realism speaking through a sensitive, tormented soul."[1] Guérard stated that Taine "is the perfect intellectual representative of his period," that "Taine is 'Second Empire' through and through; as much as the Exposition of 1867, the grand avenues hacked out by Haussmann, Garnier's Opera—and Hortense Schneider, for he too contributed to *La Vie Parisienne*."[2] The Goncourts declared him "the flesh and blood incarnation of the modern critic,"[3] and Friedrich Nietzsche called him the "*first* of living historians."[4]

Taine seemed ubiquitous in European cultural circles in the 1870s and 1880s, whether consciously or not. The Norwegian literary historian Herman Jæger (not to be confused with Hans or Henrik Jæger) stated that he saw Taine's influence everywhere: "Everyone

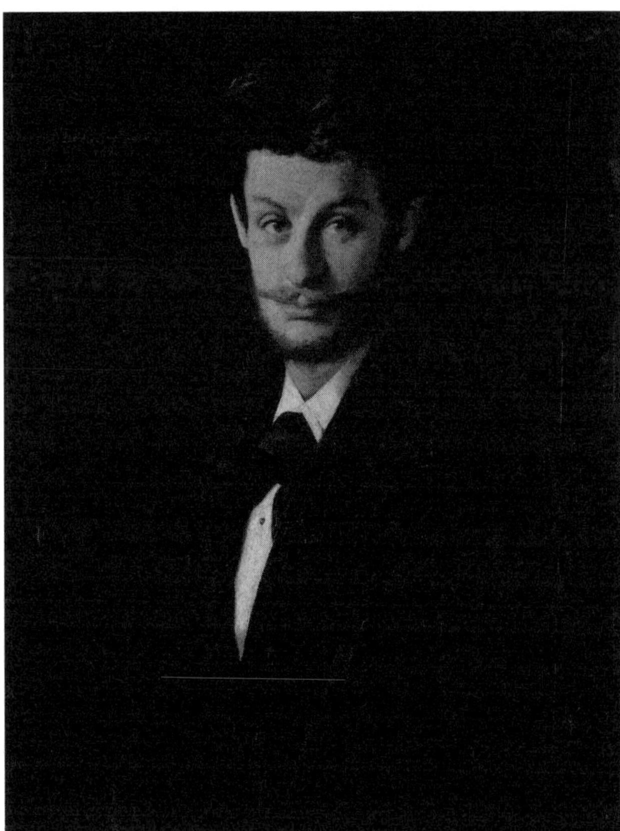

Figure 4.1.

Christian Krohg, *Georg Brandes* (1879). Oil on panel, 70.7 × 55. Photo: Art Museums of Skagen, Denmark.

from the middle of the nineteenth century is, so to speak, a student of Taine; we cannot point at one single student in the strict sense of the word, but everyone is anyway his student, because we notice in their work glimpses of Taine's way of thinking."[5] The Swedish literary historian Hellen Lindgren wrote in 1894 that Taine managed to define his own time through the topics of discussion he set for his contemporaries. Lindgren wrote that Taine awakened his era with his powerful nature: "He became a teacher for a youth without ideals."[6] Taine's books were promoted and reviewed in the Norwegian press in the 1870s, and excerpts were published in translation.[7]

Taine was also without question the most prominent and significant philosopher for naturalists in the latter half of the nineteenth century. Zola wrote of him in 1866: "He is the naturalist of the moral world. He believes that one can come to classify facts of intellectual life as one classifies the facts of physical life. . . . I love this method because it brings truth."[8] He wrote that Taine was, in the spheres of literary and artistic criticism, "the contemporary of the electric telegraph and the railways."[9] He called Taine a pure naturalist, termed Taine's method of writing history "dissecting,"[10] and concluded that Taine "is really the foremost critic we have."[11] Anatole France wrote that Taine had given him "an ardent enthusiasm, a kind of religion that I will call the dynamic cult of life."[12] Taine's naturalism

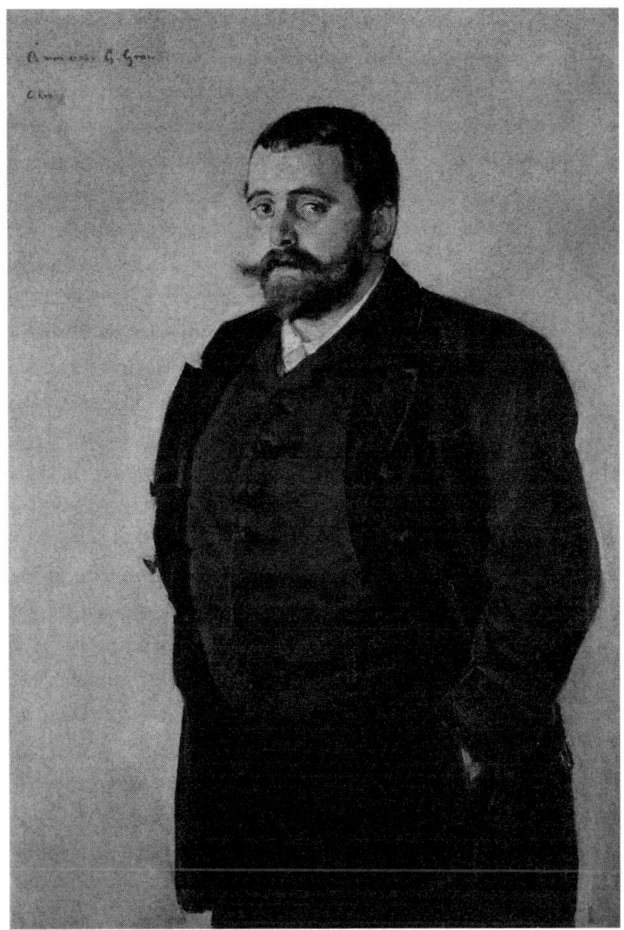

Figure 4.2.

Christian Krohg, *Gerhard Gran* (1884). Oil on canvas, 114 × 80 cm. The University of Oslo. © Photo: O. Væring Eftf. AS, Norway.

was not purely rationalist, and it has been seen as a product of romanticism, with its concern with the subject's experience of nature, interest in psychology, and relativism in values.

POÈTE-LOGICIEN: THE POET AND RATIONALIST IN CONFLICT

Taine had studied both medicine and psychiatry under the radical Lamarckian physiologist Geoffroy Saint-Hilaire, but he wanted to study philosophy instead. His *Les philosophes classiques du XIXe siècle* (1857) is the work of a young philosopher taking a stand against the establishment; it has been called a "satirical dissection of French philosophy."[13] This radical work made him interesting to Gustave Flaubert and other artists with a similar sensibility. Herman Jæger wrote that the book was not "a declaration of war. It is a crusade."[14] Taine never got his doctoral degree in philosophy, however. The committee pronounced that his "imagination is too strong for him to become a philosopher."[15] He was advised to work in the literary field instead, and he ended up completing a dissertation in literature.

Taine became a professor of aesthetics and art history at the École des Beaux-Arts in Paris and published several books and essays on aesthetics and the history of literature and art. Several of his lectures on art were published as *The Philosophy of Art* (1864) and *The Ideal in Art* (1866). The first book stressed the importance of looking at art of all eras on its own grounds, promoting the idea that art is the objective result of its time and place. The positivist art historian, Taine argued, should study works of art the way a botanist studies flowers and plants: with an impartial attitude and without judgment.[16] Each period and nation produces art that must be understood in its historical and environmental context, and not in relation to a defined standard of taste. One should examine a given era's art as a product of climatic conditions.[17] The second part, *The Ideal in Art*, in certain ways contradicts the first, because here Taine did set up defined scales of aesthetic value and emphasized the need for aesthetic judgment. Thus value judgments sneak into his writings: "We have always, and at every step, pronounced judgment."[18] Taine's aesthetics were, therefore, something of a confusing mix of realism and idealism, for which he has often been criticized.[19] Zola described him as a poet and a rationalist in conflict,[20] which Ferdinand Brunetière saw as a development rather than a contradiction: "He [Taine] gradually ascended to a view of greater generality, greater height, greater fertility."[21] The French critic Jules Lemaître called Taine a poetic logician.[22] Hellen Lindgren wrote that "Taine belongs to those who wanted to be intellectual, who wanted to be among those whom Gautier called *les cérébraux*: the brain people, while he, in his nature, was just as much a poet as a thinker."[23] He commented that "we cannot count Taine among the pure scientists. And it is precisely here that we find what is most interesting about him as a writer and person. He does not include the ideal of truth in the detached manner of a scientist, but approaches it like a poet. The combination of his two natures, the poet and the researcher, is palpable."[24] In Lindgren's view, Taine managed to combine the dispassionate approach of a scientist with a poet's strong personality. Facts are, after all, more striking if they are told beautifully. Taine was torn between the literary and the scientific, and it made his theory intellectually elastic and stimulating for artists struggling with the same issues. The contradiction in Taine's work between the romantic and the positivist is, in many ways, the intellectual power field known as naturalism in literature and painting. Zola recognized that Taine wanted to be a man of his time, but at the same time was not:

> Mr. Taine is a man neither of his times nor his body. If I did not know him, I would like to imagine him with square shoulders, dressed in grand and splendid clothing, dragging his sword somewhat, living in the midst of the Renaissance. He loves power and brilliance; he seems at ease at feasts, amongst meats and wines, at court receptions in the company of wealthy lords and beautiful ladies displaying their lace and velvet. He joyfully revels in the impulses of the flesh, in all the brutal forces of man, in silks as much as rags, in everything that is extreme. . . . And nonetheless, deep down, there is a fever. This buxom health is artificial; this love of ample and magnificent luxury is but a regret. One feels that the author is our brother, that he is frail and naked, that he assuredly belongs to our century of nerves.[25]

LIBERTÉ RÉGLÉE

One of the issues Taine contemplated was whether there were natural laws. He supported the idea of determinism and discussed a concept called *liberté réglée*—regulated freedom or free necessity. The problem with freedom is that an individual's many tendencies—habits, instincts, desires, and ideas—sometimes come into conflict, and one has to choose among them.[26] Are all our choices always determined? Taine wrote: "There is a reason even for a caprice. Within us, as without, everything is a product; exceptions, anomalies, and monstrosities are such as a result of laws as regular as those from which originate the most regular of beings and facts."[27] Taine's determinism thus presented itself as more complex than pure rationalism, since he included irrational motives in the determination of our actions. Taine was interested in psychology; in discussing human freedom in making choices, he observed: "There is nothing passive here; there is no other cause for my action besides myself. The more voluntary the action is, the more this is so. . . . It is the pure and perfect exercise of my internal energy, put into motion by an idea."[28] He connected this to morality, for, in Taine's thinking, moral responsibility was the result of determinism; we are, to paraphrase Sholom J. Kahn's summary of Taine's thought, "morally responsible for the result of our own psychologies."[29] These are difficult and complex questions, but for now it is worth noting the importance to him of the discourse on free will and determination, which the naturalists continued to explore in their art. Krohg did so particularly in his Albertine novel and paintings—in the way his heroine made the choices that led to her fall, even if her actions were seemingly shaped by others. Unlike her sister, who was able to find her way out of a life of prostitution, Albertine acquiesced in her decline. And while society may have been partially at fault, she too was an agent in her drama.

GEORG BRANDES AND THE MODERN BREAKTHROUGH

Taine believed that art should represent something real. He also claimed that literary texts gave a more truthful image of the past than historical treatises did.[30] This perspective made works of art into historical documents, though occupying a special position. Taine has been criticized for using art and literature as tools for understanding a given epoch rather than looking at them as autonomous aesthetic objects.[31] But his view paved the way for social art history. He described his approach to art as follows: "The principal point of this method consists in recognizing that a work of art is not isolated, and, consequently, that it is necessary to study the conditions out of which it proceeds and by which it is explained."[32] It is not surprising that naturalist artists of his day, including Krohg, consciously made artworks the future could use as documentation of that age.

The Danish art historian Julius Lange gave a critical lecture on Taine's philosophy of art in 1876 (and subsequently published it as a book). He went through Taine's *The Ideal in Art* and took him to task for not writing about the artist's subjectivity and the artwork's aesthetic autonomy. Lange declared that Taine only gave artworks cultural and historical value, and ignored the immediate, ravishing, stunning, and joyful aspects of art experience. In Lange's view, Taine did not have an eye for artistic personality, and did not see the value of irrationality in art: "Taine looks at and analyzes the artwork as if it were a natural product."[33] Lange's countryman Georg Brandes was of another opinion.

Georg Brandes was the voice of modernism in Scandinavia. He toured many cities, giving lectures in which he presented the newest thoughts from England, Germany, and France, and becoming a spokesperson for Scandinavian art and literature in Europe. Brandes introduced Taine to Scandinavia, and many of Taine's main works were also translated into Danish in the 1870s.[34] Through Brandes's work, the ideas of Taine and Zola possibly had an even greater impact in the Nordic countries than in France.[35] Frits Thaulow recounted an anecdote about a dinner party in Paris whose guests included Brandes, Zola, and Anatole France. The evening was alive with debates, and Brandes impressed everyone, especially Zola and France, with his "prodigious wit and phenomenal memory of all facts."[36] Naturalism, in part thanks to Brandes, became a vital aesthetic force in Scandinavia of the 1880s, just as this movement began to decline in France.

Brandes's 1871 lecture on mainstream currents in contemporary literature is often said to have ushered in the "Modern Breakthrough" in Scandinavian letters. Henrik Ibsen stated that the publication of Brandes's lectures marked a groundbreaking shift between yesterday and today.[37] The Modern Breakthrough was a literary movement that brought together aesthetics, ethics, and politics. "Modern" opposed the "established" and rejected romanticism. Radical movements in France, Germany, and England inspired the Modern Breakthrough and influenced many powerful literary creations by such writers as Ibsen, August Strindberg, and Bjørnstjerne Bjørnson. Their favorite themes were marriage, sex, and morality, exemplified by Ibsen's scandalous play *Ghosts* (1882). Krohg, with his Albertine project, was part of the Modern Breakthrough, which made Scandinavian literature famous across Europe.

Brandes became aware of Hugo, Balzac, and Darwin, as well as the theorists Sainte-Beuve, Taine, and Littré, in the 1860s, and in 1870 he wrote his doctoral dissertation on Taine.[38] Its title was "The French Aesthetics of Today" (Den Franske Æsthetik i vore Dage). Brandes attended Taine's lectures and those of other prominent philosophers when he first arrived in Paris in 1866 and wrote that of "all the contemporary French writers, I was fondest of Taine."[39] Brandes had already read Taine's *Les philosophes classiques du XIXe siècle en France* (1857) in Copenhagen, but in Paris he decided to read every book by Taine that was available at the Imperial Library. Taine was to Brandes "an antidote to German abstraction and German pedantry."[40] Brandes met Taine several times and in his memoires described the French philosopher as a mentor: "He [Taine] grew fond of me, advised me as a father or an elder brother might have done."[41] At Taine's home Brandes met many other French intellectuals, including Ernest Renan. Brandes also met John Stuart Mill for the first time in Paris, recording that as "Mill had no personal acquaintances in Paris, I was the only person he called upon."[42] Brandes encountered Mill repeatedly during his visits to England, and was very impressed by the British philosopher, especially by his boldness: "He [Mill] wished to interfere and remodel."[43] This was to Brandes an inspiring contrast to the more "defensive" French thinkers, such as Taine and Renan, who fought from behind their desks, whereas Mill wanted to be active in society. Brandes also translated Mill's *The Subjection of Women* (1869) into Danish.

Brandes believed that literature should take part in political debates, and that novels and plays should engage in social critique—a position strongly espoused by Krohg. Brandes wrote that the "failure of a literature to debate problems is the same as losing all meaning."[44] He attacked the patriarchy and supported women's rights. A common goal for Brandes and the authors of the Modern Breakthrough was to challenge the church and conservative politics, and to reform society. Krohg took an active part in this goal with his literary and artistic projects—and clearly hit a nerve, given the confiscation of his *Albertine* novel.

Brandes's main work, his six-volume *Main Currents in Nineteenth Century Literature* (1871–90), was inspired by Taine's *History of English Literature* (1864) and sought to study, through French, German, and English examples, the psychology of the nineteenth century prior to the turning point of the revolutions of 1848. Literary history was to Brandes the "history of the soul," and a work of art was a piece of the complex world in which it was created. The historian had to be as objective as possible: "The scientific view of literature provides us with a telescope of which the one end magnifies and the other diminishes; it must be so focussed as to remedy the illusions of unassisted eyesight."[45] Brandes wanted to explore the possibility of a "universally applicable scientific method of criticism, regarded as intellectual optics."[46] The challenge was to establish a technical standard of taste, so that one could claim that one thing was superior to something else. Brandes criticized Taine's early writings for looking at everything in a culture as interesting and important. Brandes seemingly suggested that it was necessary, when possible, to make aesthetic judgments in a scientific way.

BRANDES AND KROHG

Brandes met Krohg for the first time in Berlin in 1877. Krohg shared an apartment with Max Klinger and Rudolf von Voigtländer while they all studied under Karl Gussow. Krohg and Klinger were known as the two most promising Gussow students at that time. Brandes described the circle around them as "ardent nihilists, socialists, atheists, naturalists, materialists and egoists."[47] The architecture student and later painter Edvard Diriks and Bjørnstjerne Bjørnson's son Bjørn Bjørnson, an actor, were also part of that milieu. Brandes portrayed them as radicals in politics, art, and life. It was a year after their first meeting that, according to Brandes's autobiography, Krohg began his portrait:

> One day in March 1878 he [Bjørn Bjørnson] said: "Allow me to introduce a young man to you who wants to paint your portrait. He is 25 years old, Norwegian by birth, but a man of the world, very well behaved, simply not Norwegian." This was how Christian Krohg came to me. And since he shared a residence and a studio with another young artist of 21, by the name of Max Klinger, I became familiar with him also. And both quite intimately, for Krohg painted my portrait for an hour and a half each morning, and the painting took full nine months, without becoming the masterpiece it could have been if Krohg had declared it finished after one-fourth of the time.[48]

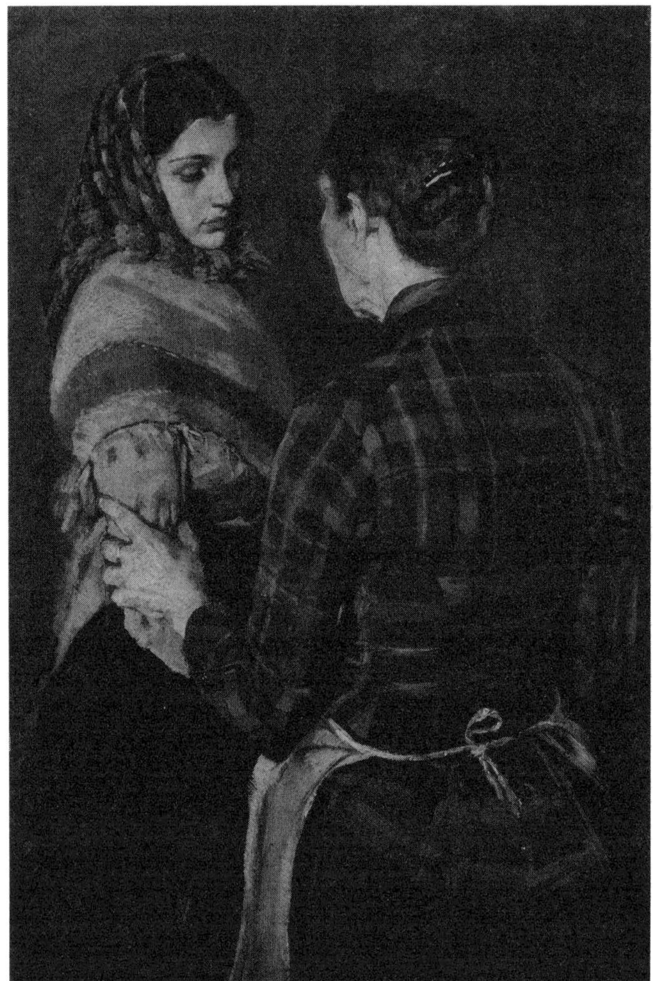

Figure 4.3.

Christian Krohg, *An Interrogation* (1884). Oil on canvas, 96.5 × 65.5 cm. SKMU Sørlandets Kunstmuseum, Kristiansand, Norway. © Photo: O. Væring Eftf. AS, Norway.

Krohg struggled with Brandes's portrait but finally exhibited it in Kristiania in 1879. He depicted Brandes as a Mephistopheles-like figure. Brandes recounted that Gussow, whom he described as the most celebrated portraitist in Berlin, came to see the painting and also found the likeness unsuccessful.[49] All the same, Krohg and Brandes spend a lot of time together while Krohg was working on the portrait, and the painter was strongly influenced by the Danish philosopher, ten years his senior, at a time when Krohg's artistic goals were being formed. In 1883 Krohg and Brandes also spent some time together in Skagen, but after 1886 their friendship became more sporadic. When Brandes turned sixty in 1902, Krohg interviewed him for the newspaper *Verdens Gang*. He was going to make a drawing of Brandes to accompany the text. But as Krohg wrote in the interview, it was not easy, since Brandes's facial expressions changed with every sentence. The solution was to draw him from behind. As Krohg quipped, "The facial expressions are less pronounced in the neck."[50] Perhaps this drawing could also be read as a comment on his failed portrait of Brandes twenty-five years earlier.

"À MON AMI G. GRAN"

Another prominent Taine disciple (and admirer of Zola) in Scandinavia was the Norwegian literary historian Gerhard Gran (1856–1925), a friend of both Krohg and Hans Jæger. Gran is probably best known for his 1918 monograph on Henrik Ibsen. But in 1880 Gran wrote a two-part article in the radical journal *Ny Illustreret Tidende* about Taine's aesthetics, and in 1883 he published a longer essay on Zola in the journal *Nyt Tidsskrift*. Krohg painted Gran's portrait in 1884 and exhibited it at that year's Autumn Exhibition in Kristiania. It is a friendship portrait, akin to the one of Brandes. Krohg wrote on the canvas, "À mon ami G. Gran." It was the year Krohg began in earnest his work on the Albertine project, and one can imagine his discussions with Gran further shaping his aesthetics, just as his conversations with Brandes had done earlier. In his article on Taine, Gran emphasized that the purpose of art was to highlight the character of whatever the artist was depicting: "We will simply say that the art aims to produce and make sensuous a main character, some salient and outstanding characteristic, a significant behavior of the object."[51] The artist's task was to capture, for example, a nation's character and temperament—how they have been formed by the climate of the land, the local diet, and daily habits. This may have been one of Krohg's motivations behind his Skagen paintings, an answer to Taine's theory about race, time, and environment. It might not be a coincidence that Krohg exhibited one of his Skagen paintings (*Mother at Her Child's Bed*, fig. 1.7, plate 3) together with his portrait of Gran at the Autumn Exhibition.

Gran began his article on Zola by linking naturalism in literature with Darwinism. He gave a thorough presentation of Zola's theories, mentioning Claude Bernard's writings as Zola's starting point and the analogy between art and medicine (he called Zola a pathologist).[52] We do not know whether Krohg had read Zola's theoretical writings by that time, but Gran's discussion of the experimental novel and the "inductive-experimental method" furnished Krohg with a recipe for the Albertine project. A large part of Gran's text was a paraphrase of Zola, and the timing of the article coincided with Krohg's early development of the Albertine paintings, including *An Interrogation* (1884, fig. 4.3). In this painting we see her mother questioning Albertine after she returns home from the city. It is clear from Krohg's literary and artistic output that he took an active part in the intellectual milieu in Scandinavia, where the ideas of Taine and Zola were not merely discussed but also shaped the Modern Breakthrough.

CHAPTER FIVE

Christian Krohg in Skagen

Painting according to Taine

KROHG's major project, the Skagen paintings, comprised more than forty pictures made over the course of several stays in the Danish fishing village of Skagen between 1879 and 1888. Krohg's main subjects in these works were the three generations of the Gaihede family: the two elders, Ane and Niels Gaihede, their son Rasmus Gaihede and daughter-in-law Tine Gaihede, and their three children, Maren Sofie, Niels Johan, and Bitt'ane. We can see them all in Krohg's strikingly honest profile portraits (figs. 5.1–5.4, plates 4 and 5). They were exhibited in one frame in 1889 in Kristiania, alongside most of the other Gaihede paintings, constituting one large "frieze of life."

I will examine the Skagen paintings in light of Hippolyte Taine's aesthetics, using the three main components of his philosophy of history: race, environment, and *le moment.* I will also look at Taine's focus on seventeenth-century Dutch art as an example of an honest and real art. All these factors were explored by Krohg in his Skagen project.

SKAGEN

Many painters had visited Skagen since the Danish artist Martinus Rørbye came there for the first time in 1833, but its "golden age" occurred in the 1870s and 1880s with artists such as P. S. Krøyer, Michael Ancher, Anna Ancher, Frits Thaulow, Carl Locher, Eilif Peterssen, Holger Drachman, and Karl Madsen—all drawn to the village's rugged beauty. Many of these painters had been to Paris and were in the process of "finding" themselves as modernist artists. As Patricia G. Berman writes, "The town of Skagen, and its commodious beaches, became a laboratory for the artists' new identities and ideas."[1] This was certainly true for Krohg and his artistic development. Taine was an important influence on this process.

Krohg had invited Georg Brandes, who first introduced Taine's ideas to Denmark, to visit him at Skagen. In a letter to Brandes, Krohg described Skagen as a paradise, adding that he had never been anywhere where he felt so good.[2] When Brandes came to Skagen in 1883, several artists made portraits of him, as is evident from P. S. Krøyer's *Oscar Björck and Eilif Peterssen Painting Portraits of Georg Brandes* (1883, fig. 5.5). He was seen as an intellectual guiding star. In his autobiography, Brandes wrote that Björck and Peterssen destroyed their portraits of him, but his likeness as captured by Krøyer and Michael Ancher survives.[3]

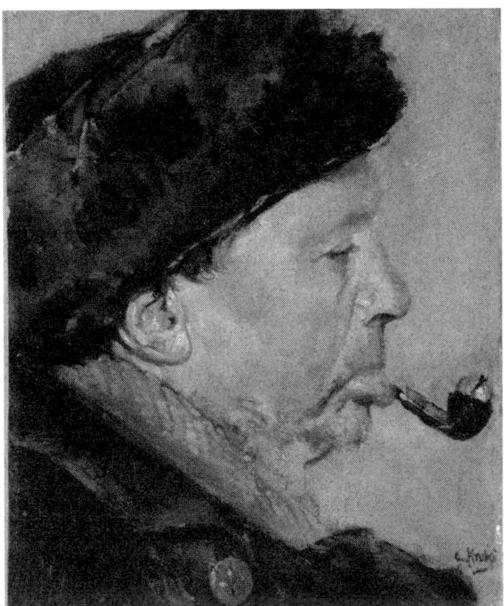

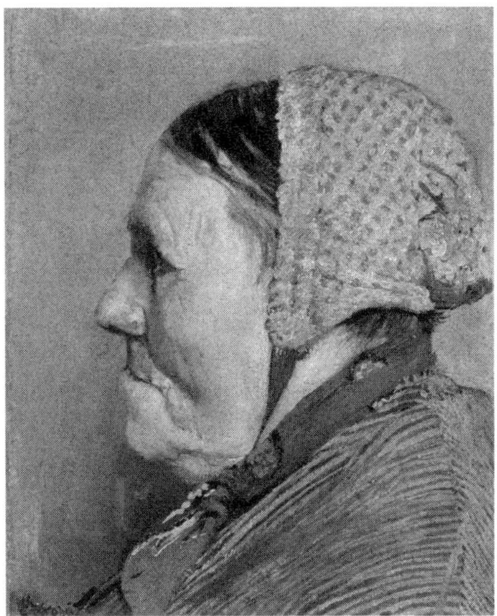

Figure 5.1 (Plate 4), *left*. Christian Krohg, *Niels Gaihede* (1888). Oil on canvas, 36 × 30.5 cm. Photo: Jacques Lathion/The National Museum of Art, Architecture and Design, Oslo.

Figure 5.2 (Plate 5), *right*. Christian Krohg, *Ane Gaihede* (1888). Oil on canvas, 36 × 30.5 cm. Photo: Knut Øystein Nerdrum/The National Museum of Art, Architecture and Design, Oslo.

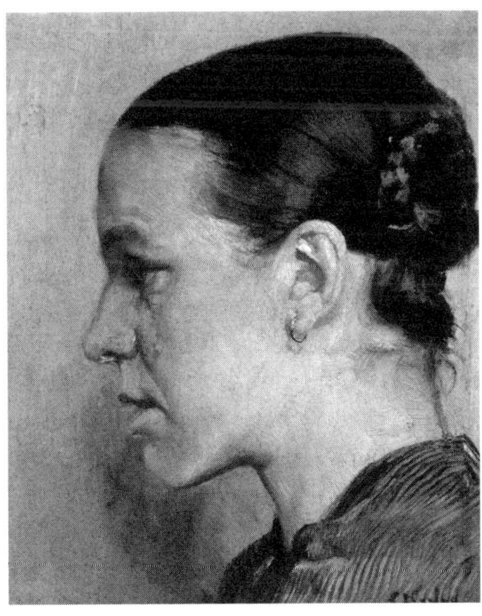

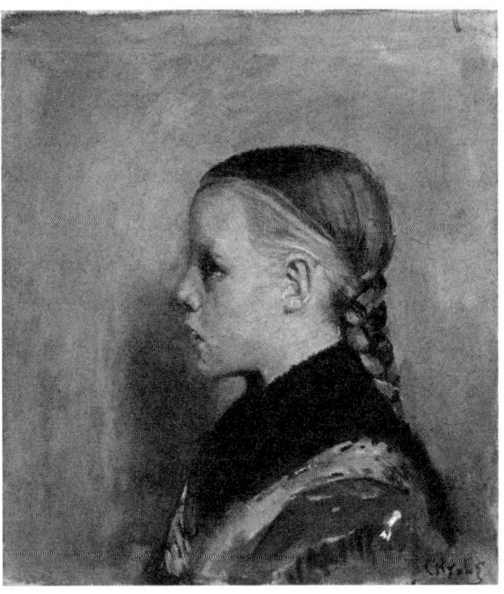

Figure 5.3. *Left*. Christian Krohg, *Tine Gaihede* (1888). Oil on canvas, 35 × 29 cm. Private collection. © Photo: O. Væring Eftf. AS, Norway.

Figure 5.4 *Right*. Christian Krohg, *Maren Sofie Gaihede* (1888). Oil on canvas, 35 × 29 cm. Private collection. © Photo: O. Væring Eftf. AS, Norway.

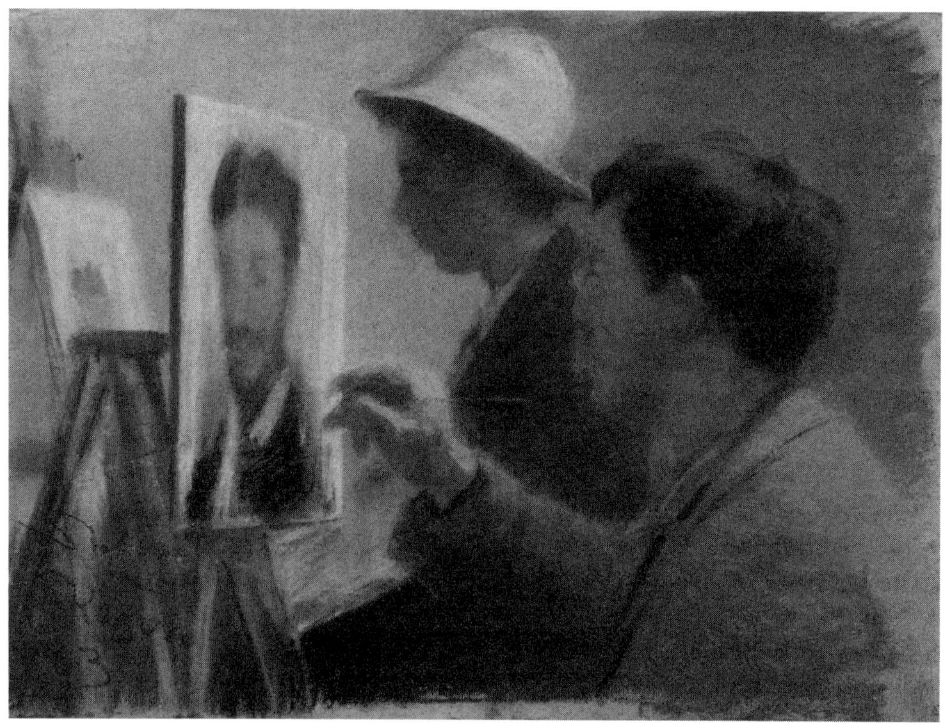

Figure 5.5. Peder Severin Krøyer, *Oscar Björck and Eilif Peterssen Painting Portraits of Georg Brandes* (1883). Pastel and oil stick on cardboard, 32 × 44.4 cm. Photo: Niels Erik Høybye, Randers Kunstmuseum, Denmark.

The painters were linked by their shared interest in French positivist aesthetics—Skagen became at this time one of the most important places for discussing the radical new ideas from Paris—as well as by the pleasures of convivilaity. Brandes described them spending all day around a table at Erik Brøndum's hotel, eating, drinking, arguing, and quarreling.[4] They constituted an informal discussion club called the "evening academy," gathering to debate artistic questions. When Brandes was there, he gave small, informal lectures.[5]

P. S. Krøyer captured the social life of the artists in many of his paintings. *Artists' Luncheon at Brøndum's Hotel* (1883, fig. 5.6) is the first large group portrait he made in Skagen. We recognize in it several key figures in this art colony: Michael Ancher is standing; Wilhelm Peters, Eilif Peterssen, and Charles Lundh are sitting on the left; on the other side are Degn Brøndum, Johan Krouthén, Oscar Björck, and Krohg—depicted at the end of the table in his characteristic painter's beret. Krøyer's more famous *Hip, Hip, Hurrah!* (1888, fig. I.2) conveys the artists' festive life in Skagen.

These artists were further united by their interest in naturalism. Though mainly an urban art style, naturalism had a rural branch devoted to the study of the everyday life of hard-

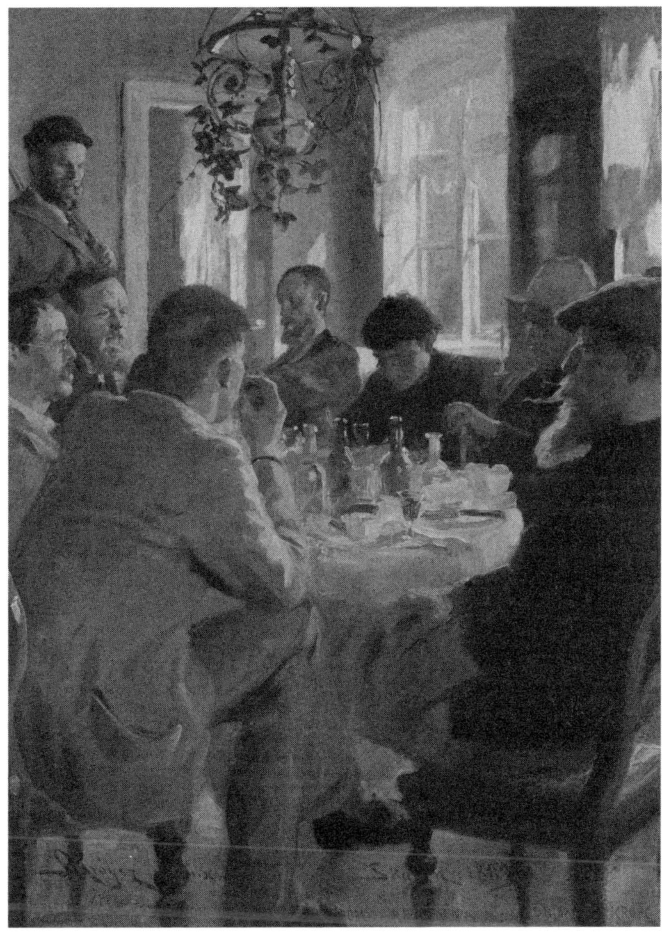

Figure 5.6.

Peder Severin Krøyer, *Artists' Luncheon at Brøndum's Hotel* (1883). Oil on canvas, 82 × 61 cm. Photo: Art Museums of Skagen, Denmark.

working farmers and fishermen. Skagen was an isolated place without connected roads or a harbor. The village's remote and rustic location made it exotic for urban artists like Krohg, and its small society, relatively cut off from the larger culture and in touch with nature and its challenges, fascinated realist and naturalist painters. As T. J. Clark writes, "For the myth, rural society is a unity, a one-class society in which peasant and master work in harmony. Rural society is, in other words, the antithesis of the community in which the bourgeois actually lived. It is a world in which social conflicts are magically resolved, in which the tensions and class divisions of the city are unknown."[6] In *Murray's Handbook for Travelers in Denmark*, published in 1875, one could read the following about Skagen: "It is one of the wildest and most desolate spots in the world, yet within a couple of hours' journey from fertile, peaceful, and idyllic rustic landsape. To the long-straggling town of Skagen the railway will never penetrate."[7] H. C. Andersen compared Skagen to Africa's deserts and Pompeii's ashes.[8] Skagen was, in other words, exotic—in its own rugged way. The Skagen art colony was nurtured by the desire of nineteenth-century painters to explore and develop new motifs that contrasted with the urban visual culture, and by many artists' wishes to experience different milieus as part of their artistic development and praxis.

ANTHROPOLOGY

Both Zola's Rougon-Macquart series and Krohg's Skagen project echoed the contemporary preoccupations of social scientists. The French sociologist Frédéric le Play (1806–1882), for example, conducted extensive research into working class families across Europe and published a series of thirty-six monographs under the title *Les ouvriers Européens* (1855). Le Play interviewed families over the course of several months. Each family was a case study, much like the Gaihede family was for Krohg. Émile Durkheim (1858–1917), often called the founder of the modern social sciences and an admirer of Auguste Comte, devoted himself to the study of social and moral life. One of his research methods was to focus on a small segment of society: for example, he studied the aborigines in Australia for his book *Les formes élémentaires de la vie religieuse* (1912). A closed and controllable group of people allowed him to investigate social patterns and behaviors. Anthropology explored cultures, societies, and civilizations by zeroing in on such manifestations of culture as speech, systems of knowledge and beliefs, customs, ideals and rules, and arts and technologies. Social heredity—how things were handed down from earlier generations—was an important part of such investigations. Rural communities shed light on different aspects of social formation compared to urban ones. The American cultural anthropologist Alfred L. Kroeber described these distinctions: "Rural condition is the underlying one, logically and historically: there must be a country area producing more food than it consumes before other people can live in cities."[9] Rural life was thus closer to tribal, "real," and original societies, and it could be linked to the contemporary fascination with primitivism.

Krohg's depictions of an extended and cross-generational family in Skagen can be read as a socio-anthropological project, and his paintings in this series as an exploration of biological and social conditions in the manner of Taine: how did race and geography, milieu and conditions under which these people lived shape their existence? Krohg sought to be an "objective" observer, a quasi-anthropologist, in his portrayal of the Gaihede family: "One can, even as a stranger, walk into any house and look around in their rooms. They don't care but continue with their meals, their sleep, or dressing completely undisturbed. One gets to know them immediately."[10] Krohg's *Oda Krohg Paints Niels Gaihede* (1888) captures the artist and her model (fig. 5.7). There was an extraordinary relationship between artists and models in Skagen. The locals were close to being professional models (they were paid), but in Krohg's paintings they appear strikingly real and authentic.

LA RACE, LE MILIEU, LE MOMENT

Taine's work came into being before anthropology was an autonomous field of research, and as the American literary critic Albert L. Guérard wrote: "Taine was satisfied with a very general hint: anthropology was still in swaddling clothes at the time."[11] But he clearly developed a proto-anthropological method.

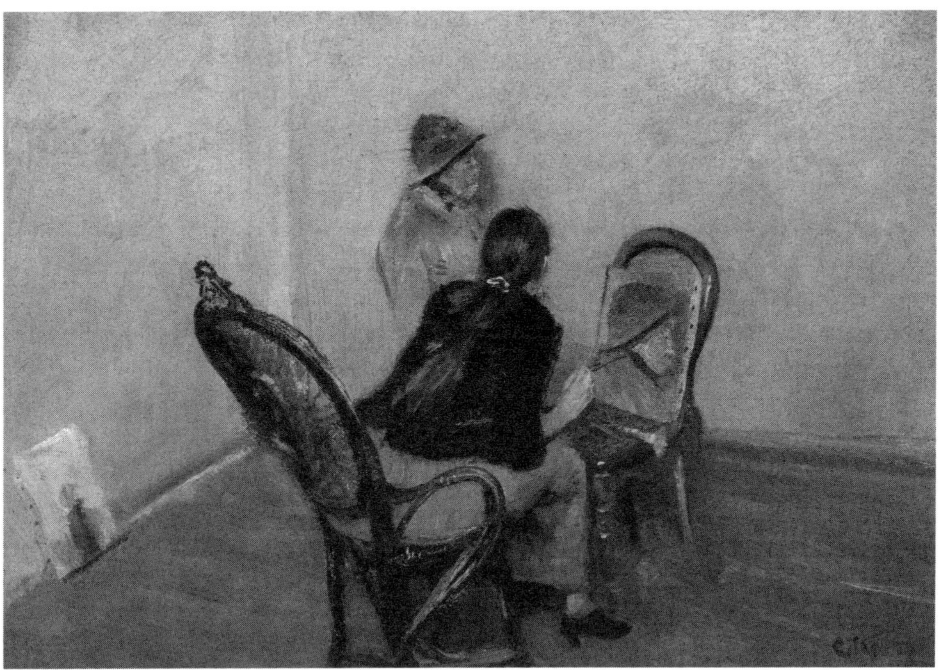

Figure 5.7. Christian Krohg, *Oda Krohg Paints Niels Gaihede* (1888). Oil on canvas, 34 × 47.5 cm. Photo: Art Museums of Skagen, Denmark.

According to Taine, art was the result of race, environment, and "le moment." Race had to do with inner factors such as psychology and people's mentality, environment with historical traditions and structures of society. The moment in a historical study reflected historical time (an era) and tradition. It was similar to zeitgeist. Race was independent of time; climate moved with geological slowness; to bring the moment into a historical discussion, Taine introduced the idea of motion and change—like a historical becoming, evolution, or just history.[12] This term, *le moment*, was complex and somewhat obscure, and I will adopt the pragmatic approach of the art historian Thomas Munro: "'Moment' is not a distinct factor or set of factors, but a name for the particular way in which other factors organize and present themselves at any one time, thus exerting a peculiar, temporary influence."[13]

In Taine's view, a work of art was predetermined by the underlying forces of race and environment.[14] A tree, for example, is determined by preestablished properties as well as environment—the local climate and geography. The same holds for works of art and human beings. In his analysis of Dutch art, Taine wrote that the artworks in museums are "both the fruit and the index of their surroundings."[15] This view on determinism was adopted by Émile Zola, who wrote in the preface to the first book in the Rougon-Macquart series, *The Fortune of the Rougons* (1871):

> My aim is to explain how a family, a small group of human beings, behaves in a given society after blossoming forth and giving birth to ten or twenty individuals who, though they may seem at first glance totally dissimilar from each other, are, as analysis shows, linked together in the most profound ways. Heredity, like gravity, has its laws.
>
> By solving the dual problem of temperament and environment, I shall attempt to discover and trace the thread that leads mathematically from one person to another. When I am in possession of every thread, and hold in my hands an entire social group, I shall describe the behaviour of this group as it plays its part in an historical period; I shall show it in action, with all its varied energies; and I shall analyse the aims and ambitions of its individual members along with the general tendency of the whole.[16]

One of the main themes in the positivist aesthetic, then, was the exploration of how characters in a novel or a play were shaped by their heritage, environment, and climate. This is just what Krohg's Skagens paintings did: they looked at three generations of one family and their daily life in the challenging climate of Skagen—a place and society cut off from the rest of Denmark and caught between two stormy oceans as a result of local geography and climate.[17] It was important for naturalist painters to place their characters in a significant contextual environment.[18] *Woman Cutting Bread* (1879, fig. 5.8, plate 6) and *Niels Gaihede Netting* (ca. 1880, fig. 5.09, plate 7), for example, present an ethnographic view of local clothing and surroundings. The concept of milieu or environment was at the center of Taine's aesthetics. It came to him from Balzac's introduction to his *Human Comedy* (1842)—and Balzac himself got it from Geoffroy Saint-Hilaire's biological writings.[19] (One should also mention Jean-Baptiste Lamarck's concept of circumstances, which is similar to environment.)[20] Balzac wrote: "Does not society make of man, following the milieus where his actions unfold, as many different men as there are varieties in zoology?"[21] *Milieu* can signify geography, social and institutional contexts, or political and economic conditions. It also encompasses ideological power structures and "moral temperature."[22] Climate was especially important to Taine because in his view it influenced the psychological and cultural "climate" of people in different places and times.[23]

HEREDITY

The idea of heredity—the transmission of character and disposition through generations—is relatively new; it developed as a scientific idea in the eighteenth century.[24] Later, anthropology and ethnography became academic disciplines especially interested in heredity—particularly as expressed in skin color and external traits.[25] Artists who preceded Krohg in Skagen were, according to art historian Walter Schwartz, concerned with depicting "in a purely ethnographic way how people there lived."[26] Martinus Rørbye's images of Skagen in the 1840s, exemplified by his drawing of a young Lars Gaihede and other local characters, can be called ethnographic studies.[27] Krohg's Skagen paintings also contained a strong ethnographic element.

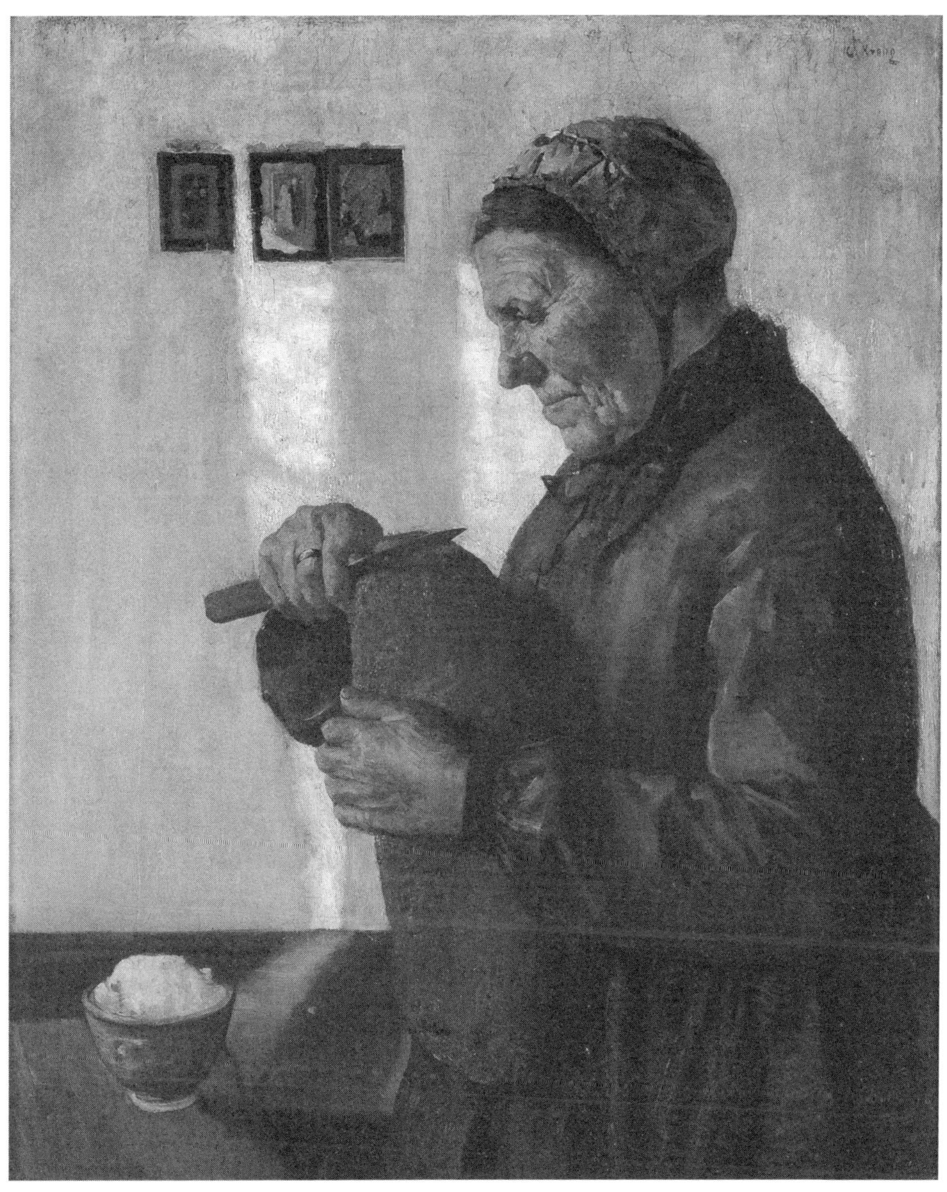

Figure 5.8 (Plate 6). Christian Krohg, *Woman Cutting Bread* (1879). Oil on canvas, 80 × 66 cm. Photo: Dag Fosse/KODE—Art Museums of Bergen, Norway.

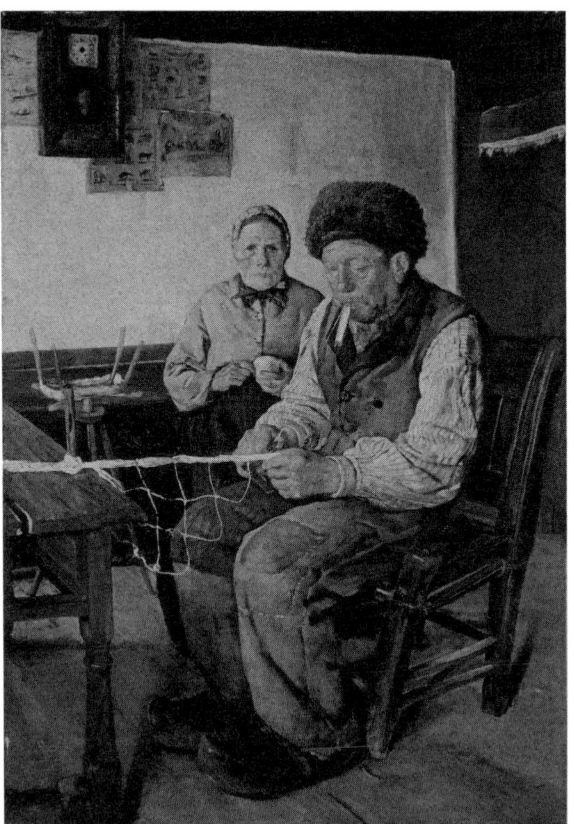

Figure 5.9

(Plate 7). Christian Krohg, *Niels Gaihede Netting* (ca. 1880). Oil on canvas, 93.5 × 67 cm. Photo: Jaques Lathion/ The National Museum of Art, Architecture and Design, Oslo.

Hippolyte Taine's *race*, like *moment*, was a somewhat ambiguous term, though its use was, generally speaking, built on two ideas. The first, related to romantic aesthetics, was that race was a form of collective heredity—it was a "national character," or *Volksgeist*.[28] The second, connected to Taine's interest in Darwin's *On the Origin of Species* (1859), was that race was a facet of biology: it was a biological disposition.[29] Taine defined race as "innate and hereditary dispositions which man brings with him into the world, and which, as a rule, are united with the marked differences in the temperament and structure of the body. They vary with various peoples. There is a natural variety of men, as of oxen and horses."[30] He continued:

> For, as soon as an animal begins to exist, it has to reconcile itself with its surroundings; it breathes and renews itself, is differently affected according to the variations in air, food, temperature. Different climate and situation bring it various needs, and consequently a different course of activity; and this, again, a different set of habits; and this, again, a different set of aptitudes and instincts. . . . So that at any moment we may consider the character of a people as an abridgment of all its preceding actions and sensations.[31]

The inhabitants of Skagen were seen as a race of their own, shaped by the challenging climate that made them look strong and weathered. Writer Holger Drachman said of the Skagen people in 1887 that "the race here is good, tenacious, immediate."[32] Krohg added, "The Skagen people is a race of its own that very much differs both in being and appearance from other Danes. Their language is very similar to Norwegian, but this is also where all similarities end. They are much freer, easier, and more sociable than Norwegians."[33] This myth about the people of Skagen has been repeated since the 1870s by artists, journalists, and historians, who have used words such as *lively*, *brave*, *strong*, *powerful*, *hardy*, *persistent*, *hardworking*, *serious*, and *cold-blooded* to describe these locals.[34] They were perceived as healthy people undistorted by modernity and civilization thanks to their close contact with nature. The hard weather had formed their bodies and features—as artists sought to show in their paintings of the fishermen and their families. In Krohg's pictures members of the Gaihede family have faces that show traces of hard work in a harsh environment and severe climate. Both men and women have large, strong workers' hands. There was, in fact, a stark contrast between how the visiting artists depicted themselves, as in Krøyer's paintings, and how they portrayed the locals: their faces and bodies seem, indeed, to belong to different races.

CLIMATE

Climate is a challenge that shapes civilizations, and Taine often invoked geography and climate in his discussions of a nation's art. He was also interested in firsthand observations of a people's native habitat.[35] In Krohg's representations of the Skagen family, life is clearly determined by geography and climate. Krohg wrote that one got an impression of something wild, hostile, and harsh when one heard the name Skagen.[36] It was a place famous for its severe storms; Krohg described their effects: "I can see shipwreck after shipwreck when I walk alone down the sunny beach. I counted sixteen wrecks over a short distance. Sixteen corpses of large ships."[37] Krohg's writings about Skagen and those of other authors are characterized by their descriptions of the climate and its effect on Skagen life.

Shipwrecks and deaths of fishermen were recurring motifs among many Skagen painters. Interestingly, although Krohg made the hard life at sea one of his main motifs throughout his career, he did not explore it in his Skagen series. For the Skagen project, he was more interested in the indoor life of women, children, and retired fishermen (figs. 5.10–5.13). He painted *A Distress Signal* in several versions, but that was his only painting from Skagen that dealt directly with accidents at sea. The character in *A Distress Signal* is probably a member of a rescue team. The Skagen rescue crews were heroes, and watching them in action on the beach was a tourist attraction. One could even buy postcards with pictures of them.[38] But Krohg was interested in less heroic protagonists, the "invisible" heroes at home: women and elders performing their duties.

THE IMPACT OF THE DUTCH SCHOOL

Dutch old master paintings were in vogue during the heyday of the Skagen art colony, and Krohg was clearly influenced by them.[39] *Braiding Her Hair* (1888, fig. 5.14, plate 8) is one

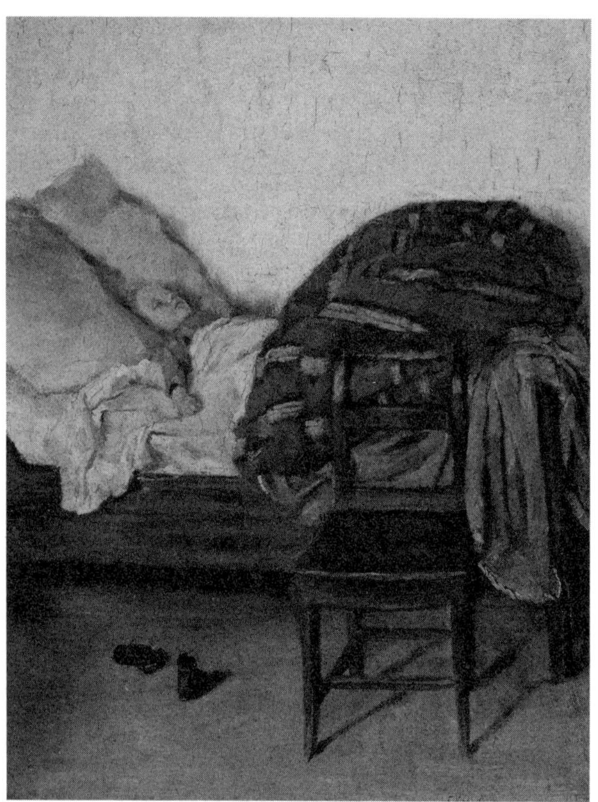

Figure 5.10.

Christian Krohg, *Sleeping Child (Maren Sophie Gaihede)* (1883). Oil on wood, 50 × 39 cm. Photo: Jacques Lathion/The National Museum of Art, Architecture and Design, Oslo.

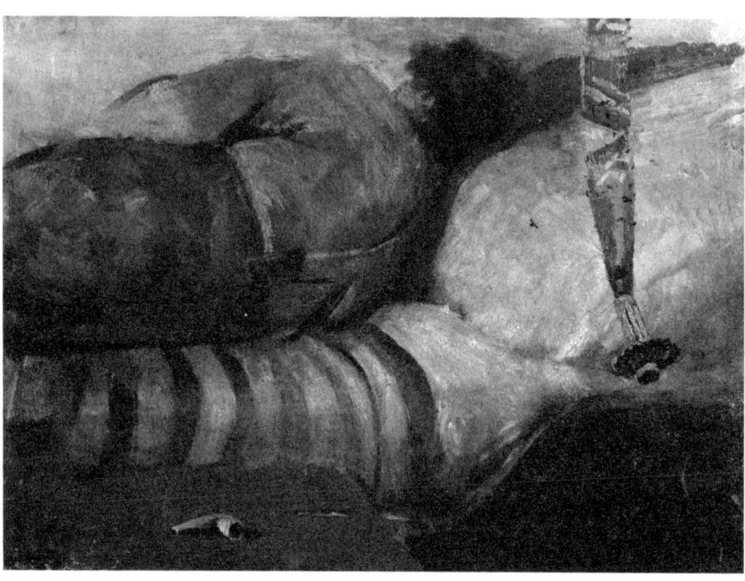

Figure 5.11. Christian Krohg, *Sleeping Fisherman (Rasmus Gaihede)* (1882). Oil on canvas, 59 × 82 cm. Private collection. © Photo: O. Væring Eftf. AS, Norway.

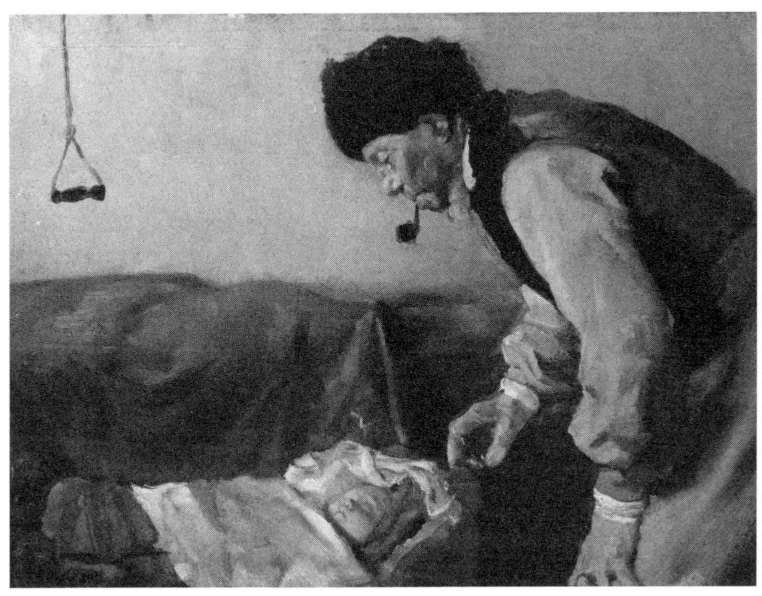

Figure 5.12. Christian Krohg, *Grandfather Rocking the Cradle* (1883). Oil on canvas, 46 × 62 cm. Private collection. © Photo: O. Væring Eftf. AS, Norway.

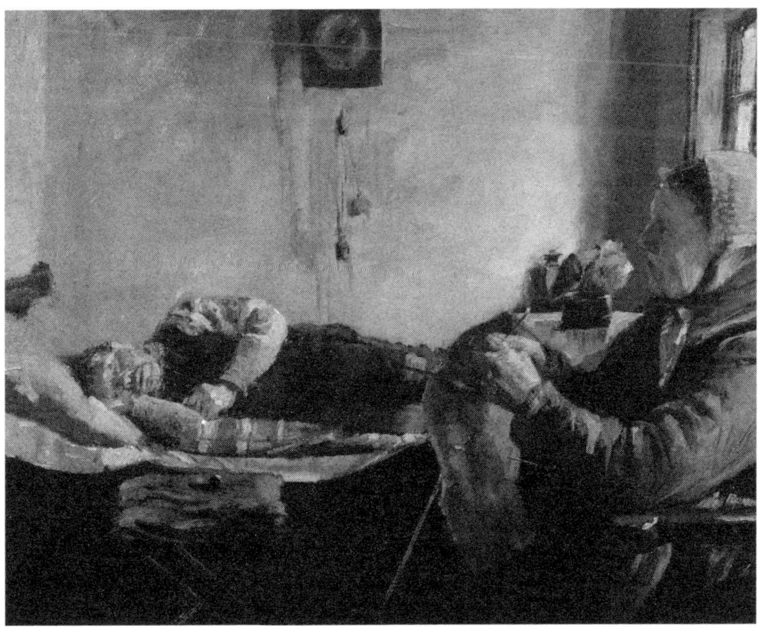

Figure 5.13. Christian Krohg, *Interior (Skagen)* (1888). Oil on canvas, 59 × 73. The National Museum, Stockholm. © Photo: O. Væring Eftf. AS, Norway.

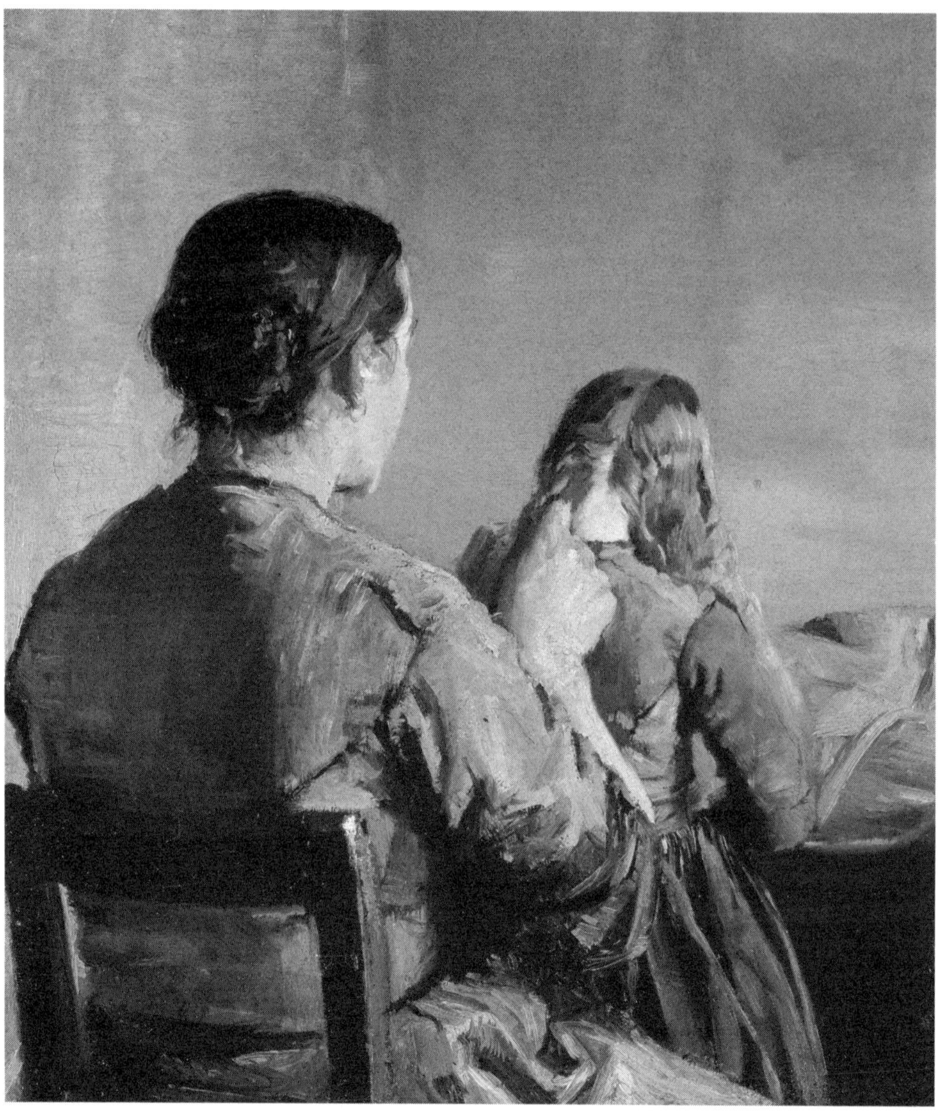

Figure 5.14 (Plate 8). Christian Krohg, *Braiding Her Hair* (1888). Oil on canvas, 56 × 49 cm. Photo: Jacques Lathion/The National Museum of Art, Architecture and Design, Oslo.

of many examples of a Skagen painting with a Dutch Golden Age feel. During his stay in Skagen in 1883, Krohg painted his first ambitious self-portrait, *Self-Portrait with Beret* (1883, fig. 5.15, plate 9). It was the first time he presented himself as an artist in a painting, gazing directly at the beholder with a confident look. He showed himself smoking a large pipe of the kind smoked by the fishermen, thus identifying himself with their habits instead of those of an urban artist-dandy, who would be smoking a cigarette or a cigar. Aritsts often

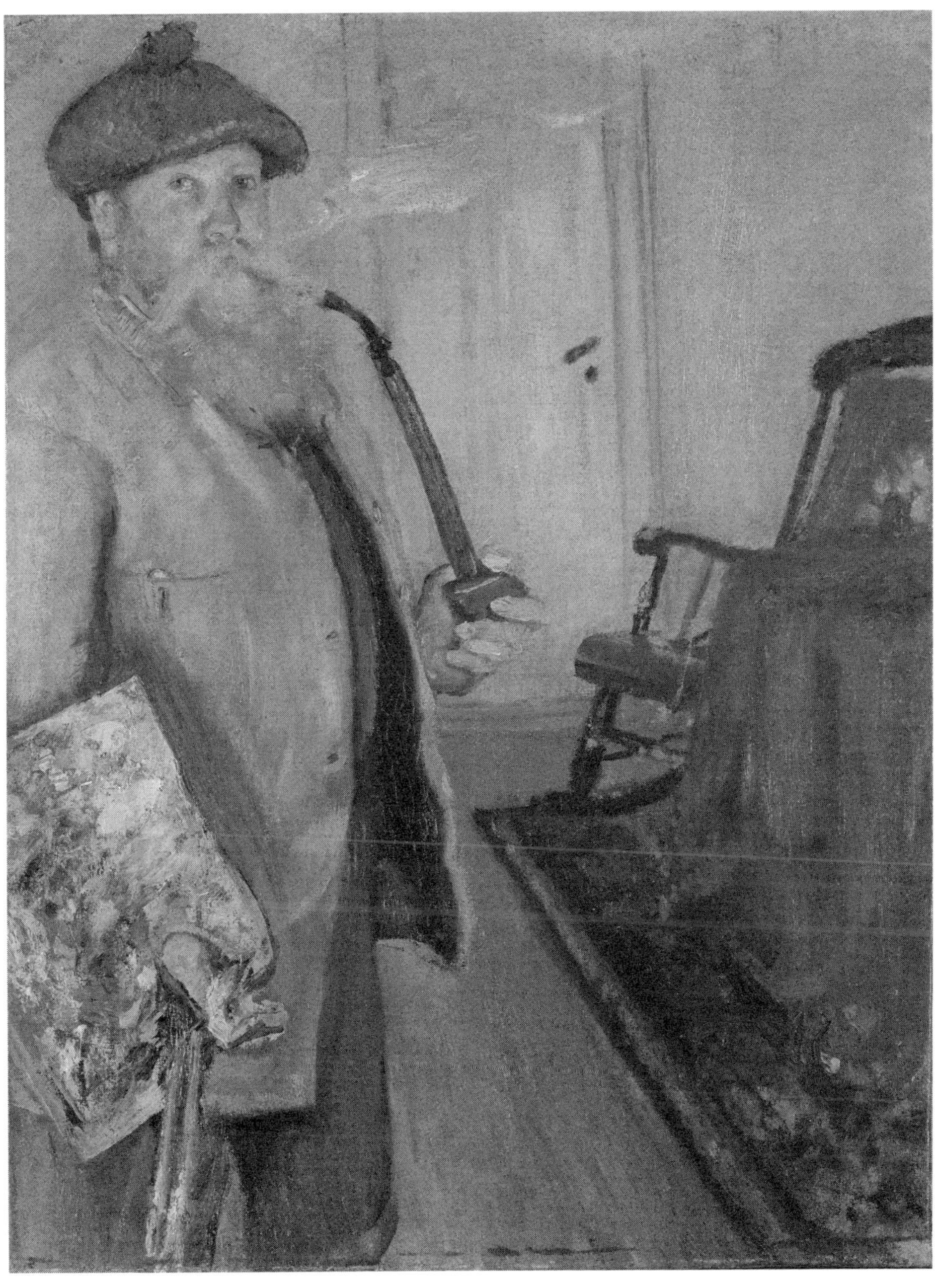

Figure 5.15 (Plate 9). Christian Krohg, *Self-Portrait with Beret* (1883). Oil on canvas, 47.5 × 36 cm. Photo: Børre Høstland/The National Museum of Art, Architecture and Design, Oslo.

depicted themselves smoking at that time, but Krohg's gesture may also reflect his interest in Dutch paintings. Pipe smoking featured in many Dutch genre scenes, and pipes frequently appeared in still lives. Krohg wrote in 1897, "Whether the Dutch smoke more than others I don't know, but tobacco smoking does play a significant role in the motifs of old masters."[40] Krohg's painting was also strikingly modern, so Krohg placed himself simultaneously in the tradition of Dutch masters and the avant-garde art of Paris. He also signaled his artistic ambitions by wearing the now-clichéd beret, which he also sported in Krøyer's aforementioned group portrait and in Eilif Petersson's 1883 Skagen portrait of him. (The most famous beret wearer in art history was of course Rembrandt, who included one in numerous self-portraits.)

Seventeenth-century Dutch painting underwent a revival in the latter half of the nineteenth century, and artists like Rembrandt, Frans Hals, and Vermeer were seen as painterly pioneers. Dutch art was considered low, compared to the classicizing paragons taught at art academies, which made it a suitable historical model for realists and naturalists. Looking back at this less familiar artistic tradition must have felt fresh and exciting to them, and it signaled a change of taste. Dutch genre painting became in the first half of the nineteenth century the only major alternative to the classicist canon of academic history painting.[41] Artists began to visit the Rijksmuseum in Amsterdam, the Mauritshuis in The Hague, and the Frans Hals Museum in Haarlem. (Frits Thaulow wrote of his visit to the Rijksmuseum that it felt like he had been invited to a very special party.)[42] Krohg studied Dutch and Flemish painting on his many trips around Europe and, like many of his contemporaries, especially admired Rembrandt and Frans Hals. Krohg called the Mauritshuis a sanctuary, and faced with Rembrandt's *The Anatomy Lesson,* he exclaimed ecstatically: "He [Rembrandt] has painted everything. Landscapes, figures, animals, marine paintings, saints, beggars, Jews, richness and poverty, sickness and misery, hospital scenes, the Bible and Greek mythology. His genius embraced everything: life and death; heaven, earth, and hell; and all artistic directions. He was an idealist and realist, romantic, symbolist, and impressionist; he was a supernatural being, a mystery, a God."[43] Brandes was no more reticent when he called Rembrandt a genius and stated: "In reality Rembrandt invented the art of painting; he is *the painter* for all painters."[44]

TAINE'S *ART IN THE NETHERLANDS*

Krohg's and Brandes's declarations echoed Taine's book on Dutch art, in which Rembrandt was characterized as "a magican and a visionary."[45] Taine described Rembrandt's work using a realist, even impressionist, vocabulary, making him into a proto-modernist.[46] Taine wrote *Art in the Netherlands* in 1868 (it was translated into Danish in 1881). Taine stated: "During the seventeenth century Holland is the first of thoughtful contries. The positive sciences here find their native soil, or the land of their adoption."[47] Taine declared that Dutch and Flemish art was the result of its people, and that these people—their bodies, features, behavior, and psychology—were shaped by their climate (including weather, temperature, and light) and geography (landscape and nature). Dutch art seemed to Taine to be more in tune with real life than French and Italian art. In contrast to the latter two,

Taine described Dutch and northern European art as "the crude and complete representation of actual life, with all its atrocious, ignoble and common-place details, its sublime and brutal instincts."[48] He explained the predisposition of Dutch artists toward sober and nonidealized realism by reference to race and environment: "He lives in a moist and equable climate, one which relaxes the nerves and develops the lymphatic temperament, which moderates the insurrection, explosions, and impetuosity of the spirit, soothing the asperities of passion and diverting the character toward sensuality and good humor."[49] Thus Taine saw Dutch seventeenth-century painting as the most successful and fully developed art form in northern Europe (ahead of Germany, Scandinavia, and England). It was a free and natural art, working directly with forms and colors rather than letting subject matter such as philosophy or theology take the lead. Dutch art, for Taine, did not allow inner ideas and feelings to obscure the execution: "The Flemings and Hollanders alone have prized forms and colors for their own sake."[50] For Dutch painters, in his view, truth was more important than décor. All this made Dutch art an important example for realist and naturalist artists of the nineteenth century, including those painting in Skagen.

Painter and writer Eugène Fromentin, in his book *Les maîtres d'autrefois* (1876), made an accurate observation about what attracted his contemporaries to Dutch masters: "Dutch painting . . . could not be anything but the portrait of Holland, its external image, faithful, exact, complete, life-like, without any adornment. The portrait of men and places, of *bourgeois* customs, of squares, streets, the countryside, of sea and sky—such was bound to be, reduced to its primary elements, the programme adopted by the Dutch school."[51] Fromentin's book was read and commented on by Skagen painter Karl Madsen and likely known to other Scandinavians artists as well.[52] In trying to characterize the Dutch school, Fromentin noted a "total absence of what we call today a subject." He continued: "What motive had a Dutch painter in painting a picture? None. And notice that he is never asked for one. A peasant with a drunken red nose looks at you with his heavy eye and laughs with open mouth showing his teeth, raising a jug."[53] The realist attitude in Dutch painting spoke to many nineteenth-century artists.[54]

Several Skagen painters explored Dutch genre painting, combining it with a modern visual language. These paintings had "a certain Dutch taste," to paraphrase Karl Madsen.[55] Krohg's series of sleeping characters, such as his *Mother and Child* (1883, fig. 5.16), recall Jan Steen's genre paintings of sick women—but without Steen's irony, humor, or sentimentality. Vermeer, another Dutch master, was "rediscovered" by Théophile Thoré in a text published in the *Gazette des beaux-arts* in 1866.[56] Emil Hannover and Karl Madsen compared Michael Ancher with Vermeer,[57] but it was Anna Ancher and Krohg who most successfully created a silent, absorbed mood similar to Vermeer: Ancher in *The Girl in the Kitchen* (ca. 1883/86) and Krohg in *Woman Cutting Bread*. Viggo Johansen's *Kitchen Interior: The Artist's Wife Arranging the Flowers* (1884) was also part of this trend. Skagen painter and art historian Karl Madsen wrote in 1884 that Vermeer was the genre painter modern painters most admired. Madsen especially focused on how Vermeer represented the beauty of daylight, of large open windows, of floor tiles and white walls draped with old maps or dark paintings.[58] These were the kinds of elements the Skagen painters included in their contemporary genre scenes.

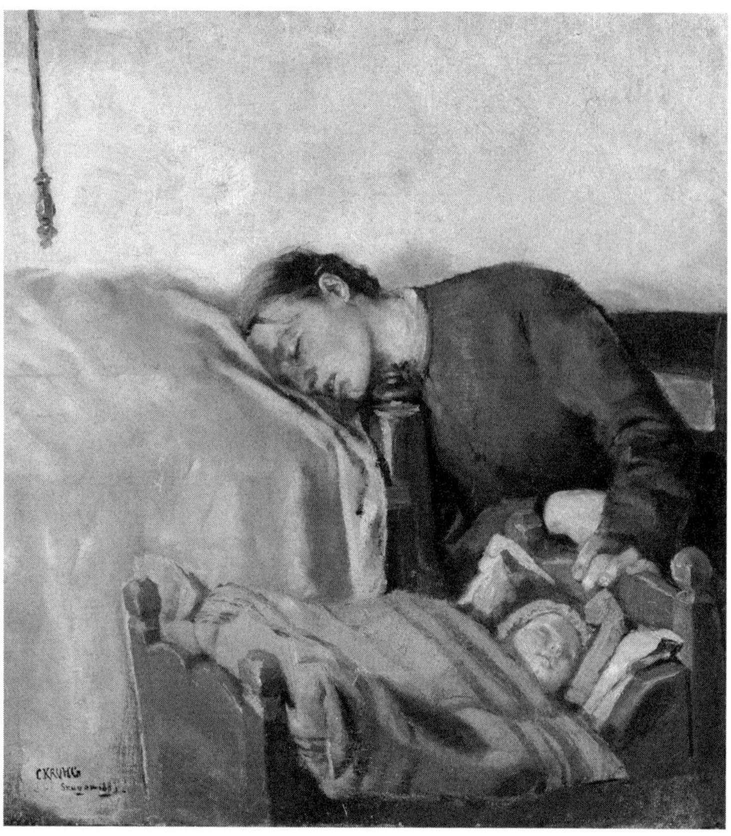

Figure 5.16. Christian Krohg, *Mother and Child* (1883). Oil on canvas, 53 × 48 cm. Photo: Jacques Lathion/The National Museum of Art, Architecture and Design, Oslo.

FRANS HALS, THE PAINTER'S PAINTER

The master who most stood out among seventeenth-century Dutchmen was Frans Hals (ca. 1582–1666). Frits Thaulow declared that Hals was a painter in the true sense of the word.[59] Eugène Fromentin stated, "Never has any one painted better nor ever will."[60] He pointed out that the name Frans Hals was "reappearing in our school at the moment when the love of the natural is coming back."[61] Hals, more than Rembrandt, was a hero to modernist painters.

Hals's importance was expressed by art critic Andreas Aubert in his presentation of Manet's art in 1888: he pointed out how much the French painter was inspired by Hals.[62] The work that brought Manet the most recognition, according to Aubert, was *Le bon bock*

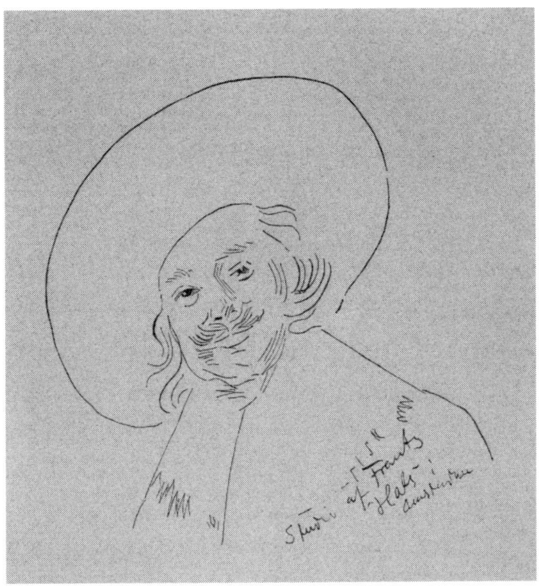

Figure 5.17.

Christian Krohg, *The Merry Drinker (after Frans Hals)* (1897). Facsimile from Christian Krohg, *I smaa Dagsreiser til og fra Paris* (1897)

(1873). It was popular among both critics and audience because, in Aubert's words, "It is hard to find in today's art a work that is so close to Frans Hals's immediate boldness in its fresh and powerful colors. Frans Hals was, so to speak, his time's 'impressionist': no one has surpassed him in perceptive power."[63] Krohg shared Aubert's view and wrote about Hals several times. He saw Hals's works on many occasions and, like Thaulow and Brandes, visited the Frans Hals Museum in Haarlem—opened in 1862 and popular with leading artists and critics in the latter half of the century, especially in the 1880s.[64] The opening of the Hals museum helped promote the old master and make him a star. His fame among the French artists may have begun with Théophile Thoré's articles about him and was further extended by other critics, among them Zacharie Astruc and Fromentin. Thoré's many essays about Hals and other Dutch painters were especially influential, and he postulated a link between Dutch masters and modern art.[65]

Krohg commented that many modern painters were inspired and influenced by Hals in their portraits. He did not mention names, but he, like Aubert, must have had in mind Manet and *Le bon bock*—painted a year after Manet's visit to the Netherlands and recognized as a pharaphrase of Hals's *The Merry Drinker* (ca. 1628–30), housed in the Rijksmuseum. Krohg drew a small sketch of *The Merry Drinker* when he visited Amsterdam in 1897 (fig. 5.17), but he knew the painting well many years earlier. It was one of Hals's most iconic and celebrated works. Hals's painting style and technique must have influenced many of the Skagen portraits, including Krohg's *Lars Gaihede Laughing* (1880, fig. 5.18).[66] Hals was admired for his portraits of people laughing, like his famous *Malle Babbe* (1633–35). Krohg honors the Dutch master with *Lars Gaihede Laughing*, just as he honors Vermeer with his *Woman Cutting Bread*, and Jan Steen with *Sleeping Mother*.[67]

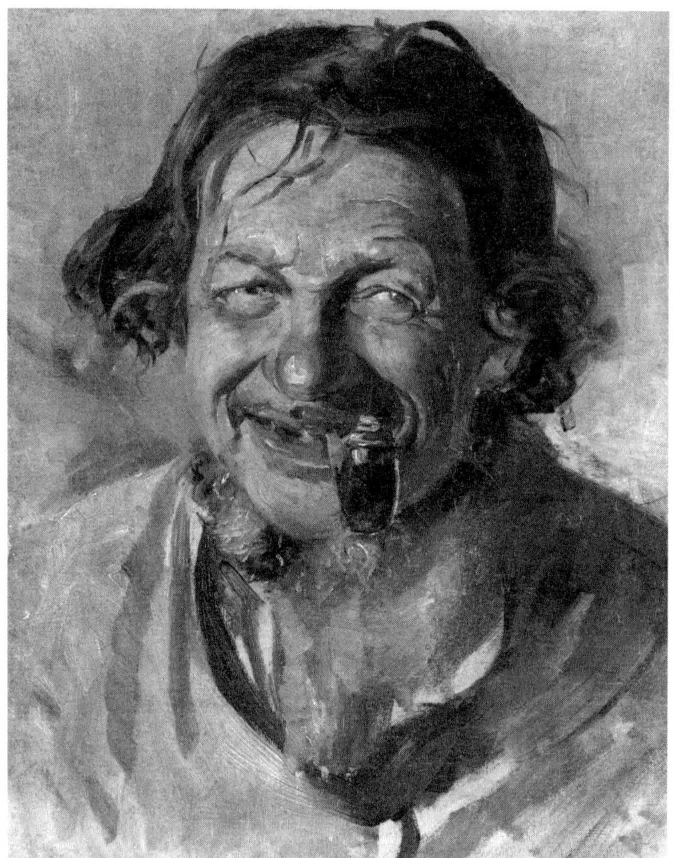

Figure 5.18. Christian Krohg, *Lars Gaihede Laughing* (1880). Oil on canvas, 41.2 × 33.2 cm. Photo: Art Museums of Skagen, Denmark.

Krohg's Skagen paintings clearly followed Taine's aesthetics, embracing his emphasis on climate and race and his admiration for Dutch old masters. They were certainly modern but carried on a fascinating dialogue with the history of art that preceded him. His art both linked Dutch naturalism with its modern incarnations and rethought old masters in light of modern intellectual and social concerns.

CHAPTER SIX

Naturalism and the Beholder

Sympathy and Theatricality

The considerations that caused him [Krohg] to have a predilection for certain subjects were not exclusively of an artistic nature. No, his quest for the painterly stemmed from a firm and original connection to a purely modern aesthetic and a purely human empathy. . . . The result is an originality in both his motifs and his execution, the likes of which we have never seen before in Norway.

HENRIK JÆGER, 1885

No matter how objective, scientific, or anthropological the artist wanted to be, the naturalist artworks of Zola or Krohg never became cold and clinical. There are many paradoxes and contradictions in naturalism—or, rather, tensions between different ambitions: to be at once objective in one's observations and subjective in one's temperament, to approach a work of art with the detachment of a scientist while striving to affect the beholder. This is especially interesting in Krohg's art, since he, more than Zola, wanted to make art of social and political importance. He wanted to make the viewer feel sympathy toward his subjects, be they Albertine, a sick girl, or the poor. One can see in Krohg's naturalist works not only a presentation of reality based on reason and argument, but also a passion for advocacy. Many of his paintings are highly emotional.

Facial expressions were of great interest to nineteenth-century scientists as well as artists—though the latter have been exploring ways to convey feelings for a long time. Charles Le Brun, for example, had focused on facial expressions in his drawings in the seventeenth century. A fascination with facial expressions in art stemmed in part from a desire to find alternatives to traditional notions of beauty.[1] Realist and naturalist artists especially strove to depict natural-looking faces that were neither too idealized nor too theatrical. The Goncourt brothers wrote in 1866: "The beauty of the ancient face was the beauty of its lines; the beauty of the modern face is the physiognomy of its passion."[2] How could inner character be expressed in the body and especially the face? How did one represent emotions realistically? This question challenged naturalist painters. Their canvases often aimed to make the beholder feel a certain way, to experience sympathy for the characters in the paintings and their hard lot—and to want to improve it.

To convey the differences between realism or impressionism and naturalism in conveying and evoking feelings, I refer to two binary sets of terms: absorption versus theatricality, and visualization of daily life versus the abnormal, the hidden, and the pathological. *Absorption* and *theatricality* come from Michael Fried's writings on modernist painting and its relationship with the beholder. The terms describe two conditions that characters in a painting can reflect. Absorption is "the state or condition of rapt attention, of being completely occupied or engrossed or . . . absorbed in what he or she is doing, hearing, thinking, feeling."[3] The goal for realist and impressionist painters was to make images of absorption, where the characters are self-forgetting and all attention is on the painting itself, without caring about any beholders. Absorption guaranteed the painting's success as a work of modernism. Theatrical images resemble stage sets, with the characters acting rather than truly experiencing something. They have a somewhat false quality: "The theatrical, implying consciousness of being beheld" is "synonymous with falseness."[4] Fried writes that the painter has to find a way to "neutralize or negate the beholder's presence, to establish the fiction that no one is standing before the canvas. (The paradox is that only if this is done can the beholder be stopped and held precisely there.)"[5] Krohg struggled with this. His Skagen paintings achieve successful absorption: subjects sleep or are so fully engaged in their daily activity that they are unaware of the beholder. The Albertine paintings, *Sick Girl*, and *Struggle for Existence* are more problematic: they address—and assume—the audience more directly.

Realism and impressionism often dealt with scenes of daily life in its most normal state: people going about their business. Naturalism, in contrast, sought to emphasize the hidden aspects of society: people's intimate lives, sickness, the misery of the poor, prostitution, and so forth. Naturalists focused on the abnormal (at least from the point of view of a middle- or upper-class observer) and on what many called the "degenerate." Krohg's *Sick Girl* (1881, fig. 6.1, plate 10) illustrates a naturalistic trend that could be called visual pathology: the representation of people in a state of disease. An important component of this type of imagery was theatricality: there had to be pathos in the image to move the beholder. As Georges Canguilhem writes, "Pathology implies pathos, the direct and concrete feeling of suffering and impotence, the feeling of life gone wrong."[6] The challenge for the naturalist artist was to find the fine line between absorption and theatricality. To be successfully realistic, a painting had to show life as it was, without giving the viewer moral instructions. A convincingly realistic artwork had to simply exist without trying to move, convert, or persuade the beholder. Naturalism often broke these rules, which is why it has been seen as second-grade modernism.

Sympathy in art aims to make the beholder feel for the depicted characters, to experience their sentiments and hardships. Artists wanted to elicit compassion, pity, and identification through their works.[7] Sympathy was seen in that era as one of the great virtues. The aesthetician Claudius Wilkens wrote that sympathy in art created ideals, rather than real feelings, in the beholder. Ideal feelings were of a greater value to Wilkens, since they were disinterested.[8] One of the issues Joris-Karl Huysmans brought up in writing about Jules Bastien-Lepage was whether the painter managed to communicate true and sincere emotions.[9]

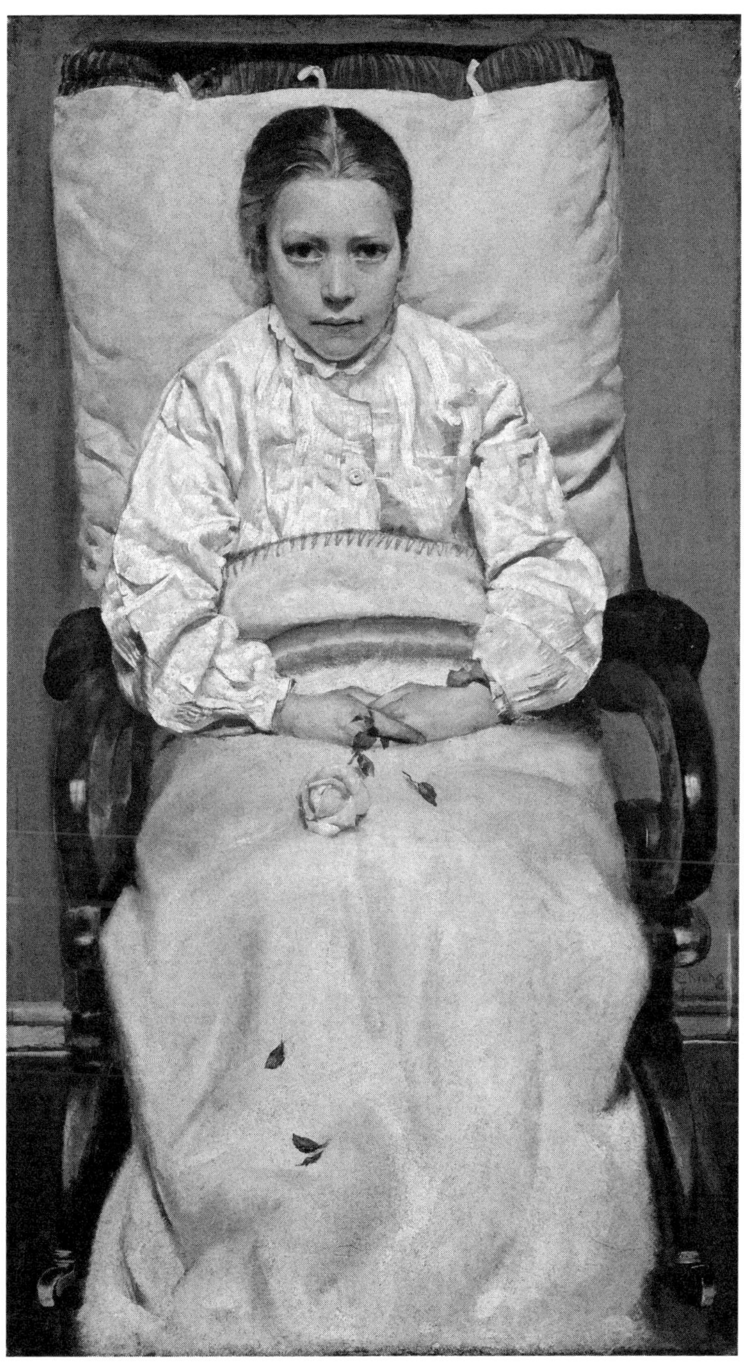

Figure 6.1 (Plate 10). Christian Krohg, *Sick Girl* (1881). Oil on board, 102 × 58 cm. Photo: Jacques Lathion/The National Museum of Art, Architecture and Design, Oslo.

I would claim that in his day, Bastien-Lepage most actively tried to find a proper balance between theatricality and absorption, and explored ways to make beholders feel *real* sympathy for the painted characters. This was the true originality of his art.

THE IMPORTANCE OF JULES BASTIEN-LEPAGE

Jules Bastien-Lepage was possibly the most influential French representative of naturalism for Nordic artists in the 1880s, but he was also an important figure on the Parisian art scene until his early death in 1884. Huysmans, who was for the most part critical of Bastien-Lepage's art, stated in *Le Salon de 1879*: "Mr. Bastien-Lepage is a painter of prodigious skill who knows his craft down to his fingertips."[10]

Zola described how Bastien-Lepage made his reputation with *Haymaking* (1877, fig. 6.2) and *October* (1878): "Two pages where one has breathed in the fresh air with a surprise full of admiration."[11] The critic Théodore de Banville named Bastien-Lepage the king of the Salon of 1879 because of *October*,[12] and the Finnish painter Albert Edelfelt called him "the hero of the Salon."[13] Frits Thaulow was clear in his opinion that Bastien-Lepage was "France and our time's most significant artist."[14] He wrote that Bastien-Lepage's paintings, made with the artist's "clear eye and sober noblesse, . . . blew like fresh air into the sultry, overperfumed salons."[15] The Danish art historian Julius Lange commented in 1879 that Bastien-Lepage was among the young artists who had an extraordinary "will to artistic honesty and truth,"[16] and in 1888 that for the last ten years Bastien-Lepage had been "one of the most famous and talked-about artist's names in the whole of Europe."[17] Norwegian art critic Andreas Aubert called Bastien-Lepage the "happy artist, who already in his youth won the sympathies of his own time. . . . Posterity will see in him one of the most energetic expressions of what, artistically speaking, has moved our time in the healthiest and most noble manner."[18] P. S. Krøyer, an enthusiastic admirer who had met the French painter a few times, called *Joan of Arc* (1879), despite the vision in the background, "by far the most beautiful modern art I have seen."[19] The Danish art historian Emil Hannover recorded: "The highlight of modern French art to us Danes was Bastien-Lepage."[20]

Bastien-Lepage was seen as Courbet's true successor.[21] He was also associated with Manet and even called an impressionist by Louis Desprez in *L'évolution naturaliste* (1884).[22] Many compared him to Millet, although Georg Nordensvan stated that "Bastien-Lepage was an individualist and detailist, whereas Millet was a synthesist and epicist."[23] Bastien-Lepage was admired as an artist who challenged academic painting and created a new visuality. As he himself declared, "We need to start again with the education of our eyes, looking sincerely at how things are in nature instead of taking for absolute truths the theories or conventions of art school."[24] He wrote in a letter: "When I came to Paris, I knew nothing at all, but at least I was ignorant of the heap of formulas with which you are perverted there. You wish to paint what you see, and instead of this, you are urged to aim at an unknown ideal, that is to say, to imitate old pictures more or less."[25]

Bastien-Lepage was perceived by his contemporaries across Europe as an ascending star. In addition to the Salons, his paintings could be seen in Paris at the Galerie Georges Petit in the spring of 1884 and at the memorial exhibition held the following year at the Hôtel de Chimay in the École des Beaux-Arts. Swedish painter Eva Bonnier visited that show

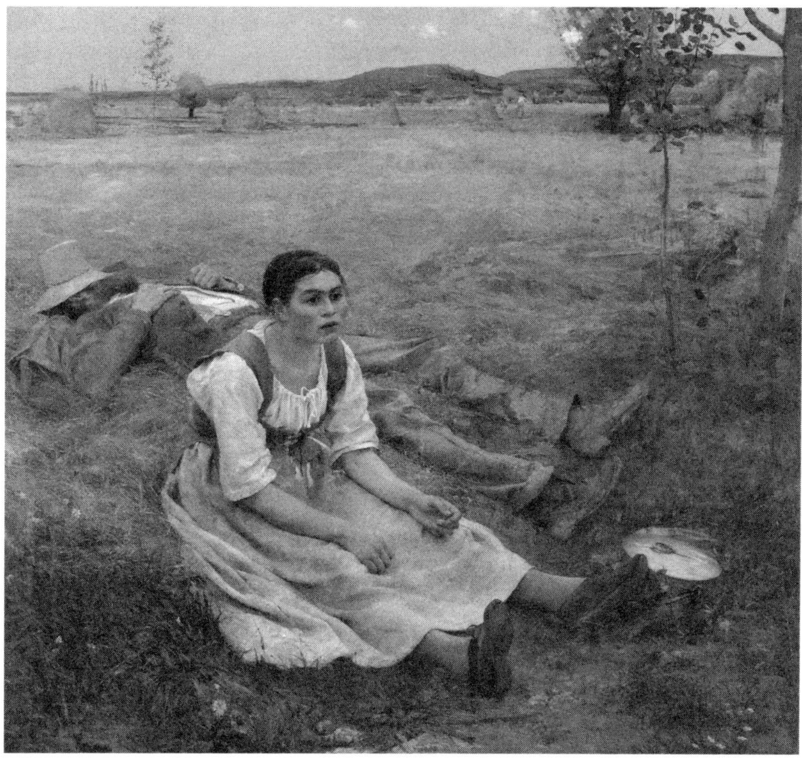

Figure 6.2. Jules Bastien-Lepage, *Haymaking* (1877). Oil on wood, 160 × 195 cm. Photo © RMN-Grand Palais (Musée d'Orsay)/Hervé Lewandowski.

and was impressed: "It was awesome, and the greatest art experience I have had in a long time. Not before one has seen all of his work collected in one place can one imagine his greatness and originality. Most striking is his productive energy. Six rooms are full of his work, although he died when he was only thirty-one, and for the last two years he was not even able to hold a brush."[26] Indeed, he died too young, in 1884, when he was only thirty-six (not thirty-one, as Bonnier wrote). Akseli Gallen-Kallela wrote after seeing the memorial exhibition, "I find he has more in common with the old masters: the same fierce passion for nature, the same fine skills of characterization, the same immaculate brushwork. His originality is the natural outcome of an aspiration to paint nature exactly as he perceived it. Art such as this will never be modern, nor will it ever grow old."[27]

The Danish art historian Emil Hannover wrote that Bastien-Lepage had "sublime artistic values," and that he was "the most noble" and "without a doubt the most gifted among all the realist painters of the nineteenth century."[28] Hannover praised Bastien-Lepage for capturing the uniqueness of his subjects while creating a harmonious whole.[29] This approach could be seen as a reaction to impressionist art, with its motifs taken from the busy world

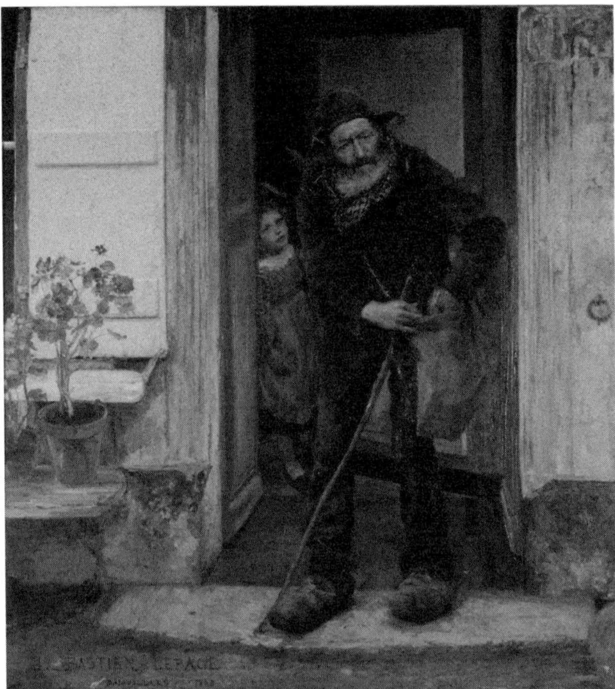

Figure 6.3.

Jules Bastien-Lepage, *The Beggar* (1880). Oil on canvas, 192.5 × 180.5 cm. Photo: Glyptoteket, Copenhagen.

and its emphasis on speed and movement expressed through the flickering painterly surface. Bastien-Lepage's great contribution, according to Hannover, was to have an extraordinary human perception based on sympathy. He was sympathetic without being soft. Hannover wrote, echoing Zola, that *October* was "a piece of nature seen through a noble and powerful temperament."[30] Julius Lange also emphasized Bastien-Lepage's heartfelt sympathy for his subjects. He wrote that the artist did not really paint portraits or genre scenes, but rather "life paintings" (*Lifsbilleder*) in which he "gives an in-depth and complete portrayal of the character."[31] Lange saw this as especially exemplified by *The Beggar* (1880, fig. 6.3).

Bastien-Lepage's *Haymaking* became the iconic naturalist image. The painting was exhibited at the 1878 Salon, and the conservative *Art Journal* reported from the show: "The rigorous realism of 'Les Foins' ('In the Hay-Field'), by Bastien-Lepage, will appeal to the critical sense even of those who do not altogether admire the aberrations and odd theories that so often lead astray the talent of this gifted young painter." The critic did find the woman in the painting vulgar: "She is a stupid-looking, bullet-headed, country clodhopper—nothing more; an unpleasant creature to look at, and one giving no hint or revelation of any of life's higher possibilities."[32] The author criticized the painting for lacking the "unconscious pathos" of a Millet canvas or the "unconscious heroism" of Antoine Vollon's *The Fisher Girl* (1876). The *Art Journal* critic far preferred Vollon's idealism to the modern realism of Bastien-Lepage. The fisher girl depicted by Vollon may have been offensive in real life, but the artist made her beautiful in his painting. Bastien-Lepage's *Joan of Arc* was moved from room to room at the Salon because no one wanted the radical "ugly" painting

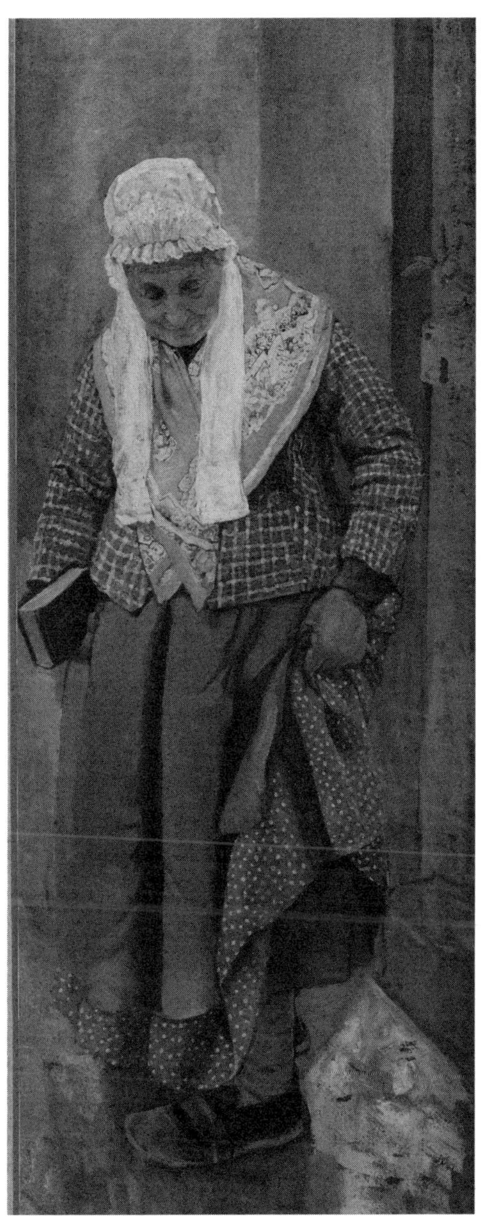

Figure 6.4.

Christian Krohg, *Old Woman (Sunday Morning)* (1882). Oil on canvas, 134.5 × 51.2 cm. National Gallery of Denmark, Copenhagen. © SMK Photo.

to hang near his or her work, ending up next to a Vollon still life of a pumpkin: "Yet such was the breadth, the dignity, the nobleness of that pumpkin, that it was Bastien's picture that suffered the neighborhood, not Vollon's."[33]

These examples of Bastien-Lepage's reception tell us something about the edge on which he and those like him were poised—between harsh realism and dignifying idealism. How beautiful or ugly should the realist make his subjects? Art historian Marnin Young has summarized the quandary of French critics before *Haymaking*: "Was she [the central, seated woman] a humble, earthy, hard-working peasant, the critics asked, or was she a repugnant, slack-jawed beast? . . . What did it mean to paint a peasant realistically?"[34] How should sympathy for one's subjects be represented? This last point was especially important to Bastien-Lepage, and here his originality as an artist showed itself. The sympathy question seemed crucial to him, his observers, and other artists who saw him as their model.

NATURALIST TYPES

At the 1882 Paris Salon, where Krohg showed two paintings that critics compared to works by Bastien-Lepage,[35] Krohg got to see Bastien-Lepage's *The Woodgatherer* (1881). Immediately afterward he went to the Scandinavian artist colony in Grez, south of Paris, close to the Fontainebleau forests, where he painted *Old Woman (Sunday Morning)* (1882, fig. 6.4). This picture was clearly inspired by Bastien-Lepage both in subject matter and execution. The woman in his painting was a typical Bastien-Lepage subject. Krohg drew special

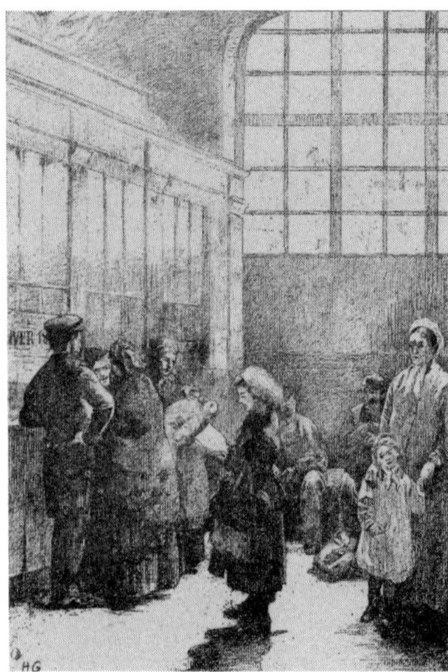

Figure 6.5.

Drawing of Henri Gervex's *A Charity Organization Office* (1883). Facsimile from F.-G. Dumas, ed., *Catalogue illustré du Salon* (1883).

attention to her big shoes—just as Bastien-Lepage did in *The Beggar*. Krohg saw Bastien-Lepage's *Rural Love* (1882) at the Salon of 1883, when he visited Paris with Max Klinger, as well as striking naturalist canvases by other masters: Léon Lhermitte's *The Harvest* (1883) and Fernand Pelez's *Homeless* (1883). Henri Gervex's *A Charity Organization Office* (1883, fig. 6.5) possibly inspired Krohg in his work on the Albertine series. In this painting, Gervex vividly depicted a shy young girl caught by the gaze of other characters in a waiting room, her body language similar to Albertine's.

Krohg completed several paintings in the 1880s with naturalist types. These canvases are his most Bastienesque, evincing a desire to create contact with the viewer and to make him or her feel empathy with the depicted characters. Krohg's *Carry for You?* (1880, fig. 6.6), for example, may have been influenced by Bastien-Lepage's paintings of children; clearly they are artistically related. In Krohg's canvas, an errand boy looks for work at the market. He carries a number sign around his neck and a big basket over his shoulder. The painting showcases a variety of objects and textures, including a still life with vegetables in the foreground. A realistic image of modern life, it contains allusions to Émile Zola's *The Belly of Paris* (1873), in which much of the story takes place at the food market in Les Halles. Some years later, Krohg painted a related *Errand Boy Drinking Coffee* (1885, fig. 6.7), which shows a boy taking a break to get something to eat and drink. He wears a number sign around his neck. In both paintings the boys are young and already engaged in labor. Many such types appear in Krohg's art in the 1880s, including *Sick Girl*.

SICK GIRL (1881)

Sick Girl (1881, fig. 6.1, plate 10) is one of Krohg's best-known paintings today, not least because it is a direct inspiration for Edvard Munch's artistic breakthrough, *The Sick Child* (1885). The two works show the closeness as well as the difference between the two artists. Both depicted a child dying of tuberculosis—a favorite naturalist theme. In Krohg's

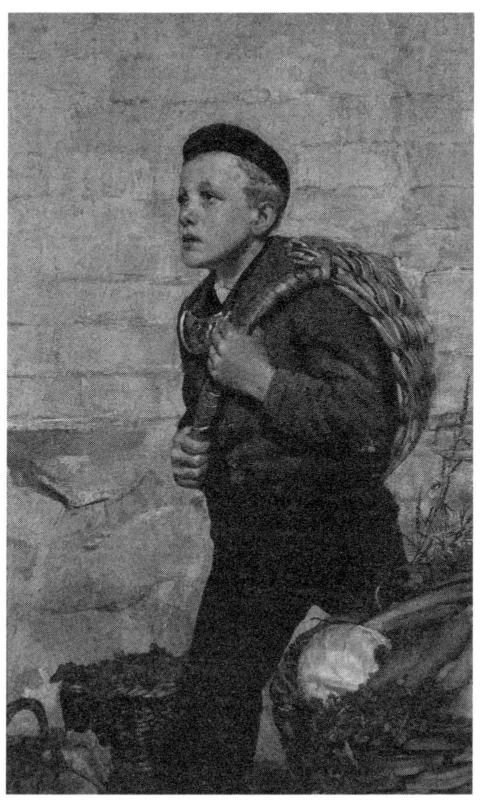

Figure 6.6.

Christian Krohg, *Carry for You?* (1880). Oil on canvas, 88 × 57.5 cm. Private collection. © Photo: O. Væring Eftf. AS, Norway.

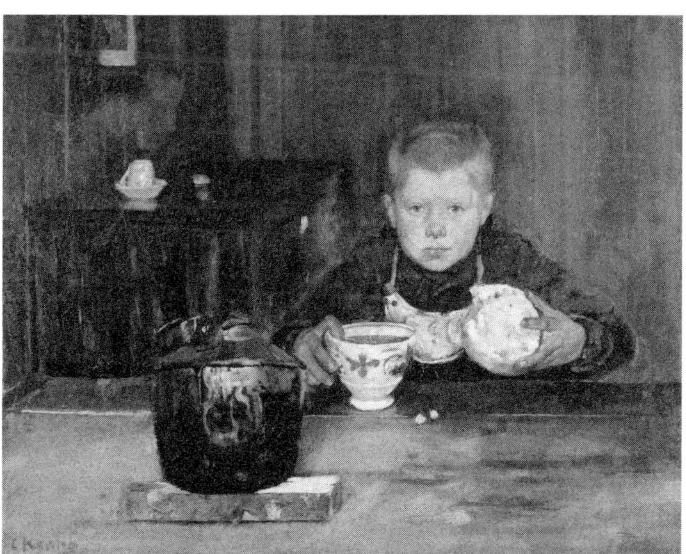

Figure 6.7. Christian Krohg, *Errand Boy Drinking Coffee* (1885). Oil on canvas, 49 × 63 cm. Photo: Gothenburg Museum of Art, Sweden.

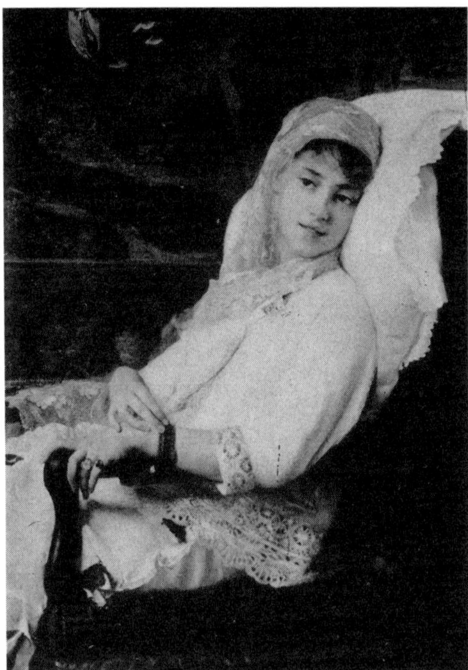

Figure 6.8.

Emile Lévy, *The Convalescence* (1883). Facsimile from Louis Énault, *Paris-Salon Triennal 1883* (1883).

painting, the rose on the girl's lap symbolizes the fragility of life and the approach of death. The outside world she longs for is accessible only in a reflection of the window in the chair's armrests. As he does in many of his paintings, Krohg pulls the figure close to the frame, but then he does something unusual: he makes the girl look straight at the viewer, directly seeking his or her sympathy. Krohg took a standard motif and turned it into a challenging image through its original composition, an almost abstract assemblage of forms, and the placement of the girl close to the beholder, so that she stares right into the viewer's eyes. The boldness of his conception becomes clearer when his picture is compared to two similar paintings shown at the 1883 Salon: Paul L. Jenoudet's *November* (1883, made popular through prints) and Émile Lévy's *The Convalescence* (1883, fig. 6.8). Louis Énault wrote in his Salon catalog that Lévy's painting became a favorite with viewers because he was such a talented artist and he made the viewers feel sympathy for the girl.[36] He described the painting as delicate, charming, pure, and brilliant—the opposite of what one might say of Krohg's version. The critics of Krohg's *Sick Child* pronounced the painting bad, aggressive, or uncanny; all one writer could see in it was a head without a body.[37]

Tuberculosis, the white plague, was perhaps the most deadly disease of the nineteenth century.[38] It was an urban illness, easily spread in the growing cities. An infection that attacks the lungs and can move to other organs, it was transmitted by contact with infected droplets emitted by the coughing patient. The symptoms of the disease include cough, sputum, fatigue, fever, emaciation, and night sweats. In Krohg's novel, Albertine's younger brother, Edvard, suffers from these symptoms. Coughing was the first sign of the illness,[39] and Edvard is constantly coughing: "He coughed hollowly and strained and spluttered, spat out something and stepped on it."[40] Thousands of children and grown-ups died of tuberculosis, and the disease provoked fear, anxiety, and shame. Before it was scientifically understood, people had no idea what caused it. The tubercle bacillus was only discovered in 1882, and in the 1870s and 1880s explanations of the disease included "hereditary disposition, unfavorable climate, sedentary indoor life, defective ventilation, deficiency of light and 'depressing emotions.'"[41] René and Jean Dubos called tuberculosis a social disease and wrote in their classic study: "The disease modifies in a peculiar manner the emotional and intellectual climate of the societies it attacks."[42] The discovery of the tuberculosis bacillus the year after Krohg painted *Sick Child* changed medical knowledge of the illness, but it took longer to alter popular understanding and imagination. Tuberculosis was such a ubiquitous problem that it shaped the development of modern society through major health and hygiene reforms. Because it affected so many people and was seen as a social ailment associated with poverty—striking especially poor children—it was a perfect subject for naturalist artists.

THE SEAMSTRESS SERIES

Another urban type depicted by Krohg was the seamstress; he also chose it because of its political potential. His first painting titled *The Seamstress* (1879) is known today only through a black-and-white photograph, but we can already see in it many of the elements that reappear in the later versions. He next showed a seamstress in *Dawn* (1880, fig. 6.9). His sister Amalie served as the model for the image, and the interior reproduced the Krohg family home. Lorentz Dietrichson writes that the girl in *Dawn* is endowed with "a portion of ugliness"—one of the main ingredients of naturalism.[43] The seamstress has fallen asleep, and it is obvious that Krohg is trying to give the image a social meaning, drawing attention to the fatigue of an overworked woman. A year later Krohg painted a larger version of this subject, also called *The Seamstress* (1881, fig. 6.10), this time using a different model. He made the motif more "naturalistic" by including a cheap and broken lamp, as well as a curtain with holes and a large rip that has been repaired but remains visible. The girl uses a different kind of sewing machine, one operated by a hand crank instead of a treadle. The social message of poverty and hard work is here more convincingly expressed than in the earlier versions.[44] When the painting was exhibited the same year, the art critic Andreas Aubert called it Krohg's most significant and skilled work.[45]

The final version of the seamstress motif is *Tired* (1885, fig. 6.11, plate 11). In that painting Krohg combined the subject of his earlier canvases with the Albertine project. In fact, he incorporated it into the Albertine series. He used the same model in *Tired* as in the Albertine paintings and made Albertine in the novel into a seamstress.

Tired shows a more mature artist at work. The space is composed in a new and effective way that draws the beholder into the picture. The brushwork is looser but confident. The scene is now convincingly poor, set in a working class home. Krohg chose not to include the dress the girl is sewing—we can only see something white on her lap—thus avoiding the cliché of a poor girl working on an expensive silk garment. It falls to the beholder to figure out the implied social contrast. The image is, thus, less didactic than the previous one and more convincingly realistic.

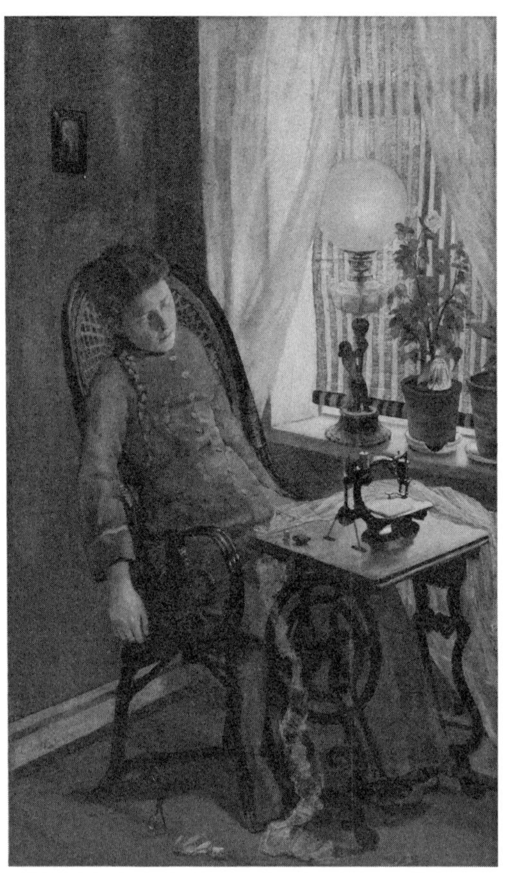

Figure 6.9. *Left.*

Christian Krohg, *Dawn* (1880). Oil on board, 135 × 81 cm. National Gallery of Denmark, Copenhagen. © SMK Photo.

Figure 6.10. *Below.*

Christian Krohg, *The Seamstress* (1881). Oil on canvas, 130 × 166 cm. Gothenburg Art Museum, Sweden. © Photo: O. Væring Eftf. AS, Norway.

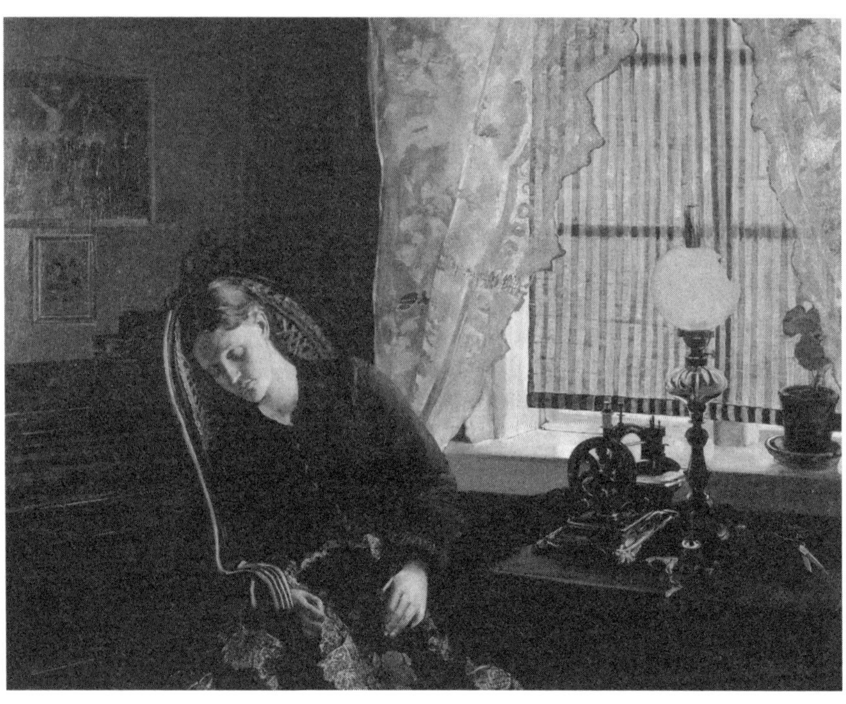

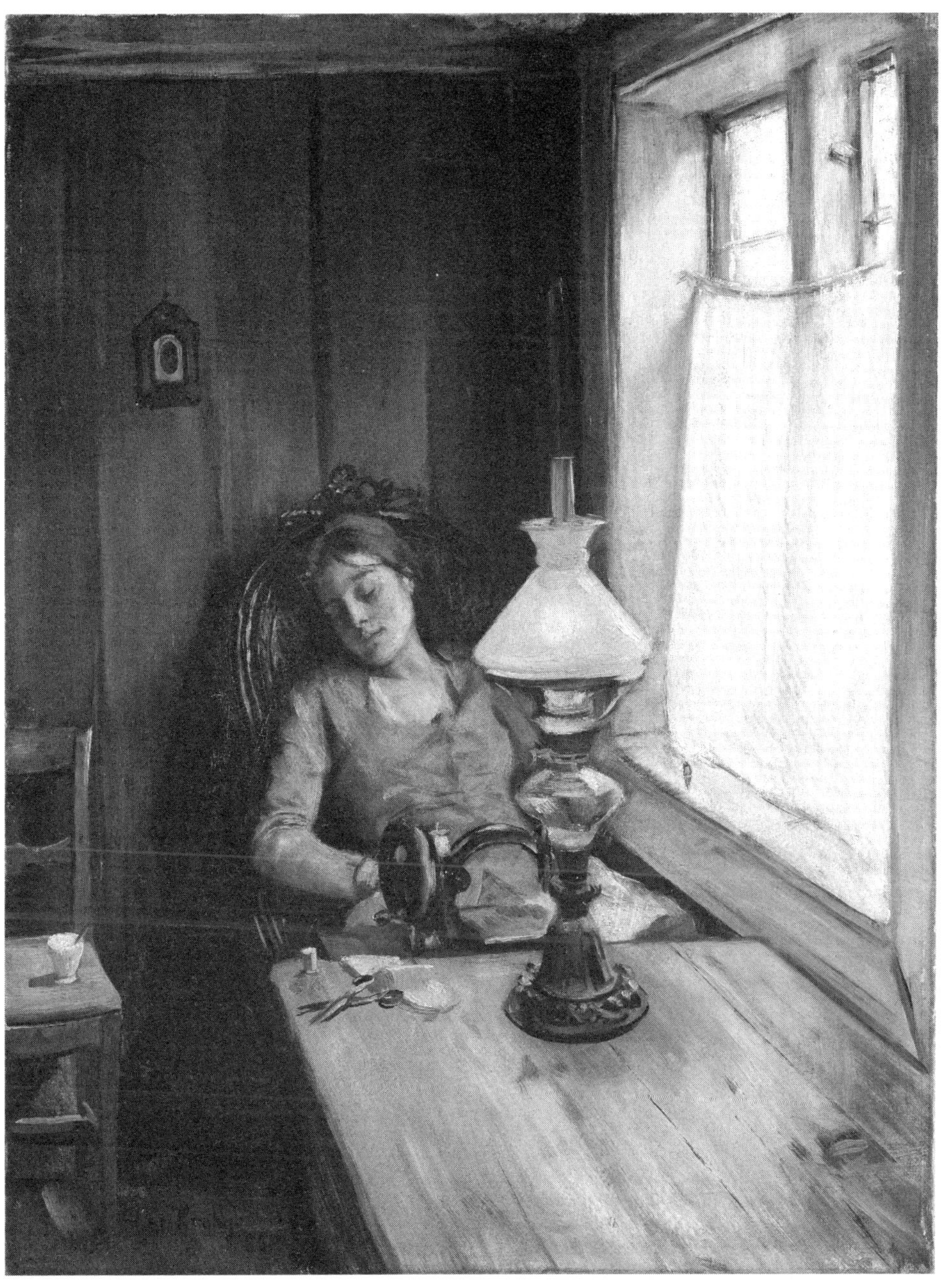

Figure 6.11 (Plate 11). Christian Krohg, *Tired* (1885). Oil on canvas, 79.5 × 61.5 cm. Photo: Jacques Lathion/The National Museum of Art, Architecture and Design, Oslo.

A girl or woman sewing has been a common motif throughout art history. Needlework is the most womanly of the manual arts, and the needle became a symbol of femininity. Sewing—the most appropriate feminine activity—appeared in many genre paintings in the early seventeenth century. Sleeping spinners and lace makers were seen as lazy women with weak morals; whether they slept or daydreamed, they abandoned their duties. They were also perceived as sexually available.[46] Sewing women continued to be ubiquitous in nineteenth-century art, for they fulfilled realist and modernist demands for an absorbed image. The sleeping seamstress appeared in realist images by masters such as Courbet, Millet, and Mentzel. Representatives of daily life, women bent over their sewing were depicted convincingly in many impressionist paintings. Krohg updated this traditional motif by showing Albertine with a sewing machine. This domestic device had become increasingly popular starting in the 1850s, and cheaper versions became available in the 1870s and 1880s, just when Krohg painted his seamstress canvases. Her sewing machine is a symbol of modernity: a product of the industrialized world and an attribute of a modern woman's life.[47] The sewing machine was the first technical device women were allowed to use, and it came to be associated with femininity.

The sewing machine was one of the very first mass-produced and mass-marketed tools for private consumers. It marked a revolution in clothing production and consumption. As the historian Judith G. Coffin writes, "Icon of modern femininity, object of desire, and emblem of modernity, the nineteenth-century sewing machine appeared startling, almost hypnotic in its promises and appeal."[48] This quote is visually demonstrated in Eilif Peterssen's *The First Sewing Machine* (1876, fig. 6.12), in which the characters have set aside their old equipment to look with wonder, surprise, and laughter at the new modern device.

The sewing machine was not only an important tool but a source of financial anxiety for poor women. It enabled them to take on more work but also put them into debt, since sewing machines, even those made for domestic use in the 1870s and 1880s, were very expensive. They could cost between one-fifth and one-half of the yearly earnings of a seamstress. Keen to sell these machines to the working class, manufacturers offered payment plans that allowed people to purchase them on credit, thus making them an important part of the new large-scale credit industry.[49] The seamstress, alas, often became entangled in a hopeless financial situation as she struggled to obtain and complete enough work to pay for the tools of her trade.

Before long, the sewing machine and women's work became a political, ethical, and medical issue prompting extensive debates. Was the machine bad for women's bodies and psyches (the noise and vibration of the machine added to their exhaustion) or was it liberating? Fatigue was a common complaint,[50] and Krohg drew attention to this problem in his paintings. His seamstresses are far from the happy "Singer girls" of commercials. Some social commentators argued that sewing machines would keep girls off of the streets and bring an end to prostitution.[51] Certain doctors, however, believed that pedal work was sexually arousing to women and could corrupt them. One Parisian doctor wrote in 1866: "For this young woman, these different movements [of the body against the machine] produced

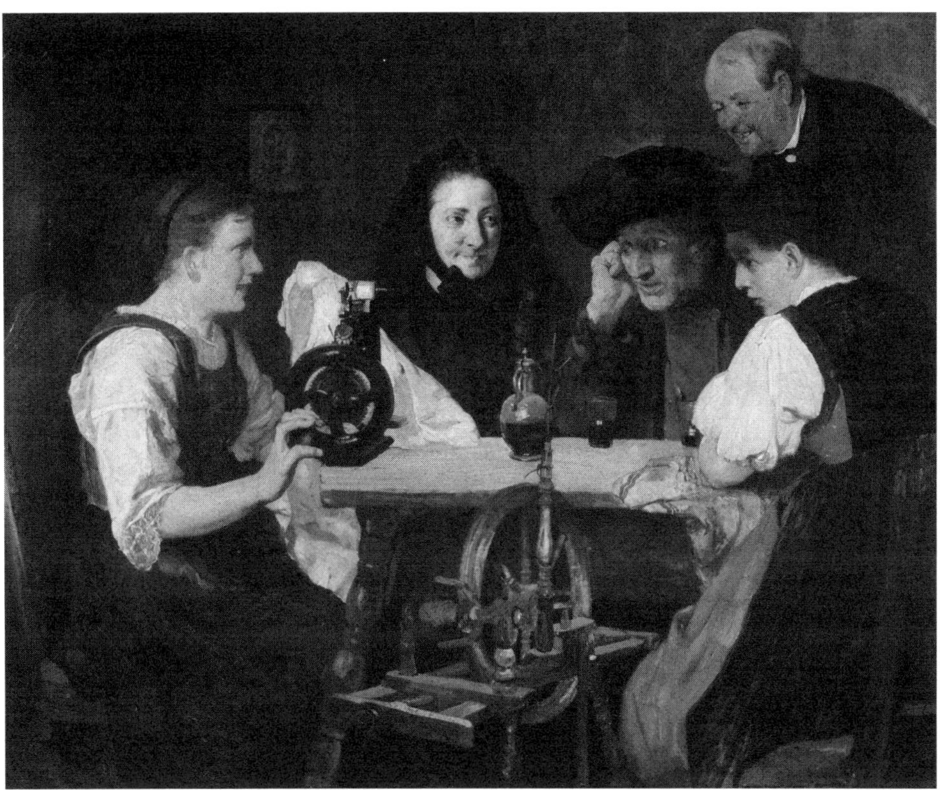

Figure 6.12. Eilif Peterssen, *The First Sewing Machine* (1876). Oil on canvas, 51 × 65 cm. Private collection. © Photo: O. Væring Eftf. AS, Norway.

a considerable genital excitement that sometimes forced her to suspend work, and it is to the frequency of this excitement and to the fatigue it produced, that she attributed her leucorrhea, weight loss, and increasing weakness."[52] It seems that many believed women got orgasms from working on their sewing machines. Thus the device became a symbol of female sexuality, as many commercials implied. In Albertine's case, the sewing machine clearly did not keep her off the streets. In fact, it was not unusual for seamstresses to become prostitutes. The Norwegian police doctor Boeck described this sad transition: "[Many] started doing licentious things little by little. This is very common for seamstresses and laundresses."[53] Statistics from France show that almost 50 percent of registered prostitutes had as their previous occupation some kind of needlework or were laundresses, ironers, or linen maids.[54] It was therefore no coincidence that Krohg made his Albertine a seamstress.

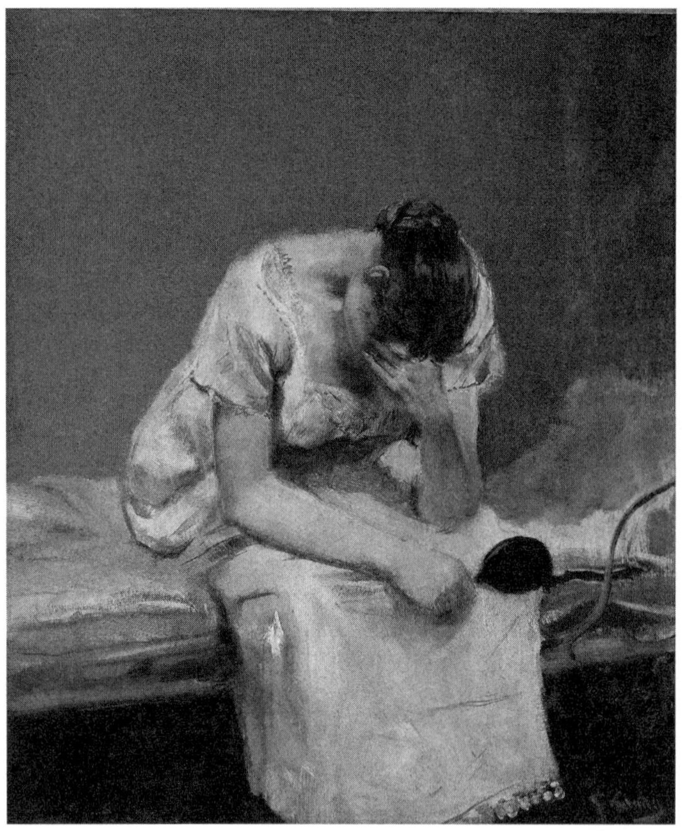

Figure 6.13. Christian Krohg, *Madeleine* (1883). Oil on board, 53 × 45 cm. Photo: Lillehammer Art Museum, Norway.

Krohg's *Madeleine* (1883, fig. 6.13) may serve as a coda to the present discussion. She is also a "naturalistic type." This painting received a great deal of attention at the Nordic exhibition in Copenhagen in 1883, and we can already see in it signs of Krohg's interest in portraying prostitution. The painting could have been executed in France the year before, and the name might be a reference to Marie Madeleine (Mary Magdalene)—often said to be a prostitute. The woman's body language makes the viewer feel sympathy for her without resorting to theatricality or drama. The painting shows Krohg's ambition to work with the contentious but highly modern subject of prostitution.

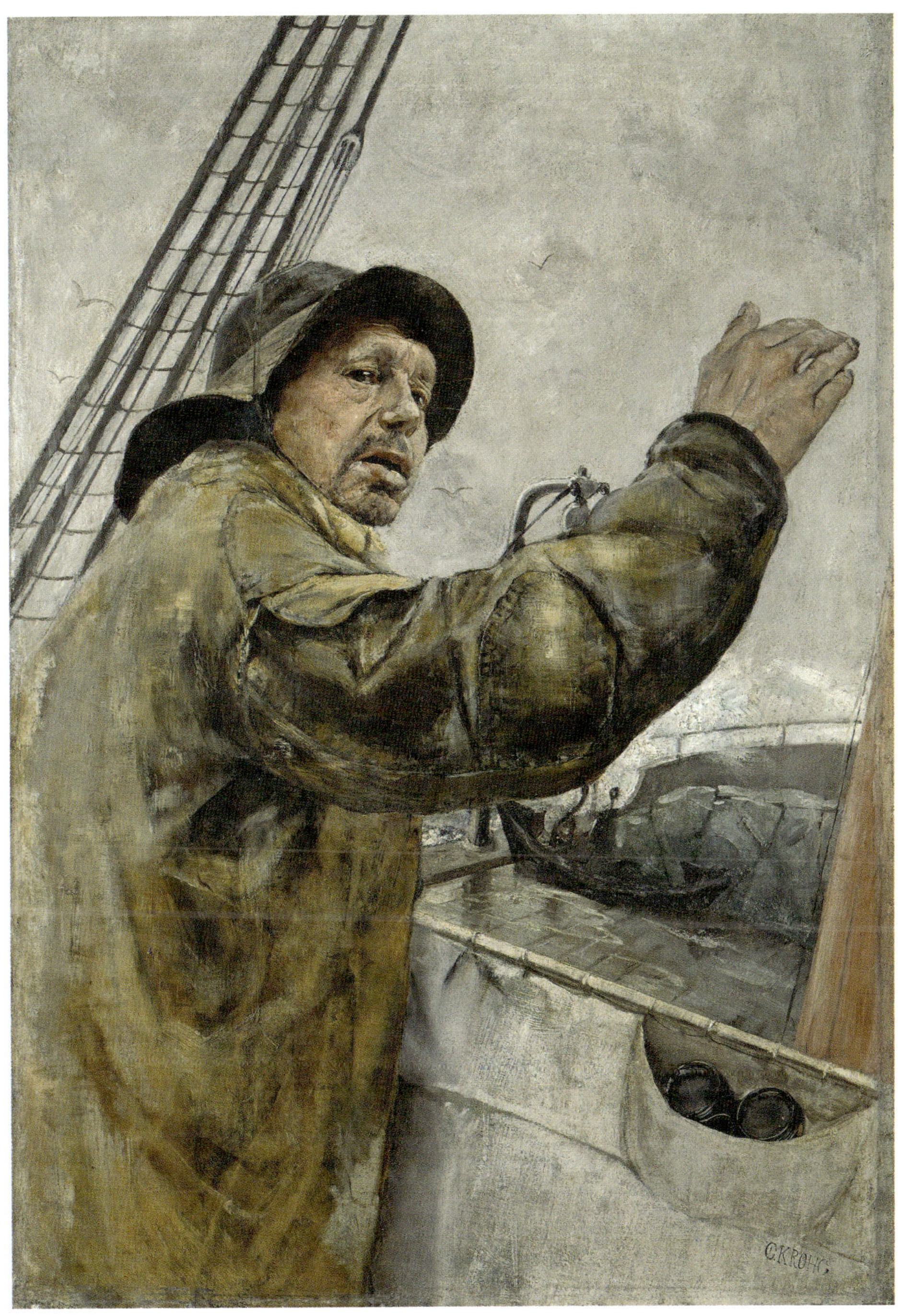

Plate 1. Christian Krohg, *Port Side!* (1879). Oil on canvas, 99 × 70 cm. Photo: Jacques Lathion/The National Museum of Art, Architecture and Design, Oslo.

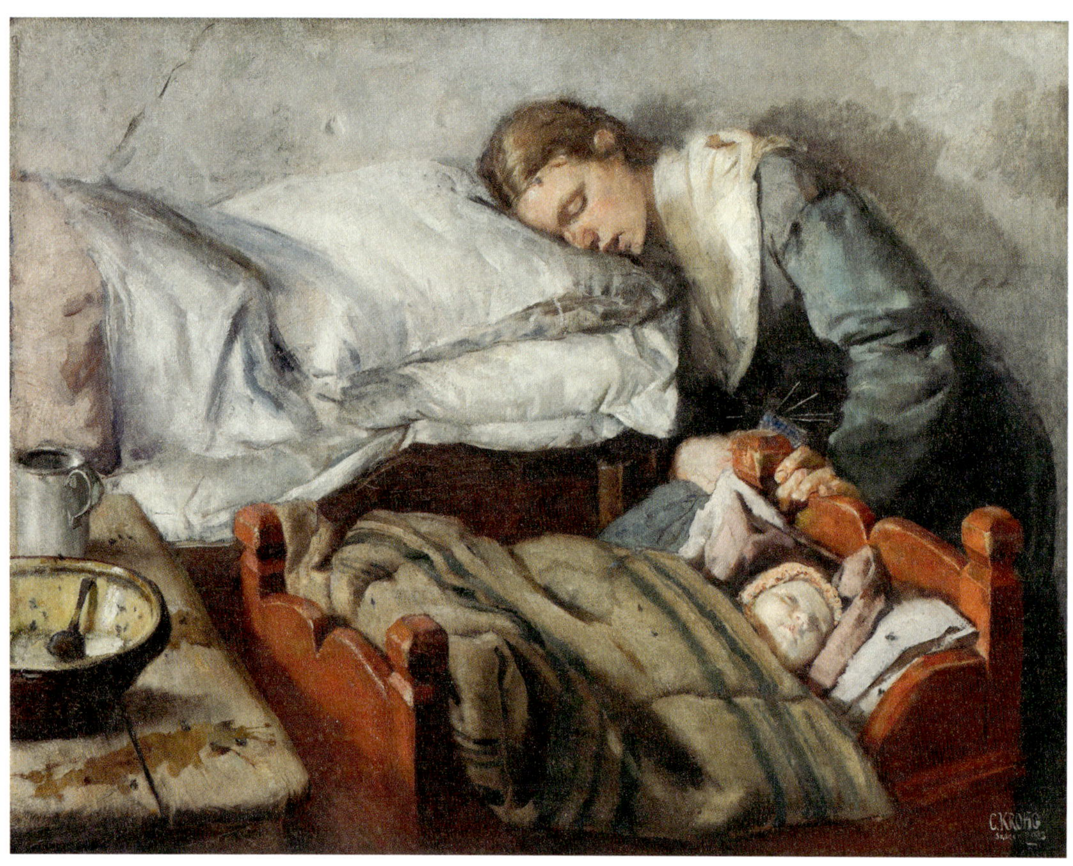

Plate 2. Christian Krohg, *Sleeping Mother* (also known as *Sleeping Fisher Family*, 1883). Oil on canvas, 107.5 × 142 cm. Photo: Dag Fosse/KODE—Art Museums of Bergen, Rasmus Meyer Collection.

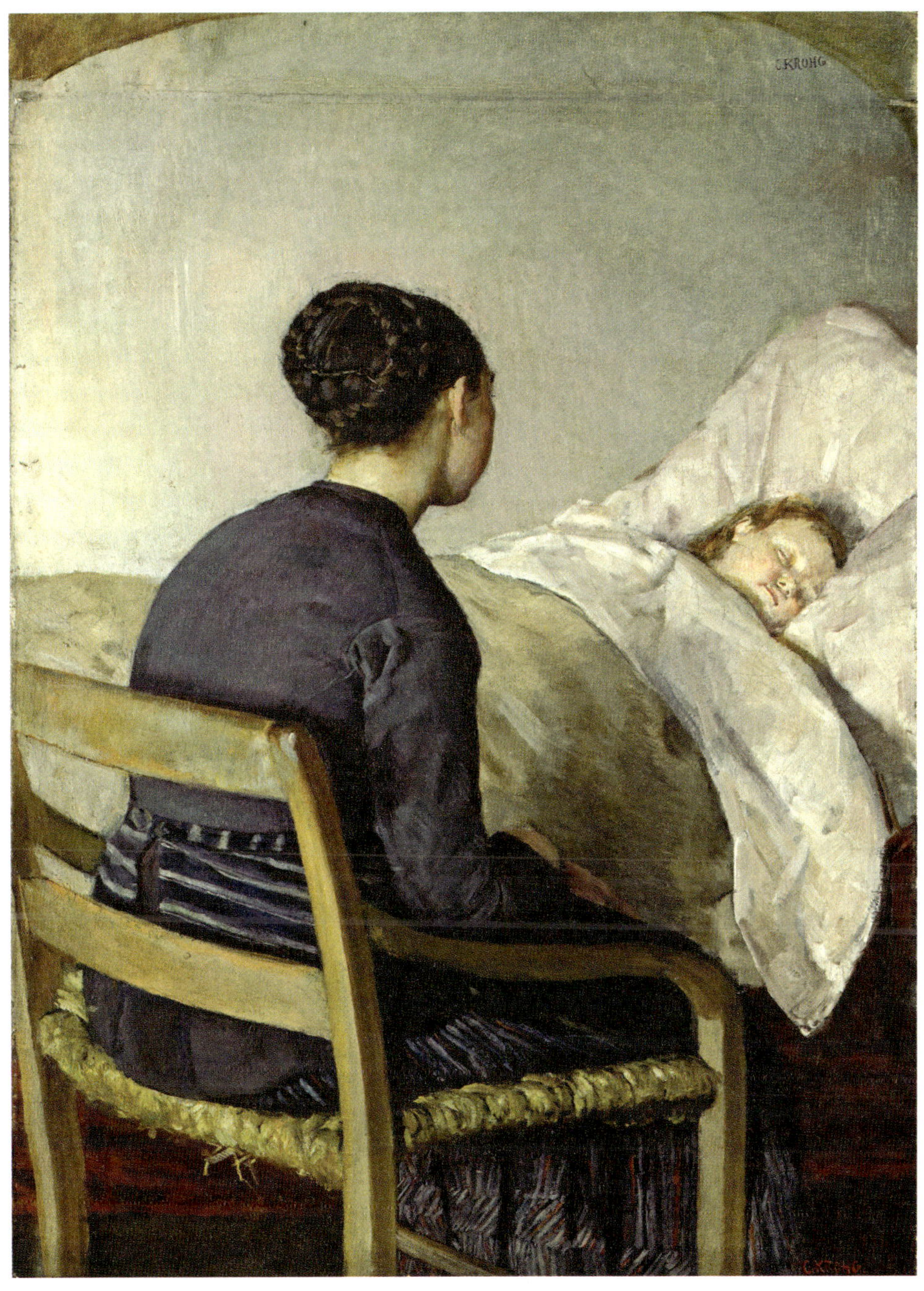

Plate 3. Christian Krohg, *Mother at Her Child's Bed* (1884). Oil on canvas, 131 × 95 cm. Photo: Jacques Lathion/The National Museum of Art, Architecture and Design, Oslo.

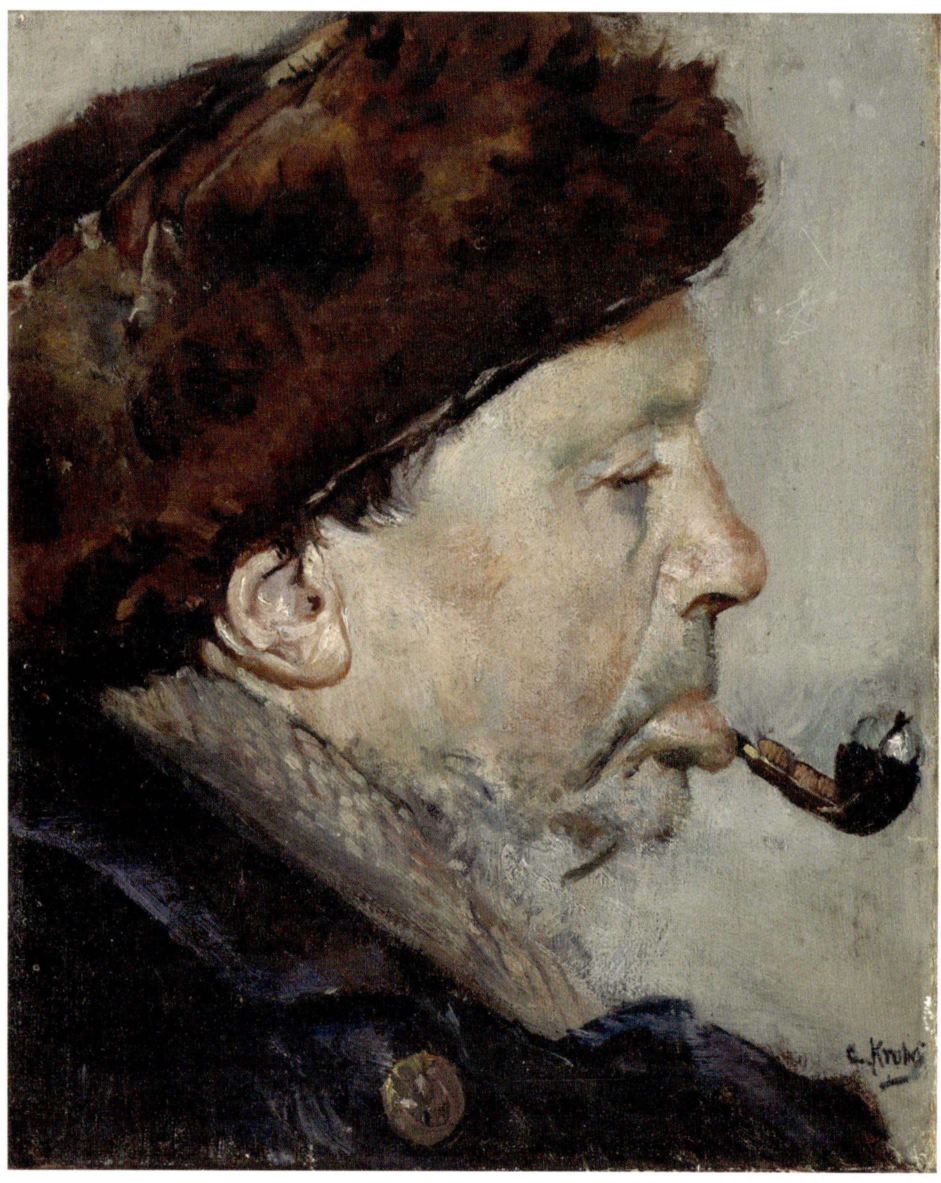

Plate 4. Christian Krohg, *Niels Gaihede* (1888). Oil on canvas, 36 × 30.5 cm. Photo: Jacques Lathion/The National Museum of Art, Architecture and Design, Oslo.

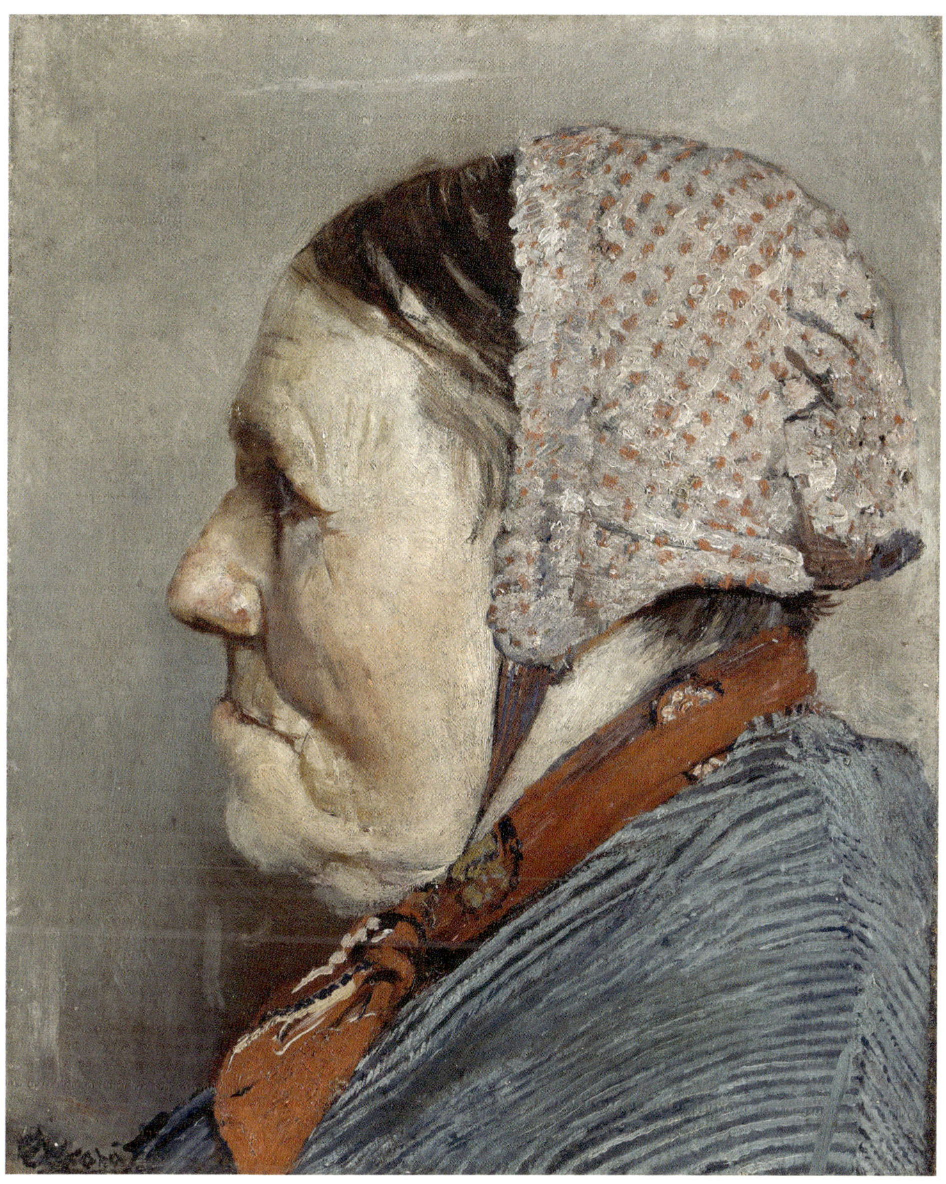

Plate 5. Christian Krohg, *Ane Gaihede* (1888). Oil on canvas, 36 × 30.5 cm. Photo: Knut Øystein Nerdrum/The National Museum of Art, Architecture and Design, Oslo.

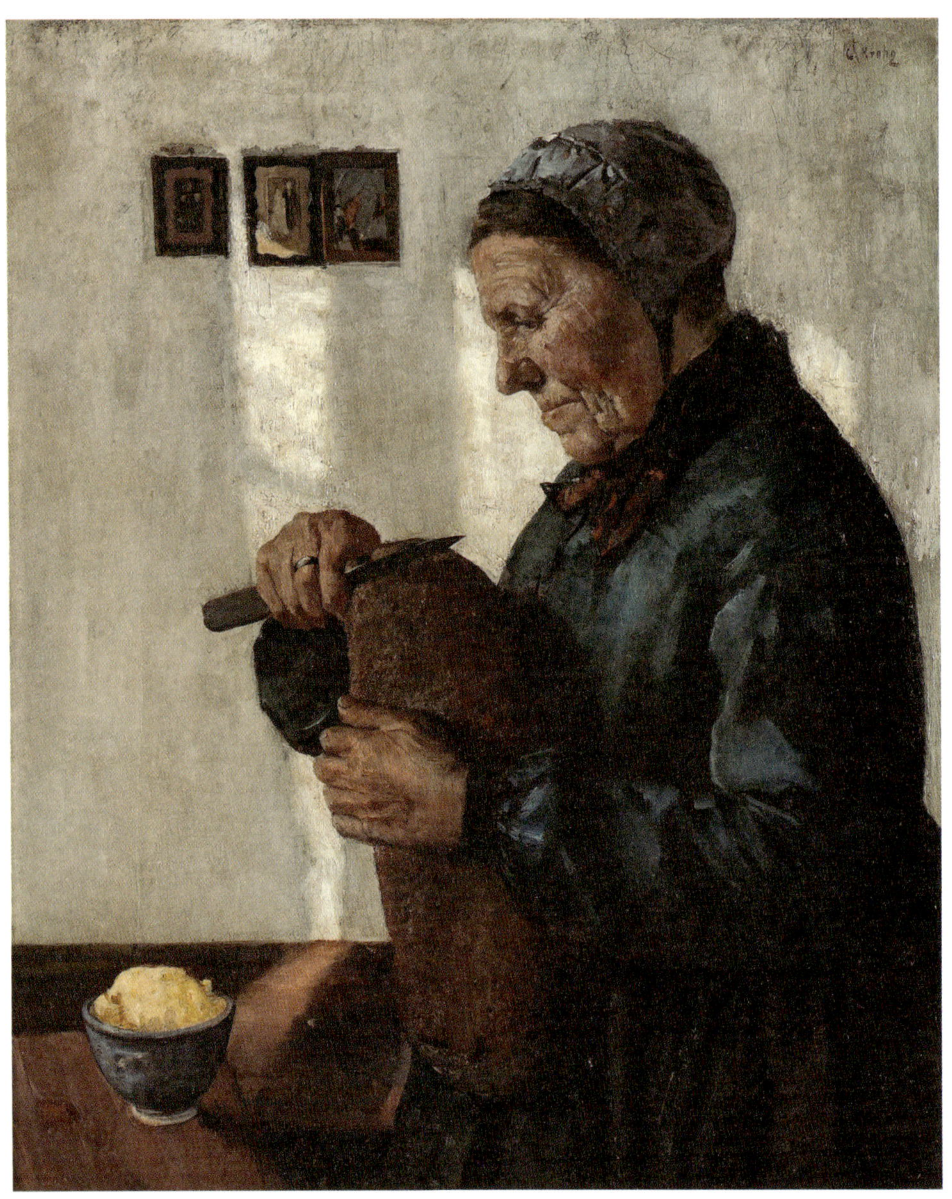

Plate 6. Christian Krohg, *Woman Cutting Bread* (1879). Oil on canvas, 80 × 66 cm. Photo: Dag Fosse/KODE—Art Museums of Bergen, Norway.

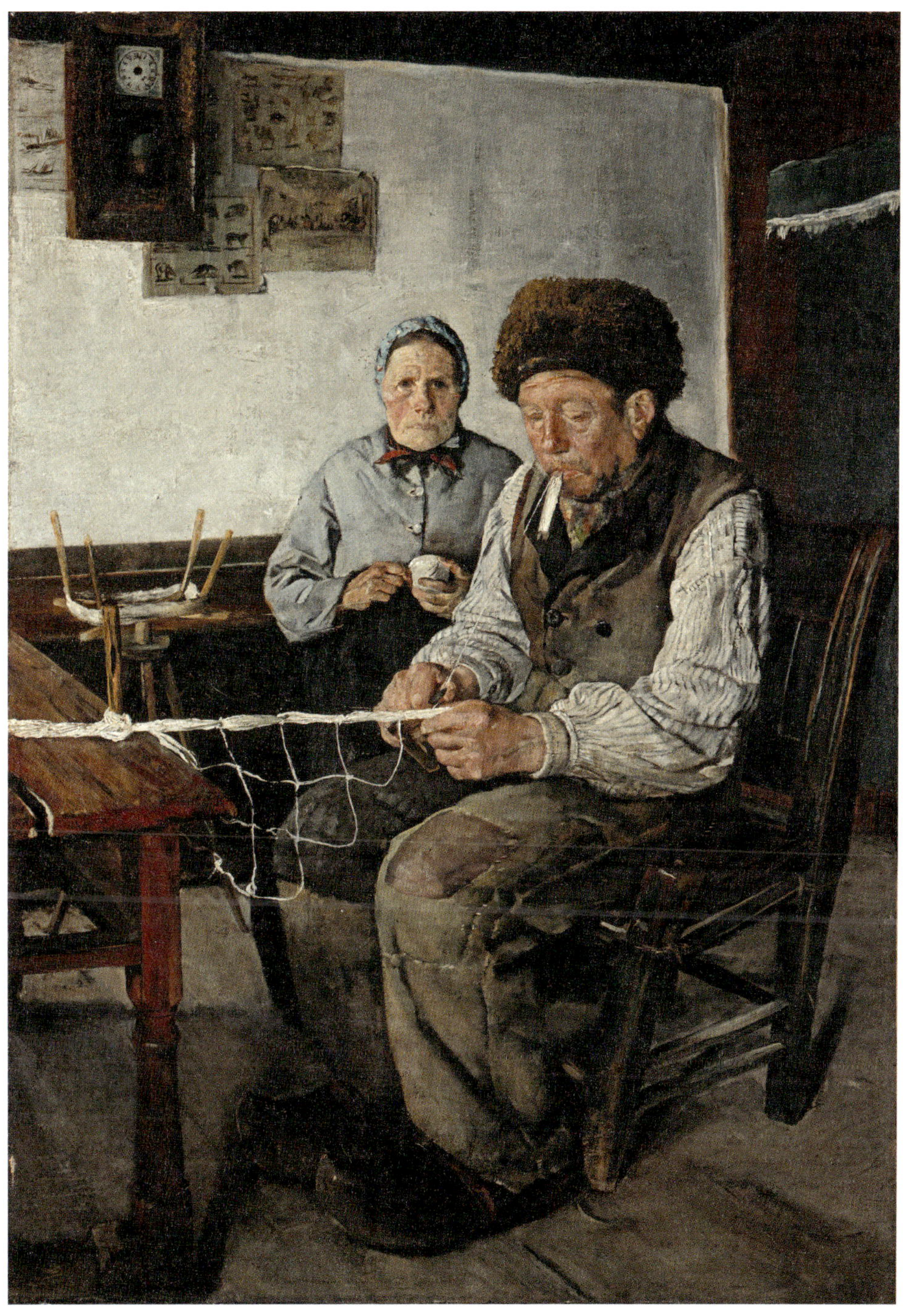

Plate 7. Christian Krohg, *Niels Gaihede Netting* (ca. 1880). Oil on canvas, 93.5 × 67 cm. Photo: Jaques Lathion/The National Museum of Art, Architecture and Design, Oslo.

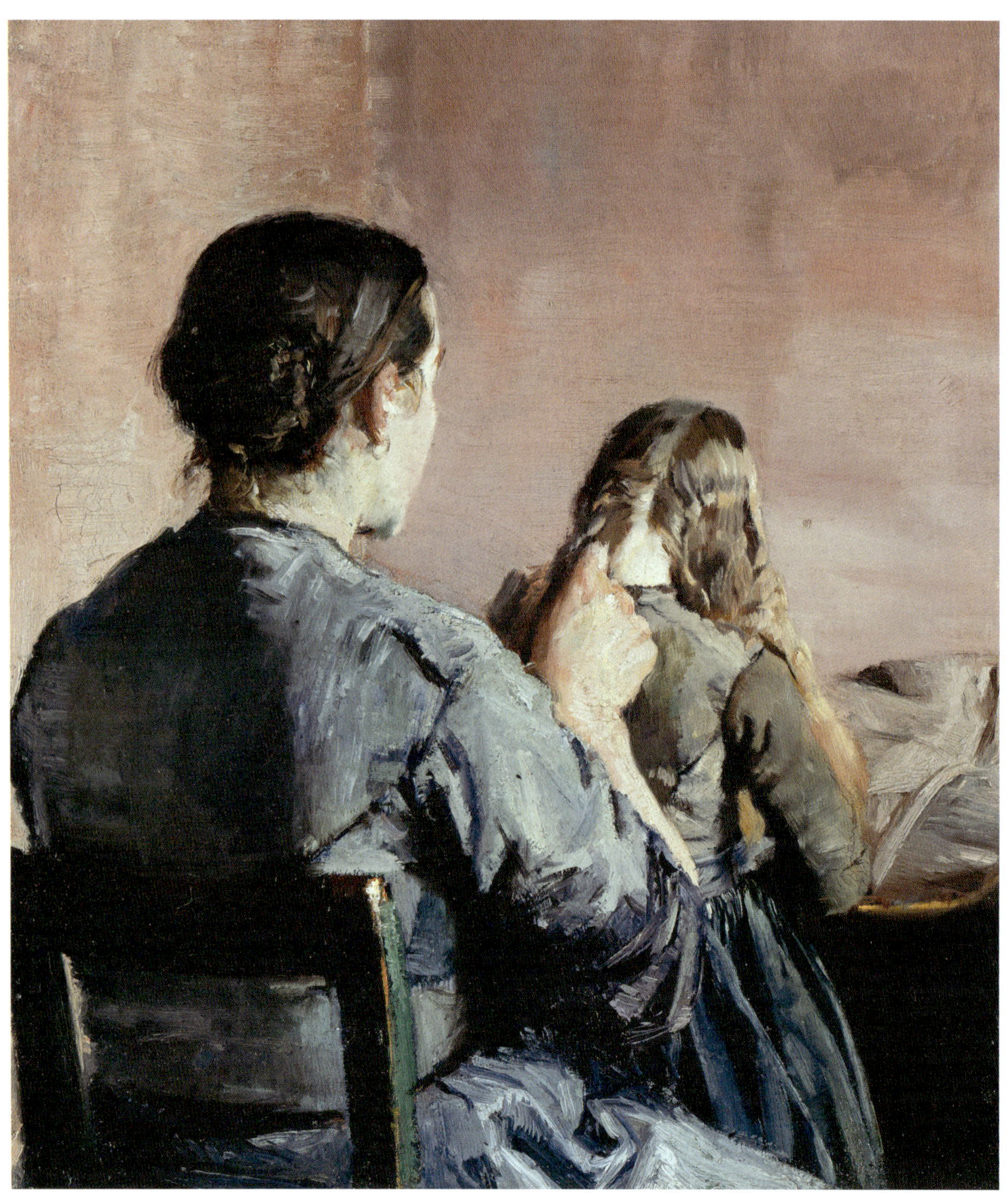

Plate 8. Christian Krohg, *Braiding Her Hair* (1888). Oil on canvas, 56 × 49 cm. Photo: Jacques Lathion/The National Museum of Art, Architecture and Design, Oslo.

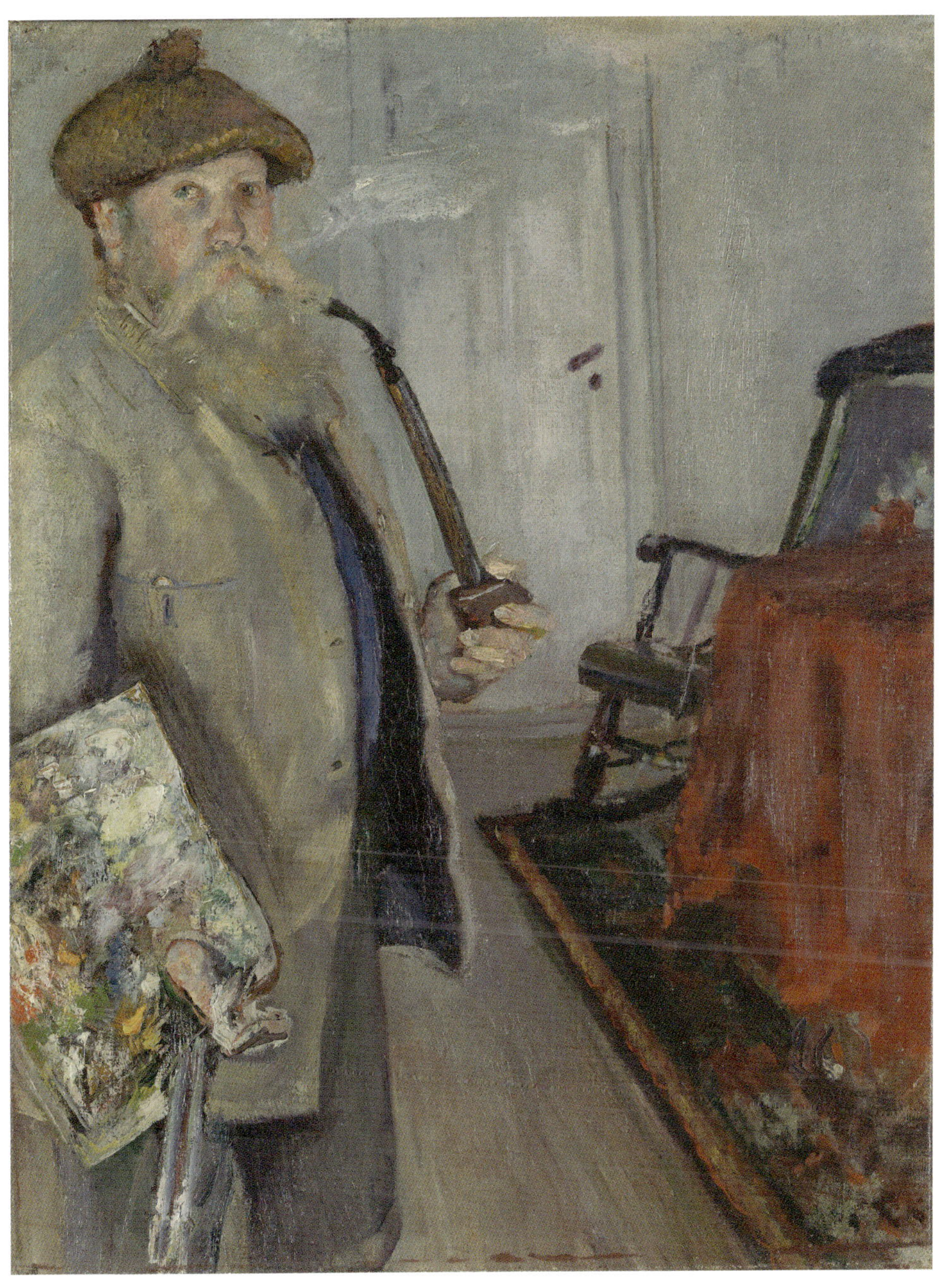

Plate 9. Christian Krohg, *Self-Portrait with Beret* (1883). Oil on canvas, 47.5 × 36 cm. Photo: Børre Høstland/The National Museum of Art, Architecture and Design, Oslo.

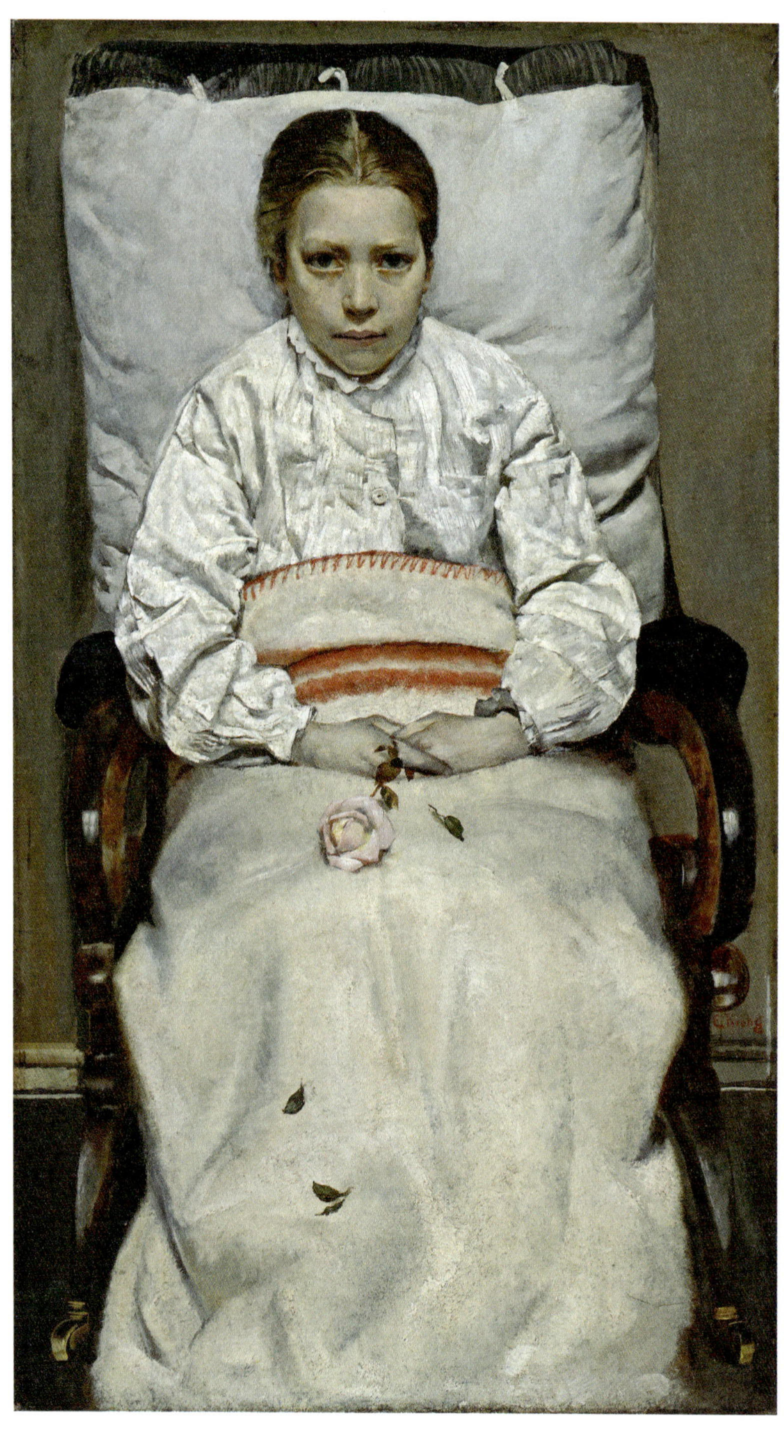

Plate 10. Christian Krohg, *Sick Girl* (1881). Oil on board, 102 × 58 cm. Photo: Jacques Lathion/The National Museum of Art, Architecture and Design, Oslo.

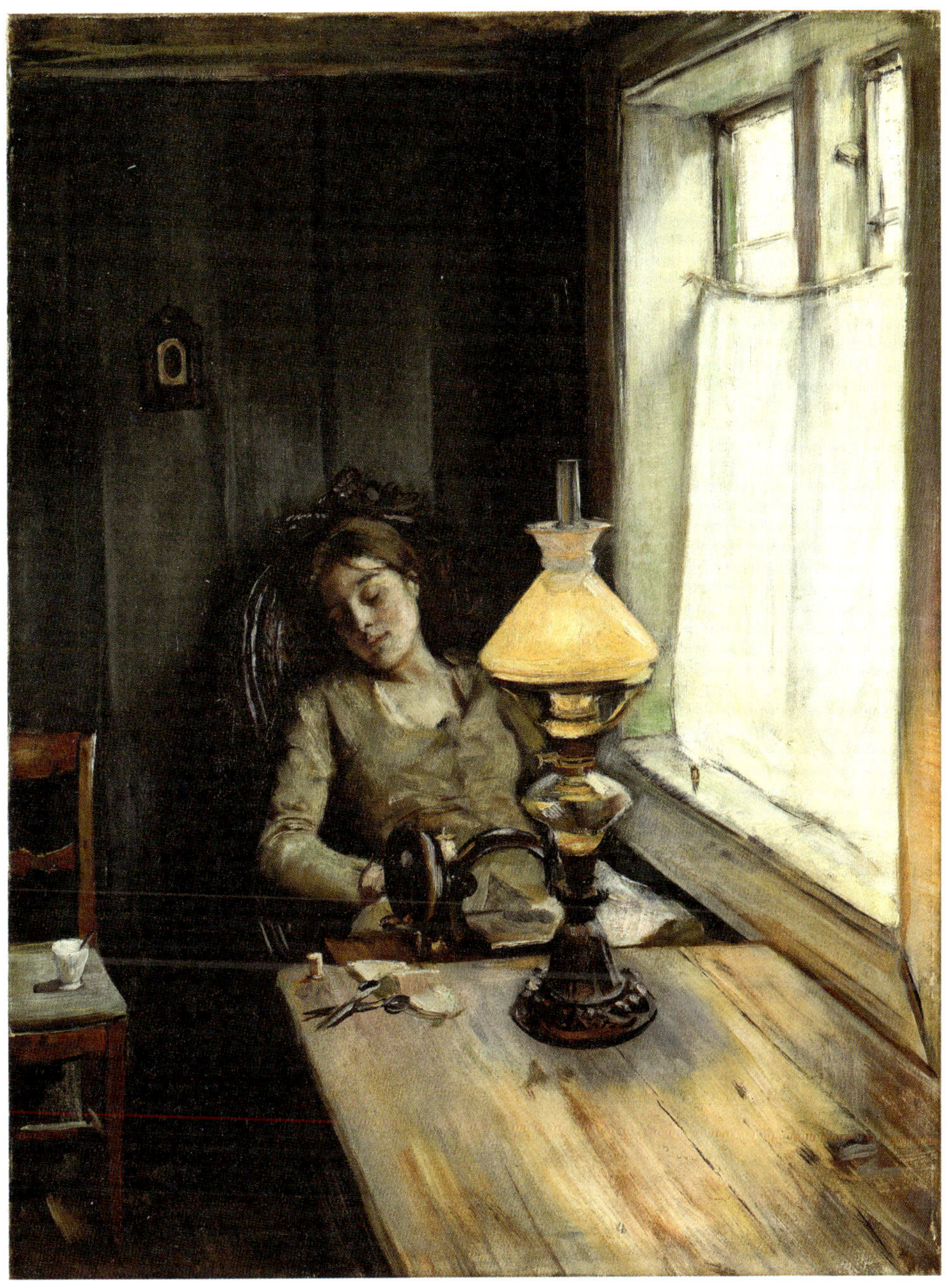

Plate 11. Christian Krohg, *Tired* (1885). Oil on canvas, 79.5 × 61.5 cm. Photo: Jacques Lathion/The National Museum of Art, Architecture and Design, Oslo.

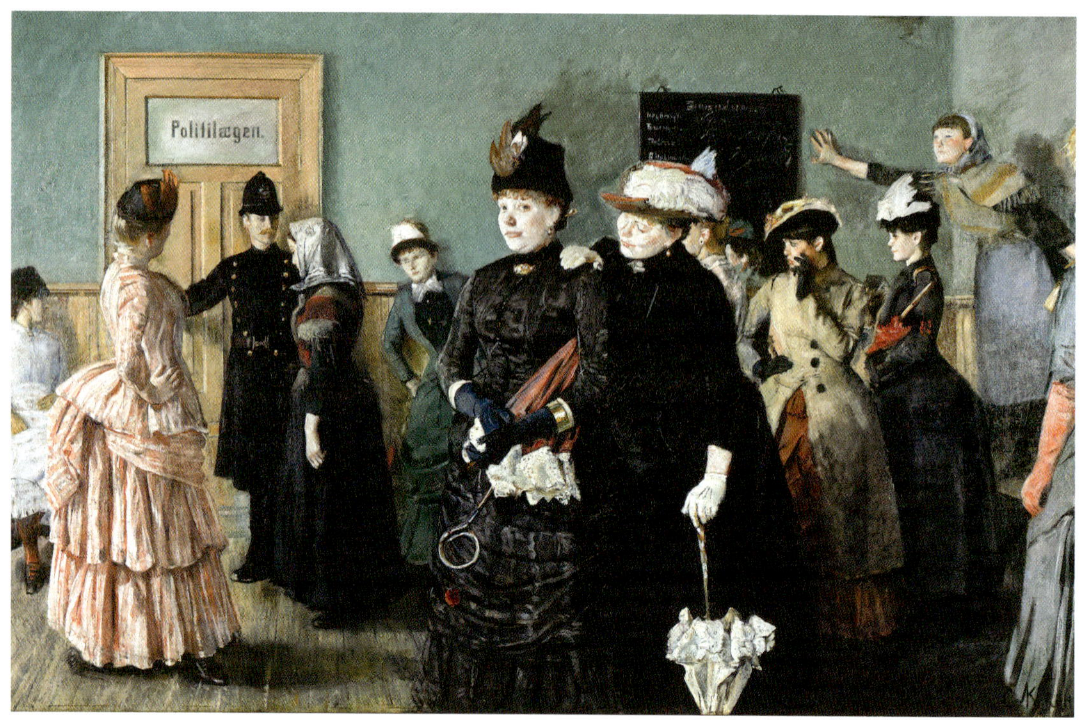

Plate 12. Christian Krohg, *Albertine in the Police Doctor's Waiting Room* (1887). Oil on canvas, 211 × 326 cm. Photo: Jacques Lathion/The National Museum of Art, Architecture and Design, Oslo.

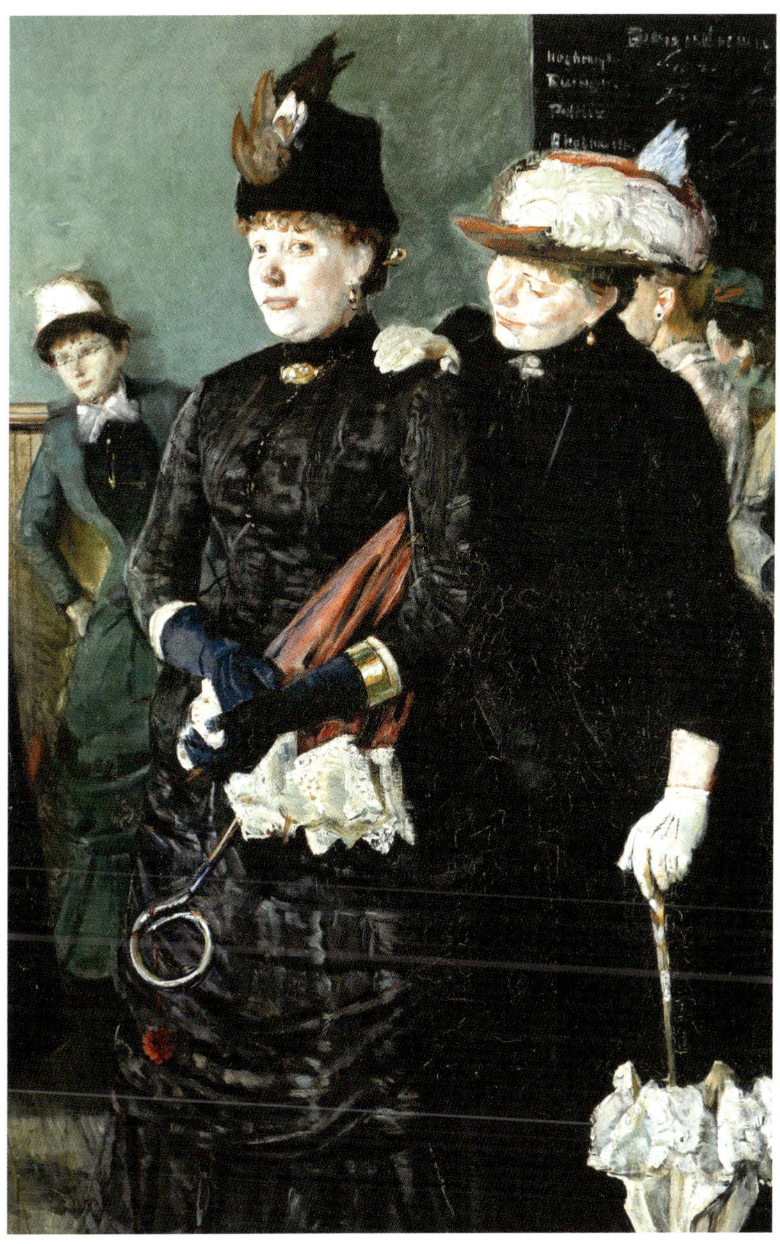

Plate 13. *Detail.* Christian Krohg, *Albertine in the Police Doctor's Waiting Room* (1887). Oil on canvas, 211 × 326 cm. Photo: Jacques Lathion/The National Museum of Art, Architecture and Design, Oslo.

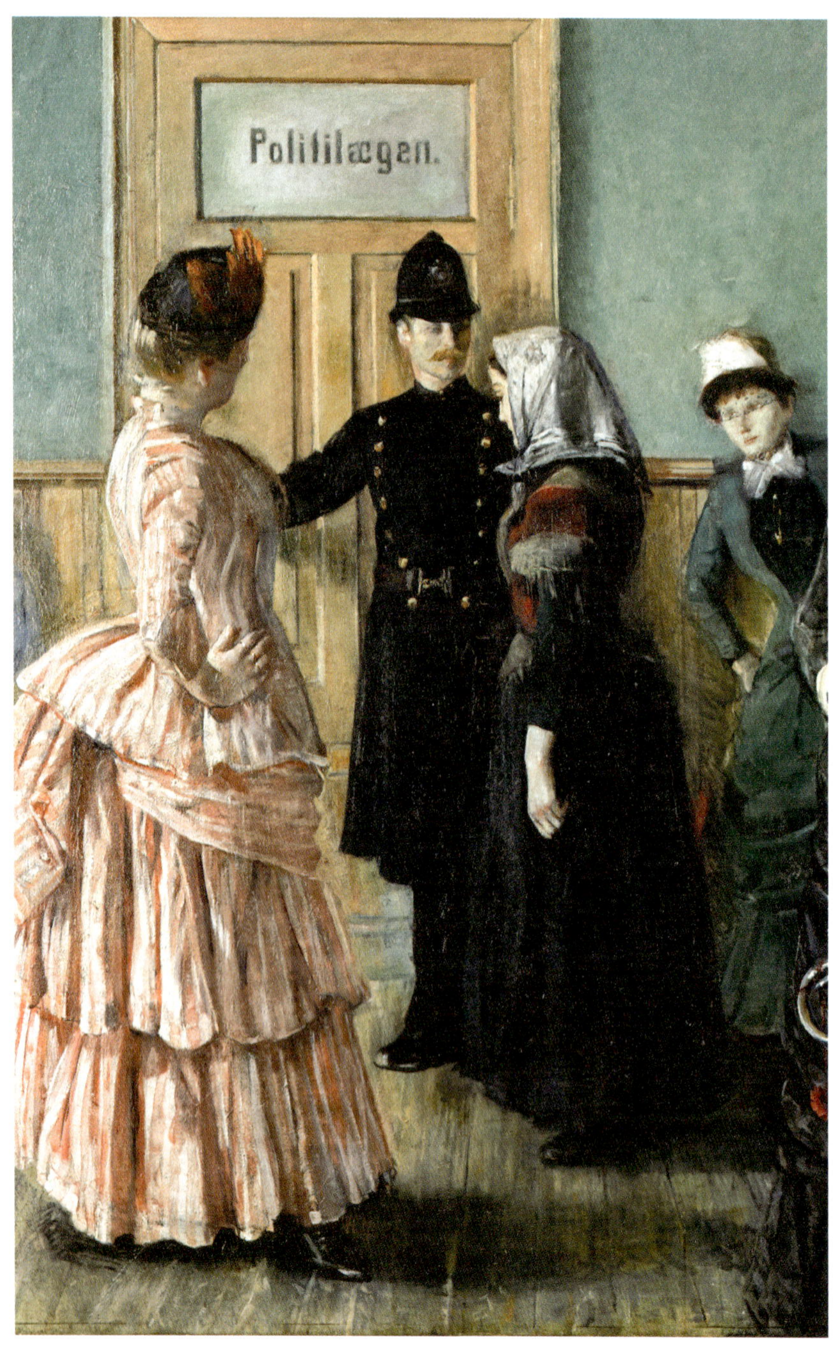

Plate 14. *Detail.* Christian Krohg, *Albertine in the Police Doctor's Waiting Room* (1887). Oil on canvas, 211 × 326 cm. Photo: Jacques Lathion/The National Museum of Art, Architecture and Design, Oslo.

CHAPTER SEVEN

Naturalist *Paragone*

Literature and Painting

One of the French literary critic Pierre Macherey's points in *A Theory of Literary Production* (1966) is that the scientific model in realist literature is a novelistic *process* rather than something that produces objective facts. The scientific model is an instrument that creates a style: "This new instrument implies that the novel has been penetrated by a *doctrine*."[1] Macherey emphasizes Honoré de Balzac's wish to fashion a new genre between political ideology and literature—between politics and aesthetics. All of this is true for naturalism, and these literary and political qualities, this penetration of a doctrine into literature, make naturalism a *discursive* art, unlike impressionism and "neutral" realism, which are *figural*. Oscar Thue (1928–1994), the primary authority on Christian Krohg, distinguished in his groundbreaking dissertation on Christian Krohg (1955) between the artist's social images and his other paintings, seeing the former as literary and the latter as visual: "In contrast to most of his other creations, Krohg's paintings concerned with social issues are almost always made on the basis of a literary idea on which he decides first, and then translated as satisfyingly and naturally as possible into an artistic form."[2] Thue's distinction between the literary and the visual is the subject of this chapter, although instead of using notions of literary images or visual paintings, I focus on the terms *discursivity* and *figurality*. I suggest that there exists a tension between the discursive and the figural, and that these two concepts offer effective ways to understand Krohg's art.

The discourse/figure concept stems from Norman Bryson's semiotic theory. Bryson examines how different sign combinations in painting create certain visualities that range from realism to symbolism (these terms are used semiotically and not art historically). Bryson defines these terms as follows: "By the 'discursive' aspect of an image, I mean those features which show the influence over the image of language. . . . By the 'figural' aspect of an image, I mean those features which belong to the image as a visual experience independent of language—its 'being-as-image.'"[3] A figural image is a painting that is experienced as highly realistic, almost like life itself, while a discursive image is as symbolic as a text. The photograph can be a paradigmatic example of the first type of image, the hieroglyph of the latter. The role of the image in a discursive picture is to serve as a substitute, as something that is controlled by the word: it has something specific to tell. The discursive image is read as artificial and *created*.

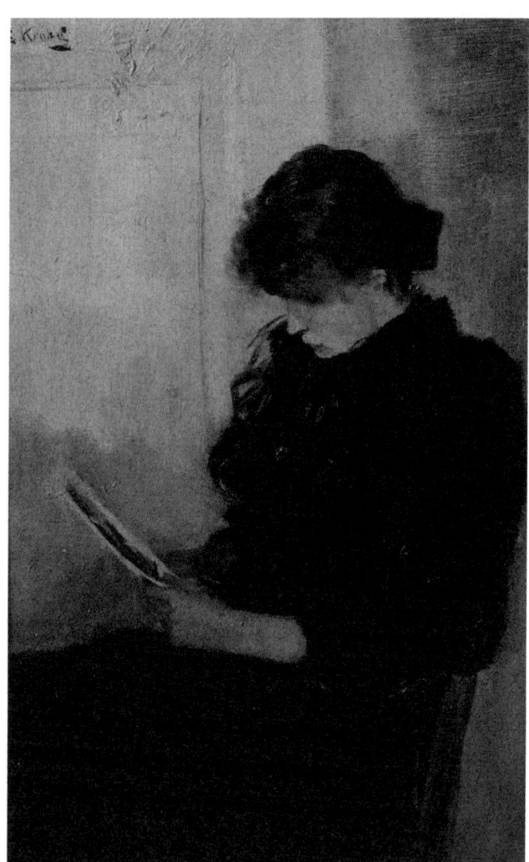

Figure 7.1.

Christian Krohg, *The Photograph* (1884). Oil on canvas, 48.5 × 32.5 cm. Private collection. © Photo: O. Væring Eftf. AS, Norway.

This does not mean, however, that the figural image is more real, or closer to "being" and farther from "meaning," compared to a discursive image. Roland Barthes's notion of *l'effet de réel* demonstrates this idea.[4] The "effect of the real" makes us read Krohg's impressionist-inspired canvas *The Photograph* (1884, fig. 7.1), with Oda Krohg absorbed in studying a photograph, as more real than his *Albertine in the Police Doctor's Waiting Room. The Photograph* looks immediate and real, like a snapshot, because of its angle and brushwork; it does not feel planned. The meaning of the work is experienced as coming from the outside and not from a process *within* the work. The realistic image hides the production of meaning and creates the illusion of a passive reproduction of reality. It is as if the meaning penetrates the work from an imagined place outside it. In discursive pictures, on the other hand, it is obvious how the mechanisms of meaning work.

Georg Clausen's analysis of Jules Bastien-Lepage's art demonstrates how naturalism constitutes a form of "literary art"—a discursive painting with a story to tell: "The literary and æsthetic sides of art were very evenly balanced in him [Bastien-Lepage]."[5] In many of Bastien-Lepage's paintings, characters enact a story rooted in his time and place but without an overt agenda. One of the naturalist's most important challenges was to balance the liter-

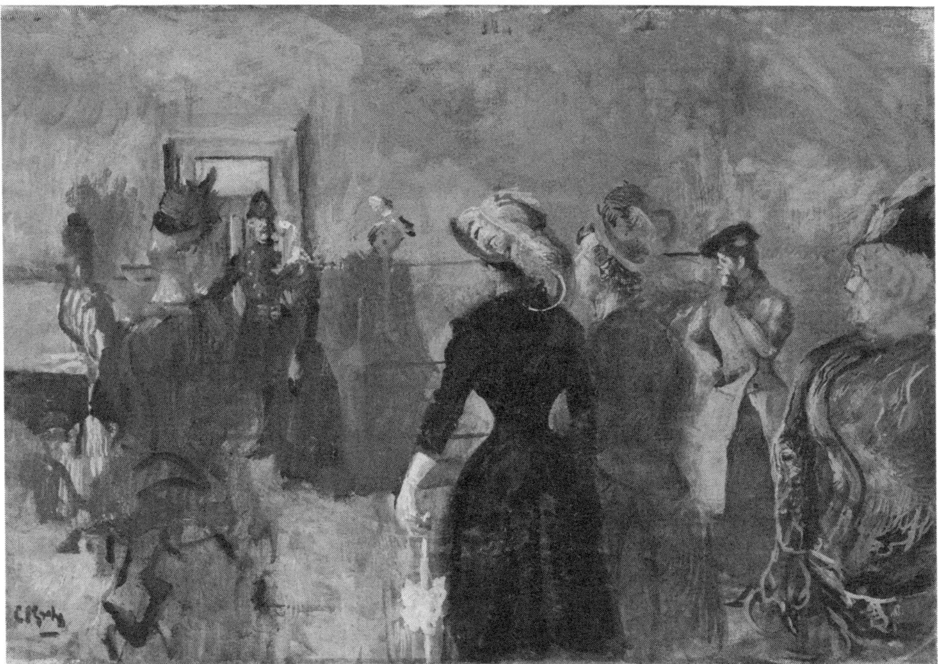

Figure 7.2. Christian Krohg, *Albertine in the Police Doctor's Waiting Room* (1917). Oil on canvas, 51 × 74.5. Photo: Jacques Lathion/The National Museum of Art, Architecture and Design, Oslo.

ary against objective realism, to give an agenda the effect of reality. The way Krohg chooses to situate Albertine in *Albertine in the Police Doctor's Waiting Room* (fig. 8.1, plate 12)—placing her off-center, in profile, amid a group of women—serves in part to conceal his meaning-production and to create an effect of the real. Whether he succeeded is a separate issue. Realism holds that truth exists not in the obvious, but in the hidden. The beholder has to stumble across the image's true meaning to be convinced. Krohg might have tried too hard to create an effect of the real in his painting: the meaning-production in the image is too obvious. That seems to have been a common problem for naturalists: they tried too hard, and their social or political message was often too obvious.

The Swedish newspaper editor Cläes Lundin wrote that the large Albertine painting was an artistic failure because it was "an appendage to a literary work without independent content."[6] Critic Andreas Aubert noted in his description of Krohg's aesthetic project that "the visual arts are reaching out a helping hand to literature and science."[7] Krohg criticized the painting in a 1920 interview for these reasons: "The composition in my large Albertine painting is wrong. It is theatrical. Some of the figures are stepping aside so that Albertine becomes visible, and everyone is afraid of turning their back to the beholders."[8] Three years earlier, in 1917, he painted a small version of the same motif (fig. 7.2), showing how he would have rendered it if he were to do it again. He placed the figures differently, encircling

Albertine, and used a looser and more expressive brushstroke. He joked in the 1920 interview that the large 1887 canvas was the sketch for the small 1917 version.

Thus, both the naturalists and the impressionists sought to create a sense of life in their works, but naturalist paintings tended to feel more like texts, while the impressionist ones conveyed an illusion of lived experience. Naturalist painters *struggled* more to hide the production of meaning as they strove to deliver social and political messages and used a scientific approach to reality and art making. Krohg's Skagen paintings, focused on scenes of daily life, can be seen from this viewpoint as a success. They present no apparent agenda and seem to be just a slice of real life. The sympathy the beholder might feel for the family stems from the depicted images themselves and is not forced on the viewer. But naturalism straddles a fine line between life and text. I suggest that the literacy of naturalist paintings was essential to their aesthetics rather than a sign of their failure. Naturalism's discursive side was its original contribution to the aesthetics of realism.

THE VISUAL NOVEL

The goal of modernist painters and novelists was to create new optics, or new kinds of representations in terms of both subject matter and form—or new modes of vision.[9] While naturalism in painting was a discursive aesthetic working with what could be called literary elements (the obvious narrative and political messages were more important to these artists than the materiality of painting), naturalist novelists seemed to want to write as if they were painters. They included different angles and scopes of vision, tangible interactions between characters, and scenes set up so vividly that they resembled paintings full of color, texture, light, and shadow. The naturalist authors' interest in visuality had its source in a combination of contemporary painting, experimental psychology, and visual perception. These writers highlighted voyeurism and narcissism, and they frequently included optical and ocular instruments such as mirrors. Visual information in literary texts sought to capture the distance or angle of sight, a panorama or a close-up view, light and movement.[10] Because of these elements, naturalist novels have been called visual novels—part of what Roland Barthes termed the pictorial code of literary mimesis.[11] Zola said in an interview that he wanted to translate impressionism into literature, and that both painting and literature should be based on observation.[12] There should be an interplay between light and color, between unclear visual information—the kind one sees in abstract impressions—and clear, in-focus identification of objects. The literary descriptions of light and shadow, colors and lines, were in many ways really descriptions of the process of painting: from light to dark areas, from background to foreground, from abstract patches to detailed descriptions, or from a first impression to a well-formed perception. The literary descriptions were to follow the chronological order of the act of looking. Because of all these elements, nineteenth-century novels could be approached as a kind of visual art form.[13]

Krohg's Albertine paintings were literary, and his novel was visual or painterly. This can be exemplified by the book's opening passage:

> Across a small, low window with many panes of glass, a worn half-curtain had been hung. She sat in front of it, bent over a sewing machine. The hard winter

> day sent a thin, bluish light along the back of her head, over her hair knot, down her neck and starched collar. The steel surface shined coldly in the poor gray light, and the white tarlatan strip she was sewing became quite blue. Her scissors lay open, and the thread spools and thimble cast shadows over the mahogany table. The light spread farther from her head, down her bent back, and then became lost in shadow. Her face disappeared in the dimness, but her profile stood out against the light curtain behind her. The bodice of her dress, made of gray corduroy, fit tightly across her shoulders; they were straight and broad. The part of her that was most brightly lit was her hand, which was large and lay on top of the shiny, cold steel surface and controlled the tarlatan strip under the needle. . . . The darkest part of the room was the corner by the stove. Mother Kristiansen stood there, busy with her doings.[14]

Notice how Krohg uses an artist's vocabulary to describe the colors, light, and shadow. He verbally paints the scene from its lightest to darkest elements, just like a painter would do, first defining the brightest and the darkest areas of the canvas. It is as if Krohg were describing one of his seamstress paintings, such as *Tired* (fig. 6.11, plate 11). His book is full of such visual and painterly descriptions, demonstrating how he used his talent as a painter in his writings, and his gift as a novelist in his paintings.

MANETTE SALOMON

Art historian Emil Hannover wrote in his memoirs that "aside from Springer and Morelli, no writers on art have made such a strong impression on me as the famous brothers Edmond and Jules. The first lecture I heard Brandes give was about them, and it produced in me an infatuation with their artistic and cultivated nature. I had, of course, already eagerly read *Manette Salomon* and *Les frères Zemganno*."[15] When Georg Brandes discussed the relationship between literature and painting in an article published in *Dagbladet* on August 30, 1879, he used as his examples three novels by the Goncourt brothers: *Soeur Philomène* (1861), *Germinie Lacerteux* (1865), and *Manette Salomon* (1867). Brandes sought to demonstrate how the Goncourts deployed visual observations in their literary descriptions and how their writings paralleled modern French painting: "They [the Goncourts] are in literature what 'the impressionists' are in modern French painting—trying to convey the strong impression of an individual moment."[16] (In 1893 Brandes would conclude that French painting in the nineteenth century developed parallel to literature, but that the art of painting had influenced poetry and prose more than the other way around.)[17] The Goncourt brothers became favorites of modern painters; their literary style was, and still is, described as impressionistic because of its "visual" language.[18] Brandes was one of those who saw their style as "impressionistic," providing sketchy literary images of Paris with emphasis on color and chaos. Their novel *Manette Salomon* was a must-read for radical and bohemian artists.[19]

Manette Salomon, published in 1867, between Balzac's *The Unknown Masterpiece* (1831) and Zola's *The Masterpiece* (1886), was a real artist's novel. Frits Thaulow recalled how Krohg was relaxing in his cabin and reading *Manette Salomon* as they sailed to an artists' meeting in Gothenburg in May 1881.[20] Krohg had been introduced to the book in Berlin some years

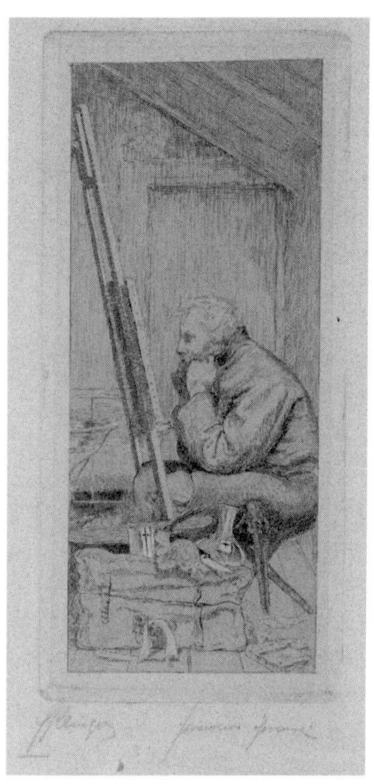

Figure 7.3.

Max Klinger, *The Artist in the Attic* (1879). Etching and aquatint, 15.2 × 7.4 cm. Photo © bpk/Staatliche Kunstsammlungen Dresden/Renate Schurz.

before. In *The Artist in the Attic* (1879, fig. 7.3), Max Klinger depicted Krohg in their shared studio staring at a canvas on an easel. In the foreground are painting tools and a book lying on the floor: it is, not coincidentally, *Manette Salomon*.[21] The novel was, to quote art historian Carol Armstrong, an "allegory of modern art."[22] Its characters were painters, it made references to many known paintings, and it addressed how painting should represent modernity—*du paysage moderne*.[23] The title of the book was probably a play on Manet's name, and the character Coriolis was based on him.

It is not surprising that the Goncourt brothers appealed to a man like Christian Krohg. They were intellectual and sophisticated, and they combined cultural refinement with a socialist-aesthetic agenda, as is demonstrated by their foreword to *Germinie Lacerteux*: "Living in the nineteenth century, in the time of universal suffrage, democracy, and liberalism, we asked ourselves if what one calls 'the lower classes' did not have rights in novels; if in this world beneath a world, the people must remain subject to literary interdiction and the disdain of authors who have hitherto remained silent on the soul and the heart they might have."[24] They found their subjects and heroes among the poor, and to them the novel was both a literary study and a sociological investigation.[25] They strove to give a nearly clinical representation of the lower classes: "Do not expect a photograph of Pleasure with a low-plunging neckline; the following study is Love's Clinic."[26] It is likely that the Goncourts' book inspired Krohg to write his own novel.

Art critic Andreas Aubert wrote in 1880: "You are not supposed to paint poetry, that is one of the essential rules on which art rests. . . . You are not supposed to first write and then paint."[27] Krohg was often criticized for painting canvases that were too literary, with more emphasis on content than form. Thaulow commented that Krohg, in contrast to his own art for art's sake, "was fighting for content."[28] Critic Irgens Hansen made a similar comment in 1889: "It has been said that a narrative painting lacks high artistic value; it is no longer art for art's sake, but rather art in the service of something else. Christian Krohg has never cared about that."[29] Art historian Jens Thiis saw Krohg's tendency to create content-based paintings as a "weakness": "Krohg is not only in possession of a pair of healthy and vigorous painter's eyes, he certainly also has a soft heart. And, as a painter, he is so unfortunate as to be gifted with a talent for writing. Sometimes he has come close to painting literature. . . . But Krohg has luckily been aware that this is his weakness since early on and has fought against it; usually his sound and perceptive painter's eye has prevailed."[30] The Swedish art critic August Brunius wrote in 1914 that Krohg's paintings were often "pure literature"; he found *The Struggle for Existence* to be the most boring artwork he knew because of its literal quality and moralizing tone. He found the large Albertine painting also too elaborately done and therefore lacking in aesthetic value.[31]

Krohg felt a need to defend himself against such criticism when, in 1915, some thirty years after his first seamstress painting, he wrote:

> [*The Seamstress*] is the first painting I made that was praised in the newspapers by a critic. But it was, of course, only because of its literary subject, and because the "democratic moment" was preoccupied with seamstresses and the "less fortunate in society." Luckily, this kind of sympathy was not the underlying reason for the painting—that would have been totally unartistic. No, the underlying motivation for this painting was only a problem of color. It was around five o'clock in the morning, on the second floor of Café Américain in Paris. Just as we were moving toward Les Halles, I saw the first cold glimpse of daylight streaming in, dampened by the curtains, and meeting the artificial light that back then was the warm cadmium of yellow gas lamps. I could not forget that peculiar coloristic mood, its disharmony. But when I returned to Norway, where neither back then nor later did we have a "[Café] Américain," I wanted to paint the aforementioned contradiction. So I had to invent something that gave me the opportunity to paint the same light effect, and thus the "Seamstress" was made.[32]

Of course, Krohg did look at paintings as coloristic experimentations, but he was, in this passage, surely exaggerating the importance of formal issues over the social content of his works. When he wrote these lines in 1915, he probably wanted to associate himself with contemporary formalist tendencies rather than with "old-fashioned" naturalism. In fact, he painted this particular work before his first trip to Paris, so the anecdote is likely invented.

One of Krohg's main points in his aesthetic writings of the 1880s was painting's superiority to the other arts—especially the novel. In a lecture in 1886, the time when he was writing the Albertine novel, he declared: "I am also working on a novel, and at some point I just could not get any further—I could not get it good enough, as good as I wished, because it [the story] was more arresting to my eye than I was able to capture in the writing, so I started painting it."[33] He claimed that it was when he began to paint the Albertine story that he was truly able to communicate what he wished, and that this proved painting's superiority as an art form.

Norwegian cultural life in the 1880s was dominated by literature, especially the works of Ibsen, Bjørnson, and others. The ambitious Krohg wanted to challenge the hegemony of literature, and he found his inspiration in Leonardo da Vinci's *paragone* discourse and in Zola's aesthetics. Krohg's arguments were not unlike those of Leonardo:

> And you, poet, should you wish to depict a story as if painting with your pen, the painter with his brush will more likely succeed and will be understood less laboriously. If you assert that painting is dumb poetry, then the painter may call poetry blind painting. . . . Painting remains the worthier in as much as it serves the nobler sense and remakes the forms and figures of nature with greater truth than the poet. . . . Painting moves the senses more rapidly than poetry. . . . A painter made a figure so that anyone who saw it immediately yawned and continued to repeat this behavior for as long as his eyes remained on the picture in which the yawning was actually portrayed.[34]

Krohg also borrowed Zola's arguments from "Naturalism on the Stage" in his discussion of the arts, but he took the argumentation a step further. Whereas Zola asserted that a novel was superior to a play, Krohg saw paintings as superior to novels. Zola wrote:

> The novelist has time and space before him; all sorts of liberties are permitted him; he can use one hundred pages, if it pleases him, to analyze at his leisure a certain character; he can describe his surroundings as much as he pleases; he can cut his story short, can retrace his steps, changing places twenty times—in a word, he is absolutely a master of his matter. The dramatic author, on the contrary, is enclosed in a rigid frame; he must heed all sorts of necessities. He moves only in the midst of obstacles.[35]

Krohg admitted in his 1886 lecture that human psychology and inner feelings could be described more adequately in literature, but argued that only modern painting could give a really striking image of society:

> When an author describes a person's appearance and milieu, he tries to write in such a way that one can *see* these things with one's eyes, as if at a momentary glance. And he can very well write like that, but in so doing will overstrain himself because the means are inadequate; he will describe and describe and get the form and color and a total impression, but if he wants more form and more color,

> his means will be insufficient. He will want to throw the pen against the wall and grab a paintbrush instead. *Then the visual artist enters.* For this is his area of expertise. He can do it even better, in a way that enables one to see it even better, so that one can see and never forget the images, so that the truth becomes even more striking, and the uncanny even more uncanny. This is the artist's mission in today's cultural movement.[36]

Krohg's original rethinking of the *paragone* debate was to use Zola's arguments to promote painting as the greater modernist art than the novel. But this was more of a theoretical position than a real practice. He used both literature and painting to communicate different aspects of the Albertine project.

Naturalism was, in many ways, a battlefield between literature and painting. It took part in modernism's version of the classic *paragone* debate. It also touched on formal properties of different art forms and on the issue of form versus content, art for art's sake, and so on. Modernism at once created a sisterhood between literature and painting and spurred their competition. Naturalism was one of the arenas in which these debates took place.

CHAPTER EIGHT

Albertine in the Police Doctor's Waiting Room

Panopticon, Spectacle, Speculum

THE morality of sex was a hot topic in Norway in the 1870s and 1880s, and sexuality became one of the most important subjects in Scandinavian literature in the works of Ibsen, Strindberg, and others. Literature verbalized sexuality in new ways, constructing a new vocabulary for it. Simultaneously, a sexual vocabulary developed in the judicial system. Politicians, the police, and the judiciary reviled prostitution as a threat to marriage and society; Krohg focused on the social factors that forced young women into a life of prostitution. Krohg's views echoed those of feminists and socialists—their position articulated by Victor Hugo in *Les misérables* (1862) and by the political activists Josephine Butler and Yves Guyot. Krohg's Albertine project can be interpreted as an attempt to support the workers' movement and its efforts to abolish the institution of prostitution.

Albertine in the Police Doctor's Waiting Room (1887, fig. 8.1, plate 12), begun in 1885, was Krohg's largest and most ambitious painting. It was part of what I term his Albertine project or Albertine experiment, which included a large number of Albertine and seamstress paintings, like the two waiting room paintings *Albertine* (1884, fig. 8.2, plate 15) and *A Meeting* (1885, fig. 8.3), the novel *Albertine* (1886), illustrations for the novel, sketches, a photograph, and theoretical lectures and essays. Krohg began working on the novel in 1885, basing its narrative on a true story he heard from one of his models. She recounted to him how one of her girlfriends, a seamstress, had been raped by a highly regarded police officer. When a journalist visited Krohg's studio in 1885, he saw the unfinished painting and wrote that it would get much attention: "It is a genre painting in the grand style, with a motif from the darker side of life. The idea behind it may be best expressed by calling the picture 'a debut in prostitution.' The scene is staged in the police station's waiting room for prostitutes. Among all the older and younger yet experienced women with impudent faces and fancy clothes, there stands a young, poorly dressed girl who has been summoned here for the first time. Her eyes are downcast, and she is scared and miserable."[1] Krohg's original intention may have been to represent one individual's destiny, but the art project, or experiment, developed into much more than that.

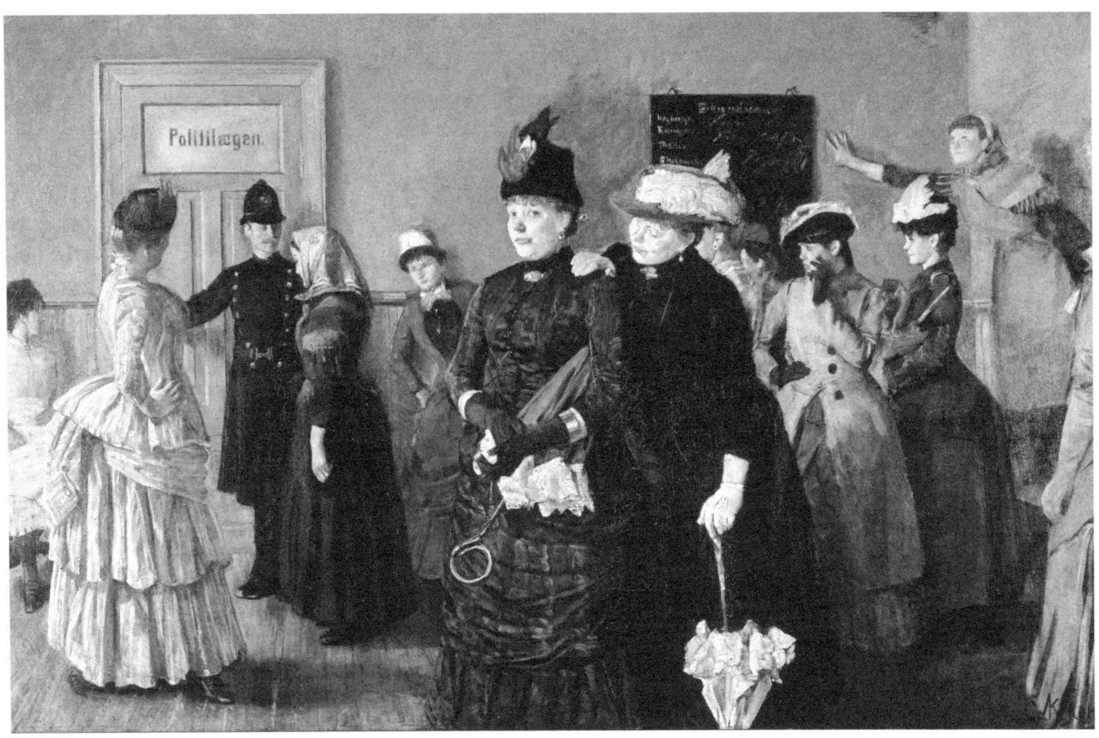

Figure 8.1 (Plate 12, *details* plates 13 and 14). Christian Krohg, *Albertine in the Police Doctor's Waiting Room* (1887). Oil on canvas, 211 × 326 cm. Photo: Jacques Lathion/The National Museum of Art, Architecture and Design, Oslo.

It was not surprising that Krohg chose prostitution as the theme for his first novel. Prostitution was considered the most shocking, and therefore the most "realistic," topic for a modern radical novel, as Émile Zola demonstrated with irony in *Nana* (1880):

> During the day she [Nana] had read a novel which was causing a sensation at the time. It was the story of a prostitute, and Nana inveighed against it, declaring that it was all untrue, and expressing an indignant revulsion against the sort of filthy literature which claimed to show life as it was—as if a writer could possibly describe everything, and as if novels weren't supposed to be written just to while away the time! On the subject of books and plays Nana had very decided opinions: she liked tender, high-minded works which could set her dreaming and uplift her soul.[2]

Krohg also had some great examples of modern art to inspire him, such as Manet's *Olympia* (1863) and Gervex's *Rolla* (1878). In these examples, the nude was modernized,

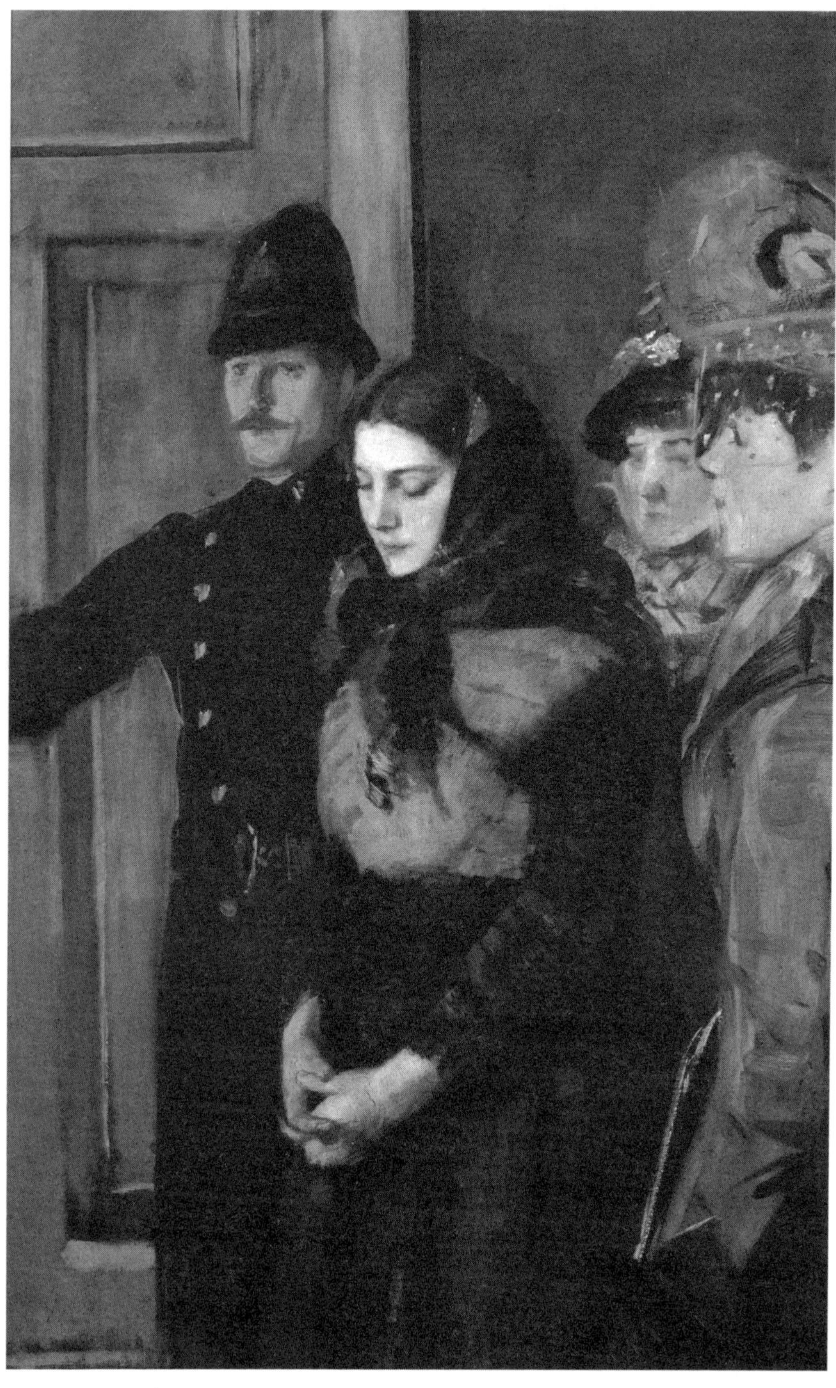

Figure 8.2 (Plate 15). Christian Krohg, *Albertine* (1884). Oil on canvas, 91 × 58 cm. National Gallery of Denmark, Copenhagen. © Photo: O. Væring Eftf. AS, Norway.

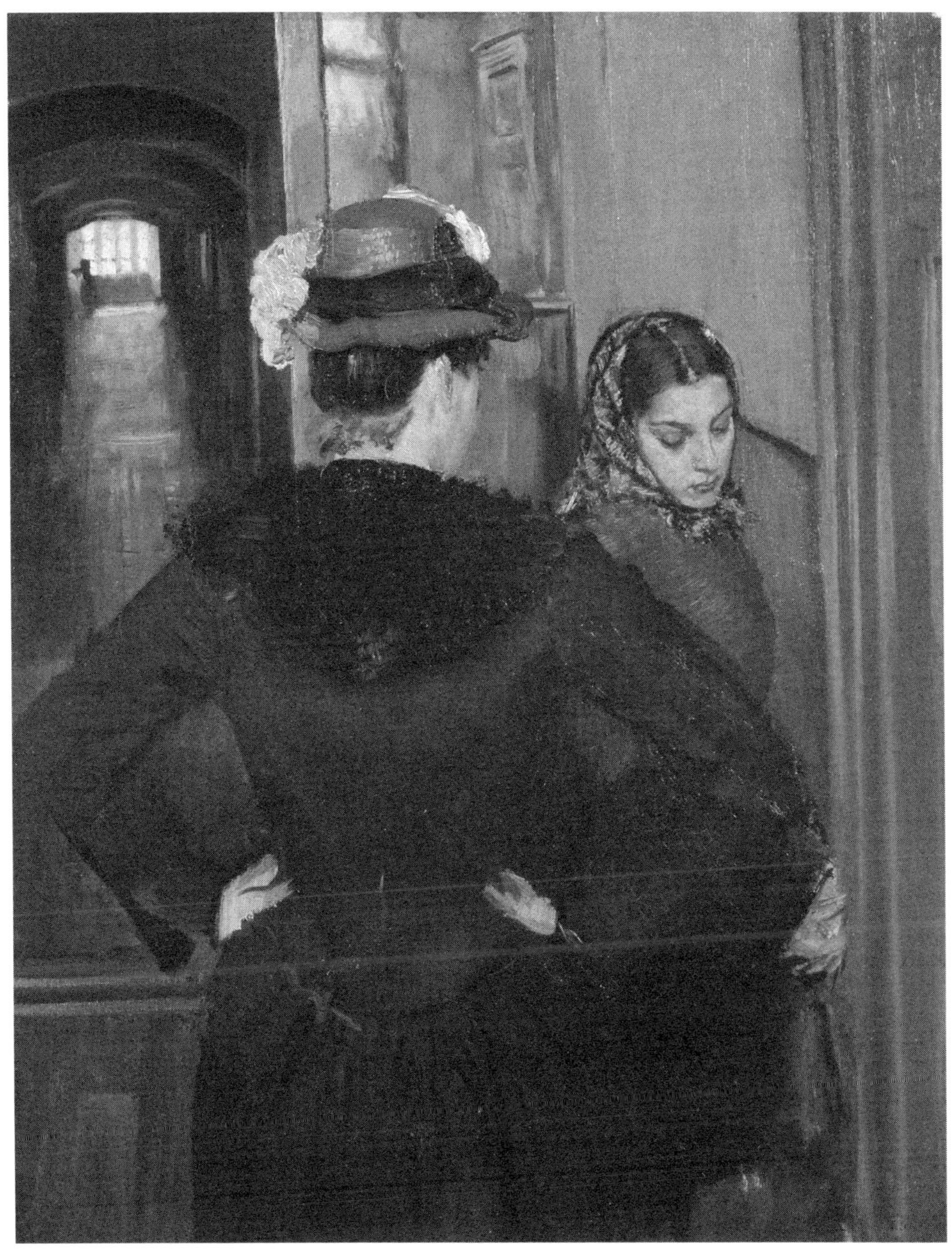

Figure 8.3. Christian Krohg, *A Meeting (Albertine)* (1885). Oil on canvas, 61.5 × 50.5 cm. Private collection. © Photo: O. Væring Eftf. AS, Norway.

creating scandal. Krohg was not interested in the nude per se, though he certainly adopted some of the aggressiveness with which Manet's painting confronted the beholder. Krohg found in the Albertine project a perfect combination of avant-garde aesthetics and actual politics.

Prostitution was a sensitive subject for bourgeois society because it intertwined sex with money. True and eloquent representation of prostitution was a challenge that inspired late nineteenth-century artists and authors. As T. J. Clark noted, the prostitute became a principal character for understanding modernism and modernity: "The category 'prostitute' is necessary, and thus must be allowed its representations. It must take its place in the various pictures of the social, the sexual, and the modern which bourgeois society puts in circulation. There is a sense in which it could even be said to anchor those representations: it is the limiting case of all three, and the point where they are mapped most neatly onto one another. It represents the danger or the price of modernity."[3] The prostitute challenges and makes fun of established class divisions and shows that they, and therefore classed society, are full of falsehoods.[4]

Krohg was not the only painter in Norway to tackle the theme of prostitution in the 1880s. Around 1880, Hans Heyerdahl (1857–1913) had painted his *Champagne Girl*—a bare-breasted woman, most likely posed in a bordello, looking straight at the viewer as she vulgarly grips a champagne glass. Heyerdahl's short article "Prostitution" appeared in the daily newspaper *Verdens Gang* only a week before Krohg published *Albertine* in December 1886. Like Krohg, he criticized the society's double standard regarding prostitution: its toleration under government control combined with a perception of prostitutes as immoral borderline criminals. Heyerdahl's response to prostitution was "Away with it!"[5] His text coincided with his painting *Black-Anna* (1887, fig. 8.4), a portrait of another bare-breasted woman. Black-Anna was a well-known prostitute in Kristiania, and Krohg had used her as his model in *Portrait of Jossa* (1886, fig. 8.5). But the two artists approached the subject of prostitution very differently. Heyerdahl depicted the woman as a sexually available object sitting in a luxurious environment smoking a cigarette (with its suggestive symbolism). Krohg's *Jossa* was much more respectable: nothing in the picture made it obvious that she was a prostitute. It was a portrait of an individual rather than a type.

One of the most striking aspects of Krohg's *Waiting Room* was the representation of the different looks, gazes, and glances exchanged by its characters, and the way they engage the beholder. The woman at the front who gazes directly out particularly provoked some beholders, much like the woman in Manet's *Olympia*. Andreas Aubert called the two women in the foreground representatives of "the most repulsive of bestial womanhood" and described the way they look at the beholders as offensive.[6] Karl Madsen wrote about the two women in a review of Krohg's painting: "Similar to how the scientist puts a rare animal on his laboratory table—the artist has here arranged two kinds of interesting species of 'la bête humaine' in order to make a thorough examination and characterization of their appearances."[7] Lorentz Dietrichson, who did not think highly of Krohg's naturalist works, wrote that the painting depicted "some abominable horrible madams and other repulsive physiognomies."[8]

The painting raises questions about sex and power, and Krohg's Albertine project as a whole focuses not on the brazenness or eroticism of prostitutes but on the power dynamics between bourgeois society and these women—explored in his painting through looks

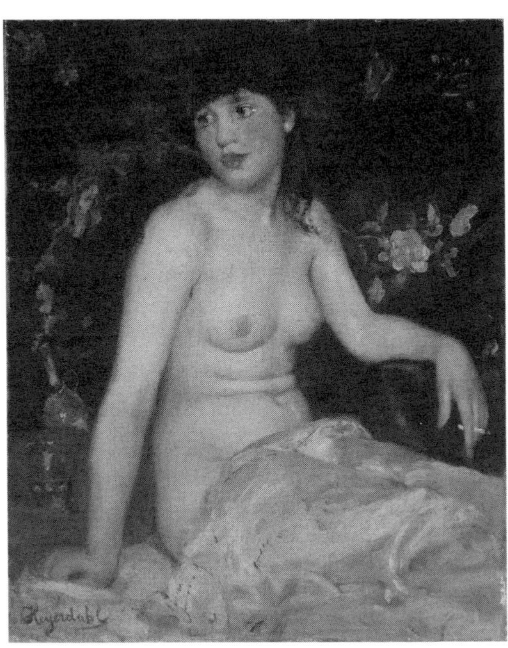

Figure 8.4.

Hans Heyerdahl, *Black-Anna* (1887). Oil on canvas, 54 × 44 cm. Photo: Andreas Harvik/The National Museum of Art, Architecture and Design, Oslo.

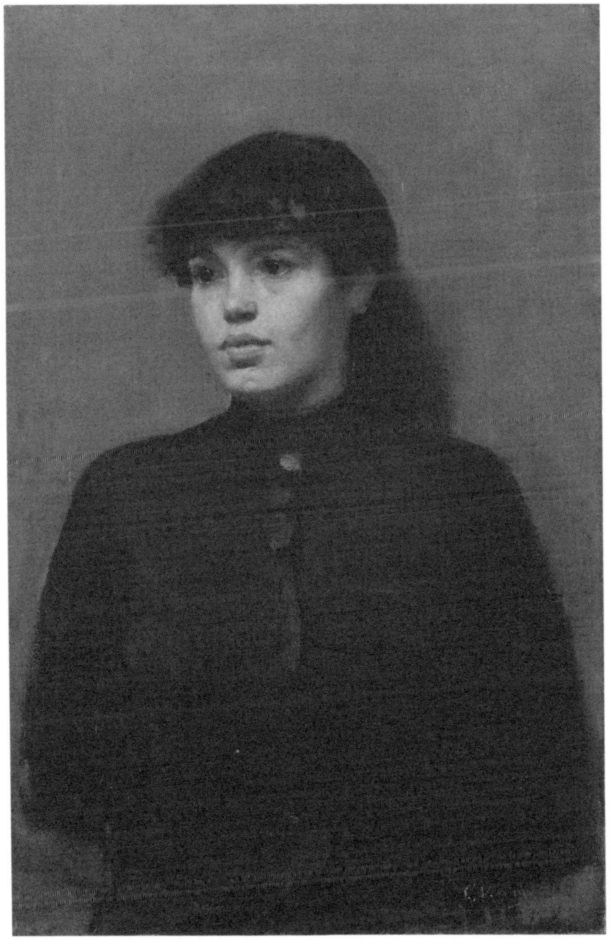

Figure 8.5.

Christian Krohg, *Portrait of Jossa* (1886). Oil on canvas, 81.5 × 54.5 cm. Photo: Jacques Lathion/The National Museum of Art, Architecture and Design, Oslo.

connecting the policeman, the doctor, and the prostitutes. Krohg's work was original in his sympathetic and sociological treatment of this explosive subject and in his use of the methods of naturalism to make his pictures into a call for change.

PANOPTICON

I propose to use the lenses of panopticon, spectacle, and speculum to explore how Krohg's *Albertine in the Police Doctor's Waiting Room* tackled visuality and modernity. In the course of the nineteenth century, European society experienced a kind of medicalization, as medical ideas shaped and colored both politics and art. The "dangerous classes" of urban society had to be controlled, disciplined, and "medicated" to make them more respectable and acceptable. Hygiene, alcoholism, tuberculosis, child mortality, and venereal diseases (with syphilis the most dreaded) were all important subjects of public debate and, increasingly, of naturalist art.[9] Because Paris was the international center of both medicine and art in this period, many ideas about social ills emanated from there. Hereditary disease became an especially popular topic in both medicine and literature.[10] Meanwhile, ailments related to social class—especially syphilis and tuberculosis—were discussed it terms of the spread of infections and their possible treatments.[11] The moral hierarchy of diseases was reflected in art, with naturalist artists focusing on the "dirtiest" and lowest ones.

All this was directly related to the development of modern statistics in France in the 1830s and 1840s. Information on age, occupation, health, criminality, political beliefs, and so on was systematically collected by social scientists and linked to natural laws and the new science of sociology.[12] Krohg's art took an active part in the period's verbalization and visualization of sexuality, as described by Michel Foucault in the first volume of *The History of Sexuality* (1976). Foucault argues that an important part of nineteenth-century medical discourse can be seen as voyeurism linked to sexuality, and that there was a striking fascination with the secret life.[13] An important project for naturalist artists was that of revealing hidden lives at the edges of bourgeois society. If the "perverse" and the "degenerate" came to light, it would be possible to deal with them rationally and to improve their lot. Krohg's art illuminated the uncomfortable relationship between power and sexuality in Kristiania in the 1880s.

Krohg's Albertine project came into being simultaneously with criminal and judicial reform in Norway that sought to criminalize prostitution.[14] Fornication was prohibited in 1842, although only women could be punished for it. In reality prostitution was tolerated, and in the 1880s the government tried to formalize this arrangement to control it better and prevent the spread of venereal diseases. Indeed, prostitution was, more than anything else, an administrative problem, an unsatisfying compromise between the legal and the illegal. In 1863 the position of police doctor was established so that prostitutes could be registered and regularly checked.[15]

As prostitution increased significantly in the nineteenth century, it became a pressing concern for the government because of the twin fear of venereal diseases and moral decay. Anatomist Alexandre Parent-Duchâtelet's book *De la prostitution dans la ville de Paris* (1836) was an important contributor to the discourse on prostitution. Parent-Duchâtelet had studied twelve thousand prostitutes and analyzed how they entered their profession and lived in it. He treated prostitution as an issue of public hygiene, and thus a subject of science and medicine. In his view, prostitution was a cultural problem resulting from the class system. He believed that the prostitutes had to be observed, registered, controlled, and regulated. Parent-Duchâtelet's book was followed by a large number of studies in the 1870s,[16] including Cesare Lombroso's research, which put heredity and instinct before the cultural hypothesis and argued that a girl was born a prostitute by nature, rather than turned into one by social circumstances.[17] This biology versus culture debate also preoccupied Krohg and Zola: could one escape one's destiny, they wondered?

The Norwegian police doctor Haakon Boeck compiled a series of annual reports on prostitution in the 1870s and 1880s.[18] He gave relatively detailed information on the backgrounds and lives of prostitutes, described how they behaved in public, and discussed the prevalence of sexually transmitted diseases among them. It is not impossible that Krohg may have known Boeck's writings and been inspired and influenced by them in his novel. He had trained as a lawyer early in his career and would have been familiar with these kinds of documents. As Charles Bernheimer notes in his authoritative book on prostitution and art, *Figures of Ill Repute* (1989), "There is no necessary break between the texts we recognize as 'literary' and those we designate officially as social, political, or legal."[19]

Boeck's research can be viewed through the lens of panopticism as described by Foucault. The term literally means "all-seeing," but in Foucault's interpretation it has become a model of social control, of the regimentation and monitoring of individual human beings by authorities: "Our society is one not of spectacle, but of surveillance. . . . We are neither in the amphitheater, nor on the stage, but in the panoptic machine."[20] The panopticon culture gave birth to statistics and government quantification of society. It is a type of surveillance that is related to the rationalization and bureaucratization of capitalism: life bureaucratized down to the smallest details. The sciences of clinical medicine, criminology, and sociology grew out of this rationalization,[21] and naturalism in art can be seen as both a symptom and a critique of the panopticon culture.

The prostitutes were required to register with the authorities and be photographed for their records; they were subjected to regular vaginal exams, and their behavior and movements in public spaces were regulated. As Foucault shows, the prostitute was placed in a field of documentation.[22] An archive of information was created, and the individual was caught in a network of documents that defined who she was. The individual became, as Foucault puts it, a "case": the registered prostitute was a *fille en carte*. These panoptic tendencies were keenly observed by artists. One of the characters in Balzac's *Splendeurs et misères des courtisanes* says to one of the prostitutes: "Since you are in the archive of the police you are only a number—separated from all other human beings in society."[23] T. J. Clark described the life of a prostitute as a labyrinth of registration, reporting, and inspection.[24]

The "visitation book," called "Bog [Book]" in Norway, was the prostitute's personal official document in Kristiania. It comprised personal information about her health and the regulations she had to follow. Every time she went for her vaginal exam, the results and her condition were written down in her "Bog." Then potential clients could consult the "Bog" to see if she was healthy or not.[25] The police also kept catalogs with photographs of prostitutes (figs. 8.6–8.7). Photography became an effective, rational, scientific medium for identifying, classifying, and controlling individuals such as prostitutes, criminals, and the mentally

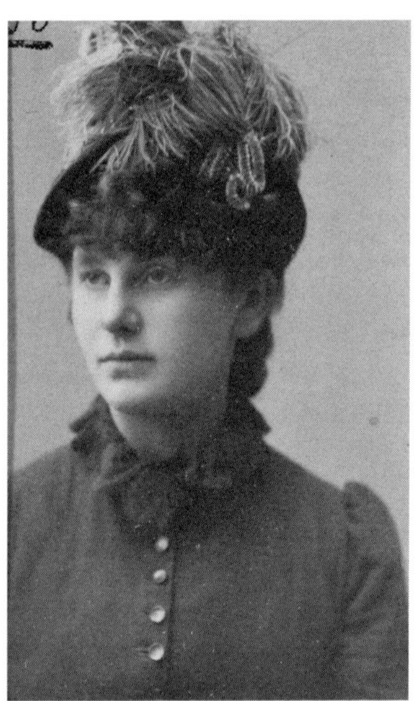

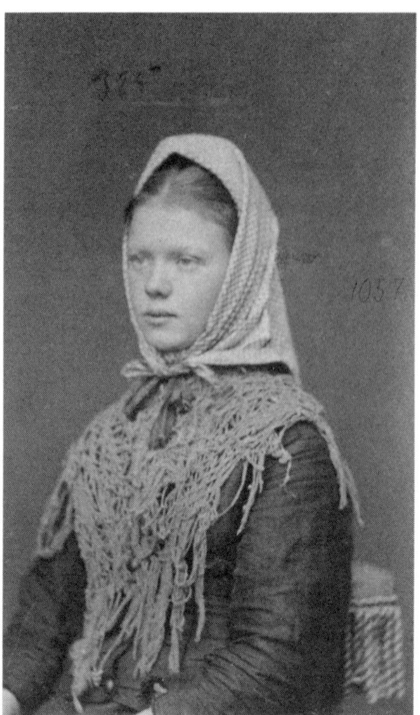

Figure 8.6. *Left. Portrait of Karoline Gustavsen* (no. 538 in the Kristiania Police's Album of Prostitutes, undated, last part of the nineteenth century). Photo: The Norwegian National Museum of Justice.

Figure 8.7. *Right.* Daniel G. Nyblinn, *Criminal Portrait of Indiane Olsen* (between 1870 and 1890). Photography, 10 × 6.3 cm. Photo: The Norwegian National Museum of Justice.

ill.[26] As Allan Sekula writes, the new photographic praxis invented the criminal body and confronted people with a double system: "A system of representation capable of functioning both honorifically and repressively."[27] These kinds of photo archives were an important part of Cesare Lombroso's anthropological work on prostitution.[28] Krohg's *Jossa* looks like one of the photographs in the police archive, although through the art of painting, the image is transformed into a portrait of a woman with dignity—lifted out of the criminal context and placed on a gallery wall in a frame for regular beholders to see.

THE *FLÂNEUSE* DISCOURSE

The modern city did not allow women to move about freely. Public spaces were the realm of men. A great deal of feminist art history over the past thirty years has dealt with the issue of how to understand women and public spaces in the nineteenth century, or the *flâneuse* discourse.[29] There was a distinction between appropriate and inappropriate behavior, and

Albertine and other women in the 1880s were testing these limits: what could be seen and what could be hidden in a public arena?

Prostitutes were objects at once of curiosity and control. Onlookers showed up to watch them arrive at and leave the police station, where the prostitutes had to follow prescribed rules of conduct. Boeck recorded one of these instructions: "When they [the prostitutes] arrive and leave the police station at appointed times, they must go one at a time and use different streets. They have to wear a simple, and under no circumstances noticeable, dress, without jewelry and without makeup."[30] In 1876 the authorities in Kristiania issued a detailed regulation regarding the prostitutes' conduct. They could not move around the city without permission, go to concerts, visit restaurants, or use the streetcar; in other words, they had to show themselves in public as little as possible. Section 8 in the regulations specifies, "They shall, when they show themselves outside their home, be decently dressed and not wear any decoration or dress that will attract attention. They must all in all behave so that they will not attract attention or offend anyone."[31] In Paris, it was reported, women on the street could be arrested for a provocative look (*oeillade*) or an obscene gesture (*geste lascif*).[32] Historian Aina Schiøtz stresses that the regulations in Kristiania were often challenged or just ignored by the women. We can see this in Krohg's large painting, where the prostitutes at the police station sport lavish dresses and hats.

A woman's attire was the most visible sign of her affluence.[33] But where does the line between luxury and tastelessness lie, and can one always tell a respectable bourgeois woman from a prostitute? Clothing, accessories, and makeup can signal class and gender roles, but prostitutes could play with them. Parent-Duchêtelet described the ambiguity of this encoded visuality in his 1836 study: "The best possible outcome is reached when men, and particularly those who seek out [prostitutes], are able to distinguish them from honest women; but the latter, and particularly their daughters, are not able to make this distinction, or at least can only do so with difficulty."[34] Clients needed to be able to recognize prostitutes, while women and children should remain unaware of them. Among the important signifiers were shawls, scarves, hats, gloves, umbrellas, and handkerchiefs, as well as makeup, which was, in Lombroso's words, "a virtual requirement of the prostitute's sad trade."[35] Looking at nineteenth-century paintings, it can be hard to distinguish between a fashionable promenade ensemble and cheap vulgarity. This is the co-called "female identification problem"—exemplified by Manet's *A Bar at the Folies Bergères* (1882), which Krohg saw at the Salon in 1882. The woman at the center of the painting presents herself through her clothing as something she might not be—there is a certain class confusion, or a confusing dress code, in her appearance. She is a "simple" sales girl, probably from the lower class, posing as a bourgeois woman to appear more pleasing and acceptable to her customers.[36] The salesgirl was part of the new petite bourgeoisie, which Zola, in *Ladies' Delight* (1883), called a vague, nameless class, "floating between the working and middle classes."[37]

SPECTACLE

Spectacle comes from Latin *spectare* (to see, or observe) and *spectaculum* (a show, or a view). The word and the concept are central to the theories of Guy Debord and T. J. Clark, who use the term *spectacle* to refer to the weight placed in modern capitalist society on superficial things, surface phenomena, and artificial behavior—where the sign is more important than the object, the copy supersedes the original, the fantasy outweighs reality, and appearance is more prized than essence. The notion of spectacle is used in particular to critique the way capitalism has created a form of theater based on commodity and mass production. Life in a capitalist society is seen as a spectacle, with people and objects put on display like a performance. Everything that used to be experienced directly is now a mere representation. The symptoms of this society are commercials, propaganda, and the entertainment industry. The industrial society is fundamentally *spectacular*.[38] This phenomenon is directly related to the growth of cities and urbanity in the nineteenth century. In the Albertine project, Krohg represents Kristiania for the first time as an urban center, a city characterized by spectacle: a place to see and be seen, one enlivened by visual desire for bodies and commodities—pretty clothes and appealing shop windows. In the novel, Albertine window-shops on Karl Johan Street, just as Zola's Nana does at the Passage des Panoramas: "She [Nana] could not tear herself away from the shop-windows."[39]

The fashion industry was an important part of the new society. It is interesting to see how the democratization of fashion at the end of the nineteenth century blurred traditional class boundaries. The honest woman and the prostitute may have never looked more alike than they did in the 1870s and 1880s.[40] Perhaps on closer scrutiny one could notice differences in the style, cut, and adornments of their garments. A prostitute's clothes were likely to be made of cheaper materials and to be more garish. The shocking thing about Gervex's painting *Rolla* was not the naked girl, Marion, but the pile of clothes lying next to the messy bed. It was a sign of paid sexual activity, and the discarded clothes signaled that the woman who shed them was a prostitute. Critics thought the naked body itself was beautifully painted, but the dirty accessories spoiled the scene and made it improper. Especially noticeable was the red corset turned inside out and draped over the chair. It was a piece of underwear, as well as a sign of modernity, when it came into fashion in the 1870s. The one in the painting could be identified as the type of cheap, ready-to-wear corset that could be bought in a shopping mall.[41]

An anonymous letter signed "An old man," published in the daily newspaper *Aftenposten* during the Albertine affair, expressed many of the day's views on women and sexual mores: working class women were clearly earning too much, since they used their extra money to buy new clothes and jewelry. The vanity of a working class girl was a disease without limits, erasing the distinctions between clothes for young ladies of different classes. In addition, as girls became more seductive, men could not help themselves. So, reading between the lines, it was the girl's fault if she was raped or became a prostitute.[42]

Police doctor Boeck similarly observed that prostitutes "exaggerate the leading fashion, and especially when it comes to the hats, which can really be funny and tasteless."[43] This fits well with Baudelaire's description of prostitutes in *The Painter of Modern Life* (1863): "Women who have exaggerated the fashion to the extent of perverting its charm and totally destroying its aims, are ostentatiously sweeping the floor with their trains and the fringes of their shawls; they come and go, pass and repass, opening an astonished eye like animals, giving an impression of total blindness, but missing nothing."[44]

Prostitutes have, over the centuries, used clothes and makeup to challenge constructs of social class and age, and to exaggerate their looks in vulgar ways. By playing with social niceties and expectations, they also reveal the arbitrary boundaries set up by society and the superficiality of its values. A fascinating convergence of prostitution and theater at the Folies-Bergère was wonderfully expressed by Guy de Maupassant in *Bel-Ami* (1885): "But Madame de Marelle was hardly looking at the stage, having eyes only for the prostitutes moving around behind her. She kept on turning around all the time, longing to touch them, to feel their dresses, their cheeks, their hair, just to discover what such women were made of."[45] The prostitute's taste for superficial pleasures was captured by Zola in *Nana* (1880): "She [Nana] adored the Passage des Panoramas. It was the passion she had felt since her youth for fancy goods, fake jewelry, gilded zinc, and cardboard made to look like leather."[46] Huysmans's Marthe also had a "craving for luxury and glamour."[47] It is interesting that the journalist Rosenkrantz Johnsen drew attention in his thorough 1887 review of Krohg's large painting to the prostitutes' exaggerated finery: their brightly colored outfits put together with failed attempts at harmony.[48] He went on to comment on the women's hats and umbrellas, gloves and jewelry, skin and eye color, hairstyles and makeup, the fabrics and colors of their clothes.

THE WAITING ROOM SPECTACLE

Krohg's *Waiting Room* is a stage on which different kinds of prostitutes are made visible: from the young factory girls to the older, more experienced women flaunting their "fancy" dresses—mimicking bourgeois elegance, or creating "a parody of fashionable clothing,"[49] to borrow the words of fashion sociologist Diana Crane. Krohg captured the carnivalesque side of prostitution and a hierarchy even among these representatives of the underclass. Krohg's painting depicts the different types of prostitutes described in Boeck's reports of the early 1880s. The two older women in the foreground of the painting fit especially well with some of Boeck's comments from 1881 and 1882:

> Gladis, 22 years old, from Bergen, thick and fat, with an animalistic face, with hands, lips, and even eyes shaking from drinking beer and hard liquor; she has had syphilis and one child. . . .
>
> If one walks into one of the bordellos in the evening, one will see a collection of women one will not soon forget. Their looks, clothing, manners are so different from all others—they form a class unto themselves. . . . Those living there are repulsive in appearance. . . .
>
> Most of the girls at the bordello have been at it a long time. One can see them year after year, meeting up twice a week for the doctor's examination. They get fatter and more amusing, and they look more and more foolish. All the elegance disappears and only the animalistic qualities remain.[50]

It seems as if Krohg had visualized these descriptions and sought to convey them in his painting.

The more experienced women in Krohg's large canvas are imitating the *chic Parisiennes* in their choice of dresses and accessories—their shoes, hats, gloves, and umbrellas. In his novel, Krohg also described nice ladies wearing silk and velvet, as well as large hats from

Paris.[51] The hat especially was an important indicator of official or aspired-to social status. As art historian Anthea Callen states, "Hats, the crowning glory of a woman's toilette, epitomized the bourgeois obsession with appearance and the outward display of luxury."[52] Hats had special social meanings, and men and women of all classes wore them with pride. It was inappropriate for women of any class to be seen outside without wearing a hat.[53] Toward the end of the nineteenth century, women could also choose among different kinds of hats beyond the traditional bonnet, and only the poorest went bareheaded. In the 1870s and 1880s hats and bonnets became higher and higher, built up with feathers of aigrette and ostrich, and with ribbons of taffeta, satin, or velvet. In Krohg's large painting, women wear a variety of hats with striking decorations; only Albertine and another poor girl on the right have mere shawls on their heads—typical of working class women. It was the size and color of hats worn by prostitutes that made them stand out, the exaggeration and vulgarization of fashion conveying their low class and crass taste.

The social meaning and importance of the hat is exemplified by paintings of milliners' shops in the impressionist era, especially the series by Edgar Degas. His millinery shop paintings illustrate a rich variety of hat colors and decorations. Milliners were typically women, and they were often associated with prostitution; they were believed to be sexually available and were seen as objects of desire.[54] Women milliners took part in the café life and were perceived as coquettes; they did not belong to the category of "good women." Yet the hats they made and sold were intended for prosperous and decorous ladies (similarly Albertine sewed opulent dresses she could only dream of owning). As the journalist Charles Benoist noted in his commentary on milliners in *Le temps* in 1895, "The woman working on luxury objects begins to desire for herself the beautiful things she makes for the rich."[55] Benoist thought this striving led a woman to prostitution—compelling her to earn with her body the money for luxuries she could not otherwise afford. Krohg clearly addressed this myth about prostitutes in his Albertine project. Albertine's vanity shows itself when her mother encourages her to take a walk outside. Albertine exclaims, "Go out? . . . Do you want me to go out with a knitted scarf and a kerchief on my head like another factory girl?"[56] Although she has been cooped up inside for almost four weeks, she refuses to be seen out in the world in her poor clothes. Notions of proper dress take up a lot of Albertine's thinking and dreaming as she is sewing rich ladies' ball gowns.

Among the noticeable things in Krohg's *Waiting Room* are large bustles on some of the women's dresses—another fashionable article in the mid-1880s, when the painting was made. (Think also of the lady standing in the foreground of Georges Seurat's *A Sunday Afternoon on the Island of La Grande Jatte* (1884–86), painted at the same time as the *Waiting Room.* Seurat's woman, often read as a prostitute, echoes the lady in pink in Krohg's painting.) The bustle was widely discussed and made fun of in satirical drawings, so it is noteworthy that Krohg gave it such a distinctive place. There is a stark contrast between the woman in the showy, vulgar pink dress and Albertine, whose dress is modest and unaffected; this contrast is also apparent in their body language—one ostentatiously confident, the other demure. They are opposites. Notably, the flesh-pink dress is painted as if it were composed of pieces of meat at a butcher's shop rather than of luxurious fabric.

Two other striking fashion details in Krohg's painting are gloves and umbrellas. Gloves were as socially important as hats, and women were expected to wear them at all times, except when eating. They constituted a huge and growing business in the 1880s,[57] and all women in Krohg's large painting wear gloves except for the two working class girls. Three of the women also carry ornate umbrellas—items that could only be bought in department stores, not made at home. They spoke of modernity and urbanity.

Krohg also drew attention to the many colors of dresses and the variety of fabrics in the *Waiting Room*: mauve, peach-pink, forest green, warm yellow, saturated blue. These beautiful hues signaled women's ambitions to belong to a higher class. Albertine's dress, in contrast, is dark and lacks style—as was typical of working class and poor girls. Dark colors were practical: they did not get visibly dirty. A black dress could also be used on various occasions: Sunday services, a funeral, or everyday garb. Middle and upper class women could afford to own a variety of lighter-colored dresses, whereas working class girls most often had only one. Blue-green was the most fashionable color in *la belle époque*, and some of the women here wear that shade. Well-to-do ladies also favored luxurious fabrics such as silk, velvet, and muslin, while working class women wore coarser and heavier wool. Albertine and the other poor girl in the *Waiting Room* wear shawls over their shoulders to add a touch of color. But Jossa, the fourth girl from the right, wears a long jacket—a very fashionable item at the time.

THE MIRROR

From a certain feminist point of view, one might argue that the modern urban culture described in this chapter makes a woman see herself through a man's gaze—that the female body becomes a fetishized icon for the woman's own narcissistic pleasure.[58] The new city and shopping culture created a new objectification of women, who adopted a male sexual gaze to see themselves. Their own narcissistic pleasure in watching themselves duplicated the male gaze. A great literary example is Madame de Burne in Guy de Maupassant's *Alien Hearts* (1890): "By dint of admiring herself, of cherishing the subtleties of her expression and the elegance of the figure, and of cultivating whatever could enhance them, discovering imperceptible nuances which made her loveliness more powerful in less accustomed eyes, by pursuing every artifice that might increase her grace, she had naturally discovered everything which might please others most."[59] Is this the woman's own perception of herself, or has she adopted a male point of view? Albertine enjoys seeing herself in the mirror, exclaiming, "I've also got a nice figure—much nicer than before."[60] From a feminist perspective. one might claim that Albertine admires herself as a man would, tricked by male capitalist society into dreaming about fancy dresses that would make her pleasing to men. This scene from *Albertine* mirrors one from *Nana*: "One of Nana's pleasures consisted of undressing in front of the mirror on her wardrobe door, which reflected her from head to foot. She used to take off all her clothes and then, stark naked, gaze at her reflection, oblivious of everything around her. A passion for her body, an ecstatic admiration of her satin skin and of the supple lines of her figure made her serious, attentive, and absorbed in her love for herself."[61] Mirror scenes were common in naturalist literature and painting. There are memorable mirror scenes in both Huysmans's *Marthe* (1876)[62] and Maupassant's *Alien Hearts* (1890).[63] The mirror is a crucial object both literally and symbolically. It is directly related to painting (as a tool) and to the new capitalist society, appearing prominently in

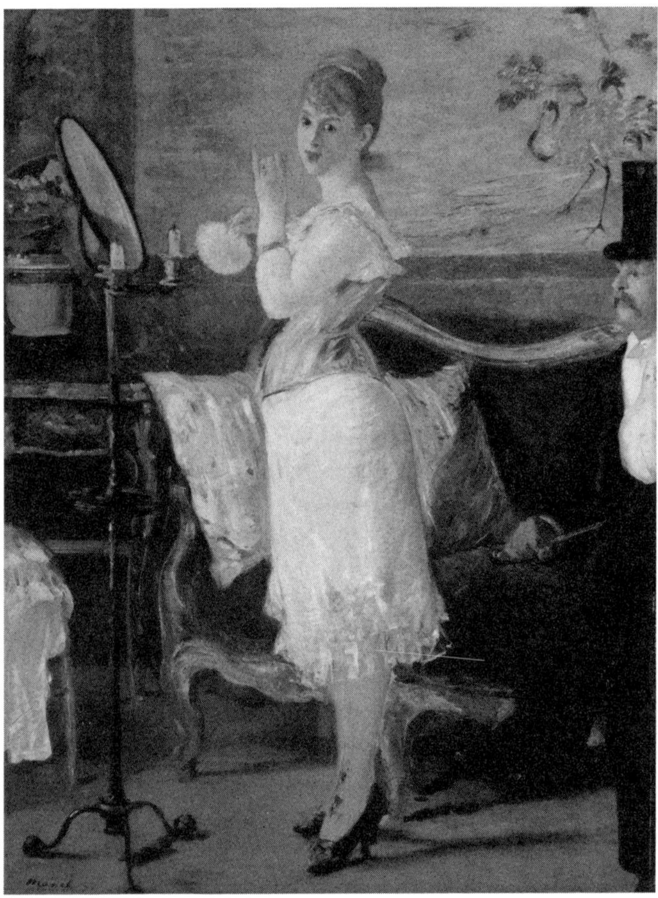

Figure 8.8. Édouard Manet, *Nana* (1877). Oil on canvas, 154 × 115 cm. Photo © bpk/Hamburger Kunsthalle/Elke Walford.

shopping malls and in brothels. Zola made those connections in *The Ladies' Delight* (1883): "Everywhere mirrors were making the shop recede further into the distance, reflecting displays together with patches of the public—inverted faces, bits of shoulders and arms."[64] Mirrors multiply desires. Manet's *Nana* (1877, fig. 8.8) brilliantly illustrates the complex constellation of sights enabled by a mirror: the prostitute is placed, or caught, between her own image in the mirror (or is it our or the customer's mirror image of her?), the customer's gaze at the right, and the painter or beholder who meets her eyes directly. Is she in control of her appearance or oppressed by multiple male eyes?

Krohg returned to the motif of a woman looking at herself in the mirror around 1912, when he created a series of paintings set in his studio that focused on the life of his female model: what she did before and after sittings, including looking at herself in the mirror and getting dressed or undressed. These paintings were related to the Albertine series in that models were often prostitutes. The most famous and praised of these paintings, *Toilette*

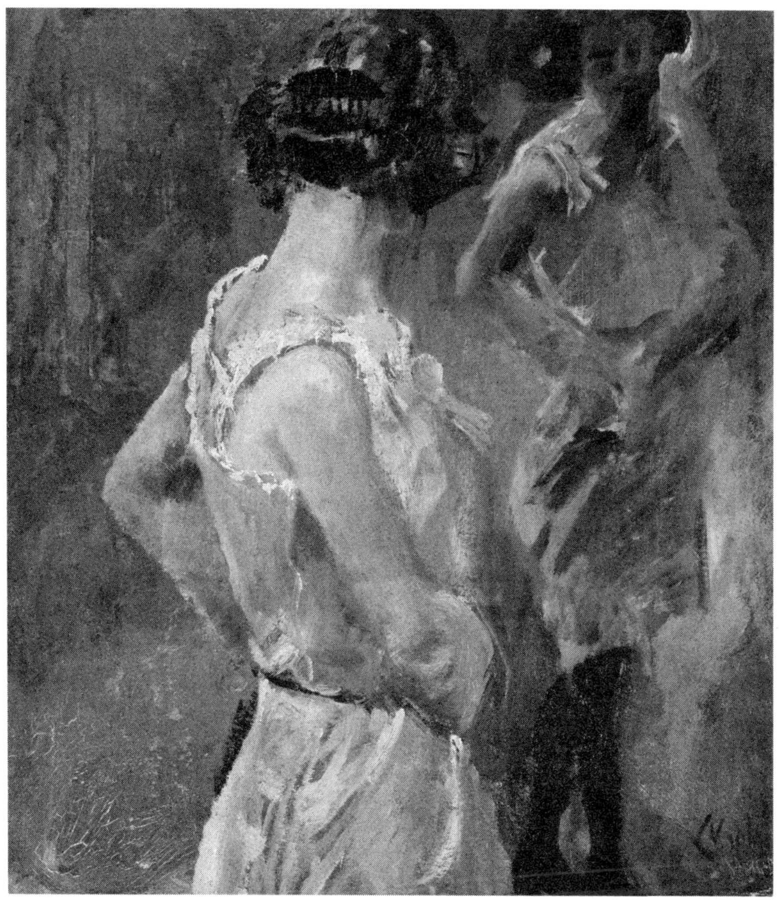

Figure 8.9. Christian Krohg, *Toilette* (1913). Oil on canvas, 58 × 52.5 cm. Photo: Jacques Lathion/The National Museum of Art, Architecture and Design, Oslo.

(1913, fig. 8.9), was possibly an homage to Manet's *Before the Mirror* (1876). But is it a woman enjoying the sight of herself in the mirror, as Albertine did in the novel? Is the model in the *Toilette* engaged in a typical feminine activity and, in the vocabulary of gender studies, performing her gender as she is expected to in a patriarchal society, or is she just using the mirror as a tool so she can fix something on her dress? The model is not sexually available to the beholder's gaze nor is she enjoying herself in the mirror.

DISCIPLINE AND POWER

Albertine is caught in a network of power relations, as well as in the gaze of several powerful people who stereotype and judge her. As Aubert wrote in his review of the painting: "The young girl's shame and paralyzing anxiety as the officer stands ready to open the door to the visitation office forms the main subject, around which the rest of the composition is grouped. Compassion, afterthought, curiosity, indifference, and contempt are the most visible expressions on other women's faces and in their attitudes. In this way compassion, which is the image's essential mood, is strengthened in us."[65] How could Albertine feel anything but shame?

The historian Alain Corbin states in his seminal study *Women for Hire: Prostitution and Sexuality in France after 1850* (1978), "The nineteenth-century prostitute does not speak to us about herself; what reality we can glean is mediated through male eyes: those of the policeman, the doctor, the judge, and the administrator."[66] We could add to this list the novelist and the artist. As Anthea Callen so poignantly shows in her writings on Degas, the man is invisible in most representations of prostitutes. We only catch momentary or elusive glimpses of the clients or male observers of these women.[67] We get to meet some male characters in the novel *Albertine*, but not in Krohg's paintings (except for the anonymous police officer at the door). The clients, policemen, and doctors are all nearly invisible to the beholder. This suggests that the visual representation we are offered is generated by a male outsider. If one of the prostitutes were to paint her version of the events, she would surely remember the doctors, for example, and give us their detailed and vivid descriptions. Henri Toulouse-Lautrec also painted prostitutes waiting for the doctor's examination. In *The Medical Inspection* (1894, fig. 8.10), two women make themselves ready for a vaginal exam. It is not a picture intended to please the beholder. The two women would most likely not meet the male gaze with anything but fake lust and real revulsion.[68] Neither in this painting nor in the *Albertine* canvas is the doctor present, and the police officer in the Krohg picture is anonymous, like an extra without a personality. Albertine notes only that the doctor had a "quiet, businesslike face," and she is stunned that he proceeds with the examination as if nothing were at stake.[69] Foucault writes that the policeman had to be like a "faceless gaze that transformed the whole social body into a field of perception: thousands of eyes posted everywhere."[70] Exercise of power is most effective when it is invisible. In Foucault's words, "In discipline, it is the subjects who have to be seen. Their visibility assures the hold of the power that is exercised over them. It is the fact of being constantly seen, of being able always to be seen, that maintains the disciplined individual in his subjection. And the examination is the technique by which power . . . holds them in a mechanism of objectification. In this space of domination, disciplinary power manifests its potency."[71] In Zola's *Nana* we read: "She [Nana] had always been afraid of the Law, that unknown power, that instrument of male vengeance which could wipe her out without anybody in the world lifting a finger to defend her. She saw Saint-Lazare as a grave, a black hole in which they buried women alive after cutting off their hair."[72]

The relationship between a prostitute and a policeman was complex and paradoxical. The policeman could become a friend and a lover, and the prostitute an informer. An important part of Krohg's work was to show the well-known but undiscussed fact that police officers also operated as pimps.[73] The policeman was always a representative of the law and could at any moment arrest a prostitute, or he could take advantage of her and abuse her, as happened in *Albertine*. This cat-and-mouse dynamic underlies *Nana*, *Albertine*, and Huysmans's *Marthe*: "This life of fear and anguish didn't give her a moment's respite."[74] In Zola's novel, Nana sleeps with a police officer: "At one time she used to go to bed with a police-

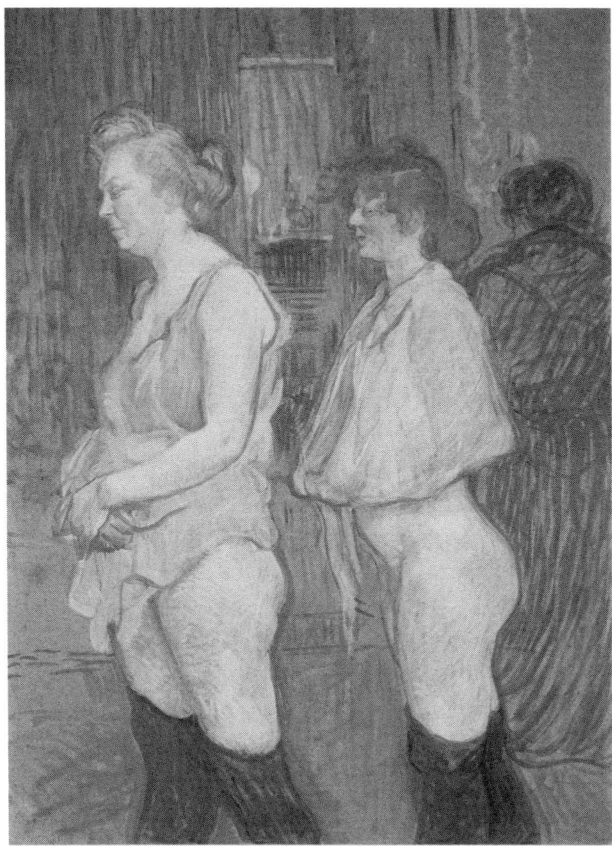

Figure 8.10.

Henri de Toulouse-Lautrec, *The Medical Inspection* (1894). Oil on cardboard on wood, 83.5 × 88.9 cm. Photo: National Gallery of Art, Washington, DC/Chester Dale Collection.

man in the public morals brigade, to make sure they left her alone; and twice he had kept her from being listed as a prostitute."[75] Not to be registered as a prostitute was the most desirable outcome, and mistaken arrests were much discussed at the time, for the police often suspected and arrested innocent girls and women—as happened with Albertine. The fact that the police sometimes made such mistakes was one of the arguments made by the abolition movement.

In Krohg's painting we are invited to take part in an uncomfortable scene in the waiting room before Albertine's examination. The wait itself is institutionalized: Albertine is one of a number of women being processed, and they are strangers to her. The exam is a form of punishment, and the waiting hall a disciplining room.[76] It is an awkward place where looks flicker from one face to another, some curious or taunting, others nervous or desperate. It is a theater of embarrassment where one feels the gazes of others scanning one's body. In the novel Albertine tries ineffectually to escape them: "She pulled away from those made-up eyes. . . . [A]ll of them looked at her and smiled mockingly."[77]

The waiting room is a space where prison and hospital converge, where law and medicine collude against the women. Albertine is shocked to find herself in this room and forced to see herself in a new light. In the examination room she is defined as a prostitute—by both the doctor and herself. As she sits in the medical chair, she becomes a prostitute, with no way back to her previous life and self. This space decides who the women in it are and who they believe themselves to be.[78]

A registered prostitute had to be checked at least twice a month, sometimes as often as twice a week. The physician needed an examination chair and a speculum to complete his check, looking at the vulva and vagina, the neck of the womb, the woman's lips, and the inside of her mouth.[79] We do not see the examination itself in Krohg's painting—that would be much too graphic. In this instance we see how text and image serve different functions and produce different effects: literature can describe what cannot be pictured, and painting can show things that cannot be described. In the novel the vaginal examination is represented in a way a painting could never convey: "Then suddenly she felt the instrument move into her naked body, she jumped, but then remained lying down in deep fear, not daring to move a muscle, her mind unnaturally clear."[80] Literary historian Christen Collin commented on this difference between painting and literature in 1894, and thought the painting to be more successful, or rather less decadent, than the novel:

> Apparently Mr. Christian Krohg, as both a painter and a narrator, has represented the same "Albertine." But his narrative representation followed her all the way into the police doctor's office—the Krohgian storytelling went all the way in with less reluctance than did the poor young girl, while his painting dared not go further than the waiting room.
>
> Now, apparently, because of the nature of narrative art, it can dare to go further into the representation of the repulsive or the uncomfortable than can the fine arts. For this reason, the narrator can touch on a thing in a fleeting moment and thereafter lead the reader further into the story, while the fine artist must paint or chisel the motif with greater elaboration, such that the beholder must stand still in front of the image.[81]

In Albertine's case the examination became a decisive moment and a turning point in her life. Researchers on prostitution concurred that the medical exam was a dramatic and degrading act. Dr. Hippolyte Mireur, in his 1882 study, called the health check a "stigma" and "an affront to human dignity," even though he saw it as necessary.[82] Albertine would never be an innocent girl again. In the Albertine story both the police and the medical establishment are represented as powerful forces that create prostitution rather than prevent it. Since discipline had failed, it was best to exercise control over the prostitutes so that society as a whole could cope with them. That is why bordellos were accepted as long as they were under official control.[83] The medical examination in a way normalized prostitution and made it almost impossible for a woman to get out of its clutches. After the examination Albertine becomes a lost case: she loses her sense of shame. This is the beginning of the same state of shamelessness that Zola's Nana reaches: "She no longer thought of anything but her beauty, forever inspecting her body, and washing and scenting herself all over, in the proud knowledge that she could strip naked at any moment and in front of anyone without any cause to blush."[84]

From the 1830s on, vaginal examinations were performed with a speculum. The Latin word *speculum* means mirror, and it comes from *specere*, "to see." The instrument made it possible for the (male) doctor to look at and penetrate farther into female genitalia. The French physiologist Joseph Récamier developed the popular version of the instrument, which consisted of two half-cylinders that could be extended to see more. The American gynecologist James Marion Sims invented his own spoon-like speculum and concluded after using it: "I saw everything as no man had ever seen before. I felt like an explorer in medicine who first views a new and important territory."[85] Sims's speculum became a standard tool after 1845. It was made of German silver (nickel silver), so that when the instrument was inserted into the woman's vagina, it reflected light shone into it: in Sims's own words, "the concave surface of the bright speculum making everything perfectly distinct."[86] The speculum was controversial, and many saw its use as immoral. The first American woman doctor, Elizabeth Blackwell, protested against its application in general gynecological examinations because she saw it as threatening women's purity.[87] In England in the mid-nineteenth century, it was reported that the virtuous woman "who has been subjected to such treatment is not the same person in delicacy and purity that she was before."[88] In other words it became an instrument associated with prostitutes and was seen as a tool of rape. It is not surprising that Albertine felt the procedure as a shock and a dramatic turning point: the speculum was a phallic eye that physically raped her, not metaphorically or narratively, but in reality. The speculum became an extreme version of the male gaze, the clinical gaze, and the disciplining gaze.

Female sexuality has long been seen as a problem in patriarchal society. Depictions of women and female bodies in art often vacillated between the Madonna and the whore. Prostitutes have been frequently portrayed as essentially animalistic, sexually hungry creatures living out the sexual instincts with which they were born. Guy de Maupassant described Madame de Burne in *Alien Hearts* (1890) in a kind of parody: "But above all she was a born coquette, and once liberated, she set about pursuing and capturing her adorers as a hunter pursues game, for the simple pleasure of bringing it down. Yet her heart did not thirst for emotions like the hearts of sentimental women; she was not searching for a man's unique love nor the gratification of a passion."[89] In Lombroso and Ferrero's study of women and prostitutes, published in 1893, the "born prostitute" was characterized by "moral insanity": "For the majority of the prostitutes, poverty and abandonment are only catalysts, while the underlying cause is their lack of modesty and moral insanity, which push them first into debauchery and then the brothel."[90] Prostitutes were described as vain, lazy, greedy, heavy drinkers and smokers, and liars. It was not a sympathetic image.

The prostitute became in this period a favorite character for exploring and fantasizing about the animalistic instincts of human beings. The red-headed prostitute was often described as an animal. Guy de Maupassant's *Bel-Ami* describes one prostitute: "Her vast bosom was bursting the seams of her dark silk dress and her lips, like a gaping red wound, gave her an extravagantly passionate appearance, animal-like but exciting."[91] Another example appears in Zola's *Nana*, where a cat is lurking in the dressing rooms as Nana and the other girls are getting ready. The cat is obviously very much at home in this environment:

"But in the midst of all the girls scurrying about on the four floors, the only thing he saw clearly was a cat, the big ginger he had seen before, which, in that musky, oven-like atmosphere, was stalking upstairs, rubbing its back against the banister, with its tail in the air."[92] (One also recalls the cat in Manet's *Olympia*.) Man is possibly an ape, the prostitute a cat.

Krohg tried to identify with his female characters, although the male artist's privilege to represent women in "his" way has been deemed problematic in a society where the power relationship between the sexes is asymmetric.[93] It is probably impossible for a man to truly convey female experience, but Krohg tried to break through this divide. Amalie Skram defended *Albertine* in 1887 and commented on a core issue in the novel: the challenge faced by a male artist seeking to represent a woman's experience.[94] In the book's pivotal rape scene, Chief Inspector Winther tricks Albertine into coming to his house, where he serves her alcohol and forces her to have sex with him. After the deed is done, he enjoys the sight of Albertine sleeping in his bed: "As the pale, oval line of her cheek disappeared down toward her neck, the warm yellow light vanished without any edges into the shadow under her ear, and then, for one last time, showed itself on the neck's stretched muscles."[95] Albertine is shown as the object of a man's (Winther) gaze and sexual craving. At the same time she becomes the painter's aesthetic object, and Krohg comments that Winther "wished that he was a painter, or that there were a painter here."[96] Krohg is aware that the two gazes—that of the rapist and the artist—can cross, and this problem becomes one of the main issues in the novel. Krohg's work is both an admission of his own gaze as speculum and a critique of it. Even though his artist's gaze is employed in the service of the good, Albertine still cannot escape the phallic eye.[97]

There are, obviously, many problems inherent in a feminism which takes for granted that there are clear gender differences between the roles men and women play in art: men are agents of action, while women are passive objects at whom the action is aimed. Laura Mulvey famously stated that a woman "stands in patriarchal culture as a signifier for the male other, bound by a symbolic order in which man can live out his fantasies and obsessions through linguistic command by imposing them on the silent image of a woman still tied to her place as a bearer, not maker, of meaning."[98] Women are added to the picture for decorative reasons, an object to rest one's eyes upon. This is true in many instances and may be a general feature of Western art. But this perspective also implies that the beholder is always a heterosexual male, projecting his erotic fantasies on the depicted women. These roles are held to be constant for all women and men, since they show the truth behind the unconscious construction of gender identities. Women in a patriarchal society are the other, caught in a symbolic order in which men are free to live out their fantasies and obsessions. It is a state of affairs that Krohg describes in his Albertine project. And in the novel and paintings Krohg comments on women's role in a patriarchal society using the means at his disposal—the male gaze, albeit a sympathetic one. Krohg's art shows how women struggled to define themselves in a modern society that finally began the difficult process of trying to create equality between the sexes—both in theory and in praxis. The Albertine project demonstrates how the modern artist struggled to represent women in art without falling back on male chauvinist clichés.

The Albertine project was a complicated experiment. On the one hand, Krohg sought to follow the evolution—or decline—in the fortunes of a typical working class girl. On the other hand he pursued a social agenda: he wanted beholders, especially the government, to feel sympathy with Albertine so as to change the lot of such girls. At the same time he struggled with how he—as a male observer and an artist—could properly represent women. His project provides an interesting example of the ambiguous relationship between power and gaze in modernist art. It is also an example of a progressive artist drawing on the philosophical, scientific, political, and aesthetic ideas of his era to forge a revolutionary art—in the sense of art that has as its goal social and political change. He uses his power—as an artist—to show and alter for the better the lot of the most dispossessed and oppressed women.

CHAPTER NINE

Modern Pessimism

From Naturalism to Symbolism

> There comes a moment of decision when naturalism must either break through to socialism or founder in fatalism, symbolism, mysticism, religiosity, and reaction.
>
> ERNST FISCHER

According to Kirk Varnedoe, one of the most striking aspects of Nordic art at the end of the nineteenth century is the muddled relationship between realism and symbolism. Varnedoe shows how many Nordic paintings are hybrid works that "refuse to conform to either/or classification; they seem to be 'both/and'—both Realist and Symbolist, both descriptive and abstract, both objective and expressive, both retrograde and avant-garde." He continues: "The painters appear to leapfrog back and forth over the familiar chain of progress to arrive at 'forward' positions independently. . . . This distinctive phenomenon of interrelation and overlap between the ostensibly opposite tendencies of Realism and Symbolism appeared in matters of content as well as aspects of tone and style in an extraordinarily diverse range of Scandinavian art."[1] In this chapter I explore the relationship between realism/naturalism and symbolism, arguing that naturalism and symbolism were not experienced as essentially disparate in Scandinavia, and I examine how Krohg dealt with this issue in his art.

Naturalism as an aesthetic started to lose its currency at the end of the 1880s. As many historians have pointed out, there was a sense that naturalism as an empirical, objective art could not go any farther. Marxist Ernst Fischer's analysis is appealing and touches upon some relevant issues: "Naturalism revealed the fragmentation, the ugliness, the surface filth of the capitalist bourgeois world, but it could not go further and deeper to recognize those forces which were preparing to destroy that world and establish socialism. . . . This is why the naturalistic writer, unable to see beyond the patchwork shoddiness of the bourgeois world, was bound—unless he moved toward socialism—to embrace symbolism and mysticism, to fall victim to his desire to discover the mysterious whole, the meaning of life, behind social realities."[2] It seems that naturalism readily moved into symbolism, as it did in the works of Zola, Ibsen, and Strindberg in literature, and Munch in painting. The shift from naturalism to symbolism was both a continuation and a reaction. Krohg's case, however, is more problematic. He stopped painting political naturalistic paintings after 1890, and his art became more self-centered and formally experimental.

DEGENERATION

Despite the ambition of the sciences to make the world a better place to live, many late nineteenth-century artists and intellectuals noticed an increasing number of negative developments as a result of the growth of cities: alcoholism, prostitution, poverty, criminality, and insanity. Scientists sought to map these social ills and propose solutions. Social critics grouped them under the rubric of degeneration.

Critics of naturalist art, such as the Paris-based German doctor Max Nordau, believed that it spurred further degeneration rather than making the world a better place. Nordau stated on the very first page of his famous book *Degeneration* (1892):

> Degenerates are not always criminals, prostitutes, anarchists, and pronounced lunatics; they are often authors and artists. These, however, manifest the same mental characteristics, and for the most part the same somatic features, as the members of the above-mentioned anthropological family, who satisfy their unhealthy impulses with the knife of the assassin or the bomb of the dynamiter, instead of with pen and pencil.
>
> Some among these degenerates in literature, music, and painting have in recent years come into extraordinary prominence, and are revered by numerous admirers as creators of a new art, and heralds of the coming centuries.
>
> This phenomenon is not to be disregarded. Books and works of art exercise a powerful suggestion on the masses. It is from these productions that an age derives its ideals of morality and beauty. If they are absurd and anti-social, they exert a disturbing and corrupting influence on the views of a whole generation.[3]

Nordau attacked writers such as Ibsen, Nietzsche, and Zola, and saw in their art—and the life they described—a sick society and declining nations. How could their works help make the world better? It was a debate that encompassed aesthetics, sociology, medicine, politics, and morals. Art, in Nordau's view, ought to be positive and uplifting, not dark and destructive.

Another powerful attack on naturalism in literature in the 1890s came from the Norwegian literary historian Christen Collin (1857–1926). He criticized Krohg, Zola, Taine, Brandes, Garborg, Kitty Kielland, and Gunnar Heiberg, and saw naturalism as a kind of aesthetic disease.[4] He thought, as did Nordau, that such art had a harmful influence on society; what he wanted instead was a therapeutic art. His favorite authors were Shakespeare and Bjørnstjerne Bjørnson, his good friend.[5] Collin's opinion about Christian Krohg was mixed: "Few, if any, of our painters have painted more vital pictures than he has. But on the other hand, he strenuously promotes the poets of sick love [like Hans Jæger]." Collin continued:

> There is, all in all, a striking contrast between most of our painting and a large amount of our newer literature. The first—painting—shines with the joy of the sun and the cheerful play of strong colors, with the unstoppable play of light and shadow. It is imbued with the spirit of mountains, forests and the sea and is our art's richest expression of the healthy outdoor life. But a large part of our newest literature reminds one of the stuffy smell of flats and bars. It is a withered smell of Berlinian and Parisian indulgence brought home. To me, Christian Krohg represents this contradiction in *one* person.[6]

Collin saw literary naturalism, which Krohg also represented, as an example of a sickly culture that could not coexist with the progress of democracy. For him this art was decadent: "The imagination of a decadent poet—whether he calls himself naturalist or *Décadent*—thrives best in representing processes of moral decay."[7] He wrote that the naturalist author enjoys the abomination of destruction and prefers to dwell on the brutal and impure aspects of life and love, including the animalistic sexual drive. Baudelaire and Flaubert were, for Collin, major decadent vectors, and Taine and Zola the worst naturalists because of their pervasive influence. In Collin's literary history, naturalism was an offspring of French romanticism, and later naturalism and symbolism were part of the same decadent art movement.[8] This is a view I share, but in a positive light.

NATURALISTIC SYMBOLISM

In France, literary naturalism lost its preeminence in the mid-1880s and came to be regarded as a dead art. Arnold Hauser gives a brilliant summary of the situation: "Naturalism, it was asserted, was an indelicate, indecent and obscene art, the expression of an insipid, materialistic philosophy, the instrument of clumsy, heavy-handed democratic propaganda, a collection of boring, trivial and vulgar banalities, a representation of reality which, in its portrayal of society, described only the wild, ravenous, undisciplined animal in man and only the works of disintegration, the dissolution of human relationship, the undermining of the family, the nation and religion, in short, it was destructive, unnatural, hostile to life."[9] There was a growing interest in the subjective, in place of the utopia of objectivity—an interest in the depth of the human soul and the mysteries of life. Artists and writers wanted to explore the unknowable, and this called for new visual languages. Symbolism became the new trend of the 1890s. And as naturalism was both a critique and a continuation of romanticism, symbolism was a critique and a continuation of naturalism—*and* impressionism.[10] It combined the subjectivity of impressionism with the darker subject matter of naturalism.

Jean Moréas stated in his 1886 manifesto that symbolism was an enemy of objective description and the realist arts.[11] To Krohg, on the other hand, symbolism was the natural development of impressionism: "The impressionists had already declared that it wasn't the object that was interesting, but the way the artist perceived it. Symbolism stands as a continuing development of and close relative of impressionism, since the symbolist emphasizes the spiritual."[12] He cited Max Klinger and Arnold Böcklin as examples of impressionism. But there was one major difference between impressionism and symbolism in Krohg's theory, and that was a shift from temperament, the artist's personality, to the more emotional *mood*. The symbolist, and Krohg meant chiefly Munch, painted his mood, rather than something from the actual world, an idea rather than reality. Impressionism was attached to a time and place; symbolism was not. The symbolist canvas was a painterly expression independent of nature. As art historian Øivind Storm Bjerke rightly remarks, "To Krohg, the Naturalist, Symbolism was a radical continuation of Naturalism, for it drew the human soul itself into the critical examination of reality."[13]

Literary historian Evert Sprinchorn uses the term *naturalistic symbolism* to describe the final stages of naturalism. His examples are works by Zola and Ibsen in the 1880s and 1890s, when their texts were more loaded with symbolic and suggestive meanings than before. It became important to suggest inner life, feelings, and the unconscious in addition to empirical and optical reality. This is why B. W. Wells could state in *The Sewanee Review* in 1893, after the publication of *Doctor Pascal*: "And yet, in spite of it all, in spite of himself, Zola is not a naturalist, but rather the greatest of living French idealists. . . . Zola is a genius; his theory is wrong, but his literary instinct is right."[14] August Strindberg is perhaps the greatest example of an author who moved from strict naturalism to symbolism. He even moved *out* of the "naturalist symbolist" zone where Ibsen and Zola dwelled. In painting, Munch's art developed along similar lines, demonstrating the close relationship between the naturalism he learned from Krohg and the symbolism he developed on his own. I agree with Sprinchorn when he emphasizes "the close connection that exists between Naturalism and Symbolism, isms that are often taken to be opposites." He continues:

> The Symbolists are pictured as lying in wait throughout the century for a chance to hurl themselves upon the naturalists. But why were they given this chance? And why at that particular time, in the late 1880s? And who gave them that opportunity? Not the scientists surely, who put no weapons in the hands of the Symbolists and who moved ever further away from a belief in a transcendental order. No, it was the naturalist writer and the naturalist painter, the Impressionist, who opened the door to the Symbolist.[15]

MODERN PESSIMISM

Frits Thaulow, in a humorous letter to his nephew Per Krohg (Christian Krohg's son and a painter in his own right), described the naturalists in Paris living on the right bank of the Seine, in Montmartre, far from the symbolists on the left bank, on Montparnasse, and "in sad ignorance about Schopenhauer and Nietzsche."[16] Ferdinand Brunetière opined in *Revue des deux mondes* in 1890 that Schopenhauer might be the most influential philosopher at the end of the century.[17] Georg Brandes's article on Arthur Schopenhauer, published in Danish in 1884, was probably widely read in Scandinavia.[18] Schopenhauer became in the latter half of the 1880s one of the most fashionable philosophers among the European intellectuals, even though he died in 1860. His writings resonated with the dark views of life and misanthropy embraced by artists and writers, with Strindberg the darkest pessimist of all.[19] The greatest literary expression of this growing negativity, and a parody of Zola's naturalism, was offered by Joris-Karl Huysmans in *Against Nature* (1884). Its neurotic protagonist Des Esseintes is described as follows: "In brief, since leaving Paris, he was moving further and further away from reality, and especially from the contemporary world which inspired an ever-growing disgust in him; this aversion had necessarily affected his literary and artistic tastes, and he distanced himself as much as possible from pictures and books whose limited subjects related to modern life."[20] In a foreword to the 1903 reissue of the novel, Huysmans was more programmatically critical of naturalism: "[Naturalism] was becoming exhausted from endlessly working over the same ground. The supply of observations that each writer had stored up, by watching himself and others, was running out. Zola, that fine painter of theatrical scenery, got along by producing bold canvases that were more or less accurate; he was very good at suggesting the illusion of movement and life; his heroes had no soul, being governed purely by impulses and instincts, which simplified the task of analysis."[21]

Many looked on naturalism as espousing a pessimistic worldview—an entropic vision exemplified by Zola and Taine. Taine's interest in psychology and the darker sides of the mind is seldom commented upon today. The French novelist and critic Paul Bourget called Taine's writings "naturalistic pessimism."[22] Taine himself wrote in *On Intelligence* (1870), "Madness is always hovering near the mind, as illness is always hovering near the body; for the normal condition is a temporary victory only; it results from and is renewed by the continual defeat of the contrary forces. Now these last are always present; an accident may give them preponderance; there is little required to enable them to assume it; a slight alteration in the proportion of the elementary affinities and the direction of the constructing process would bring on a *degeneracy*."[23] Guillermo Ferrero wrote that "Renan and Taine are perhaps the two worst pessimists I know of. . . . Taine depicts the most hideous form of human cruelty without a wink, as if he were describing the stages of development in crystallization or the metamorphoses in a plant's life."[24] And Émile Faguet meant Taine's writings were pessimistic, misanthropic, and fatalistic.[25]

The art historian Lorentz Dietrichson described how naturalist artists, inspired by Schopenhauer, portrayed the contemporary world as evil and the future as hopeless—as a time when culture and the institution of the family fail and people become like animals, driven by nature and pure instinct, and then gradually dissolve and return to the "Ur-slime."[26] When Dietrichson wrote about Krohg's *Dawn* (fig. 6.9), he emphasized the ugliness of the poor girl and concluded that it "is the necessary ingredient of the naturalist school."[27] The two key words for Dietrichson in discussing naturalism were *pessimism* and *ugliness*. He lamented that the naturalists saw their own time as difficult and poor, hopeless and declining, and he linked this pessimism to modernity and the growth of cities, in which the proletariat was crammed into small, crowded living quarters. This kind of life, the struggle for existence ("Kampen for Tilværelsen"), was producing sickness and death, alcoholism and prostitution. Dietrichson noted that realists also treated these subjects, but not with the same pessimism as naturalists. Realism still left room for hope, Dietrichson wrote, but "modern naturalism has eagerly placed itself under the flags of pessimism and is itself suffering from this illness: it is, thus, both its time's child and leader."[28] In his description of human struggle, people turned into animals, and only the strong ones triumphed. His analysis touched on one of the most important subjects in naturalism: in a world where only the strongest survive, according to Darwinism and scientism, how much could an artist really do to save the weak? Was the battle against nature hopeless?

The Danish philosopher and sociologist Claudius Wilkens (1844–1929), in "Modern Naturalism" (1888), offered one of the most fruitful analyses of naturalism and positivism in literature. He proposed an alternative to Zola's version of naturalism. For Wilkens, the difference between realism and naturalism was in the degree of pessimism. He wrote that realism engaged in a "minute, stereoscopic, mirror-like representation of everyday life."[29] When it chose subjects from the darker strata of society and began to criticize their shortcomings, it got closer to naturalism. Wilkens looked at naturalism not only as a literary movement but as a socio-spiritual phenomenon and an accurate reflection of modern currents. In Wilkens's comprehensive text, naturalism was both a symptom and a critique of positivism and science's influence on the world: "Everywhere we breathe the spirit of positivism."[30] Wilkens perceived pessimism as one of the defining features of naturalism—with its lack of belief in the goodness of human nature and the meaningfulness of life, and its exclusive focus on the darkest manifestations of human experience. The naturalist was "the dark side's author,"[31] and in the "shadow of pessimism" grew the gallery of naturalistic characters. Wilkens traced to Zola the story of the generation's dissolution: "A generation becomes a degeneration."[32] He concluded that the reason for the naturalists' interest in the gloomier aspects of society and the coarser parts of heredity (manifested in such sicknesses as syphilis, alcoholism, and madness) was that these were the only visible scientific conditions: "The heredity of the finer spiritual features is impossible to confirm: it can only be guessed."[33] This is why the naturalists often preferred ugliness to beauty and chose as subjects for their paintings the sick, the tired, the anguished, the old, and the worn out, shunning any idealization of life. In his book on modern aesthetics, also published in 1888, Wilkens discussed beauty and ugliness, concluding that the latter was naturalism's domain. Beauty is linked to desire, harmony, and freedom, whereas ugliness highlights pain, disharmony, lack of freedom, impurity, and disorder.[34] Zola himself acknowledged that his representations provided an alternative to the idealism of romanticism: "There is a tinge of the human beast in all of us, as there is a tinge of illness. These young girls who are so pure, these young men who are so loyal, represented to us in certain novels, do not belong to earth; to make them mortal everything must be told. We tell everything, we do not make a choice, neither do we idealize; and this is why they [the critics] accuse us of taking pleasure in obscenity."[35] Zola was, of course, somewhat naïve when he asserted that the naturalists did not make choices, for the latter's preoccupations and subjects were definitely deliberate.

The naturalist, as Wilkens pointed out, was interested in "the animal in man,"[36] exemplified by Zola's *The Beast Within* (1890). It is not a surprise that Wilkens saw naturalism as a continuation of romanticism: he wrote that "French romanticism was pregnant with naturalism."[37] Wilkens saw vitalism—a kind of positive naturalism—as an alternative outcome of naturalism, for it favored health, believed in the powers of the body and its movements, and possessed more humor: "The pessimism will be transformed into a modified optimism."[38] This could be a fitting description for Krohg's paintings of idyllic family life, which replaced his Skagen and Albertine cycles, and of Munch's evolution from depictions of sick people in the 1890s to his healthy, sun-filled canvases in the new century.

Georg Brandes declared in 1889: "Friedrich Nietzsche appears to me to be the most interesting writer in German literature at the present time. Though little known even in his own country, he is a thinker of a high order who fully deserves to be studied, discussed, contested, and mastered. Among his many good qualities is that of imparting his mood to others and setting their thoughts in motion."[39] Friedrich Nietzsche (1844–1900) played a vital role in the intellectual shift of the late 1880s and 1890s and was instrumental in connecting naturalism to symbolism and vitalism. Arne Garborg wrote in 1890 in the Norwegian journal *Samtiden* (paraphrasing Ola Hansson) that while Mill, Darwin, and Taine resembled small waves on the "ocean of development," Nietzsche was the real storm making huge waves.[40] Two years later, in 1892, *Samtiden* published a translation of an article from *Revue bleue* by Téodor de Wyzewa, who stated that Nietzsche was the modern philosopher who more than any other engaged the intellectual imagination of Europe.[41] Nietzsche had been influenced by both Renan and Taine and had sent the latter a copy of *Beyond Good and Evil* (1886), in which he called Taine the greatest living historian. Taine replied that the passage in question "speaks far too flatteringly of myself." This letter, dated October 17, 1886, is full of compliments on Nietzsche's book: "I shall recommend to philosophers what you say upon philosophy, but historians and critics will also find a store of new ideas."[42] Nietzsche's ideas, in fact, influenced artistic reactions against the French realist school. For Nietzsche the scientist was not a hero. Science killed art, whereas only the artist understood the world. Nietzsche's philosophy and aesthetics constituted a critique of modern society; he regarded savants as a sorry, sad, dogmatic, and shortsighted crowd.[43] The scientist was only a myopic specialist, and science an illusion originating in optimistic self-deception.[44] Literary historian Émile Faguet wrote in *En lisant Nietzsche* (1904): "Hear the words of Claude Bernard: 'If I knew any one thing thoroughly, I would know everything.' The explanations of science are therefore always so superficial that they are equivalent to a non-explanation. . . . [S]cience knows nothing."[45]

As he had done with Taine, Nietzsche sent Brandes a copy of *Beyond Good and Evil* in 1886, followed by *The Genealogy of Morals* in 1887, the year they began exchanging letters.[46] Brandes was the first European author to offer a larger introduction of Nietzsche with his article "Aristocratic Radicalism" (1889), though he was soon followed by others. (The Danish journal *Ny Jord* published a translation of seven chapters of Nietzsche's *Zarathustra* that same year.)[47] Ola Hansson published a text on Nietzsche in the German periodical *Unsere Zeit* in 1889, and reissued it as a book in Norwegian in 1890.[48] In 1894 the Swedish literary historian Hellen Lindgren linked Nietzsche to the neo-romantic movement of the 1890s and the vogue for the enigmatic and uncertain. (Crucial to Lindgren's presentation of Nietzsche was the period's catchphrase "Schopenhauer's pessimism.") To Lindgren, Nietzsche's philosophy constituted an important revival of romantic ideas after the tiresome realistic representations of daily life.[49] It is interesting to notice that many contemporaries saw Nietzsche and Taine as related philosophers, for they shared an interest in the primitive, animalistic, and psychological aspects of human life.[50] Lindgren wrote about 1890s Nietzscheanism: "Contemporary man also experiences the need to get out of the sedentary bourgeois life and to do something less specious and more instinctual. An unconquerable longing for danger and strife has arrived. One is attracted to anything that awakens strong passions. . . . The unconscious Nietzschean morals are what manifest themselves among ordinary people."[51]

A remarkable intellectual shift thus occurred around 1890. Radical intellectual journals such as *Tilskueren* and *Samtiden* now wrote about Nietzsche, Darwinism, Alfred Russell Wallace, socialism, anarchism, and mysticism. Science was no longer seen as the right track, and realism and naturalism in art were deemed boring. The scientifically minded realist artist was viewed as a child of the nineteenth century. As the new century dawned, it no longer respected old ideals.[52] The Danish literary historian Valdemar Vedel declared in an article in *Tilskueren* in 1892 that the arts needed new sources of inspiration. He claimed that naturalism had closed people's eyes to positive sides of life, and naturalist art had undermined their resilience. It was now important, according to him, to show that people really were different from how they had been represented in the works of Darwin, Taine, and Zola.[53]

Christian Krohg did not refer to Nietzsche or seem particularly interested in the German philosopher—unlike Brandes, Strindberg, or Munch, who even painted a portrait of Nietzsche in 1906. But Krohg must have been aware of him, especially while living in Berlin in the 1890s and taking part in the *Zum schwarzen Ferkel* circle alongside his aforementioned friends. The change in intellectual climate made Krohg lose interest in naturalism and its scientific, political, and pessimistic manifestations. In his article on impressionism from 1889, one can see that he was now more interested in painterly qualities and personal expression.[54] The hero of his essay, Claude Monet, managed to paint as a human being and not as an artist; he had unlearned his skill as a painter. Monet was, in a way, painting unconsciously, without thinking—just painting. Krohg was interested in this form of naivism; he would later be fascinated by Henri Rousseau and see him as the greatest painter after the impressionists, the next artist to take a step into the future.[55] In the 1889 article Krohg mentioned Paul Gauguin and Armand Guillaumin as artists he admired. He seemed to have lost his social and political ambitions.

THE AGE OF CHARLES DARWIN

Émile Zola mentioned Darwin only briefly in his text on the experimental novel, commenting that he would completely lose himself if he were to engage Darwin's theories.[56] But Darwin's ideas were certainly part of the late nineteenth-century preoccupation with heredity and environment, and they were well known in Scandinavia. It was common to think of the nineteenth century as the Darwinian century. As Arne Garborg declared in his 1882 lecture on naturalism, "It is Darwin who has marked the spirit of the century."[57] Gerhard Gran wrote in an article about Zola the following year that it was "Darwin's century," and described how the worldview had been completely changed. Humans were now seen as part of nature and not above it. He also noted that naturalism in literature was Darwinism.[58] The Danish botanist and author Jens Peter Jacobsen (1847–1885), "the first apostle of Darwinism in Denmark,"[59] introduced Darwin to a wider Scandinavian audience in 1871 with his article "Darwins Theori." Jacobsen translated *The Origin of Species* in 1872 and *The Descent of Man* in 1874–75 and used themes and motifs from Darwin's writing in his novels. Brandes wrote in *Main Currents*, "We, who live in the age of Charles Darwin, no longer accept the possibility of an original state of perfection and a fall. There is no doubt that the teaching of Darwin means the downfall of orthodox ethics, exactly as the teaching of Copernicus meant the downfall of orthodox dogma. The Copernican system deprived the Church heaven of its 'local habitation'; the Darwinian system will despoil the Church of its Paradisiac Eden."[60] Darwin also played a role in Brandes's book on Taine and French aesthetics: "Darwin adds the influential principle of natural selection to the old theories of the influence of habits, climate, and nutrition. Natural selection preserves and collects all the beneficial variations that secure the existence of the species through the trait of heritability and in that way secures for them a final victory in the struggle for life [*Kampen for livet*]."[61]

Krohg's last naturalist project referred to Darwin through its title, *The Struggle for Existence* (1889, fig. 9.1, plate 16). He had worked hard on this subject in many sketches and created several versions. The artwork's title, *Kampen for tilværelsen*, is the usual Norwegian translation of "struggle for existence" or "struggle for life." Darwin had derived his term from Robert Malthus's *Essay on the Principle of Population* (1798) and used it as part of the title of his first important book, *On the Origin of Species by Means of Natural Selection, or the Preservation of Favoured Races in the Struggle for Life* (1859). The title of Jacobsen's 1872 translation was *Om Arternes Oprindelse ved Kvalitetsvalg eller ved de heldigst stillede Formers Sejr i Kampen for Tilværelsen.* In Jacobsen's essay on Darwinism, especially "Parringsvalget" (Selection in relation to sex), the struggle for existence had to do with mating, courtship, and the importance of the sexual drive. Bjørnstjerne Bjørnson claimed that Jacobsen fueled the obsession with sexual desire of Krohg and other Scandinavian novelists in the 1880s.[62] Krohg's 1889 painting, however, addressed a simpler, more general, daily struggle for existence rather than the larger problems of the species. Interestingly, he chose the same title for the four-volume collection of his articles and papers (1920–21), as if it were the motto for his whole oeuvre.

Krohg had studied in an environment where Darwin's ideas were well known and discussed. Max Klinger (1857–1920), his best friend, fellow student, and roommate in Germany in the 1870s, was an avid reader of Darwin and Darwinist writers.[63] Darwinist texts were often published in German journals and newspapers, and Klinger made a drawing called *Darwinian Theory* in 1875. Darwinism must have been a topic of lively conversation in their apartment and school. In the 1870s and 1880s Klinger continued making graphic art that depicted the struggle for life in nature—including conflicts between the sexes. Krohg's Albertine project could be read as having been inspired by Darwinist ideas.

Hans Jæger had harshly criticized Krohg's Albertine project and pronounced it an artistic failure because, in his view, Krohg did not really know the subject he was working on: "Albertine—who is she?—a pale face glimpsed in the gloom and then gone. Where have you seen it, Krohg? You have never been down there. What do *you* know about the life that is lived down in the dark shafts right beneath our feet, where misery lives and people move about, unhappy and longing for sun and air—what do *you* know about it? You have never been down there."[64] Jæger declared that the Albertine project was an example of failed impressionism, since Krohg had never experienced or directly observed what he was depicting in his novel and paintings. Jæger labeled Krohg's art a "guess" and called the large painting nothing more than an atelier work with some brilliantly painted models.[65]

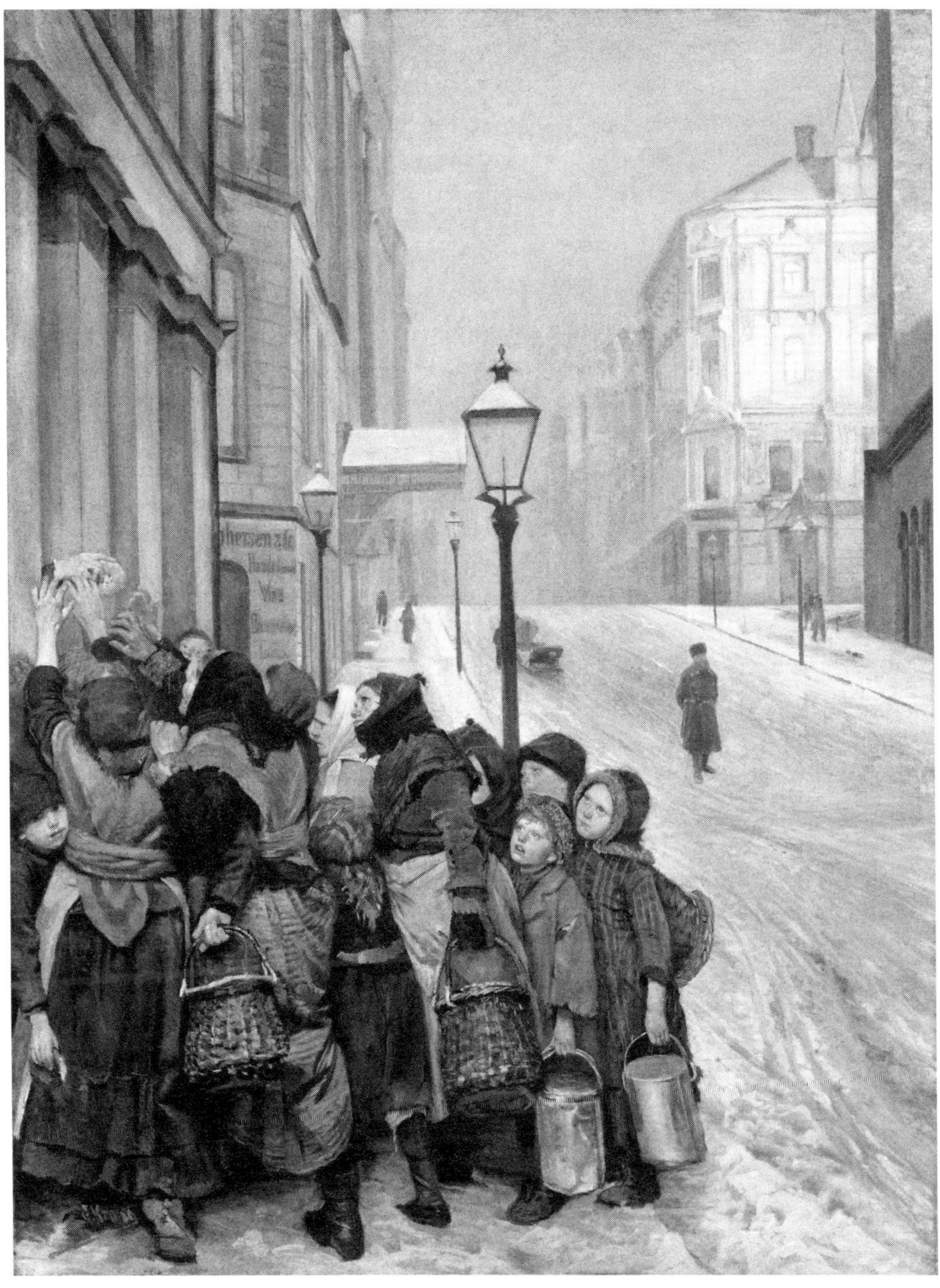

Figure 9.1 (Plate 16). Christian Krohg, *The Struggle for Existence* (1889). Oil on canvas, 300 × 225 cm. Photo: Jacques Lathion/The National Museum of Art, Architecture and Design, Oslo.

It was imperative to Jæger that art and life be the same. Interestingly he called the Albertine theme—the prostitute's struggles—a "struggle for life."[66] He advised Krohg to paint a struggle for existence *he* knew. And this is exactly what Krohg did in his next project, straightforwardly entitled *The Struggle for Existence*. Jæger was aware of it when he wrote his *Albertine* review in 1887: "What you now are about to paint, you have seen. You have stood down there at the corner of Karl Johan Street and Skippergata and observed this line of hungry women and children, where everybody is stretching their thin arms hungrily in the air when the door opens and the bread distribution begins. You have stood there, gripped by this sight, and sworn to yourself that *this* was the image you would present to the public so that they should be gripped by it the same way *you* were."[67]

Krohg's painting depicts a scene taking place along Kristiania's main thoroughfare, Karl Johan Street. A group of poor is getting day-old bread from a baker. These people are desperate, clinging together in the cold winter weather like hungry animals. A policeman—for whom Krohg used himself as a model—is walking down the street. It is unclear whether the policeman threatens the beggars or merely observes them. In any case, the anonymous eyes of the state are present.

Krohg's last naturalist canvas is pessimistic. Human evolution has not made man's conditions better—only worse. Nietzsche expressed the same pessimism in 1888: "Man as a species is not progressing."[68] Krohg's Karl Johan Street painting of hopelessness and desperation was echoed in Edvard Munch's *Evening on Karl Johan Street* (1892, fig. 9.2). This was not the happy world of the buzzing boulevards bathed in sunlight. As Kirk Varnedoe rightly assessed Krohg's *Struggle for Existence* and Munch's *Evening on Karl Johan Street*: "The initially striking dissimilarity of these two works on practically all levels of technique and mood, in fact masks a strong similarity, at point of origin, in structure of conception."[69] Here we see naturalism and symbolism melt together and for a moment overlap. Munch turns his group of figures toward us. Krohg's painting is absorbed in itself. Munch's vision is theatrical and confrontational. Krohg gives visual form to the hard and traumatic life of the lower classes. Munch visualizes the traumas of his own class and milieu, most of all himself, in a personal, subjective experience of the world. As Varnedoe writes, "Here, painting the same street, literally on the other side of the hill, Munch transformed a story of urban cruelty in the third person, Krohg's picture about what others suffer, into a confrontational image of the city in the first person: a picture about what the artist suffers."[70]

Lorentz Dietrichson called Krohg's painting a "parody," since in reality the bread was given away for free and the poor did not have to fight for it. He criticized it for working against all rules of composition: the group of people is lumped together in the corner and appears out of balance, while the empty street is a failure of perspective.[71] The conservative critic in *Aftenposten* wrote that the painting gave a "humorous impression [*humoristisk Indtryk*]."[72] But both Dietrichson and the *Aftenposten* critic seem to miss the point. The painting showed that the world in 1889 was not a better place, and Krohg's message seemed to be that society should take care of those who fall outside it. The painting received a very positive review in the newspaper *Verdens Gang*, whose art critic stated that in this painting Krohg "reaches farther than he has before."[73] He found the image heartbreakingly true and convincing, and praised the way the artist represented the motif with remarkable power and fervency. The Danish art historian Julius Lange described the work in 1892:

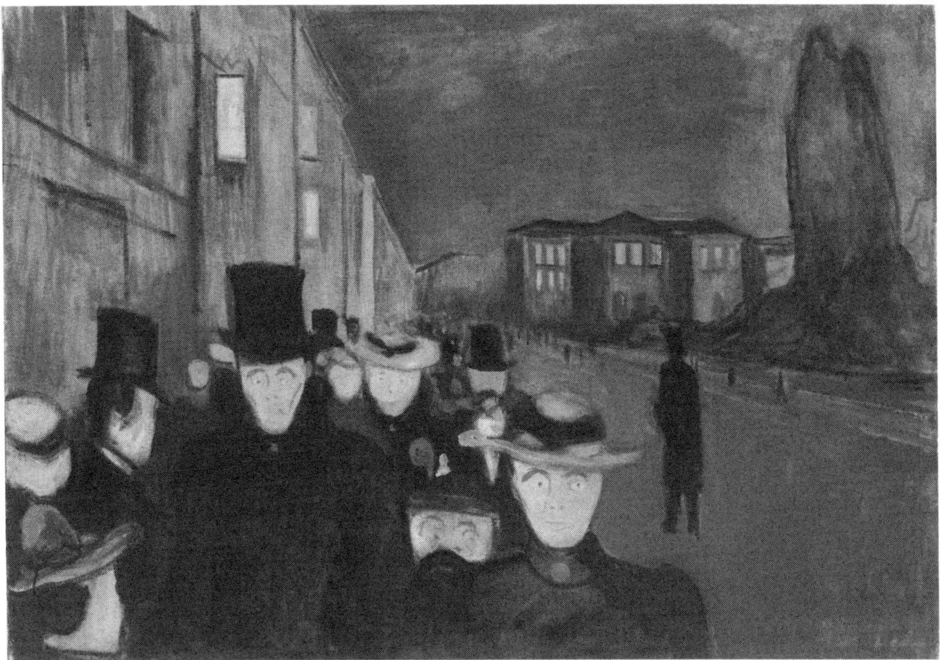

Figure 9.2. Edvard Munch, *Evening on Karl Johan Street* (1892). Oil on canvas, 84.5 × 121 cm. Photo: Dag Fosse/KODE—Art Museums of Bergen, Rasmus Meyer Collection.

> The treatment of the image is broad, energetic and bold, and the figures' expressions are superbly felt: the little girl who is pushed all the way to the back of the group is an image of resigned and fervent expectation; the boy at her side with the unhealthy complexion and the greedy glance of one fantasizing about warm wheat bread—his mouth is watering and he wants to throw himself like a wolf on the prey when his time comes; the women are reaching out and sending prayers and hungry glances to the goddess Ceres who is handing out her gifts. It is the fervor of hunger, which comes from the stomach. It is neither as beautiful nor as deep as the one originating from the heart. Even though old Odysseus was right when he said that nothing is as insensible to disgrace as the stomach, so its hunger can still be satisfied from day to day, while the heart's hunger just grows and grows continuously. But the fervor of hunger has—God help us—a very big place in real life; and if art seriously wants to penetrate those forces that are at work in contemporary life and society, then it will undoubtedly also notice hunger, that large ugly vulture with glowing eyes and sharp claws.[74]

This description of humans as animals (the beast in man) and the interest in human instinct were typical of naturalism. Taine paved the way for this focus on the irrational in man and on the role of underlying unconscious structures, or forces, in shaping human beings. Zola was profoundly engaged with these issues. In the preface to the second edition of *Thérèse Raquin* (1868), he wrote that his aim "has been to study temperaments and not characters. That is the whole point of the book."[75] Zola's goal was to look at the characters as human animals and nothing more: "I have endeavored to follow these animals through the devious working of their passions, the compulsion of their instincts, and the mental unbalance resulting from a nervous crisis."[76] Zola wanted to "uncover the animal side" through a scientific approach. Krohg's *Struggle for Existence* must be read as a critique of social Darwinism, and it might also be a confession of the failure of modern society and capitalism. The positivist's dream also consists of many nightmares. Darwinist views of the relationship between man and nature played a major role in the thoughts and works of Krohg and his contemporaries: if man is a beast, should he fight the beast in himself?

Naturalism took as its subject the darker sides of society. A naturalist image had a scientific, political, or ethical mission as it documented modern society. It was an art about human dignity and its loss, free will and the fight against determinism. At its best, it was about animalist instincts and human ethics, sexuality, and class. Symbolism moved farther into the personal and psychological territory and explored sexuality and instinct in new visual languages. Naturalism paved the way for symbolism, as can be seen in the artistic relationship between Krohg and Munch and the evolution of the latter's art. Krohg was interested not in "moods" but in the observation of the world, and once the predominant trend shifted away from naturalism, he was, in a sense, "painted out" of the place he used to occupy in art and had no interest in adopting symbolism. Instead, he went on to engage with everyday life around him, in paintings of family and friends and journalistic writings.

Epilogue

Naturalism Is Dead, Long Live Naturalism!

In his writings, Krohg mentioned both Bastien-Lepage and Zola as important naturalists but criticized them for being too focused on details: Bastien-Lepage in how he painted texture and fabrics, Zola in his overly detailed descriptions of scenes. Krohg wrote about Bastien-Lepage: "Bastien-Lepage painted each fold and each wrinkle of the skin, it was as if one could touch it and feel every little shape, even the smallest form—especially the smallest form."[1] About Zola, Krohg commented: "And when Zola is describing a Parisian evening mood, he starts to mention every building and every church tower, and if he is telling about the smells in Les Halles, he mentions every kind of smell, he dissects the smell."[2] Krohg thought that this focus on details did not really create an image of the time, but merely gave the reader or the viewer an assemblage of minutiae. But there was one artist who managed to move beyond Bastien-Lepage's and Zola's detailed realism to adequately present an image of the time: "And then came Manet—the French painter Manet."[3] To Krohg, Manet was the only artist who knew no authorities:

> *Manet* wanted the same as the realists, he wanted to depict the time in which he lived, but he understood and was aware that it was not enough to imitate nature, and it was impossible to *make* nature. One first had to learn to see it, dare to see it with one's own eye and with the eye of the time, and then paint what one had seen as freshly as possible, so that each brushstroke was colored by one's *goal*, and one of *the most fundamental things was to stop*—not to paint more than what one saw. One ought not to look for something.[4]

Krohg wrote that the artist's work was "not about painting as much as possible, but as little as possible."[5]

The critique of Zola's extreme thoroughness of detail is often repeated.[6] Eugène Véron stated in his *Æsthetics* (1878) that "however important we may consider absolute truth, we are not obliged to tell everything. . . . There can be no art without selection; and upon such selection the total impression must always depend. Some of the descriptions of M. Zola remind us of pictures in which the painter, from sheer ignorance of what should be left out, has finished by compromising the truth of everything. Everything is there, but there is no salient point."[7] The Norwegian journalist Johan Vibe, in his 1884 book about Zola, wrote a whole chapter about the writer's obsession with detail. He presented long quotes from Zola's novels and showed how meticulously the French author described his scenes. Vibe opined that Zola tried to be a painter instead of a writer—and that his attempt could never succeed. A literary description could never compete with a painting of real life—it could never give the same experience.[8] Krohg agreed with this view, which is why he claimed that painting was more fitting as a naturalistic art form than was literature. (It was the only thing on which Krohg and Vibe agreed.)

Krohg lost interest in Zola and Bastien-Lepage by the end of the 1880s, commenting, "First I tried to paint like Bastien-Lepage, then like the Impressionists. I wanted to be part of the radical program."[9] His encounter with Manet's art freed Krohg from detail-obsessed naturalism—and, actually, from naturalism in general. His brushstrokes became broader and his colors brighter. The motifs no longer came from the darker sides of society, nor were they filled with political and moral messages. As he said, he wanted to be part of the radical program, and in the 1890s post-impressionist artistic ideas were seen as radical. As Krohg rejected the models of Bastien-Lepage and Zola and turned toward formalist aesthetics and the materiality of painting—to form over content—he moved away from naturalism. But this did not mean that naturalism in art was dead.

PHOTOGRAPHY AS THE DEFINITIVE NATURALIST ART

Carl Gustaf Estlander, a Finnish professor of aesthetics and comparative literature, opened his 1891 book *Naturalismen enligt Zola* (Naturalism according to Zola) with these words: "Now that naturalism seems surely over . . . it is time to begin investigating what its task has been in art and art history."[10] By 1891 it was clear that naturalism belonged to the past. As Lilian R. Furst and Peter N. Skrine wrote in their small book *Naturalism* (1971), it had been an extremist movement: "The theories of Naturalism, if taken literally, amount in fact to a formidable anti-aesthetics in their deliberate exclusion of the creative power of the artist's individual imagination."[11] Of course, naturalist artists like Zola and Krohg did not follow their own theories slavishly—this is also one of Estlander's points. Slowly, perhaps without knowing it, the naturalists departed from their aesthetic agendas. Around 1890 they moved toward a more subjective art: symbolism and expressionism. Zola wrote *Une page d'amour* (1878); Ibsen, *When We Dead Awaken* (1899); and Strindberg, *Dream Play* (1901). On the Norwegian art scene, Edvard Munch's symbolism garnered a great deal of attention—mostly with Krohg's support.

Many historians have argued for the existence of various modernisms and realisms. Raymond Williams suggested that there were also many naturalisms. Unlike Estlander, he did not claim that naturalism ended by 1891, but rather argued that it took a new form. According to Williams (under the influence of August Strindberg), naturalism strove to express the experience of reality, and this impulse could take many shapes:

> For it is clear, in practice, that naturalism means several different things. In its widest sense, it is an absorbed interest in the contemporary everyday world, and a corresponding rejection or exclusion of any supposed external design or system

of values. It is, then, an absorbed recreation of the ways in which people, within human limits, actually speak, feel, think, behave, act. By these criteria, many of the supposed rejections of naturalism are in fact variations of it. Conventions are changed, not because some other view of the world, or some other creative purpose is now proposed, but because existing conventions are no longer *true enough*, by essentially similar criteria. It must be obvious that what is meant by "rejection of naturalism" is ordinarily a rejection of its earliest particular conventions.[12]

He continues by quoting Strindberg, who contrasts "false naturalism, which believes that art consists simply of sketching a piece of nature in a natural manner; . . . [and] true naturalism, which seeks out those points in life where the great conflicts occur, which rejoices in seeing what cannot be seen every day."[13] Naturalism was an aesthetic and philosophical attitude, not a technique, a style, or an artistic convention. The driving force behind naturalism was not realistic reproduction of the world, but, according to Williams, "a passion for truth, in strictly human and contemporary terms."[14] In the search for this truth, old conventions were rejected. From this perspective, symbolism and early expressionism constituted not a break with naturalism, but rather its continuation: "What was still, in the patient reproduction of naturalism, a self-evidently man-made world, is now a phantasmagoria, a hostile projection, a parody of order. Out of this structure of feeling—in historical terms, out of the failure of bourgeois revolt against bourgeois society—comes a new confidence: a confidence of despair."[15] Both traditional naturalism and psychological expressionism were, for Williams, historically connected structures of feeling. This makes a lot of sense if we compare Munch to Krohg.

Williams's main point is that there was never a real break in naturalism. I would not, however, call symbolism and expressionism versions of naturalism. Rather, I would suggest that naturalism as an aesthetic power—an ambition to document one's own time in an uncomplicated visual language with a special interest in the darker sides of society—continued to exist in art, but in the medium of photography. Photography was technical, scientific, and objective, and it gave a convincingly real image of the world; it was based not on the artist's inner emotions and subjectivity, but on outer reality. Naturalism strove to document the hidden sides of its own time in an aesthetically meaningful way, but not in the detached manner of pure journalism or scientific documentation. Photography offered a perfect combination of art and science.

Naturalism and photography already had a shared history before the 1890s. In fact, Lorentz Dietrichson claimed that naturalism and impressionism would look different—have other forms—if photography had not come into existence.[16] He saw impressionism as a child of the snapshot aesthetic, and photographic influences made both naturalism and impressionism different from earlier realisms. The photograph became an important tool for naturalists. They used it because of its objective accuracy and potential to avoid or bypass style. The photographic image became a metaphor for being modern and scientific. A tool that intersected different worlds, it was used by naturalist artists, law enforcement authorities, and scientists, among others.[17] Photography inspired artists to experiment with perspective, composition, and cropping. Krohg used photography as a tool in painting, but he was intent on making his pictures look like paintings, not like colored, blown-up photographs. He accomplished this through his imaginative cropping of scenes, surprising perspectives, and visible brush strokes.

The relationship between painting and photography had been one of the main issues in realism, impressionism, and naturalism. The Swedish art historian Georg Nordensvan wrote in 1900 that the realistic study of nature has often been called photographic art or the transcript of nature. Photography had indeed exercised an immense influence on the art of the 1870s and 1880s,

> but the camera gave abstract images of reality and never a personal impression, and it is primarily the personal perception that makes a picture of nature into a work of art. Taine, in his *Philosophie de l'art,* had already emphasized that the artist's task when studying nature is to present an object's "caractère essentiel," and that to stress this determining character, he must overlook or exclude superfluous elements that would interfere with the essential character. The photograph has thus helped us sharpen our eye for those elements that the camera itself *cannot* correctly render in its soulless interpretation of reality. The photograph uncritically and thoughtlessly gathers everything into an image without differentiating between the main and the secondary subject. The artist, on the other hand, *chooses*, he sees nature through his temperament.[18]

Nordensvan was echoing a view presented by Claudius Wilkens some years earlier, when he discussed realism, objectivity, and photography: "But this reality principle should not be construed as meaning that the artist must be a photographer who only copies reality or possesses a copying temperament that only mirrors with his soul the documents of human life. The Zolaesque doctrine that an artwork is a piece of reality mirrored in a temperament is, as his own examples show, incorrect or vague."[19] Wilkens's point was that the artist's imagination moves beyond reality and an inner truth could also be found in mythical works. The relationship between naturalism and photography was complex, entailing a negotiation between photographic objectivity and artistic subjectivity. A naturalist painting as a whole did not look like a single photograph, but rather, as Krohg's large Albertine painting demonstrates, consisted of smaller photographs, life studies, and artistic imagination.[20]

Despite the criticism of photography as unartistic, many photographers continued the naturalist tradition. This was convincingly demonstrated when the Danish-born photographer Jacob A. Riis (1849–1914) published *How the Other Half Lives* in 1890. Riis, a contemporary of Krohg, made the subject of his book the hidden slum life of New York City. It was a work composed of journalistic texts illustrated with photographs and drawings based on photographs. Riis used many of his photos, often taken with the new flash technology, in slide shows he projected during his lectures on New York slums. The extreme realism of these pictures powerfully affected the beholders, making them feel sympathy for the poor. Photographs such as *Street Arabs at Night, Mulberry Street* (1890), and *Sewing and Starving in an Elizabeth Street Attic* (1890) were deeply moving. Riis's work clearly demonstrates that around 1890, photography naturally and logically took the baton from naturalist painting.

Many other photographers of the same generation were part of this trend, notably Alfred Stieglitz and Peter Henry Emerson. Emerson's widely read book *Naturalistic Photography*

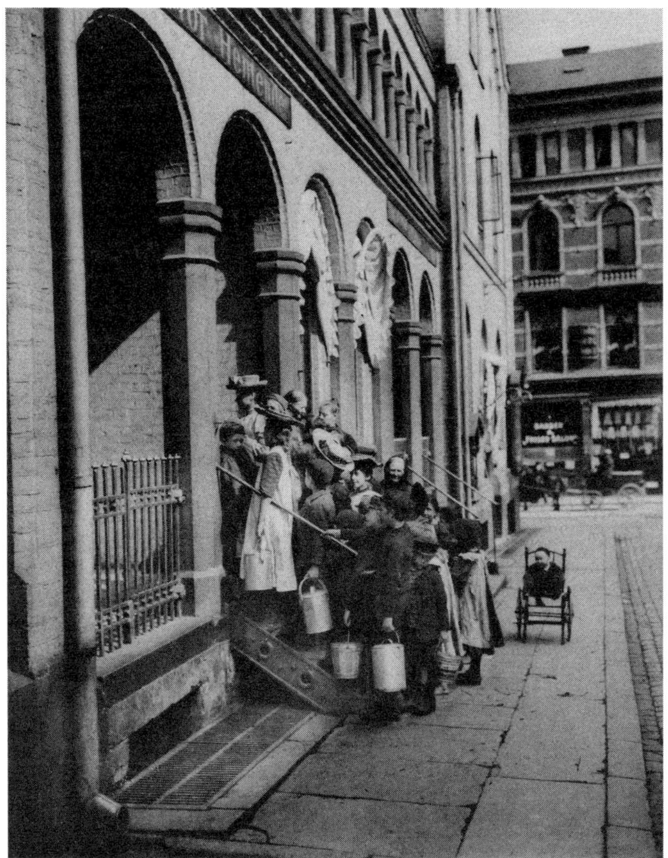

Figure E.1.

Anders Beer Wilse, *In Line for Food* (1907). Photo: Anders B. Wilse/ Oslo Museum.

for Students of the Art in 1889 discussed extensively the relationship between painting and photography, and the ways they influenced one another. He advised young photographers to make yearly pilgrimages to the Salon in Paris, and among the naturalist painters he especially praised Lhermitte and Breton.[21] Emerson's own photographic works were strikingly close to the rural naturalism of these two French painters.

In Norway, the photographer Anders Beer Wilse (1865–1949) demonstrated the same shift. His set out to document all parts of Norwegian society in careful detail, and many of his pictures resembled Krohg's paintings: Wilse's *In Line for Food* (1907, fig. E.1), for example, is very close to Krohg's *Struggle for Existence*. Wilse knew Krohg personally and was quite familiar with his work. He had photographed many of Krohg's paintings and made several photographic portraits of him. In fact, Krohg based several self-portraits on these photographs. Krohg owned a camera in the 1890s, most likely a Krügener Taschenbuch, and his assistant, Carl Brunskow, took many photos to be used both as models for Krohg's compositions and as actual painting surfaces. (Andreas Aubert even commented in 1890 that some of Krohg's paintings had an unpleasant flavor of photography.)[22] These experiments engaging photography were natural developments for the post-naturalist Krohg.[23] But this is another chapter in his art, and it falls outside the scope of this book.

Notes

ACKNOWLEDGMENTS

Epigraph: Hippolyte Taine, *The Philosophy of Art*, trans. John Durand (New York: Holt and Williams, 1873), 37–38. Durand's translation is here slightly modified. Original: "La méthode modern que je tâche de suivre, et qui commence à s'introduire dans toutes les sciences morales, consiste à considérer les œuvres humaines, et en particulier les œuvres d'art, comme des faits et des produits dont il faut marquer les caractères et chercher les causes; rien de plus. Ainsi comprise, la science ne proscrit ni ne pardonne; elle constate et explique. Elle ne vous dit pas: 'Méprisez l'art hollandais, il est trop grossier, et ne goûtez que l'art italien.' Elle ne vous dit pas non plus: 'Méprisez l'art gothique, il est maladif, et ne goûtez que l'art grec.' Elle laisse à chacun la liberté de suivre ses prédilections particulières, de préférer ce qui est conforme à son tempérament, et d'étudier avec un soin plus attentif ce qui correspond le mieux à son propre esprit." Hippolyte Taine, *Philosophie de l'art*, vol. 1 (Paris: Hachette, 1895), 14–15.

INTRODUCTION

1 Guillermo Ferrero, "Er vi syge?," *Samtiden* 4 (1893): 362. Original: "Lærde, digtere, kunstnere, alle, som tænker og producerer, henter sine inspirationer og sit stof fra degenerationens former."
2 Ibid., 363. Original: "De er brødre, og saaledes kan man forklare den gjensidige beundring, de nærer for hverandre, og som sant at sige ikke er ganske uden egoisme, Taines beundring for Lombroso, Lombrosos beundring for Zola, Ibsen, Flaubert, Dostojewskij, Taine; Zolas beundring for Lombroso. De har allesammen, uden at vide det, arbeidet paa det samme arbeide, det vil sige paa at opreise det store mindesmærke over dette *fin-de-siècle's* degeneration, som for det 19de aarhundredes historieskrivere vil være et af de merkligste fænomener."
3 Henrik Jæger, *Kristiania og Kristianienserne* (Kristiania: F. Beyers, 1890), ch. 1.
4 I am inspired by the methodological perspective presented in George Levine, *Darwin and the Novelists: Patterns of Science in Victorian Fiction* (Cambridge, MA: Harvard University Press, 1988), 3.
5 I am paraphrasing ibid., 13.
6 "Modern French Painting," *Art Critic* 1, no. 2 (1894): 28.
7 Christian Brinton, "Introduction," in *Scandinavian Art Illustrated*, ed. Carl Laurin, Emil Hannover, and Jens Thiis (New York: American-Scandinavian Foundation, 1922), 30.
8 Ibid., 11.

9 T.J., "Exposition Universelle des Beaux-Arts d'Anvers," *Courrier de l'art* 5 (1885): 361. Original long quote: "Chose curieuse, il y a dans ce petit recoin du nord de l'Europe un sentiment artistique vivement et profondément marqué, mais qui n'a pu, jusqu'à présent, trouver chez les peintres norvégiens une expression bien caractéristique de la race et des mœurs . . . et que Paris voit accourir, des parages du pôle nord, une nuée d'affamés du 'plein air.' Les impressionnistes, les naturalistes, et jusqu'aux impossibilistes ont là des fervents passionnés: les plus grandes audaces de Manet sont de timides tentatives à côté de certaines toiles de M. Krohg et de M. Wentzel."

10 *Exposition Universelle des Beaux-Arts 1885, catalogue général, première partie: Belgique—Autriche—Espagne—France—Hollande—Norvège—Suisse* (Anvers: J.-E. Buschmann, 1885).

11 Louis Edmond Duranty, "Suède. Norvège. Danemark. Russie," in *L'art moderne à l'exposition de 1878*, ed. Louis Gonse (Paris: A. Quantin, 1879), 130. Original: "Dans ces régions du Nord, nous nous trouvons en face des phénomènes de la nature. La peinture y est tant soit peu météorologique. Des montagnes rouges, des cascades vertes, des rochers bleus, des soleils noirs, en un mot, toutes sortes de dérangements, de renversements et de bouleversements des choses y constituent un genre antipictural, antiharmonieux, qui trouble beaucoup les yeux et l'esprit, quoiqu'il puisse enrichir de faits curieux un traité d'optique."

12 Maurice Hamel, "La peinture du Nord," *Gazette des Beaux-Arts* 38 (1888): 403. Original: "M. Krohg, lui, n'est pas un silencieux, mais un tempérament tout en dehors épris de force et d'action. Il connaît le mer et les marins, la lutte de l'homme et du flot. Ses coins de bateaux hardiment découpés, avec le barreur qui s'enlève en force sur la mer ou sur le ciel, bien lancés dans leur mouvement, font deviner la vague, le roulis et le tangage presque sans les montrer. Très original d'effet, et largement brossé ce matelot sortant à mi-corps de l'entrepont pour observer le temps qui fraichit. Le coloris souvent rêche s'assouplit à l'occasion pour peindre une petite pécheuse charmante sous une fraîche lumière de printemps. Ce violent a de jolies tendresses de pinceau."

13 André Michel, "Af *Journal des Débats*, 27de August 1889," in *Beretninger om Norges Deltagelse i Verdensudstillingen i Paris 1889* (Christiania: W. C. Fabritius, 1891), xxxxvi. Translated from the Norwegian version: "Deres lille Flok danner i vort gamle Europa en af de mest homogene og mest livskraftige Skoler, inden hvilken forresten hver Gruppe, Nordmændenes, Svenskernes og Danskernes—og man kan dertil føie Finlænderne—bevarer sit selvstændige Fysiognomi."

14 Maurice Hamel, "Danemark. Suède. Norvège. Finlande. Russie. Suisse," in *Exposition universelle de 1889: Les beaux-arts et les arts décoratifs*, ed. Louis Gonse and Alfred de Lostalot (Paris: Journal de Temps, 1889), 228. Original: "L'art n'étant que l'expression idéale du rêve de bonheur que fait chaque groupe humain, les conditions de la vie sociale le déterminent aussi bien que les milieux naturels, et l'on observera que le naturalisme familier du Nord revêt des aspects différents dans trois pays tout proches par les origines, la religion et la langue."

15 A number of French reviews of the Universal Exhibition 1889 are collected and translated into Norwegian in *Beretninger om Norges Deltalgelse*, xxxxiii–xxxxx.

16 Georges Lafanestre, "Af Indberetningen fra den internationale Jury for Klasse 1 og 2 (Maleri og Tegninger)," in *Beretninger om Norges Deltagelse*, xxxxiv. Translated from the Norwegian version: "Her er der en hel Gruppe af virkelig individuelle, overbeviste, interessante Kunstnere, der fra sit Hjemland bringe os saa meget Eiendommeligt og Fængslende."

17 Charles Ponsonailhe, *Les artistes scandinaves à Paris* (Paris: Grande Revue/Nilson, 1889),

5. Original: "La Suède, la Norvège et le Danemark, libres de traditions picturales, peuples tout palpitants d'une belle et féconde jeunesse, ont eu tôt fait de peser l'inanité de l'enseignement académique; sans hésitation aucune, ils ont adopté le plein-airisme qui était à la fois d'accord avec leur raison et leur tempérament."

18 Ibid., 27. Original: "La Norvège reste un peuple plus autonome, ayant gardé un accent très personnel, un peu rude, mais point banal." The author doesn't write much about Krohg, but adds on page 29: "La mère veillant son fils, la vieille cousant près de son mari, qui goûte la sieste, prouvent un superbe tempérament de peintre chez M. C. Krogh [*sic*]. Qu'il apprenne son métier, débarbouille sa couleur, cette lourde pâte,—rappelant avec plus de vigueur le genre de M. van Strydonck;—qu'il pousse plus loin que l'ébauche, et il obtiendra tous nos applaudissements."

19 Maurice Hamel, *The Salons of 1902*, trans. Paul Villars (Paris: Goupil, 1902), 67.

20 Ibid., 68. Krohg's *The Pilot* was also mentioned in *Le petit Parisien*, March 29, 1902.

21 Brinton, "Introduction," 30.

22 Thor J. Mednick, "Danish Internationalism: Peder Severin Krøyer in Copenhagen and Paris," *Nineteenth Century Art Worldwide* 10, no. 1 (2011): n.p., http://www.19thc-artworldwide.org/spring11/danish-internationalism-peder-severin-kroyer-in-copenhagen-and-paris, accessed June 3, 2014.

23 Brian Dudley Barrett, *Artists on the Edge: The Rise of Coastal Artists' Colonies 1880–1920* (Amsterdam: Amsterdam University Press, 2010), 54.

24 Eva Bonnier, *Pariserbref* (Stockholm: Klara, 1999), 107. Original: "Norrmännen äro dock de enda af skandinaverna, som försöka hålla tillsammans."

25 Patricia G. Berman, *In Another Light: Danish Painting in the Nineteenth Century* (London: Thames and Hudson, 2013), 11.

26 "Introduction," in *European and Nordic Modernisms*, ed. Mats Jansson, Jakob Lothe and Hannu Riikonen (Norwich: Norvik Press, 2004), 12–13. Literary historian Elisabeth Oxfeldt has also shown how Scandinavian literature(s) are unique responses to French impulses, and she brilliantly discusses the complex relations between self-other and centers-peripheries. Elisabeth Oxfeldt, *Nordic Orientalism: Paris and the Cosmopolitan Imagination 1800–1900* (Copenhagen: Museum Tusculanum Press, 2005), 9–20.

27 Berman, *In Another Light*, 8.

28 Toril Moi, *Henrik Ibsen and the Birth of Modernism: Art, Theater, Philosophy* (Oxford: Oxford University Press, 2008), 3.

29 Ibid., 26–30.

30 Hollis Clayson, "*Avant Garde* and *Pompier* Images of 19th Century French Prostitution: The Matter of Modernism, Modernity and Social Ideology," in *Modernism and Modernity: The Vancouver Conference Papers*, ed. Benjamin H. D. Buchloh, Serge Guilbaut, and David H. Solkin (Halifax: Press of the Nova Scotia College of Art and Design, 2004), 61.

31 Michael Fried, "Caillebotte's Impressionism," *Representations* 66 (1999): 2.

32 Ibid., 16.

33 Kirk Varnedoe, *Gustave Caillebotte* (New Haven, CT: Yale University Press, 2000), 14.

34 Fried, "Caillebotte's Impressionism," 28.

1. CHRISTIAN KROHG, THE RADICAL NATURALIST

Epigraphs: Georg Brandes, *Levned: Et Tiaar* (Copenhagen: Gyldendalske, 1907), 296. Original: "Han havde paa Ungdommens Vis Munden fuld af Teorier, og søgte den yderligste gaaende Synsmaade op for at vedkende sig den." Bjørn Bjørnson, *Bare ungdom* (Oslo: Aschehoug, 1934),

54. Original: "Hans skråsikre urokkelighet imponerte mig meget. Jeg har aldri møtt nogen som mere finpusset og blankt holdt sine meninger og sin fanatisme frem i lyset som han gjorde det." Julius Lange, "Norsk, svensk, dansk Figurmaleri: Indtryk og Overvejelser," *Tilskueren* 9 (1892): 252. Original: "Som Forfatter—jeg mener endog blot som Forfatter om Kunst—er han som bekendt en Fanatiker, ja en sand Muhammedaner for Modernismen, og det er Modernisme, der er drevet til en saa tankeløs Yderlighed, at den ikke kan gaa ti Skridt hen av Landevejen uden at falde over sine egne Ben. Han synes for Alvor at tro, at Menneskehedens Udvikling og Arbejde kan gaa saaledes for sig, at Nu'et idelig løsriver sig fra sin Fortid og vender sig fuldstændig vragende mod det nærmest forudgaaende for at funkle i isoleret Herlighed og atter straks igjen at slukkes."

1 The term is borrowed from Maurice Bigeon's book *Les révoltés scandinaves* (Paris: L. Grasilier, 1894), dedicated "au maître" Émile Zola, in which Bigeon wrote about people such as Georg Brandes, August Strindberg, and Henrik Ibsen.

2 Quoted in Oscar Thue, *Christian Krohg* (Oslo: Aschehoug, 1997), 55. Thaulow wrote in a letter to Eilif Peterssen in January 1880: "Christian og jeg ere nok til en Del Rædsel for de gode Borgere, vi male Posthushjørner, øvre Volds etc. og existere i Publicums Bevisthed som et Firma, der skrives Krohg og Th. og har sat sig til Opgave at iritere den gode Smag."

3 Lorentz Dietricson, *Svundne Tider af en Forfatters Livserindringer*, vol. 4 (Christiania: Cappelen, 1917), 298.Original: "Maleren Christian Krohg, som, da Jæger forsvandt fra Skuepladsen, blev den ledende Kraft paa denne vor sociale Radicalismes yderste venstre Fløj."

4 Andreas Aubert, *Aftenposten*, November 1, 1884.

5 Andreas Aubert, "Manet: Et Bidrag til Sujetets og Koloritens Historie i den nyere Tid," *Tilskueren* 5 (1888): 670.

6 Quoted in Mette Bøgh Jensen, *At male sit privatliv: Skagensmalernes selviscenesættelse* (Skagen: Skagens Museum, 2005), 53. Original: "Krohg kom lige fra Max Klingers Kreds og var aller radikalest paa alle Omraader."

7 Olaf Hansson, "Krohgs og Werenskiolds Maleriudstilling," *Dagbladet*, March 22, 1885. Original: "Djærvere og djærvere er han bleven, og det baade i Valget af sine Motiver og i Udførelsen."

8 Ibid. Original: "Med større og større Intensitet og med barmhjertig Sandhed har han gjennen en Række Kunstværker af høj Rang fremstillet Kampen for Livet."

9 Carl G. Laurin, *Nordisk konst: Danmarks och Norges konst från 1880 till 1925* (Stockholm: Norstedt, 1925), 228. Original: "Som 80-talets målare är han i hela Norden den, som bäst givit oss vad perioden önskade få sagt, och han har i sin över ett halvt sekel räckande produktion i vissa avseende gjort den största konstnärliga insatsen i nordisk konst." See also Carl G. Laurin, *Stamfränder* (Stockholm: Norstedt, 1925), 209–10.

10 Laurin, *Nordisk konst*, 238.

11 Eilif Peterssen, "Christian Krohg og Antwerpenerudstillingen," *Aftenposten* September 3, 1885. Original: "Enhver, som har fulgt vor Kunst med Interesse, ved hvor isoleret Krohg staar med sit Talent—mere end nogen anden maaske."

12 Hans Jæger, "Tre lyse billeder fra universitetet og et sort," in *Bohem mot Borger: Et utvalg fra Hans Jægers og Christian Krohgs "Impressionisten,"* ed. Anne Siri Bryhni (Oslo: Universitetsforlaget, 1971), 131.

13 For more on Krohg's study days in Berlin see Nils Ohlsen, "Christian Krohg's Student Years in Berlin," in *Christian Krohg: Bilder som griper/Pictures That Captivate*, ed. Vibeke

Waallaann Hansen, Erik Mørstad, Birgitte Sauge, and Marianne Yvenes (Oslo: Nasjonalmuseet for Kunst, Arkitektur og Design, 2012), 175–87.

14 Adolf Rosenberg, *Geschichte der Modernen Kunst*, vol. 3 (Leipzig: Fr. Wilh. Grunow, 1889), 233. Original: “Noch nie zuvor war in der deutschen Malerei ein so kühner, rücksichtsloser Realist aufgetreten, welcher der Natur so energisch zu Leibe ging, wie Gussow, und der in seinem Bestreben, der Natur möglichst nahe zu kommen, vor dem Hässlichsten nicht zurückschreckte, wofür der ‘Blumenfreund’, ein alter Mann mit kupferfarbenem Angesicht, der seine Blumentöpfe auf dem Fensterbrett besichtige, ein drastisches Zeugniss ablegte.”

15 The letter is quoted in Thue, *Christian Krohg*, 26.

16 Ohlsen, “Christian Krohg’s student years,” 181.

17 See Thue, *Christian Krohg*, 45.

18 *Verdens Gang*, January 19, 1884. Original: “Hans Billede vakte stor Opsigt blandt Kunstnerne og i Pressen og blev regnet blandt de beste Billeder paa Salonen det Aar.”

19 “Salon de 1882,” *Courrier de l’art*, June 15, 1882. Original: “De beaucoup un des meilleurs tableaux du Salon.”

20 L. Gastine, “Salon de 1882,” *La presse*, May 22, 1882.

21 Krohg wrote in a letter to Julius Middelthun, dated June 2, 1882, from Grez-par-Nemours, that Goupil had gotten the reproduction rights but that he had not received any payment for it or for a drawing that he made for an art journal. The letter is quoted in Thue, *Christian Krohg*, 208n70.

22 Paul Leroi, “Salon de 1882,” *L’art : Revue hebdomadaire illustré* 29, no. 2 (1882): 153. Original: “M. Christian Krohg, né à Christiania, débute au Salon par un coup de maître. Je ne parle pas de *Mer calme*, œuvre insignifiante qu’il était parfaitement inutile d’envoyer, mais de *Bâbord!* morceau excellent à louer sans restriction aucune.

La mer est mauvaise; on la devine plutôt qu’on ne la voit; le capitaine, représenté à mi-corps—grandeur nature—se penche à bâbord et commande la manœuvre d’un geste résolu. L’expression du visage, la vérité du mouvement, l’accent du dessin, la largeur de la touche d’une sûreté impeccable, l’harmonie de l’ensemble composé d’un bouquet de gris d’une extrême finesse se fondant dans une gamme blonde d’une coloration exquise, tout concourt à faire de la toile du peintre norwégien une œuvre d’élite.

Bâbord! est bien mieux qu’un tableau de genre. C’est une page puissante détachée du poème de la mer.”

23 In 1884 he showed one painting, titled *Digestion,* in the catalog. See *Explication des ouvrages de peinture, sculpture, architecture, gravure et lithographie* (Paris: Bernard, 1884), 120. This work is today known as *Sleeping Mother* (1883). *Courrier de l’art* has March 28, 1884, a list of artworks sent to the Salon, and among them, a work by Krohg titled *L’enfant malade*. This painting is today known as *Mother at Her Child’s Bed* (1884), and it was refused. See Andreas Aubert, “Breve fra Parisersalonen,” *Aftenposten*, May 7, 1884.

24 *Catalogue illustré du Salon de 1902* (Paris: Baschet, 1902), xvii, illustrated on page 66.

25 Krohg continued to paint the hard life at sea for the rest of his life. His large series of marine paintings about life and death could also be seen as a naturalistic project, but this group of works is so complex and extensive in its own right that it falls outside the scope of this study.

26 Erik Werenskiold, “Christian Krohg,” *Samtiden* 36 (1925): 531.

27 For more on this, see Kirk Varnedoe, “Christian Krohg and Edvard Munch,” *Arts Magazine* 53, no. 8 (1979): 88–95.

28 Erik Werenskiold, *Kunst—Kamp—Kultur* (Kristiania: Cammermeyers, 1917), 64.

29 Varnedoe, "Christian Krohg," 88.

30 Quoted in Sixten Strömbom, *Konstnärsförbundets historia*, vol. 1 (Stockholm: Bonnier, 1945), 159. Original: "Här i Grèz-sur-Loing, under dessa sorglösa och roliga vårdagar är det Krohgs lilla porträtt av mig (nu i Nasjonalgalleriet, Oslo) kommit till. Vi hade båda nyss studerat impressionismkonst på en utställning i Paris och hade hjärnorna fulla av de nya, starka intrycken. Krohg såg mig nu efteråt en dag stå där i det öppna fönstret till mitt rum, i den blå kostymen mot den solbelysta trädgården därutanför. Han bad mig ivrigt stå stilla i min pose, sprang efter en duk och de andra remedierna och om några ögonblick var arbetet utan vidare i full gång."

31 Karl Madsen, "Foraarsudstillingen 1887," *Politiken*, April 22, 1887. Original: "Mere Sandhed! Større Alvor! Dybere Ærlighed!"

32 Henrik Jæger, *Kristiania og Kristianienserne* (Kristiania: Beyers, 1890), 105. Original: "I det tiaar, som netop er slut, har de gaaet socialisterne en høi gang baade med hensyn til demonstrationer og agitationer."

33 Henrik Jæger, *Illustreret Norsk Litteraturhistorie*, vol. 2 (Kristiania: Hjalmar Biglers, 1896), 678. Original: "Alt, hvad der var skeet ude i verden i det sidste tiaar, havde gjort et underligt indtryk herhjemme. Det havde skræmt og jaget gemytterne op; pariserkommunen bevirkede her som andetsteds, at man blev ræd alt det nye og uprøvede, som var dukket op ude i de store kulturlande, og hvad der bidrog til at gjøre frygten end kraftigere, var den omstændighed, at mange af de nye ideer, begyndte at dukke op herhjemme dristigere og talrigere end nogensinde."

34 Gerhard Gran, *Henrik Ibsen: Liv og Verker*, vol. 2 (Kristiania: Aschehoug, 1918), 97–98.

35 Gerhard Gran, *Alexander L. Kielland og Hans Samtid* (Stavanger: Dreyer, 1992), 148–51.

36 For more on this see Elias Bredsdorff, *Den store nordiske krig om seksualmoralen* (Oslo: Gyldendal, 1973).

37 Jacques St-Cère, "La polygamie en Scandinavie," *Le Figaro*, January 11, 1888. Original: "Pour la polygamie, la monogamie, la question de mariage, la prostitution, tout un ensemble qui a pris, dans la langue politique des pays scandinaves, le nom de 'question sexuelle.'"

38 "Vor literatur," in *Bohem mot Borger*, ed. Bryhni, 54. Original: "Den moderne ungdom maa altsaa præstere en naturalistisk literatur. Derved og derved alene kan den gjøre *sin* vilje til almenhedens vilje, bli en virkende drivkraft i udviklingens maskineri og saaledes manifestere sig som 'moderne.'"

39 Ibid., 62. Original: "Hvorfor husker jeg alle Zolas romaner, fra 'Les Rougon' og til 'L'oeuvre,' hvorfor husker jeg Guy de Maupassants 'Une vie' og 'Belami' og et las af hans noveletter—mens jeg har glemt omtrent alt hvad Kjelland har skrevet?—Fordi det *de* gir er livet selv, det levende pulserende liv, men det *han* gir er flade Kjellandske fortællinger om livet. Zola og Guy de Maupassant, de lod mig høre og føle med de mennesker de skrev om, de lod mig leve disse menneskers liv med; de gav mig levende kjød og blod, og ikke døde fortællingsabstraktioner som Kjelland. Og derfor er det, *de* har grebet mig, men ikke han."

40 Hans Jæger, *Fra Kristinia-Bohemen*, vol. 1 (Oslo: Bokklubbene, 1997), 5. Original: "Naturalismen er—kort definert—deterministisk digtning."

41 Ibid., 7–8.

42 See *Bergens Adressecontoirs Efterretninger*, August 10, 1878; Max Nordau, "La Bohème," *Romsdals Amtstidende*, September 7, 1878; *Aftenposten*, January 25, 1879; *Aftenposten*, April 12, 1879; "Den franske Forfatter Zola som Politiker," *Aftenposten*, April 25, 1879; *Bergens*

Adressecontoirs Efterretninger, May 16, 1879; "Dagsnyt fra Frankrig," *Aftenposten*, November 1, 1879; *Dagbladet*, November 6, 1879; *Aftenposten*, March 24, 1880; "Franske Romaner og Romanforfattere," *Aftenposten*, September 11, 1880; "To franske Nutids-Romaner," a series of articles published in *Stavanger Amtstidende og Adresseavis*, September 1880. A critic in the conservative newspaper *Morgenbladet* wrote that Amalie Skram, with her novel *Constance Ring* (1885), had managed to write a book more obscene than Zola's *Nana*. Kielland was more positive when, in a letter to Edvard Brandes, he called Constance Ring "Nana of the north." Quoted in Bredsdorff, *Den store nordiske krig*, 145. Kielland's original: "Constance er en Nana under nordlig Bredde."

43 Quoted in Nils Messel, *Tekster om norsk kunst og kunsthistorie* (Oslo: Labyrinth, 2013), 73. Original: "Det er en vældig kunst, den går helt tilbunds i den menneskelige natur."

44 Ibid., 73.

45 Andreas Aubert, "Breve fra Parisersalonen," *Aftenposten*, May 7, 1884. Original: "Ikke raa, men djerv."

46 See the comment "Øjebliksfotografier," *Dagbladet*, March 24, 1885.

47 *Dagbladet*, March 23, 1885.

48 Henrik Jæger, "Christian Krohg og hans Emner," *Christiania Intelligentssedler (Dagens Nyheder)*, March 26, 1885. Original: "Han giver mere af sin Personlighed i sine Billeder end nogen anden."

49 Hansson, "Krohgs og Werenskiolds Maleriudstilling." Original: "'Karl Johans Gade' er en liden lystig Impression, saavidt jeg ved det eneste af den Slags Billeder, som norske Malere har udstillet herhjemme. Flagsmykket er Gaden og en Mængde Mennesker paa Benene. Gaar man lige indpaa, virker det som en sindsforvirrede Mængder Klatter; men set paa Afstand er der Liv i Folkemassen, Sporvognene er i Fart, og Flagene blaffer for Vinden."

50 Christian Skredsvig, *Dager og netter blant kunstnere* (Oslo: Andresen og Butenshøn, 2010), 57. Original: "Så stod han en morgen lenet op mot et staffeli. Mørk, elegant, skilt hår, korte mustasjer. Nesten frastøtende fremmedartet. Hans portrett vilde vært en glede i en fotografs utstillingsskap."

51 Laurin, *Stamfränder*, 156.

52 Yngvar Nielsen, *Christiania og Omegn: Illustreret Haandbog for Reisende* (Christiania: Grønneberg/Cammermeyer, 1894), 10. Original: "*Grand Hotel*, elegant, meget søgt; et fortræffelig Sted for den, som vil studere den norske Hovedstads daglige Liv."

53 Wilhelm Peters, *Hvad jeg saa og hvem jeg mødte: Erindringer fra et kunstnerliv* (Kristiania: Gyldendalske, 1914), 21.

54 Much of the information on Karl Johan Street is from Øystein Sørensen, *1880-årene: Ti år som rystet Norge* (Oslo: Universitetsforlaget, 1984), 8–10.

55 Henrik Jæger, *Kristiania og Kristianienserne*, 111. Original: "I kunstnerisk henseende var da Kristiania ligesaa uopdaget som det indre af Afrika var det i geografisk før Livingstones og Stanleys ekspeditioner."

56 Christian Krohg, *Albertine* (Oslo: Bokklubben, 1995), 15–16. Original: "Det var vår og deilig vær, og Karl Johan lå for henne. I Studenterlunden under de lysegrønne trærne hørte hun musikken, som spilte Kadettmarsjen—oppe for enden av Slottsbakken lå slottet stort og hvitt. . . . Masse folk på gaten, som gikk opp og ned—mest fine—det var hverdag. Hun selv gikk langsomt oppover, - på hodet hadde hun en brun fruehatt med perlebesetning og rød parasoll av de moderne og notemappe i armen, som det sto *Musikk* på med forgylte bokstaver,—for hun var en fin frøken."

57 Andreas Aubert, "Høstudstillingen II," *Dagbladet*, October 2, 1887. Original: "I det experimentelle Studium af Lyset er Krohg for Tiden uden Tvil den første indenfor den nordiske Kunst. Selv indenfor den franske gaar han i forreste Geled. Han lægger sit selvstændige Bidrag til Udviklingen."

58 Rosenkrantz Johnsen, "Krohgs Maleri 'Albertine,'" *Dagbladet*, March 17, 1887. Original: "Albertine er et mægtigt Kunstværk. Med dette Billede har vort Lands moderne Kunst gjort et betydeligt Skridt fremad. Og derfor kan det siges om Krohg, at han har gjort hvad ikke mange opnaar at gjøre—han har flyttet Grændser."

59 Andreas Aubert, "Vor egen Kunst paa Kjøbenhavnerudstillingen II," *Dagbladet*, June 17, 1888.

60 Andreas Aubert, "Chr. Krohgs Udstilling," *Dagbladet*, February 10, 1889.

61 Aubert, "Høstudstillingen II." Original: "'Nordenvind' af *Christian Krohg* viser en hensynsløsere Dristighed i Anvendelsen af den impresjonistiske Methodes to Hovedgrundsætninger end noget tidligere Arbejde herhjemme. Aldrig har det momentane i Betragtningen vært kraftigere betonet i Sujettet, eller en voldsommere Farvedekomposition benyttet i Tekniken."

62 Andreas Aubert, "Krohgudstillingen," *Dagbladet*, February 9, 1890.

63 My presentation of the publication of *Albertine* is paraphrased from Oscar Thue, "Fra Albertine-striden," *Samtiden* 65 (1956): 662–70.

64 *Pall Mall Gazette*, January 6, 1887.

65 Eva Bonnier, *Pariserbref* (Stockholm: Klara, 1999), 211. She writes, "Allt hvad jag har fått i år är 'Albertine'. Den håller på att göra ronden. För närvarande är den hos Vallgrens, der Ville V. sitter och läser den högt för Spada och Pelle Ekström, som lyssna med hopknäppta händer."

66 For some reviews and commentaries on the case, see *Stavanger Amtstidende og Adresseavis*, August 7, 1888; and "Fra Norge," *Social-Demokraten*, January 21, 1888. For a presentation of the discussion in the many newspapers, see the chapter on Krohg's *Albertine* in Bredsdorff, *Den store nordiske krig*.

67 *Romsdals Amtstidende*, October 19, 1886; and *Romsdals Amtstidende*, December 28, 1886.

68 Georg Brandes, "Aabent Brev til Christian Krohg," *Politiken*, December 27, 1887. Original: "Dette er utvivlsomt et af de bedst anlagte og bedst gennemførte Studier i nyere nordisk Literatur. Kunde Edmond de Goncourt læse den Bog, vilde han trykke Deres Haand for den."

69 Margrete Vullum, "Christian Krohgs Bog," reprinted in *Gjennom kvinneøyne*, ed. Åse Hjort Lervik (Tromsø: Universitetsforlaget, 1980), 78. Original: "Alle skulde læse denne Bog. Der burde foranstaltes en billig Folkeudgave af den."

70 Lervik, ed., *Gjennom kvinneøyne*, 81.

71 Amalie Skram, "Om 'Albertine,'" in *Samlede verker*, vol. 7 (Oslo: Gyldendal, 1993), 412. See also "Literaturtidende," *Dagbladet*, December 22, 1886; Gina Krog, "Albertine" and Ragna Nielsen, "Albertine," both in *Dagbladet*, December 24, 1886; "Literaturtidende," *Dagbladet*, December 22, 1886.

72 *Hedmarkens Amtstidende*, January 14, 1887.

73 *Hedmarkens Amtstidende*, January 14, 1887. See also *Fædrelandet*, January 13, 1887.

74 "Folketoget til Stiftsgaarden," *Kristianiaposten*, January 18, 1887.

75 Arne Garborg, "Hr. Statsraad Dr. Blix," *Dagbladet*, December 22, 1886. Original: "Vi har en Forening til Prostitutionens Afskaffelse; den vil ikke udrette saa meget paa ti Aar, som Krohg har udrettet i denne ene Bog."

76 *Dagbladet*, March 18, 1887. Original: "Mange Folk, baade Damer og Herrer fra alle Samfundslag."

77 For a discussion of Krohg's theories, see Erik Mørstad, "Christian Krohgs kunstteori i 1880-årene," *Kunst og Kultur* 74, no. 2 (1991): 69–101.

78 René Wellek, "Hippolyte Taine's Literary Theory and Criticism," *Criticism* 1, no. 1 (1959): 11–13.

79 Christian Krohg, *Kampen for tilværelsen* (Oslo: Gyldendal, 1954), 11.

80 See Raffaëlli's essay in *Catalogue illustré des oeuvres de Jean-François Raffaelli* (Paris, 1884).

81 Krohg, *Kampen for tilværelsen*, 5. Original: "Når vi ser oss omkring, så ser vi en rastløs uro og utilfredshet på alle kanter."

82 Ibid., 6.

83 Ibid.

84 Arne Garborg, G. V. Lyng, and Henrik Jæger, *Betegner den moderne naturalisme i poesien et fremskridt eller et forfald?* (Kristiania: Studentersamfundet, 1882), 6. Original: "Digtningen kan ikke løse problemet, og det gjør naturalismen hellerikke fordring på; men den kan og skal gjennem levende billeder holde sandheden således frem for os, at vi tvinges til å tænke."

85 "Vor literatur," 64.

86 Krohg, *Kampen for tilværelsen*, 11.

87 Ibid., 17. Original: "Din plikt er det å ta det gjenstridige publikum i kraven og få det til å stanse og se på hva du har å vise det."

88 Ibid., 4–5. Original: "Og så er det oss, som tror at den bildende kunst er aldeles uunnværlig for ethvert fremskritt i menneskenes utvikling."

89 Gabriel P. Weisberg, *Beyond Impressionism: The Naturalist Impulse* (New York: Harry N. Abrams, 1992), 250.

90 Ibid., 273.

91 Quoted in Leif Østby, *Fra Naturalisme til Nyromantikk* (Oslo: Gyldendal, 1934), 26. Original: "Man vil nemlig ikke her gjenfinne den voldsomme anarkist, der hånler av alt som heter autoritet eller skole."

2. NATURALISM, THE DARK SIDE OF REALISM

Epigraphs: Aftenposten, April 12, 1879. Original: "Det er altsaa ikke Realismen, vi skal frygte for, det er Naturalismen og Materialismen." Frits Thaulow, *I Kamp og i Fest* (Kristiania: Gyldendalske, 1908), 146. Original: "Naturalismen var en Religion, og vi var dens fanatiske Bekjendere."

1 Harald Høffding, "Om Realisme i Videnskab og Tro," *Tilskueren* 1 (1884): 20.

2 Ernst Fischer, *The Necessity of Art*, trans. Anna Bostock (London: Verso, 2010), 121.

3 Leo Berg, *Der Naturalismus* (Munich: Verlag der Münchner Handelsdruckerei & Verlagsanstalt M. Poessl, 1892), 3. Original: "'Naturalismus,' 'Realismus,' 'Impressionismus,' 'Symbolismus,' 'Verismus,' 'Décadence,' 'Fin de siècle'! O diese Fremdwörter!" Berg, a Berlin-based journalist, was part of the avant-garde group *Der Verein Durch*, or just *Durch*. It was his wish to "cut through" the field of conventions. Naturalism was certainly looked upon as an avant-garde aesthetics. In addition to his book on naturalism, Berg wrote *Henrik Ibsen und das Germanentum in der modernen Litteratur* (1887), *Das sexuelle Problem in der modernen Litteratur* (1890), *Die Moderne* (1891), and *Deutsche Gesammt-Ausgabe von Emile Zola's kritisch-theoretischen Werken* (four volumes, 1890s).

4 "Christian Krohg om gammel og ny kunst og den evige kunst," *Nationen*, November 20, 1920. Original: "Og alle disse gloser som impressionisme og ekspressionisme er da bare gloser, noget som er fundet op for at enkelte mennesker skal faa noget at sysle med."
5 Émile Zola, *The Experimental Novel and Other Essays*, trans. Belle M. Sherman (New York: Haskell House, 1964), 44. For the original text, see Émile Zola, *Le roman expérimental* (Paris: Charpentier, 1880), 43.
6 Terry Eagleton, *Marxism and Literary Criticism* (Berkeley: University of California Press, 1976), 30.
7 Georg Lukács, *Studies in European Realism*, trans. Edith Bone (New York: Howard Fertig, 2002), 6.
8 Eagleton, *Marxism*, 30.
9 Lukács, *Studies*, 89.
10 Eagleton, *Marxism*, 31.
11 Zola, *The Experimental Novel*, 310; *Le roman expérimental*, 308.
12 This is an extreme simplification of Williams's discussion of modernism. See Raymond Williams, *Politics of Modernism* (London: Verso, 2007), 32–33. See also Raymond Williams, "A Lecture on Realism," *Afterall Journal* 5 (Spring/Summer 2002), n.p., www.afterall.org/journal/issue.5/lecture.realism, accessed May 27, 2014.
13 Tony Pinkney, "Editor's Introduction: Modernism and Cultural Theory," in Williams, *Politics of Modernism*, 8. See also Williams, "A Lecture on Realism."
14 Williams, *Politics of Modernism*, 53.
15 Ibid., 84.
16 Ibid.
17 Ibid., 85.
18 Quoted in Toril Moi, *Henrik Ibsen and the Birth of Modernism: Art, Theater, Philosophy* (Oxford: Oxford University Press, 2008), 108 and 109.
19 T. J. Clark, *Image of the People: Gustave Courbet and the 1848 Revolution* (London: Thames and Hudson, 1988), 130.
20 Boris Röhrl, *Kunsttheorie des Naturalismus und Realismus: Historiche Entwicklung, Terminologie und Definitionen* (Hildesheim: Georg Olms, 2003), 1.
21 Jules-Antoine Castagnary, *Salons (1857–1870)*, vol. 1 (Paris: Charpentier, 1892), 289–90. Original: "Le mot *naturalisme*, dont je me sers pour définir les tendances actuelles, n'est pas nouveau dans l'histoire de l'art, et c'est une des raisons qui me le font préférer au mot *réalisme*. Chaque fois qu'il s'est rencontré dans le monde une nation, ou dans une nation un groupe d'hommes, donnant pour objet immédiate à la peinture, l'interprétation de la vie environnante et s'efforçant de reproduire aux yeux l'image de la société envisagée dans son cadre naturel, cet art a été, cet art s'est appelé naturaliste. Le naturalisme est à vrai dire le caractère de l'art dans la majeure partie des temps modernes."
22 Ibid., 104–5. Original: "Les naturalistes, jeunes, ardents, convaincus, insoucieux des coups à donner ou des coups recevoir, montent à l'assaut de tous côtés; et déjà leurs têtes hasardeuses se montrent à tous les sommets de l'art. . . . L'école naturaliste affirme que l'art est l'expression de la vie sous tous ses modes et à tous ses degrés, et que son unique but est de reproduire la nature en l'amenant à son maximum de puissance et d'intensité: c'est la vérité s'équilibrant avec la science."
23 Richard Shiff, *Cézanne and the End of Impressionism* (Chicago: University of Chicago Press, 1984), 3–4. See also George Boas, ed., *Courbet and the Naturalistic Movement* (Baltimore, MD: Johns Hopkins Press, 1938).
24 For a definition of naturalism, see Raymond Williams, *Keywords: A Vocabulary of Culture*

and Society (London: Fontana, 1990), 216–19. See also chapter 7 on realism in Raymond Williams, *The Long Revolution* (London: Chatto and Windus, 1961).

25 Adolf J. Schmoll gen. Eisenwerth, "Naturalismus und Realismus: Versuch zur Formulierung verbindlicher Begriffe," in *Epochengrenzen und Kontinuität: Studien zur Kunstgeschichte* (Munich: Prestel, 1985), 264.

26 John Gage, *A Decade of English Naturalism: 1810–1820* (Norwich: Norwich Castle Museum and Victor and Albert Museum, 1969), 8.

27 Boris Röhrl discusses the development of the naturalist's Baroque painting and "Genre-Realismus." See Röhrl, *Kunsttheorie des Naturalismus und Realismus*, model on p. 31.

28 Anthony Savile, "Naturalism and the Aesthetic," *British Journal of Aesthetics* 40, no. 1 (2000): 46.

29 Quoted in S. R. Koehler, "Wilhelm Leibl," *American Art Review* 1, no. 11 (1880): 478.

30 Zola, *The Experimental Novel*, 114; *Le roman expérimental*, 114–15.

31 Edmond and Jules de Goncourt, *Pages from the Goncourt Journals*, trans. Robert Baldick (New York: New York Review of Books, 2007), 167.

32 For more on this, see Lilian R. Furst, "Zola's Art Criticism," in *French 19th Century Painting and Literature*, ed. Ulrich Finke (Manchester: Manchester University Press, 1972), 164–81.

33 Gabriel P. Weisberg, "Reframing Naturalism," in *Illusion of Reality: Naturalist Painting, Photography, Theatre and Cinema, 1875–1918*, ed. Gabriel P. Weisberg, David Jackson, and Willa Z. Silverman (Amsterdam: Van Gogh Museum, 2010), 22.

34 Émile Zola, *Écrits sur l'art* (Paris: Gallimard, 1991), 295–96. Original: "Manet est un artiste moderne, un réaliste, un positiviste. . . . Je le répète, l'incompréhension du public se dissipe peu à peu, et Manet apparaît ce qu'il est en réalité, le peintre le plus original de son temps, le seul depuis Courbet qui se soit distingué par des traits vraiment originaux annonçant cette école naturaliste que je rêve pour le renouveau de l'art et l'élargissement de la création humaine." For more on Zola's use of naturalism in painting, see E. Paul Gauthier, "Zola on Naturalism in Art and History," *Modern Language Notes* 70, no. 7 (1955): 514–17.

35 Zola, *Écrits sur l'art*, 305. Original: "De la jeune école naturaliste."

36 Ibid., 349. Original: "C'est un naturaliste, un analyste. Il ne saurait ni chanter ni philosopher. Il sait peindre, et voilà tout, et c'est un don si rare qu'il a suffi pour faire de Manet l'artiste le plus originale des quinze dernières années."

37 Ibid., 423–24. Original : "C'est un flot montant de modernité, irrésistible, qui emporte peu à peu l'École des beaux-arts, l'Institut, toutes les recettes et toutes les conventions. Le branle est donné, le mouvement continue, par une force fatale, sans que personne puisse l'enrayer; et ce n'est d'ailleurs pas une entente, c'est simplement le souffle du siècle qui passe, qui pousse et réunit les individualités."

38 Ibid., 424. Original: "Si tous les jeunes peintres ne sont pas des maîtres, tous, du moins, appliquent la même formule, chacun avec son tempérament différent."

39 Ibid., 427. See also Charles-Albert Arnoux Bertall, "Impressionism in France," *American Art Review* 1, no. 1 (1879): 35.

40 Quoted in Richard Thomson, *Art of the Actual: Naturalism and Style in Early Third Republic France, 1880–1900* (New Haven, CT: Yale University Press, 2012), 240.

41 Zola, *Écrits sur l'art*, 429. Original: "Donc, si nous étudions M. Bastien-Lepage peintre, nous voyons qu'il doit beaucoup aux impressionnistes; il leur a pris leurs tons clairs, leurs simplifications et même quelques-uns de leurs reflets; mais il leur a pris tout cela comme devait le faire un élève de M. Cabanel, avec une habileté extrême, et en fondant toutes

les accentuations dans une facture équilibrée, qui fait la joie du public. C'est l'impressionnisme corrigé, adouci, mis à la portée de la foule."

42 Ibid., 430.

43 Ibid., 438. Original: "Chaque année, à chaque Salon, on peut voir l'évolution s'accuser davantage. Les peintres de la tradition académique se lassent, produisent, des œuvres de plus en plus médiocres, dans l'isolement qui s'élargit autour d'eux; tandis que toute la vie, toute la force viennent aux peintres de la réalité et de la modernité."

44 Guy de Maupassant, *Bel-Ami*, trans. Douglas Parmée (London: Penguin, 2012), 133; Guy de Maupassant, *Fort comme la mort* (Paris: Louis Conard, 1908), 147.

45 Arnold Hauser, *The Social History of Art: Vol. 4, Naturalism, Impressionism, the Film Age* (London: Routledge, 1993), 160–61.

46 Alfred Stoeckius, "Naturalism in the Recent German Drama" (PhD diss., Columbia University, 1903), 3.

47 Ralph Barton Perry, *Present Philosophical Tendencies* (New York: Longmans, Green, 1912), 76.

48 This is a paraphrasing of ibid., 76.

49 Karl Pearson, *The Grammar of Science* (London: Adam and Charles Black, 1900), 41.

50 Ralph Barton Perry, *Present Philosophical Tendencies,* 80.

51 Henri Poincaré, *The Foundations of Science*, trans. George Bruce Halstad (Cambridge: Cambridge University Press, 2015), 127.

52 George S. Morris, "The Philosophy of Art," *Journal of Speculative Philosophy* 10, no. 1 (1876), 14.

53 For a brilliant presentation and discussion of the relationship between experiment and avant-garde art, see Allison Morehead, "Creative Pathologies: French Experimental Psychology and Symbolist Avant-Gardes, 1889–1900" (PhD diss., University of Chicago, 2007).

54 Zola, *The Experimental Novel*, 9–10; *Le roman expérimental*, 9.

55 Zola, *The Experimental Novel*, 11; *Le roman expérimental*, 10–11.

56 Philip Gilbert Hamerton, *Thoughts about Art* (Boston: Roberts Brothers, 1871), 311–12.

57 Gustave Courbet, *Letters of Gustave Courbet*, trans. Petra ten-Doesschate Chu (Chicago: University of Chicago Press, 1992), 103.

58 Quoted in Clark, *Image of the People*, 9.

59 Quoted in ibid., 134.

60 Hamerton, *Thoughts about Art*, 319.

61 Thaulow, *I Kamp og i Fest*, 215. Original: "Krohg søgte at fremstille Modsætningen mellem Rigdommen og Fattigdommen. Jeg tror endog, han mente, at han skulde virke for Socialismen."

62 Erik Werenskiold, "Christian Krohg," *Samtiden* (1925): 531.

63 Andreas Aubert, "I Anledning af Christian Krohgs store Komposition: Fra Politilægens Venteværelse," *Dagbladet*, March 22, 1887.

64 Quoted in ibid. The original can be found in Jean-François Raffaëlli, "Étude des mouvements de l'art moderne et du beau caractériste," in *Catalogue illustré des oeuvres de Jean-François Raffaelli suivi d'une étude du beau caractériste* (Paris, 1884), 24. Original: "À une société nouvelle, il faut un art nouveau. À une société égalitaire et démocratique, à l'homme scientifique moderne, il faut un art en mouvement constant."

65 "Que les passionnés aillent prendre les derniers et qu'ils nous montrent leur beauté et leur misère à laquelle il faudra remédier; ou le danger dans lequel ils mettent notre société;

que les fortunés nous montrent leurs amis, qu'ils aiment et connaissent; que les provinciaux nous montrent leurs voisins, avec sérieux; et que partout s'organise une étude attentive, passionnée, acharnée des tous ces caractères et dans cette idée, sous cet idéal, de l'homme libre, ou sous cette même idée: dans la critique de son individu." Raffaëlli, "Étude des mouvements de l'art moderne," 65.

66 "The Rafaëlli Exhibition," *Art Amateur*, June 1, 1884.

67 Alexandra Thaulow, *Mens Frits Thaulow Malte* (Oslo: Gyldendal, 1929), 100–101. It is not clear whether Krohg had ever met Raffaëlli, but the French painter did arrange large parties in Paris, and Thaulow seems to have attended a few of them. Raffaëlli was certainly well known and respected by the Norwegian artists.

68 Henrik Jæger, "Christian Krohg og hans Emner," *Christiania Intelligentssedler (Dagens Nyheder)*, March 26, 1885. Original: "Paa denne Maade giver Krohg en Definition af Arbeidet, der ikke stemmer overens med den gjængse gamle Talemaade, at 'Arbeidet er en Velsignelse.' Talemaaden kan være sand, naar den bruges om Arbeide, hvortil der kræves specielt Talent og speciel Interesse; men om det haarde legemlige Slit, Krohg fremstiller, gjælder den ikke. Det lignere snarere en Ulykke eller en uretfærdig Straf, hvortil man uforskyldt er bleven dømt for Levetiden."

69 "Chr. Krohg: Kampen for Tilværelsen," *Aftenposten*, May 10, 1889.

70 Quoted in David Owen Evans, *Social Romanticism in France 1830–1848* (Oxford: Clarendon Press, 1951), 27–28.

71 Georg Brandes, "Literære Studier II: Emile Zola som Kritiker," *Dagbladet*, Aug. 23, 1879.

72 Charles Bigot, "L'esthétique naturaliste," *Revue des deux mondes* 35 (Sept. 1, 1879): 415–32.

73 For Zola's response to Bigot, see Zola, *The Experimental Novel*, 291–98.

74 Bigot, "L'esthétique naturaliste," 424–25. Original: "Deux traits caractérisent proprement la littérature naturaliste. D'un côté, elle s'attache surtout à la peinture du vice, à la laideur morale, à la maladie répugnant à voir du corps ou de l'âme; de l'autre, elle emprunte de préférence les sujets de ses peintures aux classes inférieures de la société."

75 Lorentz Dietrichson, *Betegner den moderne Naturalisme i Poesien et Fremskridt eller et Forfald?* (Kristiania: Studentersamfundet, 1882), 7.

76 Ibid., 18. Original: "Og denne Naturalistens Kjæphest synes at være Betragtningen af Raadne, Slette i Menneskenaturen, hans Sanser synes at være begavede med en særlig Affinitet til det Hæslige, det Lave."

77 Ibid., 26. Original: "Den tror for fuldt Alvor, at den Methode, der duer for den videnskabelige Granskning, ogsaa maa due for den digteriske Skildring. Den er øjensynlig bleven beruset af de store Resultater, Naturvidenskaben har vundet i vor Tid, den vil studere Pathologie, foretage Diagnose og øve Therapi."

78 Ibid., 27.

79 Ibid.

80 Ibid., 28.

81 Arne Garborg, G. V. Lyng, and Henrik Jæger, *Betegner den moderne naturalisme i poesien et fremskridt eller et forfald?* (Kristiania: Studentersamfundet, 1882), 6. Original: "Digtningen kan ikke løse problemet, og det gjør naturalismen hellerikke fordring på; men den kan og skal gjennem levende billeder holde sandheden således frem for os, at vi tvinges til å tænke."

82 Christian Krohg, *Kampen for tilværelsen* (Oslo: Gyldendal, 1954), 16.

83 Garborg, Lyng, and Jæger, *Betegner den moderne naturalsime*, 14.

84 Johan Vibe, *Nogle Bemærkninger i Anledning af Naturalismen* (Kristiania: Malling, 1884), 12.

Original: "Selv den tarveligste Afhandling af en dygtig Læge ved en Sindsygeanstalt vil have mere videnskabelig Værd end den vidløftigste Roman af en skjønliterær Forfatter."

85 Ibid., 26.

86 Ibid., 82. Original: "Literaturen er i vore Dage faldt i hænderne paa syge Folk, hvis Verker er ligesaa bedrøvelige som de er fantasiforladte. Det er aandelige Patienter, der skriver om aandelige Patienter for aandelige Patienter. Enhver ny Fortælling er en ny Begrædelsernes Bog, eller et Pulterkammer for trættende og triviel psykologisk Analyse."

87 Christian Skredsvig, *Dager og netter blandt kunstnere* (Oslo: Andresen og Butenschøn, 2010), 117.

88 Ibid., 118. Original: "Navne som Manet, Monet, Bastien Lepage knitret som vimpler i storm!"

89 I am paraphrasing some of the points from Georg Nordensvan, *De Bildande Konsternas Historia under 19: De Århundradet* (Stockholm: Hugo Gebers, 1900), 301.

90 Christian Krohg, "Impresjonistene," in *Christian Krohg 1852–1925* (Åmot i Modum: Stiftelsen Modums Blaafarveværk, 1993), 70. Original: "Vi som trodde at vi var de radikaleste av de radikale, vi som påtok oss å male også det stygge—ja selv det styggeste i naturen."

91 Ibid. Original: "Hadde vi en stille indre bevissthet om at vi var den ytterste forpost i kunsten."

92 Thomson, *Art of the Actual*, 1.

3. THE HEROISM OF THE SCIENTIST

Epigraph: Giacomo Barzellotti, *La Philosophie de H. Taine*, trans. Auguste Dietrich (Paris: Félix Alcan, 1900), 236. Original: "Cette littérature est une grande clinique des maladies du siècle."

1 C.-A. Sainte-Beuve, *Causeries du Lundi*, vol. 13 (Paris: Garnier, n.d.), 363. Original: "Car en bien des endroits, et sous des formes diverses, je crois reconnaître des signes littéraires nouveaux: science, esprit d'observation, maturité, force, un peu de dureté. Ce sont les caractères que semblent affecter les chefs de file des générations nouvelles. Fils et frère de médecins distingués, M. Gustave Flaubert tient la plume comme d'autres le scalpel. Anatomistes et physiologistes, je vous retrouve partout!"

2 Quoted in Richard G. Olson, *Science and Scientism in Nineteenth-Century Europe* (Urbana: University of Illinois Press, 2008), 42.

3 Quoted in ibid., 43.

4 Quoted in ibid., 44.

5 Émile Zola, "Preface to the Second Edition (1868)," in *Thérèse Raquin*, trans. L. W. Tancock (Harmondsworth: Penguin, 1968), 24.

6 Émile Zola, *Le docteur Pascal* (Paris: Charpentier, 1893), 40. Original: "En somme, le docteur Pascal n'avait qu'une croyance, la croyance à la vie. La vie était l'unique manifestation divine. La vie, c'était Dieu, le grand moteur, l'âme de l'univers. Et la vie n'avait d'autre instrument que l'hérédité, l'hérédité faisait le monde; de sorte que, si l'on avait pu la connaître, la capter pour disposer d'elle, on aurait fait le monde à son gré."

7 Georg Brandes, *Dualismen i vor nyeste Philosophie* (Copenhagen: Gyldendalske, 1866), 11. Original: "Men det 19de Aarhundrede er tillige Naturvidenskabens og de store Opdagelsers Tidsalder."

8 Herman Jæger, *Taine: En Tænkerprofil* (Kristiania: Aschehoug, 1917), 4. Original: "Alt det et enkelt slegtled hadde magtet! Og hele den uendelige forskjellighet bundet sammen om

én enkelt ting, metoden. Paa alle felter er det ved eksperimentets hjælp man har kunnet bygge. Nævne navn — Pasteur, Cuvier og Geoffroy St. Hilaire, Berthelot."

9 Émile Zola, *The Experimental Novel and Other Essays*, trans. Belle M. Sherman (New York: Haskell, 1964), 32. Original: "Puisque la médecine, qui était un art, devient une science, pourquoi la littérature elle-même ne deviendrait-elle pas une science, grâce à la méthode expérimentale?" Émile Zola, *Le roman expérimental* (Paris: Charpentier, 1880), 30.

10 Georg Brandes, *Den Franske Æsthetik i Vore Dage: En Afhandling om H. Taine* (Copenhagen: Gyldendalske, 1870), 142. Original: "De store Mesteres Geni bestaaer i at være Physiologer i samme Grad, som de store Skribenter ere Psychologer."

11 Ibid., 194. Original: "Litteraturens Formaal er det at optegne og opbevare Følelser, og jo flere betydningsfulde følelser en Bog opbevarer, des høiere er dens historiske Rang. Den ligner da de ypperlige Apparater, ved Hjælp av hvilke Physikerne udsondre og maale de fineste indre Forandringer i et Legeme. Det er da især gjennem Litteraturstudiet, at man kan naae til Kundskaben om de psychologiske Love, af hvilke Historien afhænger, og det er for at paavise og fremstille disse, at Taine er bleven Litteraturhistoriker."

12 Arne Garborg, G. V. Lyng, and Henrik Jæger, eds., *Betegner den moderne naturalisme i poesien et fremskridt ellet et forfald?* (Kristiania: Studentersamfundet, 1882), 7. Original: "Den naturalistiske methodes 'videnskabelighed' består blot i, at digteren, gående ud fra almindelige videnskabelige grundsætninger, bygger sin skildring på *iagttagelser*, videnskabelig nøiaktige iagttagelser, og at han forholder sig videnskabeligt nøgtern — objektiv — i sin skildring. Han bygger på iagttagelse, men skaber billeder; — han er og bliver altså kunstner."

13 "Ces perturbations quelconques constituent, pour l'organisme social, l'analogue exact des maladies proprement dites de l'organisme individuel." Auguste Comte, *Cours de philosophie positive*, vol. 4 (Paris: Baillière, 1869), 309.

14 Olson, *Science and Scientism*, 42.

15 For examples of this, see Anthea Callen, *The Spectacular Body: Science, Method and Meaning in the Work of Degas* (New Haven, CT: Yale University Press, 1995), 22.

16 Claudius Wilkens, *Æsthetik i Omrids: Med særlight Hensyn til Moderne Æsthetik* (Copenhagen: Gyldendalske, 1888), x.

17 Thomas Sergeant Perry, "Science and the Imagination," *North American Review* 137, no. 320 (1883): 54.

18 Eugène Véron, *Æsthetics*, trans. W. H. Armstrong (London: Chapman and Hall, 1879), 86. For the original text, see Eugène Véron, *L'esthétique* (Paris: Vrin, 2007), 123.

19 Véron, *Æsthetics*, 86–87; *L'esthétique*, 123.

20 Guy de Maupassant, *Alien Hearts*, trans. Richard Howard (New York: New York Review of Books, 2009), 14.

21 Lorraine Daston and Peter Galison, *Objectivity* (New York: Zone Books, 2010), 217.

22 Michel Foucault, *Speech Begins after Death*, trans. Robert Bononno (Minneapolis: University of Minnesota Press, 2013), 34.

23 Ivan Illich, *Limits to Medicine* (London: Marion Boyars, 1995), 162–73.

24 More examples of paintings focused on doctors are mentioned by Shelley Wood Cordulack, *Edvard Munch and the Physiology of Symbolism* (Madison, WI: Fairleigh Dickinson University Press, 2002), 15.

25 Mary Hunter, "'Effroyable réalisme': Wax, Femininity, and the Madness of Realist Fantasies," *RACAR* 33, nos. 1–2 (2008): 56.

26 Gabriel P. Weisberg, *The Realist Tradition: French Painting and Drawing 1830–1900* (Cleveland, OH: Cleveland Museum of Art and Indiana University Press, 1980), 17.

27 Thomas Munro, "Meanings of 'Naturalism' in Philosophy and Aesthetics," *Journal of Aesthetics and Art Criticism* 19, no. 2 (1960): 133.

28 Roy Wood Sellars, *Evolutionary Naturalism* (Chicago: Open Court, 1922), viii.

29 D. G. Charlton, *Positivist Thought in France during the Second Empire 1852–1870* (Oxford: Clarendon, 1959), 11–12. See also F. A. Hayek, *The Counter-Revolution of Science: Studies on the Abuse of Reason* (New York: Free Press, 1955).

30 Henry Smith Williams, *A History of Science*, vol. 4 (New York: Harper, 1904), 54–55.

31 Ferdinand Brunetière, *Brunetière's Essays in French Literature*, trans. D. Nichol Smith (London: T. Fisher Unwin, 1898), 221.

32 Peter J. Bowler, *Evolution: The History of an Idea* (Berkeley: University of California Press, 2009), 98 and 107.

33 Auguste Comte defined positivism the following way: "[In] the positive state, the mind has given over the vain search after Absolute notions, the origin and destination of the universe, and the causes of phenomena, and applies itself to the study of their laws—that is, their invariable relations of succession and resemblance. Reasoning and observation, duly combined, are the means of this knowledge. What is now understood when we speak of an explanation of facts is simply the establishment of a connection between single phenomena and some general facts, the number of which continually diminishes with the progress of science." August Comte, *The Positive Philosophy of Auguste Comte*, vol. 1 (London: John Chapman, 1853), 1–2. Comte's philosophical positivism should be understood as a theory of knowledge, and all knowledge is, in this theory, based on what we can observe or can logically deduce from observation (empirical verification). The idea is that all phenomena in the world are connected in terms of cause and effect, and that's why a positivist thinker would say that the world of phenomena is a determined world.

34 Bowler, *Evolution*, 120–21.

35 Hippolyte Taine, *Les philosophes classiques du XIXe siècle en France* (Paris: Hachette, 1905), vii. Original: "Les positivistes . . . déclarent ne rien savoir ni sur la cause de la vie, ni sur la cause de l'univers. Ils se bornent à noter la somme et la direction des réactions chimiques et les actions physiques qui composent la vie, et à grouper les lois expérimentales qui résument tous les faits observés dans notre univers." This is an early book by Taine, written as a polemic against the spiritualistic trends in French philosophy, and especially against the best-known French philosopher of the time, Victor Cousin (1792–1867). See Martha Wolfenstein, "The Social Background of Taine's Philosophy of Art," *Journal of the History of Ideas* 5, no. 3 (1944): 336. Cousin is also known for the phrase *l'art pour l'art*, later made into a slogan by Gautier.

36 Julius Lange, *Udvalgte Skrifter*, vol. 2 (Copenhagen: Det Nordiske Forlag, 1901), 360. Original: "Fordringen gaar kun ud paa, at man under Arbejdet skal være i saa umiddelbart og uafladeligt Samkvem med sit Æmne som mulig."

37 Leo Weinstein, *Hippolyte Taine* (New York: Twayne, 1972), 35.

38 Charles Baudelaire, *The Painter of Modern Life and Other Essays*, trans. Jonathan Mayne (London: Phaidon, 2003), 13. Original: "Il est sans doute excellent d'étudier les anciens maîtres pour apprendre à peindre, mais cela ne peut être qu'un exercice superflu si votre but est de comprendre le caractère de la beauté présente. . . . En un mot, pour que toute *modernité* soit digne de devenir antiquité, il faut que la beauté mystérieuse que la vie humaine y met involontairement en ait été extraite." Charles Baudelaire, *L'art romantique* (Paris: Louis Conard, 1925), 67–68.

39 Linda Nochlin, *Realism* (London: Penguin, 1990), 103.

40 Gustave Courbet, *Letters of Gustave Courbet*, trans. Petra ten-Doesschate Chu (Chicago: University of Chicago Press, 1992), 203.

41 Jean-François Raffaëlli, "Études des mouvements de l'art moderne et du beau caractériste," in *Catalogue illustré des oeuvres de Jean-François Raffaëlli* (Paris, 1884), 24.

42 Véron, *Æsthetics*, xii; *L'esthétique*, 28.

43 Christian Krohg, *Kampen for tilværelsen* (Oslo: Gyldendal, 1954), 6. Original: "*Tidens bilde er først og fremst et bilde av menneskeheten på den tid.*" His italics.

44 Krohg, *Kampen for tilværelsen*, 18. Original: "Det samme pulsslag som er felles for hele det store liv vi kaller samtiden, det må føles litt av i det kunstverk som skal ha betydning for samtiden."

45 Gustave Courbet, "Statement on Realism," in *Art in Theory 1815–1900: An Anthology of Changing Ideas*, ed. Charles Harrison, Paul Wood, and Jason Gaiger (Oxford: Blackwell, 2003), 372.

46 *Aftenposten*, July 20, 1861.

47 Williams, *A History of Science*, 260–61.

48 P. V. Rubow writes: "This great scientist [Bernard] was for Taine and his generation a guiding star and his *Introduction to the Study of Experimental Medicine* was their bedside book." Quoted in Reino Virtanen, *Claude Bernard and His Place in the History of Ideas* (Lincoln: University of Nebraska Press, 1960),107.

49 Bernard writes: "The sceptic disbelieves in science and believes in himself; he believes enough in himself to dare deny science and to assert that it is not subject to definite, fixed laws. The doubter is a true man of science; he doubts only himself and his interpretations, but he believes in science; in the experimental sciences, he even accepts a criterion or absolute scientific principle. This principle is the determinism of phenomena, which is as absolute in the phenomena of living bodies as in those of inorganic matter." Claude Bernard, *An Introduction to the Study of Experimental Medicine*, trans. Henry Copley Greene (New York: Macmillan, 1927), 52.

50 Ibid., 221.

51 "Les phénomènes vitaux ont bien leurs conditions physico-chimiques rigoureusement déterminées; mais en même temps ils se subordonnent et se succèdent dans un enchaînement et suivant une loi fixée d'avance: ils se répètent éternellement, avec ordre, régularité, constance, et s'harmonisent, en vue d'un résultat qui est l'organisation et l'accroissement de l'individu, animal ou végétal.

"Il y a comme un dessin préétabli de chaque être et de chaque organe, en sorte que si, considéré isolément, chaque phénomène de l'économie est tributaire des forces générales de la nature, pris dans ses rapports avec les autres, il révèle un lien spécial, il semble dirigé par quelque guide invisible dans la route qu'il suit et amené dans la place qu'il occupe." Claude Bernard, *Leçons sur les phénomènes de la vie*, vol. 1 (Paris: Baillière, 1885), 51.

52 Ibid., 43.

53 Henri Bergson, *The Creative Mind: An Introduction to Metaphysics*, trans. Mabelle L. Andison (Mineola, NY: Dover, 2007), 171. It is the creative aspect that interests Bergson in Bernard's thinking. Bernard writes that "life is creation" and that in "every living germ is a creative idea which develops and exhibits itself through organization" (Bernard, *Introduction*, 93). But what Bernard describes is not a kind of vitalism but rather a way of talking about scientific life. The creative play is the scientist's play and not the organism's. The positivist scientist cannot doubt the principle of determinism—the phenomenon's regularity in the world in relationship to its surrounding conditions. See J. M. D. Olmsted

and E. Harris Olmsted, *Claude Bernard and the Experimental Method in Medicine* (New York: Henry Schuman, 1952), 148.

54 Bergson, *The Creative Mind*, 171.

55 "Le physique agit sur le métaphysique (l'engendre-t-il? ou le modifie-t-il?) mais jamais le métaphysique n'agit sur le physique." Quoted in Virtanen, *Claude Bernard*, 28.

56 Quoted in ibid., 28. Original: "Jamais la métaphysique ne disparaîtra: c'est encore une erreur de la philosophie positiviste."

57 Quoted in ibid., 29.

58 Henri Testard, "Preface," in Edmond About, *L'homme à l'oreille cassée* (London: Hachette, 1899), ix.

59 Olmsted and Olmsted, *Claude Bernard*, 110–11.

60 Bernard, *Introduction*, 43.

61 Victor Hugo, *William Shakespeare*, trans. Melville B. Anderson (Chicago: McClurg, 1891), 100, 102 and 105.

62 Ibid., 114–15.

63 Bernard, *Introduction*, 142.

64 David Baguley, *Naturalist Fiction: The Entropic Vision* (Cambridge: Cambridge University Press, 2005), 55.

65 Fiorenzo Conti and Silvana Irrera Conti, "On Science and Literature: A Lesson from the Bernard-Zola Case," *BioScience* 53, no. 9 (2003): 867.

66 Zola, *The Experimental Novel*, 1; *Le roman expérimental*, 2.

67 Ferdinand Brunetière writes: "It would be easily proved that the author of *La bête humaine* and *L'assommoir* owes almost everything, not to Balzac, nor even to Flaubert, but to M. Taine, to M. Taine's essay on *Balzac*, and the *History of English Literature*." *Brunetière's Essays in French Literature*, trans. D. Nichol Smith (London: T. Fisher Unwin, 1898), 230.

68 Bernard, *Introduction*, 14.

69 Emile Zola, "From Naturalism in the Theatre," trans. Albert Bermel, in *The Theory of the Modern Stage,* ed. Eric Bentley (London: Penguin, 1992), 368–69.

70 Hippolyte Taine, *History of English Literature*, trans. H. Van. Laun (New York: American Book Exchange, 1880), 19; Hippolyte Taine, *Histoire de la littérature anglaise*, vol. 1 (Paris: Hachette, 1863), viii–ix.

71 Zola, *The Experimental Novel*, 154; *Le roman expérimental*, 153.

72 Zola, *The Experimental Novel*, 19; *Le roman expérimental*, 18.

73 François Jacob, *The Logic of Life: A History of Heredity*, trans. Betty E. Spillmann (New York: Pantheon, 1973), 178–81; Bernard, *Introduction*, 18.

74 Zola, "Preface to the Second Edition (1868)," in *Thérèse Raquin*, 20.

75 Paul Alexis, *Émile Zola: Notes d'un ami* (Paris: Charpentier, 1882), 156–67.

76 Gabriel P. Weisberg, *Beyond Impressionism: The Naturalist Impulse* (New York: Harry N. Abrams, 1992), 22.

77 Zola, *The Experimental Novel*, 8; *Le roman expérimental*, 7.

78 Bernard, *Introduction*, 3.

79 Ibid., 5.

80 Ibid., 6.

81 Virtanen, *Claude Bernard*, 15.

82 The idea that the naturalist artwork is a thought experiment is paraphrased from Anthony Savile, "Naturalism and the Aesthetics," *British Journal of Aesthetics* 40, no. 1 (2000): 51.

83 J. G. Patterson, *A Zola Dictionary* (London: Routledge, 1912), xiii.

84 Daston and Galison, *Objectivity*, 10.
85 Ibid., 37.
86 Georg Brandes, "Literære Studier II: Emile Zola som Kritiker," *Dagbladet*, August 28, 1879.
87 Rosenkrantz Johnsen, "Krohgs Maleri 'Albertine,'" *Dagbladet*, March 17, 1887. Original: "Man ser paa dette Billede med en velgjørende illusjon af, at Figurerne bevæger sig frit, snakker, aander, lever;—og med en Overbevisning om, at det er 'et Stykke Natur, seet tvers gjennem et Temperament.'"
88 Quoted in Weisberg, *The Realist Tradition*, 1.
89 Edmond Duranty, *La nouvelle peinture à propos du groupe d'artistes qui expose dans les galeries Durand-Ruel* (Paris: Dentu, 1876), 24. Original: "Avec un dos, nous voulons que se révèle un tempérament, un âge, un état social; par une paire de mains, nous devons exprimer un magistrat ou un commerçant; par un geste, toute une suite de sentiments."
90 Émile Zola, *Écrits sur l'art* (Paris: Gallimard, 1991), 125. Zola's italics.
91 Zola, *The Experimental Novel*, 111.
92 Quoted in Richard Shiff, *Cézanne and the End of Impressionism* (Chicago: University of Chicago Press, 1984), 29.
93 Quoted in ibid.
94 Charles Baudelaire, *The Painter of Modern Life and Other Essays*, trans. Jonathan Mayne (London: Phaidon, 2003), 3. Original: "Dans l'œuvre la plus frivole d'un artiste raffiné appartenant à une de ces époques que nous qualifions trop vaniteusement de civilisées, la dualité se montre également; la portion éternelle de beauté sera en même temps voilée et exprimée, sinon par la mode, au moins par le tempérament particulier de l'auteur." Charles Baudelaire, *L'art romantique* (Paris: Louis Conard, 1925), 53.
95 Joris-Karl Huysmans, *Écrits sur l'art* (Paris: Flammarion, 2008), 69. Original: "Tel qu'il est, et tel qu'il sera surtout, l'art impressionniste montre une observation très curieuse, une analyse très particulière et très profonde des tempéraments mis en scène."
96 Charles Baudelaire, *Art in Paris 1845–1862: Salons and Other Exhibitions*, trans. Jonathan Mayne (London: Phaidon Press, 1965), 45.
97 Zola, *Écrits sur l'art*, 108. Original: "Je veux qu'on fasse de la vie, moi; je veux qu'on soit vivant, qu'on crée à nouveau, en dehors de tout, selon ses propres yeux et son propre tempérament. Ce que je cherche avant tout dans un tableau, c'est un homme et non pas un tableau."
98 Joris-Karl Huysmans, *Against Nature*, trans. Margaret Mauldon (Oxford: Oxford University Press, 2009), 145.
99 Krohg, *Kampen for tilværelsen*, 420.
100 Ibid., 178. Original: "Visstnok skulle naturen sees gjennom et temperament, men det var naturen som var hovedsaken, ikke temperamentet. Og det var temperamentet som noe konstant, ikke temperamentets enkelte flyktige uttrykksformer, der hadde betydning som seglass. Man hadde kun *et* glass, men Munch har mange hundre og lager stadig nye. Han lager dem selv. Enkelte forstørrer, andre forminsker, enkelte forvrir, andre igjen splitter."
101 Olmsted and Olmsted, *Claude Bernard*, 94.
102 Daston and Galison, *Objectivity*, 235 and 243–45.
103 Ibid., 245.
104 Bernard, *Introduction*, 23.
105 Ibid., 25.
106 Quoted in Richard Thomson, *Art of the Actual: Naturalism and Style in Early Third Republic*

France, 1880–1900 (New Haven, CT: Yale University Press, 2012), 314n49. Original: "Nous aurons gré au réaliste de nous retracer notre propre image et de préparer pour les siècles à venir des documents sur l'âge dans lequel nous vivons."

107 Paul Bourget, "Brev fra Paris: Et Overblik over den franske Literatur i Aaret 1884," *Tilskueren* 2 (1885): 59. Original: "Saaledes bliver 'Chérie' slet og ret en Protokol over en ung Piges Timer lige fra hendes spædeste Barndom til hendes tyvende Aar."

108 Emil Hannover, *Erindringer fra Barndom og Ungdom* (Copenhagen: Forening for Boghaandværk, 1966), 129. Original: "Kulthistorisk-videnskabeligt Dokument."

109 Herman Jæger, *Taine: En Tænkerprofil* (Kristiania: Aschehoug, 1917), 40.

110 Zola, *The Experimental Novel*, 9; *Le roman expérimental*, 8.

111 Quoted in Paul E. Gauthier, "Zola on Naturalism in Art and History," *Modern Language Notes* 70, no. 7 (1955): 517.

112 Honoré de Balzac, "Avant-Propos," in *Oeuvres complètes de H. de Balzac*, vol. 1 (Paris: Michel Levy, 1875), 5. Original: "La société française allait être l'historien, je ne devais être que le secrétaire."

113 Ibid., 6.

114 Zola, *The Experimental Novel*, 10; *Le roman expérimental*, 10.

115 Claude Bernard, *Principes de medicine expérimentale* (Paris: Presses Universitaires de France, 1947), xxvi. Bernard's emphasis. Original: "Moi, je suis le *secrétaire* de la nature."

116 Olin H. Moore, "The Literary Methods of the Goncourts," *PMLA* 31, no. 1 (1916): 45.

117 Émile Zola, *The Fortune of the Rougons*, trans. Brian Nelson (Oxford: Oxford University Press, 2012), 3.

118 Zola, *The Experimental Novel*, 210; *Le roman expérimental*, 206–7.

119 Zola, *The Experimental Novel*, 263; *Le roman expérimental*, 259.

120 "Modern French Painting," *Art Critic* 1, no. 2 (1894): 28.

121 Wynford Dewhurst, *Impressionist Painting: Its Genesis and Development* (London: Georges Newnes, 1904), 65.

122 "La vie seule intéresse, pour la vie, et la vérité suffit comme beauté. On analyse, on dissèque les individus ou les milieux sociaux comme un médecin disserte sur des cas pathologiques; on classe les types d'humanité, on étudie leurs tares suivant leur condition, leur passé ancestral, et l'on opère le même travail de laboratoire à l'examen mental des collectivités." Léonce Bénédite, "Alfred-Philippe Roll," *Art et décoration* 24 (July–Dec. 1908): 73. Roll is discussed alongside Flaubert, Maupassant, Courbet, Zola, Manet, and the impressionist painters.

123 But Krohg actually managed, according to Kirk Varnedoe, to tell the whole story in *Albertine in the Police Doctor's Waiting Room*. Varnedoe suggests that the painting is not "the representation of a single moment in the Albertine story, but an expanded narrative, one moment synthesizing the story as a whole. In the Justice Department's indictment of Albertine, three parts of the book were found objectionable: the initial seduction of Albertine by a policeman, which damaged her virtuous modesty; her encounter with the police doctor, which destroyed her feminine dignity; and the last chapter, which depicted her, bereft of shame, totally debased, transformed into a hardened whore. In his defense, Krohg argued that these were precisely the aspects of the story that had most deeply moved him and which he felt compelled to communicate; and they are, it seems, the three stages he tried to contain in this scene." Kirk Varnedoe, "Christian Krohg and Edvard Munch," *Arts Magazine* 53, no. 8 (1979): 90.

124 Bernard, *Introduction*, 2.

125 Zola, "Preface to the Second Edition (1868)," in *Thérèse Raquin*, 21.
126 Ferdinand Brunetière, "The Experimental Novel," trans. Janice Best, in *Critical Essays on Emile Zola*, ed. David Baguley (Boston: G. K. Hall, 1986), 34.
127 Ibid., 39.
128 Claudius Wilkens, "Moderne Naturalisme," *Tilskueren* 5 (1888): 500–501.
129 Georg Lukács, *Studies in European Realism*, trans. Edith Bone (New York: Howard Fertig, 2002), 90.
130 Ibid., 91.
131 Baguley, *Naturalist Fiction*, 92.
132 Quoted in Virtanen, *Claude Bernard*, 3–4.

4. HIPPOLYTE TAINE AND THE MODERN BREAKTHROUGH IN SCANDINAVIA

Epigraph: Ferdinand Brunetière, *L'évolution des genres dans l'histoire de la littérature* (Paris: Hachette, 1890), 246. Original: "Mais il faut dire, et si nous l'avons dit, il faut le répéter, que, depuis Hegel, personne peut-être en Europe n'a jeté dans la circulation, sur l'histoire de la littérature et de l'art, plus d'idées nouvelles, fortes ou profondes—et vraies ou fausses d'ailleurs, mais en tout cas *suggestives* et provocatrices—que l'auteur de la *Philosophie de l'art*."

1 Albert Guérard, *Literature and Society* (New York: Cooper Square, 1970), 33.
2 Albert Guérard, "Foreword," in Sholom J. Kahn, *Science and Aesthetic Judgment: A Study in Taine's Critical Method* (New York: Columbia University Press, 1953), vii.
3 Edmond and Jules de Goncourt, *Journal des Goncourt: Mémoires de la vie littéraire*, vol. 2 (Paris: Charpentier, 1887), 96. Original: "L'incarnation en chair et en os de la critique modern."
4 Friedrich Nietzsche, *Beyond Good and Evil*, trans. R. J. Hollingdale (London: Penguin, 2003), § 254.
5 Herman Jæger, *Taine: En Tænkerprofil* (Kristinia: Aschehoug, 1917), 174. Original: "Paa denne maate blir saa at si alle fra det 19. aarhundredes midte elever av Taine; vi kan ikke paapeke en eneste elev i egentlig forstand; men allikevel er alle sammen hans elever, fordi vi i deres virke merker glimtene fra Taines tankegang."
6 Hellen Lindgren, *Vittra Stormän: Kritiker och Porträt* (Stockholm: Carl Deleen, 1894), 90. Original: "Han blef läraren för en ungdom utan ideal."
7 For some articles on Taine, see "Literatur," *Bergens Adressecontoirs Efterretninger*, March 23, 1874; "Literatur," *Bergens Adressecontoirs Efterretninger*, November 30, 1874; *Bergens Adressecontoirs Efterretninger*, November 11, 1875; Christopher Bruun, "Svar til H. Lassons Omtale af 'Folkelige Grundtanker,'" *Nordre Bergenhus Amtstidende*, October 31, 1878; "Fra Paris," *Bergens Adressecontoirs Efterretninger*, February 4, 1880. Examples on excerpts can be found in *Fedraheim*, September 30, 1882, and *Bergens Adressecontoirs Efterretninger*, December 29, 1884.
8 Quoted in David Baguley, *Naturalist Fiction: The Entropic Vision* (Cambridge: Cambridge University Press, 2005), 55. Original: "Il est le naturaliste du monde moral. Il croit qu'on peut arriver à classer les faits de la vie intellectuelle comme on classe les faits de la vie physique." "Je l'aime, cette méthode, parce qu'elle apporte la vérité."
9 Émile Zola, *Écrits sur l'art* (Paris: Gallimard, 1991), 82. Original: "Le contemporain du télégraphe électrique et des chemins de fer."
10 E. Paul Gauthier, "Zola on Naturalism in Art and History," *Modern Language Notes* 70,

no. 7 (1955): 517. Original: "Un ardent enthousiasme, une sorte de religion, que j'appellerai le culte dynamique de la vie."

11 Émile Zola, *The Experimental Novel and Other Essays*, trans. Belle M. Sherman (New York: Haskell, 1964), 225.

12 Quoted in Alan Pitt, "The Irrationalist Liberalism of Hippolyte Taine," *Historical Journal* 41, no. 4 (1998): 1036.

13 Pitt, "The Irrationalist Liberalism," 1036.

14 Herman Jæger, *Taine*, 6. Original: "Taine's 'Philosophes français du 19. siècle' er ikke en krigserklæring. Den er et felttog."

15 Quoted in Patrizia Lombardo, "Hippolyte Taine between Art and Science," *Yale French Studies* 77 (1990): 119.

16 For discussions on Taine's aesthetics and values, see O. B. Frothingham, "The Morally Objectionable in Literature," *North American Review* 135, no. 311 (1882): 323–38; Stefan Morawski, "The Problem of Value and Criteria in Taine's Aesthetics," *Journal of Aesthetics and Art Criticism* 21, no. 4 (1963): 407–21.

17 Martha Wolfenstein, "The Social Background of Taine's Philosophy of Art," *Journal of the History of Ideas* 5, no. 3 (1944): 332.

18 Hippolyte Taine, *The Ideal in Art*, trans. J. Durand (New York: Henry Holt, 1874), 25. Original text: Hippolyte Taine, *De l'idéal dans l'art* (Paris: Baillière, 1867), 15.

19 Kahn, *Science and Aesthetic Judgment*, 3.

20 Zola, *Écrits sur l'art*, 63–83.

21 Ferdinand Brunetière, *Discours de combat* (Paris: Perrin, 1904), 221. Original: "Il s'est progressivement élevé à une vue plus générale, plus haute, et plus féconde."

22 Jules Lemaître, *Les contemporains*, vol. 6 (Paris: Lecène, Oudin, 1896), 311.

23 Lindgren, *Vittra Stormän*, 105. Original: "Taine hör till dem, som vilja vara en hjärna, som vilje höra till dem, som Gautier kallade *les cérébraux*: hjärnmänniskorna, medan han dock till sin natur är lika mycket diktare som tänkare."

24 Ibid., 96. Original: "Vi kunna dock ej räkna Taine till de rena vetenskapsmännen. Häri ligger det interessanta hos honom som författarpersonlighet. Han omfattar ej sanningsidealet på forskares vanliga lugna sätt utan som diktare. Föreningen hos honom af två personer och två naturer, diktarens och forskarens, är påtaglig."

25 Zola, *Écrits sur l'art*, 64–65. Original: "M. Taine n'est pas l'homme de son temps ni de son corps. Si je ne le connaissais, j'aimerais à me le représenter carré des épaules, vêtu d'étoffes larges et splendides, traînant quelque peu l'épée, vivant en pleine Renaissance. Il a l'amour de la puissance, de l'éclat; il semble à l'aise dans les ripailles, parmi les viandes et les vins, au milieu des réceptions de cour, en compagnie de riches seigneurs et de belles dames étalant leurs dentelles et leurs velours. Il se vautre avec joie dans les emportements de la chair, dans toutes les forces brutales de l'homme, dans la soie comme les guenilles, dans tout ce qui est extrême. . . . Et cependant, tout au fond, il y a de la fièvre. Cette santé plantureuse est factice; cet amour du luxe large et magnifique n'est qu'un regret. On sent que l'auteur est notre frère, qu'il est faible et nu, qu'il appartient bien à notre siècle de nerfs." See also Pitt, "The Irrationalist Liberalism," 1043–44.

26 Taine: "They are opposed to one another, the tendencies enter into conflict: that is deliberation. Then that fluctuation ceases, a tendency has emerged victorious; my entire being, hitherto divided, is concentrated on one single point, oriented in a single direction. At that moment, my will is determined. . . . Its nature, being general and not restricted, contains within itself possibilities of all sorts. In this sense, it is free." Quoted in Kahn, *Science and Aesthetic Judgment*, 22.

27 Quoted in ibid.
28 Quoted in ibid.
29 Ibid.
30 "A great poem, a fine novel, the confession of a superior man, are more instructive than a heap of historians with their histories. I would give fifty volumes of charters and a hundred volumes of state papers for the memoirs of Cellini, the epistles of St. Paul, the Table-talk of Luther, or the comedies of Aristophanes. In this consists the importance of literary works: they are instructive because they are beautiful; their utility grows with their perfection; and if they furnish documents it is because they are monuments." Hippolyte Taine, *History of English Literature*, trans. H. Van Laun (New York: American Book Exchange, 1880), 30–31. Original text: Hippolyte Taine, *Histoire de la littérature anglaise*, vol. 1 (Paris: Hachette, 1863), xlv.
31 Leo Weinstein, *Hippolyte Taine* (New York: Twayne, 1972), 51.
32 Hippolyte Taine, *The Philosophy of Art*, trans. John Durand (New York: Holt and Williams, 1873), 19. Original text: Hippolyte Taine, *Philosophie de l'art*, vol. 1 (Paris: Hachette, 1895), 2.
33 Julius Lange, *Om Kunstværdi: To Foredrag* (Copenhagen: G. E. C. Gad, 1876), 128.
34 Some important examples include *Den Italienske Kunsts Filosofi* in 1873 [*Voyage en Italie* (1866)]; *Kunstens Filosofi* in 1873 [*Philosophie de l'art* (1865)], *Den Engelske Literaturs Historie* (1874–77) [*Histoire de la littérature anglaise* (1864)]; *Om Idealet i Kunsten* (1874) [*De l'idéal dans l'art* (1867)]; *Rejse i Pyreneerne* (1876) [*Voyage aux Pyrénées* (1855–1860)]; *Pariser-Skildringer* (ed. Taine, 1876); *Jakobinernes Ledere* (1880); *Den Nederlandske Kunsts Filosofi* (1881) [*Philosophie de l'art dans les Pays-Bas* (1868)].
35 Ross Shideler, *Questioning the Father: From Darwin to Zola, Ibsen, Strindberg, and Hardy* (Stanford, CA: Stanford University Press, 1999), 49.
36 Alexandra Thaulow, *Mens Frits Thaulow Malte* (Oslo: Gyldendal, 1929), 99. Original: "Frits fortalte om en herremiddag, hvor han havde været saman med Zola og Georg Brandes. Der havde udfoldet sig en meget spændende discussion, hvor alle havde kappes i vid og spiritualitet. Brandes vandt, fortalte han, ved sin uhyre slagfærdighed og fænomenale hukommelse om alle fakta. France og selv Zola forstummede overfor al den viden."
37 Edvard Beyer, F. J. Billeskov Jansen, Hakon Stangerup, and P. H. Traustedt, eds., *Verdens Litteraturhistorie*, vol. 9 (Oslo: Cappelen, 1978), 268. See also "Brev fra Kjøbenhavn," *Bergens Adressecontoirs Efterretninger*, November 25, 1871.
38 The following presentation of Brandes's biography is built on information found in Shideler, *Questioning the Father*, 45–57; Julie K. Allen, *Icons of Danish Modernity: Georg Brandes and Asta Nielsen* (Seattle: University of Washington Press, 2012), chapter 2.
39 Georg Brandes, *Reminiscences of My Childhood and Youth* (New York: Duffield, 1906), 176.
40 Ibid.
41 Ibid., 244.
42 Ibid., 270.
43 Ibid.
44 Georg Brandes, *Hovedstrømninger i det 19de Aarhundredes Litteratur: Emigrantlitteraturen* (Copenhagen: Gyldendalske, 1872), 15.
45 Georg Brandes, *Main Currents in Nineteenth Century Literature*, vol. 1 (New York: Macmillan, 1906), vii–viii.
46 Brandes, *Reminiscences*, 228.
47 Georg Brandes, *Samlede Skrifter*, vol. 7 (Copenhagen: Gyldendalske, 1901), 672. See also Bjørn Bjørnson, *Bare ungdom* (Oslo: Aschehoug, 1934), 53–63.

48 Georg Brandes, *Levned: Et Tiaar* (Copenhagen: Gyldendalske, 1907), 296. Original: "En Dag i Marts 1878 sagde han [Bjørn Bjørnson; son of Bjørnstjerne Bjørnson]: 'Tillad mig at indføre en ung Mand hos Dem, der gjerne vil male Deres Portræt; han er 25 Aar gammel, norsk af Fødsel, men en Verdensmand, meget velopdragen, slet ingeng Nordmand'.—Saaledes kom Christian Krohg til mig. Og da han havde baade Bolig og Atelier sammen med en anden ung Kunstner, paa 21 aar, ved Navn Max Klinger, lærte jeg samtidigt denne at kende. Og begge ret intimt, thi paa det Portræt af mig, som Krohg begyndte, malte han i Regelen en halvanden Time hver Formiddag, og Maleriet tok fulde ni Maaneder, uden derfor at blive det Mesterværk, det maaske var blevet, ifald Krohg havde erklæret det for færdigt, da en Fjerdedel af Tiden var gaaet."

49 Ibid.

50 Christian Krohg, *Kampen for tilværelsen* (Oslo: Gyldendal, 1954), 623. Original: "I nakken er minespillet ikke så sterkt."

51 Gerhard Gran, "Taine og hans Kunstphilosophi," *Ny Illustreret Tidende*, April 18, 1880. Original: "Vi vil simpelthen sige, at Kunsten har til Maal at fremstille og sanseliggjøre en Hovedkarakter, en eller anden fremspringende og fremragende Egenskab, en væsentlig Væremaade hos Gjenstanden."

52 Gerhard Gran, "Emile Zola," *Nyt Tidsskrift* 2 (1883): 302.

5. CHRISTIAN KROHG IN SKAGEN

1 Patricia G. Berman, *In Another Light: Danish Painting in the Nineteenth Century* (London: Thames and Hudson, 2013), 135.

2 Letter is quoted in Erik Mørstad, "Krohg and Brandes: Friendship and Professional Dialogue," in *Christian Krohg: Bilder som griper/Pictures That Captivate*, ed. Vibeke Waallaann Hansen, Erik Mørstad, Birgitte Sauge, and Marianne Yvenes (Oslo: Nasjonalmuseet for Kunst, Arkitektur og Design, 2012), 194.

3 Georg Brandes, *Levned: Snevringer og Horizonter* (Copenhagen: Gyldendalske, 1908), 66.

4 Ibid.

5 See Wilhelm Peters, *Hvad jeg saa og hvem jeg mødte: Erindringer fra et kunstnerliv* (Kristiania: Gyldendalske, 1914), 156 and 162–63.

6 T. J. Clark, *Image of the People: Gustave Courbet and the 1848 Revolution* (London: Thames and Hudson, 1988), 151.

7 Quoted in Berman, *In Another Light*, 133.

8 Ibid., 138.

9 A. L. Kroeber, *Anthropology: Culture Patterns and Processes* (New York: Harbinger, 1963), 89.

10 Christian Krohg, *Kampen for tilværelsen* (Oslo: Gyldendal, 1954), 524. Original: "Man kan som fremmed for eksempel gå inn i hvilket som helst hus man vil og se seg om i deres stuer. De gjør ingen omstendigheter, fortsetter sitt måltid, sin søvn eller sin påkledning aldeles ugenert. Man er straks kjent med dem."

11 Albert Guérard, *Literature and Society* (New York: Cooper Square, 1970), 43.

12 Ibid., 103–4.

13 Thomas Munro, *Evolution in the Arts and Other Theories of Culture History* (Cleveland, OH: Cleveland Museum of Art, 1963), 109. *Le moment* is a surprisingly abstract concept without a clear meaning. It can be both a short time—a literal moment—and a long stretch, like an epoch. It is often translated as "momentum" and can be understood as

a unique combination of forces coming from within (the race) and from without (the environment). One can say that national character (or race) and the surrounding circumstances (or environment) cannot operate on an empty stage, but always act in a historical time, or moment. Pascale Seys, *Hippolyte Taine et l'avènement du naturaliste: Un intellectuel sous le Second Empire* (Paris: L'Harmattan, 1999), 249. See also Leo Weinstein, *Hippolyte Taine* (New York: Twayne, 1972), 83–85. Momentum is created by race and environment, and at the same time leaves visible traces on them, almost like zeitgeist. (Therefore *le moment* is sometimes understood as an epoch.) The meaning of *le moment* must, thus, be kept open and seen as ambivalent. In literary critic René Wellek's view, *le moment*'s "main function is to serve as a reminder that history is dynamic while *milieu* is static." René Wellek, "Hippolyte Taine's Literary Theory and Criticism," *Criticism* 1, no. 1 (1959): 6.

14 "On peut donc se représenter la température et les circonstances physiques comme *faisant un choix* entre les différentes espèces d'arbres, et ne laissant subsister et se propager qu'une certaine espèce à l'exclusion plus ou moins complète de toutes les autres. La température physique agit par éliminations, par suppressions, par *sélection* naturelle. Telle est la grande loi par laquelle on explique aujourd'hui l'origine et la structure des diverses formes vivantes, et elle s'applique au moral comme au physique, dans l'histoire comme dans la botanique et la zoologie, aux talents et aux caractères comme aux plantes et aux animaux." Hippolyte Taine, *Philosophie de l'art,* vol. 1 (Paris: Hachette, 1895), 60.

15 Hippolyte Taine, *The Philosophy of Art: Art in the Netherlands*, trans. J. Durand (New York: Leypoldt and Holt, 1871), 83. Hippolyte Taine, *Philosophie de l'art dans les Pays-Bas* (Paris: Germer Baillière, 1869), 69. Original: "Les créatures imaginaires comme les formes vivantes sont à la fois les produits et les indices de leur milieu."

16 Émile Zola, *The Fortune of the Rougons*, trans. Brian Nelson (Oxford: Oxford University Press, 2012), 3. Zola stated in *The Experimental Novel*: "Without daring, as I say, to formulate laws, I consider that the question of heredity has a great influence in the intellectual and passionate manifestations of man. I also attach considerable importance to the surroundings." Émile Zola, *The Experimental Novel and Other Essays*, trans. Belle M. Sherman (New York: Haskell, 1964), 19; Émile Zola, *Le roman expérimental* (Paris: Charpentier, 1880), 18.

17 Christian Krohg, "Havets land: 1910," in *Christian Krohg og Skagen*, ed. Annette Johansen and Mette Bøgh Jensen (Skagen: Skagens Museum, 2004), 61.

18 Gabriel P. Weisberg, *Beyond Impressionism: The Naturalist Impulse* (New York: Harry N. Abrams, 1992), 19.

19 Sholom J. Kahn, *Science and Aesthetic Judgment: A Study in Taine's Critical Method* (New York: Columbia University Press, 1953), 104.

20 François Jacob, *The Logic of Life: A History of Heredity*, trans. Betty E. Spillman (New York: Panhtheon, 1973), 86.

21 Honoré de Balzac, "Avant-Propos," in *Oeuvres complètes de H. de Balzac*, vol. 1 (Paris: Michel Lévy, 1875), 2. Original: "La société ne fait-elle pas de l'homme, suivant les milieux où son action se déploie, autant d'hommes différents qu'il y a de variétés en zoologie?"

22 Munro, *Evolution in the Arts*, 108.

23 Weinstein, *Hippolyte Taine*, 82; Munro, *Evolution in the Arts*, 105.

24 Staffan Müller-Wille and Hans-Jörg Rheinberger, "Heredity—the Formation of an Epistemic Space," in *Heredity Produced: At the Crossroads of Biology, Politics, and Culture, 1500–1870* (Cambridge, MA: MIT Press, 2007), 3–34; Jacob, *The Logic of Life*, 19–20.

25 Müller-Wille and Rheinberger, "Heredity," 22.
26 Walter Schwartz, *Malere ved Staffeliet* (Copenhagen: Gyldendalske, 1941), 10. Original: "Skildringen af det rent etnografiske i Folkelivet."
27 Knud Voss, *Skagensmalerne* (Oslo: Grøndahl Dreyer, 1996), 18.
28 Wellek, "Hippolyte Taine's Literary Theory and Criticism," 37.
29 Kahn, *Science and Aesthetic Judgment*, 87–88.
30 Hippolyte Taine, *History of English Literature*, trans. H. Van Laun (New York: American Book Exchange, 1880), 23; Hippolyte Taine, *Histoire de la littérature anglaise*, vol. 1 (Paris: Hachette, 1863), xxiii.
31 Taine, *History of English Literature*, 24; *Histoire de la littérature anglaise*, xxiv.
32 Mette Bøgh Jensen, *At male sit privatliv: Skagensmalernes selviscenesættelse* (Skagen: Skagens Museum, 2005), 115.
33 Krohg, *Kampen for tilværelsen*, 524. Original: "Skagboerne er en rase for seg, som atskiller seg meget i vesen og utseende fra de øvrige danske. Sproget ligner temmelig meget norsk, men her hører også likheten opp. De er meget friere, lettere og selskapligere anlagt enn nordmenn."
34 Jensen, *At male sit privatliv*, 115–16.
35 Kahn, *Science and Aesthetic Judgment*, 90.
36 Krohg, *Kampen for Tilværelsen*, 505.
37 Ibid., 509. Original: "Vrak står ved vrak eftersom jeg vandrer alene henover den solbeskinnende strand. Like til seksten vrak talte jeg på et kort stykke. Seksten store skipslik."
38 Jensen, *At male sit privatliv*, 160–66.
39 For a good example on the leading view of Dutch masters, see Karl Madsen, *Billedkunsten* (Copenhagen: Frem, 1901), 137–50.
40 Christian Krohg, *I Smaa Dagsreiser til og fra Paris* (Kristiania: Aschehoug, 1897), 53. Original: "Om Hollænderne røger mer end andre, ved jeg ikke, skjønt vistnok Tobaksrøgning spiller en stor Rolle som Motiver paa deres gamle Malerier."
41 For an excellent discussion of Dutch painting and realism, see Peter Demetz, "Defenses of Dutch Painting and the Theory of Realism," *Comparative Literature* 15, no. 2 (1963): 97–115.
42 Frits Thaulow, *I Kamp og i Fest* (Kristinia: Gyldendalske, 1908), 213.
43 Krohg, *I Smaa Dagsreiser*, 57 and 59–60. Original: "Han har malt alting. Landskaber, Figurer, Dyr, Mariner, Helgener, Tiggere, Jøder, Rigdom og Fattigdom, Sygdom og Elendighed, Hospitalscener, Illustrationer til Bibelen og den græske Mythologi, hans Geni omspændte alt, Livet og Døden, Himlen, Jorden og Helvede, og alle Retninger, han var Idealist og Realist, Romantiker, Symbolist, Impressionist, han var et overnaturlig Væsen, en Gaade, en Gud."
44 Georg Brandes, "Et Besøg i Holland," *Tilskueren* (August 1892): 583. Original: "I Virkeligheden har Rembrandt opfundet Malerkunsten; han er *Maleren* for alle Malere." See also Julius Lange, *Udvalgte Skrifter*, vol. 2 (Copenhagen: Det Nordiske Forlag, 1901), 366–76.
45 Taine, *The Philosophy of Art: Art in the Netherlands*, 181; *Philosophie de l'art dans les Pays-Bas*, 162. Original: "En magicien et en visionnaire."
46 "Supérieur à tous les peintres par la délicatesse et l'acuité natives de ses perceptions optiques, il a compris et suivi dans toutes ses conséquences cette vérité, que pour l'œil toute l'essence d'une chose visible est dans la tache, que la plus simple couleur est infiniment complexe, que toute sensation visuelle est un produit de ses éléments et en outre de ses alentours, que chaque objet dans le champ visuel n'est qu'une tache modifiée par

d'autres taches, et qu'ainsi le principal personnage d'un tableau est l'air coloré, vibrant, interposé, dans lequel les figures sont plongées comme les poissons dans la mer." Taine, *Philosophie de l'art dans les Pays-Bas*, 162–63.

47 Taine, *The Philosophy of Art: Art in the Netherlands*, 172; *Philosophie de l'art dans les Pays-Bas*, 153–54. Original: "Pendant le XVIIe siècle, la Hollande est le premier des pays pensants. Les sciences positives y trouvent leur sol natal ou leur patrie d'emprunt."

48 Taine, *The Philosophy of Art: Art in the Netherlands*, 32; *Philosophie de l'art dans les Pays-Bas*, 21. Original: "La représentation crue et complète de la vie réelle avec tous les détails atroces, ignobles et plats, avec tous les instincts sublimes et brutaux."

49 Taine, *The Philosophy of Art: Art in the Netherlands*, 43; *Philosophie de l'art dans les Pays-Bas*, 31–32. Original: "Il vit dans un climat humide et uniforme, qui détend les nerfs, développe le tempérament lymphatique, modère les révoltes, les explosions et les fougues de l'âme, émousse l'âpreté des passions et tourne le caractère du côté de la sensualité et de la belle humeur."

50 Taine, *The Philosophy of Art: Art in the Netherlands*, 64; *Philosophie de l'art dans les Pays-Bas*, 52. Original: "Seuls, les Flamands et les Hollandais ont aimé les formes et les couleurs pour elles-mêmes."

51 Eugène Fromentin, *The Masters of Past Time, or Criticism on the Old Flemish and Dutch Painters* (New York: E. P. Dutton, 1913), 131.

52 Karl Madsen, "I Holland," *Tilskueren* (December 1892): 896.

53 Fromentin, *The Masters of Past Time*, 146 and 154.

54 Painting like a Dutch or a Flemish master became a compliment. As one conservative critic wrote about Rafaëlli in 1881, "[Rafaëlli's art] has a sincerity, a truth, an extraordinary naturalness: he is an observer like the Flemish, with a Parisian spirit: his workers, his beggars, his déclassés are of a stunning realism." Quoted in Marnin Young, "Heroic Indolence: Realism and the Politics of Time in Raffaëlli's *Absinthe Drinkers*," *Art Bulletin* 90, no. 2 (2008): 238. Courbet's pictures, such as *After Dinner at Ornans* (1848–49), were also compared to those of Dutch and Flemish masters; and François Bonvin was especially known for the way he combined contemporary realism with the aura of Dutch golden age paintings, as he did in his *Woman Cutting Bread for Soup*. Clark, *Image of the People*, 70, 72–73; Gabriel P. Weisberg, "The Traditional Realism of François Bonvin," *Bulletin of the Cleveland Museum of Art* 65, no. 9 (1978): 288–89.

55 When Madsen wrote about one of Michael Ancher's Skagen paintings, he used the expression "a certain Dutch taste" in his description of Ancher's treatment of chiaroscuro and light falling on the floor through an open door. Karl Madsen, "Michael Ancher," *Tilskueren* 3 (1886): 217.

56 Vermeer was presented in a series of three articles by Théophile Thoré. See William Bürger [Théophile Thoré], "Van der Meer de Delft," *Gazette des Beaux-Arts* 21 (1866): 297–330, 458–79, and 542–75. For the French reception of Vermeer, see Christiane Hertel, *Vermeer: Reception and Interpretation* (Cambridge: Cambridge University Press, 1996).

57 Emil Hannover, "Nogle Indtryk fra Foraarsudstillingen paa Charlottenborg," *Tilskueren* 4 (May 1887), 376.

58 Karl Madsen, "Van der Meer fra Delft," *Tilskueren* 1 (1884): 972–73 and 974–75. Madsen is relying on Thoré's text from 1866 and on Henry Havard, *Histoire de la peinture hollandaise* (Paris: A. Quantin, 1882).

59 Thaulow, *I Kamp og i Fest*, 133.

60 Fromentin, *The Masters of Past Time*, 226.

61 Ibid., 222. See also Eugène Véron, *Æsthetics*, trans. W. H. Armstrong (London: Chapman and Hall, 1879), 277–78. For original text, see Eugène Véron, *L'esthétique* (Paris: Vrin, 2007), 302–4.

62 Andreas Aubert, "Manet: Et Bidrag til Sujetets og Koloritens Historie i den nyere Tid," *Tilskueren* 5 (1888): 680–81.

63 Ibid., 682. Original: "Man skal vanskelig i Nutidskunsten finde et Værk, der er kommet Frans Hals nærmere i umiddelbar Djærvhed, i frisk og kraftig Farve. Frans Hals var saa at sige sin Tids 'Impressionist': ingen har overgaaet ham i Anskuelsens Energi."

64 Petra ten-Doesschate Chu, "Nineteenth-Century Visitors to the Frans Hals Museum," in *The Documented Image: Visions in Art History*, ed. Gabriel P. Weisberg and Laurinda S. Dixon (Syracuse: Syracuse University Press, 1987).

65 For more about Hals's revival and Thoré, see Frances Suzman Jowell, "Thoré-Bürger and the Revival of Frans Hals," *Art Bulletin* 56, no. 1 (1974): 101–17. Claude Monet visited the Hals Museum in 1871, and Édouard Manet did so the year after. Naturalists such as Jules Breton, Léon Lhermitte, and Alfred Roll also made that pilgrimage. Eilif Peterssen had been there as early as 1876 and that same year painted a self-portrait likely inspired by Dutch paintings in its use of colors and brush strokes. Carl Locher had, with Karl Madsen, visited the museum in April 1879, when they were working in Skagen. Julius Lange paid a visit in 1882 and wrote two years later that Hals's paintings sparkled. Lange, *Udvalgte Skrifter*, 364. Lange included a long and laudatory passage on Hals in his account of Netherlandish art. (He also linked Taine with Hals.) It became common in the late nineteenth century to compare Hals and his technique with modern art. When Krohg visited the Hals Museum in 1897, he wrote that he was intrigued by Hals's modernity and found him the easiest to understand among the Dutch old masters because for a contemporary viewer he was "less different from modern artists" and "could very well hang in the Spring Exhibition" Krohg, *I Smaa Dagsreiser*, 65 and 66. Hals appeared so modern because he painted like a "blotch painter." He seemed contemporary and fresh: "It is in his blotch paintings that one finds his true importance as a great artist. In the way he places the patches—no one has done it before or after. There is an intensity of life in every single stroke, and one can fall into rapture over the jolly mood in those highlights which he had dabbed on a tip of a nose or in the corner of an eye." Krohg, *I Smaa Dagsreiser*, 69. Original: "Men i dette Klattemaleri ligger hans egentlige Betydning som stor Kunstner. Slig som han placerer Klatterne, har ingen kunnet gjøre det før eller siden. Det er Livets Intensitet i hver eneste af dem, og man kan falde i Henrykkelse over det gode Humør i de Glanslys, som han slængte hen paa en Næsetip eller i en Øiekrog."

66 There has been some discussion on who painted this portrait. For a long time it was attributed to Michael Ancher, but now it is given to Krohg. See Johansen and Bøgh Jensen, eds., *Christian Krohg og Skagen*, cat. no. 10. See also Oscar Thue, *Christian Krohg* (Oslo: Aschehoug, 1997), 51. Thue dates the painting to 1885 and the Skagen catalog to 1880. I rely on the Skagen Museum's dating.

67 Other Skagen painters also made Hals-inspired portraits, among them Krohg's Skagen flatmate Oscar Björck. Together with other artists, they shared a house in 1883, and that year Björck painted *Cheers* (1883), which seems like a mash-up of several Hals paintings, including *Jester with a Lute* (1620–25) in the Louvre, *Boy with a Lute* (ca. 1625), and *Young Man and Woman in an Inn* (1623). Michael Ancher's *Fisherman Lars Gaihede* (1880) likewise seems to have been influenced by Hals.

Epigraph: Henrik Jæger, "Christian Krohg og hans Emner," *Christiania Intelligentssedler (Dagens Nyheder)*, March 26, 1885. Original: "De hensyn der bringer ham til at vælge de Emner, han med Forkjærlighed behandler, er ikke udelukkende af kunstnerisk Natur, Nei, Blikket for det maleriske har hos ham indgaaet en fast og eiendommelig Forbindelse med en rent moderne og rent menneskelig Medfølelse. . . . Resultatet er bleven en Originalitet baade i Motiver og Udførelse, hvortil vi herhjemme ikke har noget Sidestykke."

1 For more on this, see Anthea Callen, *The Spectacular Body: Science, Method and Meaning in the Work of Degas* (New Haven, CT: Yale University Press, 1995), 3–4.

2 Edmond and Jules de Goncourt, *Journal des Goncourt: Mémoires de la vie littéraire*, vol. 3 (Paris: Charpentier, 1888), 33. Original: "La beauté du visage ancien était la beauté de ses lignes; la beauté du visage moderne est la physionomie de sa passion."

3 Michael Fried, *Absorption and Theatricality: Painting and Beholder in the Age of Diderot* (Chicago: University of Chicago Press, 1988), 10.

4 Ibid., 100.

5 Ibid., 108.

6 Georges Canguilhem, *The Normal and the Pathological*, trans. Carolyn R. Fawcett (New York: Zone Books, 2007), 137.

7 For more on this, see David Marshall, *The Surprising Effects of Sympathy: Marivaux, Diderot, Rousseau, and Mary Shelley* (Chicago: University of Chicago Press, 1988), introduction.

8 Claudius Wilkens, *Æsthetik i Omrids: Med særlight Hensyn til Moderne Æsthetik* (Copenhagen: Gyldendalske, 1888), 133.

9 Joris-Karl Huysmans, *Écrits sur l'art* (Paris: Flammarion, 2008), 72–73.

10 Huysmans, *Écrits sur l'art*, 72. Original: "M. Bastien-Lepage est une peintre d'une prodigieuse habilité, qui connaît son métier sur le bout du doigt."

11 Émile Zola, *Écrits sur l'art* (Paris: Gallimard, 1991), 427. Original: "Deux pages où l'on a respiré le grand air avec une surprise pleine d'admiration."

12 Quoted in Fr. Crastre, *Bastien-Lepage*, trans. Frederic Taber Cooper (New York: Frederick A. Stokes, 1914), 46.

13 Albert Edelfelt, *Ur Albert Edelfelts Pariserbrev till sin Mor* (Stockholm: Albert Bonniers, 1917), 188. Edelfelt had met and become a close friend of Bastien-Lepage as early as 1875, and wrote a glowing article about the French painter for the journal *Finsk Tidsskrift* in 1879. Edelfelt mentions Bastien-Lepage many times in his letters. See Edelfelt, *Pariserbrev*; and Albert Edelfelt, *Ur Albert Edelfelts Brev. Liv och Arbete* (Stockholm: Almqvist & Wiksells Förlag, 1926).

14 Quoted in Knut Berg, "Naturalisme og nyromantikk 1870–1900," in *Norges malerkunst*, vol. 1, ed. Knut Berg (Oslo: Gyldendal, 2000), 395. Original: "Frankrikes og vår tids betydeligste kunstner."

15 Frits Thaulow, *I Kamp og i Fest* (Kristiania: Gyldendalske, 1908), 80. Original: "Bastien Lepages Friluftsbilder blæste netop den gang frisk Luft ind i de lumre, overparfumerede Saloner. Hans klare Øine og nøgterne Noblesse."

16 Julius Lange, *Vor Kunst og Udlandets: Et Foredrag* (Copenhagen: P. G. Philipsen, 1879), 13.

17 Julius Lange, *Bastien Lepage og andre Afhandlinger* (Copenhagen: P. G. Philipsen, 1889), 1. Original: "Jules Bastien Lepage's Navn har i den sidste halve Snes Aar hørt til de bekendteste, mest omtalte Kunstnernavne i hele Europa."

18 Quoted in Lange, *Bastien Lepage*, 2. Original: "[Bastien-Lepage er] den lykkelige Kunstner, der alt i sin Ungdom har vundet sin Samtids Sympathi, og i hvem Eftertiden vil se et af de mest energiske Udtryk for, hvad der kunstnerisk har bevæget vor Tid, hvad der har bevæget den sundest og ædlest."

19 Quoted in Marianne Saabye, "Krøyer and Bastien-Lepage," *Krøyer: An International Perspective* (Skagen: Skagens Museum, 2011), 27.

20 Emil Hannover, *Erindringer fra Barndom og Ungdom* (Copenhagen: Forening for Boghaandværk, 1966), 145. Original: "Højdepunktet af moderne fransk Kunst var for os danske Bastien Lepage. Ogsaa Roll beundrede vi."

21 Boris Röhrl, *Kunsttheorie des Naturalismus und Realismus: Historiche Entwicklung, Terminologie und Definitionen* (Hildesheim: Georg Olms, 2003), 77.

22 "Il y a un terme appliqué depuis longtemps à la peinture de Manet et de M. Bastien-Lepage qui caractérise certainement mieux la manière des Goncourt, de M. Daudet, de M. Zola, et même de Flaubert et de Balzac. C'est le terme d'impressionnisme." Louis Desprez, *L'évolution naturaliste* (Paris: Tresse, 1884), 94. In Mayer's *Konversationslexikon* from 1878, one can read the following about "Naturalismus": "In der Malerei nennt man Naturalismus als Gegensatz des Idealismus diejenige Kunstrichtung, welche in der möglichst treuen Nachahmung der Natur und des wirklichen Lebens die höchste Aufgabe der Kunst sieht. . . . Zu einer platten Naturnachahmung ohne poetische Elemente artete Naturalismus erst im 19. Jahrhundert durch die Franzosen Courbet, Manet und die Impressionisten sowie durch die so genannten Naturalisten (Bastien-Lepage, L'Hermitte u.a.)." Quoted in Röhrl, *Kunsttheorie*, 77.

23 Georg Nordensvan, *De Bildande Konsternas Historia under 19: De Århundradet* (Stockholm: Hugo Gerber, 1900), 302. Original: "Bastien-Lepage var individualist och detaljist, Millet var syntetiker och epiker." See also Georg Nordensvan, "Bastien-Lepage: Till hans tafla: Ett kärlekspar," *Ny Illustrerad Tidning* 4, no. 41 (1883); and Georg Nordensvan, "Franskt Måleri och Tyskt: Några Anmärkningar," *Nordisk Tidsskrift för Vetenskap, Konst och Industri* 9 (1886).

24 Quoted in Richard Thomson, *Art of the Actual: Naturalism and Style in Early Third Republic France, 1880–1900* (New Haven, CT: Yale University Press, 2012), 128.

25 Quoted in Julia Cartwright, "J. Bastien-Lepage," in *The Portfolio: Monographs on Artistic Subjects*, ed. P. G. Hamerton (London: Seeley and Macmillan, 1894), 19.

26 Eva Bonnier, *Pariserbref* (Stockholm: Klara, 1999), 105–6. Original: "Det var kolossalt, och den största konstuppbyggelse, jag har haft på länge. Förr än man sett på detta hans arbete samladt kan man ej göra sig någon föreställning om hans storhet och originalitet. Märkvärdigast verkar hans produktionskraft. Sex salar äro fulla af hans arbeten, och ändå dog karlen vid 31 år, af hvilka de 2 sista, han ej kunde röra en pensel."

27 Quoted in David Jackson, "Natural North: Russia and Nordic Countries," in *Illusion of Reality: Naturalist Painting, Photography, Theatre and Cinema, 1875–1918*, ed. Gabriel P. Weisberg, David Jackson, and Willa Z. Silverman (Amsterdam: Van Gogh Museum, 2010), 104.

28 Emil Hannover, "Nogle Billeder paa den Franske Udstilling," *Tilskueren* 5 (1888): 563. Hannover wrote: "Det forekommer En ufatteligt, at der har været en Tid, da der var mere end én Mening om Bastien-Lepages sublime kunstneriske Værdier. Han er ikke blot med sine to Billeder *Tiggeren* og *Kartoffelhøsten* paa denne franske Udstilling den ædleste, den fineste og den størst begavede blandt alle sine Landsmænd, men han er overhovedet den ævnerigeste Kunstner blandt alle det nittende Aarhundreds realistiske Malere."

29 Ibid. Hannover wrote: "Hvad der betegner hans Billeder mere end noget andet, er den

Dvælen ved Tingen, som des værre er saa sjælden i moderne Kunst. Han dvæler ved en Ting, saa længe denne Ting alene ejer endnu en eneste lille Ejendommelighed. Han jager Virkeligheden, til han holder den fangen og bunden i sin Bevidsthed, og han lader ikke sin Haand slippe eller hvile, saa længe den ikke har meddelt alt, hvad han selv har sét."

30 Ibid., 564. Original: "Et Stykke Natur set igennem et ædelt og kraftigt Temperament, der er af de sjældne."

31 Lange, *Bastien Lepage*, 6. Original: "Giver han en dyptgaaende og fuldt gennemført Karakterskildring."

32 Lucy H. Hooper, "The Paris Salon of 1878," *Art Journal* 4 (1878): 255.

33 Kenyon Cox, "Antoine Vollon: A Painter's Painter," *Manhattan Magazine* 2 (1883): 558.

34 Marnin Young, "The Motionless Look of a Painting: Jules Bastien-Lepage, *Les Foins*, and the End of Realism," *Art History* 37, no. 1 (2014): 41.

35 "Remarquons attentivement tout cela, et si ces artistes continuent, dans cette voie, M. Bastien Lepage ne sera bientôt plus que leur égal." "Salon de 1882," *Paris moderne: Revue littéraire et artistique* 1 (1881–82): 4. See also Charles de Feir, *Guide de Salon de Paris 1882* (Paris: Au Bureau du Moniteur des Arts, 1882), 15–16.

36 Louis Énault, *Paris-Salon: Triennal 1883* (Paris: E. Bernard, 1883), 50.

37 For a discussion of the critiques, see Oscar Thue, *Christian Krohg* (Oslo: Aschehoug, 1997), 66.

38 My information on tuberculosis is gathered from Aina Schiøtz, *Folkets helse—landets styrke 1850–2003* (Oslo: Universitetsforlaget, 2003), 65–71; and Hilde Bondevik and Knut Stene-Johansen, *Sykdom som litteratur* (Oslo: Unipub, 2011), ch. 5.

39 Austin Flint, *A Treatise on the Principles and Practice of Medicine* (Philadelphia: Henry C. Lea, 1873), 287.

40 Christian Krohg, *Albertine* (Oslo: Bokklubben, 1995), 10. Original: "Han hostet hult og anstrengt og harket, spyttet ut noe og trådte på det."

41 René and Jean Dubos, *The White Plague: Tuberculosis, Man, and Society* (New Brunswick, NJ: Rutgers University Press, 1996), 69.

42 Ibid., xxxvii.

43 Lorentz Dietrichson, *Norges kunsts historie i det nittende århundre* (Oslo: Messel, 1991), 168.

44 Thue, *Christian Krohg*, 61.

45 Andreas Aubert, *Morgenbladet*, January 11, 1882.

46 For more on this, see Linda Nochlin, *Representing Women* (London: Thames and Hudson, 1999), 88–89. One should also mention Rozsika Parker's important book on the association between embroidery and women: *The Subversive Stitch: Embroidery and the Making of the Feminine* (London: I. B. Tauris, 2010).

47 Karl Marx, *Capital*, vol. 1, trans. Ben Fowkes (London: Penguin, 1990), 602–4.

48 Judith G. Coffin, "Consumption, Production, and Gender: The Sewing Machine in Nineteenth-Century France," in *Gender and Class in Modern Europe*, ed. Laura L. Frader and Sonya O. Rose (Ithaca, NY: Cornell University Press, 1996), 112. I draw on Coffin's informative and thorough research for my discussion of the sewing machine. See also Judith Coffin, "Social Science Meets Sweated Labor: Reinterpreting Women's Work in Late Nineteenth-Century France," *Journal of Modern History* 63, no. 2 (1991): 230–70; Judith G. Coffin, "Credit, Consumption, and Images of Women's Desires: Selling the Sewing Machine in Late Nineteenth-Century France," *French Historical Studies* 18, no. 3 (1994): 749–83; Judith G. Coffin, *The Politics of Women's Work: The Paris Garment Trades 1750–1915* (Princeton, NJ: Princeton University Press, 1996).

49 Coffin, "Consumption, Production, and Gender," 117–18.

50 See Coffin, *The Politics of Women's Work*, 108.
51 See ibid., 67 and 107.
52 Quoted in ibid., 109.
53 Quoted in Aina Schiøtz, "Prostitusjonen i Kristiania ca. 1870–1890: En sosialhistorisk undersøkelse" (master's thesis, University of Oslo, 1977), 69.
54 Alain Corbin, *Women for Hire: Prostitution and Sexuality in France after 1850*, trans. Alan Sheridan (Cambridge, MA: Harvard University Press, 1990), table 7.

7. NATURALIST *Paragone*

1 Pierre Macherey, *A Theory of Literary Production*, trans. Geoffrey Wall (London: Routledge, 2006), 290.
2 Oscar Thue, "Christian Krohgs sosiale tendenskunst" (Magister degree diss., University of Oslo, 1955), 107. Original: "I motsetning til det meste av hans øvrige produksjon har utarbeidelsen av Krohgs sosiale tendensbilder således nesten uten unntagelse bestått i å gi et (på forhånd) bestemt litterært innhold en mest mulig dekkende, naturlig og kunstnerisk fullverdig form."
3 Norman Bryson, *Word and Image: French Painting of the Ancien Régime* (Cambridge: Cambridge University Press, 1981), 6.
4 "The Reality Effect" can be found in Roland Barthes, *The Rustle of Language*, trans. Richard Howard (Berkeley: University of California Press, 1989), 141–48.
5 George Clausen, "Jules Bastien-Lepage as Artist," in André Theuriet, *Jules Bastien-Lepage and His Art: A Memoir* (London: T. Fisher Unwin and Macmillan, 1892), 114.
6 Quoted in Thue, "Christian Krohgs sosiale tendenskunst," 46. Original: "Ett bihang till ett litterært alster utan självständigt innehåll."
7 Andreas Aubert, "I Anledning af Christian Krohgs store Komposition: Fra Politilægens Venteværelse," *Dagbladet*, March 22, 1887. Original: "Her er det den bildende Kunst træder Literaturen og Videnskaben tilhjælp."
8 "Christian Krohg om gammel og ny kunst og om den evige kunst," *Nationen*, November 20, 1920. Original: "Kompositionen i mit store 'Albertine'-billede (Hos politilægen) i galleriet f.eks. er gal. Den er teatralsk. Nogen av figurene gaar nemlig til side for at man skal se Albertine, og alle sammen er rædde for at vende ryggen til publikum."
9 For more on this, see Philip Walker, "The Mirror, the Window, and the Eye in Zola's Fiction," *Yale French Studies* 42 (1969): 52–67. There are many excellent articles and books on the relationship between naturalist fiction and painting, including Lloyd James Austin, "Mallarmé and the Visual Arts" (on the artistic collaboration between Mallarmé and Raffaëlli), in *French 19th Century Painting and Literature*, ed. Ulrich Finke (Manchester: Manchester University Press, 1972), 232–57; Marian S. Robinson, "Zola and Monet: The Poetry of the Railway," *Journal of Modern Literature* 10, no. 1 (1983): 55–70.
10 My understanding of a visual novel is based on William J. Berg's research on Zola, and many of my points are derived from William J. Berg, *The Visual Novel: Emile Zola and the Art of His Times* (University Park: Pennsylvania State University Press, 1992). I have also consulted Walker, "The Mirror, the Window, and the Eye," 52–67.
11 Roland Barthes, *S/Z*, trans. Richard Miller (Oxford: Blackwell, 2000), 54–56.
12 See Berg, *The Visual Novel*, 9.
13 Ibid., 271.
14 Christian Krohg, *Albertine* (Oslo: Bokklubben, 1995), 9. Original: "Tvers over det lille,

lave vinduet med de mange rutene i var spent et utslitt halvgardin. Foran det satt hun, bøyet mot symaskinen under den innsigende vinterdag, som sendte et tynt blålig randlys nedover det fine bakhodet, over hårknuten og nakken og den stivete strimlen. Stålflaten skinte koldt i det grå, fattige lyset, og den hvite tarlatansremsen som hun sydde på, ble ganske blålig. Saksen lå og sprikte ved siden av, og snellene og fingerbølet kastet slagskygger bortover mahogniplaten. Randlyset gled videre fra hodet og nedover den bøyde rygg og tapte seg i skyggen. Hennes ansikt ble borte i halvmørket, men profilen trådte frem mot det lyse halvgardinet bak. Kjolelivet var av grå kord og satt stramt over skuldrene, og de var rette og brede. Det som lyste mest, var hånden, som var stor og lå oppe på den blanke, kolde stålflaten og styrte tarlatansremsen under nålen. . . . I kroken ved ovnen var det mørkest. Mor Kristiansen sto og stelte der."

15 Emil Hannover, *Erindringer fra Barndom og Ungdom* (Copenhagen: Forening for Boghaandverk, 1966), 128. Original: "Næst efter Springer og Morelli havde overhovedet endnu ingen Kunstskribenter gjort saa stærkt Indtryk paa mig som de to berømte Brødre Edmond og Jules. Det første Foredrag, jeg havde hørt af Brandes, havde gældt disse og havde allerede medført et Sværmeri hos mig for deres kunstneriske gennemkultiverede Væsen. *Manette Salomon* og *Les frères Zemganno* havde jeg naturligvis forlængst slugt."

16 Georg Brandes, "Literære Studier III: Naturalisme i Frankrige," *Dagbladet*, August 30, 1879. Original: "De svare til 'Impressjonisterne' i det moderne franske Maleri, der ligeledes forsøge at gjengive det enkelte Øjebliks stærle Indtryk."

17 Georg Brandes, *Udenlandske Egne og Personligheder* (Copenhagen: Gyldendalske, 1893), 63.

18 Beverly Jean Gibbs, "Impressionism as a Literary Movement," *Modern Language Journal* 36, no. 4 (1952): 175–83.

19 Ambroise Vollard, "Cezanne and Zola," *Soil* 1, no. 1 (1916): 13. See also Theodore Reff, "Degas and the Literature of His Time—I," *Burlington Magazine* 112, no. 810 (1970): 586–89: and Evert van Uitert, "Vincent van Gogh and Paul Gauguin in Competition: Vincent's Original Contribution," *Simiolus: Netherlands Quarterly for the History of Art* 11, no. 2 (1980): 96.

20 Frits Thaulow, *I Kamp og i Fest* (Kristiania: Gyldendalske, 1908), 50.

21 Georg Brandes, *Levned: Et Tiaar* (Copenhagen: Gyldendalske, 1907), 297–98.

22 Carol Armstrong, *Manet Manette* (New Haven, CT: Yale University Press, 2002), 68. *Manette Salomon* is analyzed and discussed by Armstrong, and several of my points are based on her reading. See also chapter 5, "Models, Monkeys, Naturalism: The Goncourt Brother's *Manette Salomon*," in Marie Lathers, *Bodies of Art: French Literary Realism and the Artist's Model* (Lincoln: University of Nebraska Press, 2001).

23 Louis Desprez wrote: "Dans *Manette Salomon*, ce sont des vues d'Orient et de Rome, un dîner de carnaval, une synagogue, etc. Des tableaux que l'on pourrait retrancher du livre sans lui enlever rien d'essentiel. À vrai dire, l'action n'est qu'un prétexte: un roman des Goncourt ressemble à une exposition de maître-peintre." *L'évolution naturaliste* (Paris: Tresse, 1884), 88–89.

24 Edmond and Jules de Goncourt, *Germinie Lacerteux* (Paris: Charpentier, 1875), vi. Original: "Vivant au dix-neuvième siècle, dans un temps de suffrage universel, de démocratie, de libéralisme, nous nous sommes demandé si ce qu'on appelle 'les basses classes' n'avait pas droit au Roman; si ce monde sous un monde, le peuple, devait rester sous le coup de l'interdit littéraire et des dédains d'auteurs qui ont fait jusqu'ici le silence sur l'âme et le cœur qu'il peut avoir."

25 "Le public aime les romans faux: ce roman est un roman vrai. Il aime les livres qui font semblant d'aller dans le monde: ce livre vient de la rue." Ibid., v.

26 Ibid., v–vi. Original: "Qu'il ne s'attende point à la photographie décolletée du Plaisir: l'étude qui suit est la Clinique de l'Amour."

27 Quoted in Anne Wichstrøm, *Kvinneliv, Kunstnerliv: Kvinnelige malere i Norge før 1900* (Oslo: Gyldendal, 2000), 91–92. Original: "Man skal ikke male Poesi, det er en af de simple Sætninger, hvorpaa al Kunst hviler . . . der skal ikke først digtes og saa males."

28 Thaulow, *I kamp og i Fest*, 214.

29 Irgens Hansen, "Krohgs Maleri," *Verdens Gang*, May 8, 1889. Original: "Det er bleven sagt, at et Maleri som fortalte noget netop herved blev mindre Kunst; det blev ikke længre Kunst for Kunstens Skyld, men var Kunst i Tjeneste hos andre Formaal. Det har Christian Krohg aldrig bryd sig om."

30 Jens Thiis, *Norske malere og billedhuggere* (Bergen: John Griegs Forlag, 1904), 254. Original: "Krohg er nemlig ikke bare i besiddelse av et par sunde og nydedygtige malerøine, han har sikkerlig også et blødt hjærte. Og han er som maler så uheldig at være begavet med forfattertalent. Af og til har han været inde på det at male litteratur. . . . Men Krohg har heldigvis været sig denne sin svaghed bevidst og tidlig kjæmpet mot den; som regel har hans sunde sanselige malerøie seiret."

31 August Brunius, "Norsk Kolorisme: Fra Jubilæumsutstillingen," *Morgenbladet*, October 11, 1914.

32 Christian Krohg, *Kampen for tilværelsen* (Oslo: Gyldendal, 1954), 130. Original: "['Sypiken'] er det første maleri av meg som er blitt rost i avisene av en kritiker. Men det var naturligvis kun for det litterære motivs skyld, og dernest for det 'demokratiske moment' sypikene, med de 'små i samfunnet.' Heldigvis lå der ikke noen sådan sympati til grunn for bildet, ti det ville jo være helt og holdent ukunstnerisk. Nei, det som lå til grunn for bildet, var kun et koloristisk problem. Jeg hadde ved femtiden om morgenen i annen etasje på Café Américain i Paris, like før vi skulle begi oss til hallene, sett det første kolde skjær av dagslys strømme inn, dempet av gardinene, og møte det kunstige lys som ennu den gang var det varme cadmiumgule gasslys. Den merkelige koloristiske stemningen, en disharmoi, kunne jeg ikke glemme. Men da jeg senere, hjemme i Norge, hvor man verken den gang eller senere hadde noen 'Américain,' ville male den omtalte motsetning, så måtte jeg finne på noe som ga anledning til samme lyseffekt, og således ble 'Sypiken' til."

33 Ibid., 11. Original: "Jeg holder også nemlig på med en bok, og i denne kunne jeg til sist ikke komme lenger—jeg kunne ikke få det godt nok til, så godt som jeg forlangte, fordi det hadde grepet mitt øye enda frappantere enn jeg orket å skrive det, og så ga jeg meg til å male det."

34 Leonardo da Vinci, *Leonardo on Painting*, trans. Martin Kemp and Margaret Walker (New Haven, CT: Yale University Press, 2001), 20–21 and 28.

35 Émile Zola, *The Experimental Novel and Other Essays*, trans. Belle M. Sherman (New York: Haskell, 1964), 145; Émile Zola, *Le roman expérimental* (Paris: Charpentier, 1880), 144.

36 Krohg, *Kampen for tilværelsen*, 6–11. Original: "Når en forfatter skildrer menneskenes ytre, deres miljø, så forsøker han å skrive således at man *ser* det for sitt ytre øye i et momentant bilde. Og han kan godt skrive slik, men undertiden overanstrenger han seg, midlet slår ikke til, han skildrer og skildrer, han får frem form og farve og glans og totalinntrykk, men vil han ha mer form og mer farve, da slår midlet ikke mer til, han vil gjerne kyle pennen i veggen og ta en pensel i stedet. *Så kommer den bildende kunstner*. For det har han

greie på. Han kan gjøre det enda bedre, så man ser det enda bedre, så man ser det slik at man aldri glemmer det, så det sanne blir enda mer skjærende, så det uhyggelige blir enda mer uhyggelig. Der har vi kunstens misjon i den nærværende kulturbevegelse."

8. ALBERTINE IN THE POLICE DOCTOR'S WAITING ROOM

1 Quoted in Arne Brenna, "Albertine igjen," *Kunst og Kultur* 63, no. 1 (1980): 63. Original: "Det er en Genre i den store Stil, hentet i sit Motiv fra Livets Natside. Tanken udtrykkes maaske bedst ved at kalde Billedet: 'En Debut i Prostitutionen.' Scenen er henlagt til Politistationens Ventesal for Kvinder henhørende under Prostitutionen. Mellem alle de ældre og yngre, men rutinerende med frække Ansigter og fjonge Toiletter staar en ung, ussel klædt Pige, som for første Gang er opkaldt, med nedslagne Øjne, forskræmt og ulykkelig."

2 Émile Zola, *Nana*, trans. George Holden (London: Penguin, 1972), 336–37. Original: "Elle avait lu dans la journée un roman qui faisait grand bruit, l'histoire d'une fille; et elle se révoltait, elle disait que tout cela était faux, témoignant d'ailleurs une répugnance indignée contre cette littérature immonde, dont la prétention était de rendre la nature; comme si l'on pouvait tout montrer! comme si un roman ne devait pas être écrit pour passer une heure agréable! En matière de livres et de drames, Nana avait des opinions très arrêtées: elle voulait des œuvres tendres et nobles, des choses pour la faire rêver et lui grandir l'âme." Émile Zola, *Nana* (Paris: Charpentier, 1893), 368–69.

3 T. J. Clark, *The Painting of Modern Life: Paris in the Art of Manet and His Followers* (London: Thames and Hudson, 2003), 103.

4 Ibid., 111.

5 Hans Heyerdahl, "Prostitutionen," *Verdens Gang*, December 11, 1886.

6 Andreas Aubert, "I Anledning af Christian Krohgs store Komposition: Fra Politlægens Venteværelse," *Dagbladet*, March 22, 1887. Original: "Den mest motbydelige bestialiserte Kvindelighet."

7 Quoted in Oscar Thue, "Christian Krohgs sosiale tendenskunst," Magister Degree diss., University of Oslo, 1955, 46. Original: "Paa lignende Maade som Videnskabsmanden legger et sjældent Dyr paa sit Laboratorie-Bord—har Kunstneren her opstillet to Typer af en interessant Art af 'la bête humaine' for grundigt at studere og karakterisere disse Fremtoninger."

8 Lorentz Dietrichson, *Norges kunsts historie i det nittende århundre* (Oslo: Messel, 1991), 168. Original: "Nogle afskyelig fæle Madamer og andre frastøtende Fysiognomier."

9 Ann La Berge and Mordechai Feingold, *French Medical Culture in the Nineteenth Century* (Amsterdam: Rodopi, 1994), 1.

10 John Waller, "'The Illusion of an Explanation': The Concept of Hereditary Disease, 1770–1870," *Journal of the History of Medicine and Allied Sciences* 57, no. 4 (2002): 410–48.

11 For more on this, see Aina Schiøtz, *Folkets helse—landets styrke 1850–2003* (Oslo: Universitetsforlaget, 2003), 59–60.

12 For more on this, see Aaron Sheon, "Parisian Social Statistics: Gavarni, 'Le Diable à Paris,' and Early Realism," *Art Journal* 44, no. 2 (1984): 139.

13 John Rajchman, "Foucault's Art of Seeing," *October* 44 (1988): 106.

14 Svein Atle Skålevåg, "Kjønnsforbrytelser: Sedelighet, seksualitet og strafferett 1880–1930," *Tidsskrift for kjønnsforskning*, 33, nos. 1–2 (2009): 8.

15 Oscar Thue, "Fra Albertine-striden," *Samtiden* 65 (1956): 669.

16 Stephen Kern, *Eyes of Love: The Gaze in English and French Paintings and Novels 1840–1900*

(London: Reaktion Books, 1996), 140. For the best presentation and discussion of Parent-Duchâtelet and other scientists writing on prostitution in nineteenth-century France, see Alain Corbin, *Women for Hire: Prostitution and Sexuality in France after 1850*, trans. Alan Sheridan (Cambridge, MA: Harvard University Press, 1990). See also Jill Harsin, *Policing Prostitution in Nineteenth-Century Paris* (Princeton, NJ: Princeton University Press, 1985), chapter 3.

17 Anthea Callen, *The Spectacular Body: Science, Method and Meaning in the Work of Degas* (New Haven, CT: Yale University Press, 1995), 43.

18 My information on Boeck is based on Aina Schiøtz's master's thesis, "Prostitusjonen i Kristiania ca. 1870–1890: En sosialhistorisk undersøkelse," University of Oslo, 1977.

19 Charles Bernheimer, *Figures of Ill Repute: Representing Prostitution in Nineteenth-Century France* (Cambridge, MA: Harvard University Press, 1989), 2.

20 Michel Foucault, *Discipline and Punish: The Birth of the Prison*, trans. Alan Sheridan (London: Penguin, 1991), 217. For a critical discussion of the panopticon concept, see Anne Brunon-Ernst, ed., *Beyond Foucault: New Perspectives on Bentham's Panopticon* (Farnham: Ashgate, 2012).

21 Bryan S. Turner, *The Body and Society: Explorations in Social Theory* (London: Sage, 1996), 161–64.

22 Foucault, *Discipline and Punish*, 189. I have also drawn information from Michel Foucault, *The Birth of the Clinic: An Archeology of Medical Perception*, trans. A. M. Sheridan Smith (New York: Vintage, 1994).

23 Honoré de Balzac, *Splendeurs et misères des courtisanes*, vol. 1 (Paris: Potter, 1845), 122. Original: "Comme vous êtes, dans les cartons de la police, un chiffre en dehors des êtres sociaux."

24 Clark, *The Painting of Modern Life*, 106.

25 Schiøtz, "Prostitusjonen i Kristiania," 103.

26 Simon Popple, "Photography, Crime and Social Control," *Early Popular Visual Culture* 3, no. 1 (2005): 95.

27 Allan Sekula, "The Body and the Archive," *October* 39 (1986): 6.

28 Cesare Lombroso and Guglielmo Ferrero, *Criminal Woman, the Prostitute, and the Normal Woman*, trans. Nicole Hahn Rafter and Mary Gibson (Durham, NC: Duke University Press, 2004), chapter 17.

29 Janet Wolff, "The Invisible *Flâneuse*: Women and the Literature of Modernity," *Theory, Culture & Society* 2, no. 3 (1985): 37–46. See also Aruna D'Souza and Tom McDonough, eds., *The Invisible Flâneuse?: Gender, Public Space, and Visual Culture in Nineteenth-Century Paris* (Manchester: Manchester University Press, 2008). One should also here mention Griselda Pollock, *Vision and Difference: Femininity, Feminism and the Histories of Art* (London: Routledge, 2000), ch. 3.

30 Quoted in Schiøtz, "Prostitusjonen i Kristiania," 104. Original: "Naar de til regelmessige Tider Fremmødede gaar til eller fra Politikammeret, maa de gaa hver for sig og benytte forskjellige Gade. De maa være iført en simpel, ikke i nogen Henseende fremtredende Dragt, uden Guldstads og uden at være sminket."

31 Quoted in ibid., 99. Original: "De skal, naar de viser sig udenfor deres Bopæl, være anstændig klædte og ikke iført nogen Pynt eller Dragt, der tildrager dem Opmærksomhed, ligsom de i det Hele taget stedse maa opføre sig saaledes, at de ikke vækker Opsigt eller forulemper nogen."

32 Harsin, *Policing Prostitution*, 20.
33 Judith R. Walkowitz, *Prostiution and Victorian Society: Women, Class, and the State* (Cambridge: Cambridge University Press, 1989), 26–27.
34 A.-J.-B. Parent-Duchâtelet, *De la prostitution dans la ville de Paris* (Paris: Baillière, 1857), 344. Original: "On arrivera au terme de la perfection et du possible en ce genre, en obtenant que les hommes, et en particulier ceux qui les recherchent, puissent les distinguer des femmes honnêtes; mais que celles-ci, et surtout leurs filles, ne puissent pas faire cette distinction, ou ne la fassent du moins qu'avec difficulté."
35 Lombroso and Ferrero, *Criminal Woman*, 143.
36 Ruth E. Iskin, *Modern Women and Parisian Consumer Culture in Impressionist Painting* (Cambridge: Cambridge University Press, 2007), 37.
37 Émile Zola, *Ladies' Delight*, trans. April Fitzlyon (London: Oneworld Classics, 2008), 152.
38 Guy Debord, *Society of the Spectacle* (Detroit: Black and Red, 1983), ch. 1.
39 Zola, *Nana* (1972), 215; Zola, *Nana* (1893), 229. Window-shopping is also described in Zola's *The Beast in Man*: "She [Séverine] loved window-shopping and the excitement of buying lavishly at the Bon Marché." Emile Zola, *The Beast in Man*, trans. R. G. Goodyear and P. J. R. Wright (London: Neil Mentor, 1975), 9.
40 Hollis Clayson, "Avant-Garde and Pompier Images of 19th Century French Prostitution: The Matter of Modernism, Modernity and Social Ideology," in *Modernism and Modernity: The Vancouver Conference Papers*, ed. Benjamin H. D. Buchloh, Serge Guilbaut, and David H. Solkin (Halifax: Press of the Nova Scotia College of Art and Design, 2004), 47. A memorable scene in Zola's *The Kill* demonstrates this phenomenon: "With the salacious cunning that was the dominant trait of his [Maxime's] character, he tried to embarrass his stepmother by asking her for details about the prostitutes, whom he pretended to mistake for authentic socialites. With a moral and serious air Renée would tell him that these were frightful creatures whom he must carefully avoid" (97–98).
41 Clayson, "Avant-Garde and Pompier Images," 48 and 56.
42 "Til Sædelighedsforeningen," *Aftenposten*, January 12, 1887.
43 Quoted in Schiøtz, "Prostitusjonen i Kristiania," 115. Original: "Men de overdriver den herskende Mode, især gjelder dette Hatten, som kan være overordentlig fiffig og smagløs."
44 Charles Baudelaire, *The Painter of Modern Life and Other Essays*, trans. Jonathan Mayne (London: Phaidon, 2003), 36; Charles Baudelaire, *L'art romantique* (Paris: Louis Conard, 1925), 102.
45 Guy de Maupassant, *Bel-Ami*, trans. Douglas Parmée (London: Penguin, 2012), 112–13. Original: "Mais Mme de Marelle ne regardait guère la scène, uniquement préoccupée des filles qui circulaient derrière son dos; et elle se retournait sans cesse pour les voir, avec une envie de les toucher, de palper leur corsage, leurs joues, leurs cheveux, pour savoir comment c'était fait, ces êtres-là." Guy de Maupassant, *Bel-Ami* (Paris: Louis Conard, 1910), 165.
46 Zola, *Nana* (1972), 215. Original: "Elle adorait le passage des Panoramas. C'était une passion qui lui restait de sa jeunesse pour le clinquant de l'article de Paris, les bijoux faux, le zinc doré, le carton jouant le cuir." Zola, *Nana* (1893), 229.
47 J.-K. Huysmans, *Marthe: The Story of a Whore*, trans. Brendan King (Sawtry: Dedalus, 2006), 39.
48 Rosenkrantz Johnsen, "Krohgs Maleri 'Albertine,'" *Dagbladet*, March 17, 1887.

49 Diana Crane, *Fashion and Its Social Agendas: Class, Gender, and Identity in Clothing* (Chicago: University of Chicago Press, 2000), 107.

50 Quoted in Schiøtz, "Prostitusjonen i Kristiania," 112 and 123. Original: "Gladis, 22 Aar gammel, fra Bergen, tyk og fed, med et dyrisk Ansigt, med Hænder, Leber, selve Øinene skjælver af Øl- og Brændevinsdrik, hun har havt Syphilis og et Barn." "Hvis man gaar ind om Aftenen paa et af de herværende Huse, vil man se en Samling af Kvinder, som man ikke snart glemmer. Deres Udseende, Dragt, deres Manerer er saa ulig enhver Andens, at de danner fuldstændig en Klasse for sig . . . Beboerskerne er afskrækkende i sit Ydre." "Bordellpigerne bliver staaende for det meste meget lenge. Aar efter Aar kan man se dem møde 2 Gange ugentlig til Visistaion. De bliver tykkere og triveligere og ser mere og mere idiotiske du. Alt det dandige forsvinder, og kun det dyriske bliver tilbage."

51 Christian Krohg, *Albertine* (Oslo: Bokklubben, 1995), 18.

52 Callen, *The Spectacular Body*, 34–35.

53 Crane, *Fashion and Its Social Agendas*, 53. I am drawing on Crane's study for my discussion of women's dresses, hats, and accessories, esp. 48–58.

54 For more on Degas's milliner paintings, see Eunice Lipton, *Looking into Degas: Uneasy Images of Women and Modern Life* (Berkeley: University of California Press, 1988), ch. 3.

55 Quoted in ibid., 161.

56 Krohg, *Albertine*, 11. Original: "'Gå ut? . . . Vil du jeg skal gå med strikketørkle og hodeplagg som en annen fabrikkjente—kanskje?'"

57 Iskin, *Modern Women*, 11.

58 Unni Langås, *Kroppens betydning i norsk litteratur 1800–1900* (Bergen: Fagbokforlaget, 2004), 156. Other important feminist and gendered readings of *Albertine* include Irene Iversen, "Blikk, Speil, Begjær: To impresjonistiske kvinneportretter," *Skrift: Skriftserie for litteraturvitenskap ved Universitetet i Oslo* 15 (1995): 34–54; Irene Iversen, "Kjønnet sprengjer det moderne," *Syn og Segn* 3 (1997): 195–208; Christine Hamm, "'Sjælemalerier': Amalie Skram leser Albertine," *Edda* 106, no. 3 (2006): 254–68.

59 Guy de Maupassant, *Alien Hearts*, trans. Richard Howard (New York: New York Review of Books, 2009), 30.

60 Krohg, *Albertine*, 115. Original: "Pen figur har jeg også—mye penere enn før."

61 Zola, *Nana* (1972), 220. Original: "Un des plaisirs de Nana était de se déshabiller en face de son armoire à glace, où elle se voyait en pied. Elle faisait tomber jusqu'à sa chemise; puis, toute nue, elle s'oubliait, elle se regardait longuement. C'était une passion de son corps, un ravissement du satin de sa peau et de la ligne souple de sa taille, qui la tenait sérieuse, attentive, absorbée dans un amour d'elle-même." Zola, *Nana* (1893), 235.

62 "Then her [Marthe's] vision cleared and she saw herself in a huge Venetian glass mirror, shamelessly sprawled on a banquette, her hair fixed up as if she were going to a ball, bare flesh emphasized by lace underwear that was spiced with a strong perfume.

"She could not believe this image was herself. She looked in astonishment at her powdered arms, her charcoaled eyebrows, her lips red as bloody meat, her legs sheathed in cherry-colored silk stockings, her heaving and tremulous breasts, at all the disturbing allure of her flesh which quivered beneath the frills of her dressing gown. Her eyes frightened her, rimmed with black eyeliner." Huysmans, *Marthe*, 48.

63 "She [Madame de Burne] walked toward the mirror where she saw three young women approaching her in the three hinged panels. When she was quite close she stopped short, made a slight bow, smiled, and nodded as if to say, 'Pretty—very pretty!' . . . Then she remained standing in front of herself, enveloped by the triple reflection of her body which

she found so charming, delighted by what she saw and taking a physical satisfaction in her beauty, savoring it with a sort of tenderness almost as sensual as that of a man." Maupassant, *Alien Hearts*, 29–30.

64 Zola, *Ladies' Delight*, 244.

65 Aubert, "I Anledning af Christian Krohg." Original: "Den unge Piges skam og lammende Angst, idet Konstabelen staar rede til paa Ordre at aabne Visitationsværelsets Dør, danner Hovedmotivet, hvorom den øvrige Komposition grupperer sig. Medfølelse, Eftertanke, ved Siden af Nysgjerrighed, Likegyldighed og Haan er de mest fremtrædende Udtryk i de øvrige Kvinders Ansigt og Holdning. Derved blir Medfølelsen med dobbelt Styrke betonet ogsaa hos os som selve Fremstillingens Grundstemning."

66 Corbin, *Women for Hire*, viii.

67 Callen, *The Spectacular Body*, 36 and ch. 3.

68 Kern, *Eyes of Love*, 141.

69 Krohg, *Albertine*, 126.

70 Foucault, *Discipline and Punish*, 214.

71 Ibid., 187.

72 Zola, *Nana* (1972), 274. Original: "Elle avait toujours tremblé devant la loi, cette puissance inconnue, cette vengeance des hommes qui pouvaient la supprimer, sans que personne au monde la défendît. Saint-Lazare lui apparaissait comme une fosse, un trou noir où l'on enterrait les femmes vivantes, après leur avoir coupé les cheveux." Zola, *Nana* (1893), 297.

73 Nils Rune Langeland, *Siste ord: Høgsterett i norsk historie 1814–1965*, vol. 1 (Oslo: Cappelen, 2005), 395.

74 Huysmans, *Marthe*, 74.

75 Zola, *Nana* (1972), 273–74. Original: "Autrefois, elle couchait avec un agent des mœurs, pour qu'on la laissât tranquille; à deux reprises, il avait empêché qu'on ne la mît en carte; et, à present, elle tremblait, car son affaire était claire, si on la pinçait encore." Zola, *Nana* (1893), 296–97.

76 I'm here inspired by Foucault, *Discipline and Punish*, 141–49.

77 Krohg, *Albertine*, 123. Original: "Hun trakk seg tilbake for alle disse sminkende øyne" and "De så på henne alle sammen og småsmilte."

78 John Rajchman writes: "We are surrounded by spaces which help form the evidence of the ways we see ourselves and one another. Where we 'dwell,' how we are housed, helps in this way to determine who and what we think we are—and so they involve our freedom. We are beings who are 'spatialized' in various ways; there is a historical spatialization of ourselves as subjects." Rajchman, "Foucault's Art of Seeing," 103.

79 This is a paraphrase from Corbin, *Women for Hire*, 90–91.

80 Krohg, *Albertine*, 126. Original: "Så plutselig følte hun instrumentet mot sitt blottede legeme, og hun skvatt til, men ble så liggende der i dyp redsel uten å tore røre en muskel og med en rent unaturlig klar bevissthet."

81 Christen Collin, *Kunsten og Moralen: Bidrag til kritik af realismens digtere og kritikere* (Copenhagen: Gyldendalske, 1894), 50–51. Original: "Vistnok har Hr. Christian *Krohg* baade som Maler og som Fortæller fremstillet den samme 'Albertine.' Men hans fortællende Fremstilling fulgte hende helt ind i Politilægens Kontor—den Krohgske Fortællerkunst gikk derind mindre modstræbende end den ulykkelige unge Pige—, mens hans Malerkunst ikke vovede sig længere end til Venteværelset.

"Nu ligger det vistnok i den fortællende Kunsts Væsen, at den kan vove sig længere end Billedkunsten i Fremstillingen af det modbydelige eller det rædsomme. Af den

Grund, at Fortælleren kan berøre en Ting flygtig og derpaa føre Læseren videre, medens Billedkunstneren maa udmale eller udmeisle omstændelig og ovenikjøbet maa lade Tilskueren blive staaende stille foran Billedet."

82 Quoted in Corbin, *Women for Hire*, 88.

83 Foucault, *Discipline and Punish*, 279–80; Michel Foucault, *The History of Sexuality: An Introduction*, trans. Robert Hurley (New York: Vintage, 1990), 4.

84 Zola, *Nana* (1972), 324. Original: "Et, au milieu de cet abandon d'elle-même, elle ne gardait guère que le souci de sa beauté, un soin continuel de se visiter, de se laver, de se parfumer partout, avec l'orgueil de pouvoir se mettre nue, à chaque instant et devant n'importe qui, sans avoir à rougir." Zola, *Nana* (1893), 354.

85 Quoted in Kern, *Eyes of Love*, 142.

86 Quoted in Michael J. O'Dowd and Elliot E. Phillip, *The History of Obstetrics and Gynaecology* (New York: Parthenon, 1994), 399.

87 Kern, *Eyes of Love*, 142.

88 Quoted in Walkowitz, *Prostitution and Victorian Society*, 57.

89 Maupassant, *Alien Hearts*, 26.

90 Lombroso and Ferrero, *Criminal Woman*, 213.

91 Maupassant, *Bel-Ami* (2012), 17. Original: "Sa poitrine, trop forte, tendait la soie sombre de sa robe; et ses lèvres peintes, rouges comme une plaie, lui donnaient quelque chose de bestial, d'ardent, d'outré, mais qui allumait le désir cependant." Maupassant, *Bel-Ami* (1910), 22.

92 Zola, *Nana* (1972), 168. Original: "Mais, au milieu de cette débandade de filles lâchées à travers les quatre étages, il n'aperçut distinctement qu'un chat, le gros chat rouge, qui, dans cette fournaise empoisonnée de musc, filait le long des marches en se frottant le dos contre les barreaux de la rampe, la queue en l'air." Zola, *Nana* (1893), 175–76.

93 Linda Nochlin, *Courbet* (London: Thames and Hudson, 2007), 172.

94 Amalie Skram, "Om 'Albertine,'" *Samlede verker*, vol. 7 (Oslo: Gyldendal, 1993), 410–11.

95 Krohg, *Albertine*, 98. Original: "Eftersom kinnets bleke, ovale linje gled forsvinnende nedover mot halsen, tapte det varme gule lys seg uten noen grense i skyggen nedenfor øret og kom så for siste gang igjen på halsens strakte muskel."

96 Ibid. Original: "Ville ønske at han var en maler, eller at han hadde en maler her."

97 It should be mentioned that *speculum* is a central term in Luce Irigaray's psychoanalytical vocabulary, but I will not dwell here on that field. See Luce Irigaray, *Speculum of the Other Woman*, trans. Gillian C. Gill (Ithaca, NY: Cornell University Press, 1986).

98 Laura Mulvey, *Visual and Other Pleasures* (Bloomington: Indiana University Press, 1989), 15.

9. MODERN PESSIMISM

Epigraph: Ernst Fischer, *The Necessity of Art*, trans. Anna Bostock (London: Verso, 2010), 92.

1 Kirk Varnedoe, *Northern Light: Realism and Symbolism in Scandinavian Painting 1880–1920* (New York: Brooklyn Museum, 1982), 19 and 25.

2 Fischer, *The Necessity of Art*, 94.

3 Max Nordau, *Degeneration* (Lincoln: University of Nebraska Press, 1993), v–vi.

4 Christen Collin, *Kunsten og Moralen: Bidrag til kritik af realismens digtere og kritikere* (Copenhagen: Gyldendalske, 1894), 157.

5 Max Nordau, "Bjornson's Paris Days," *Bookman* 32, no. 1 (1910): 63–67.

6 Collin, *Kunsten og Moralen*, 13–14. Original: "Neppe nogen af vore Malere har malet mere livsfriske Billeder end han [Krohg]. Men paa den anden Side gjør han den mest energiske Reklame for den syge Kjærligheds Digtere og skriver om det barbariske i at stænge Natkafeer. I det Hele er der en paafaldende Modsætning mellem det meste af vor Malerkunst og en temmelig stor Del af vor nyeste Skjønliteratur. Den første—Malerkunsten—udstraaler Solglæde og Jubel over stærke Farvespil, over Lysets og Skyggernes uudtømmelige Leg. Den aander af Fjeld og Skog og Sjø og er vor Kunsts rigeste Udtryk for den sunde Friluftsliv. Men en ikke liden Del af vor nyeste Digtning minder snarere om indestængt Hybel- og Kneipeluft. Den dufter vissent af hjemført berlinsk og parisisk Nydelsessyge. Christian Krohg forekommer mig at repræsentere denne Modsætning i én Person."

7 Ibid., 15. Original: "Den dekadente Digter—hvadenten han kalder sig Naturalist eller *Décadent*—er den, hvis Fantasi trives bedst i Fremstillingen af moralske Opløsningsprocesser."

8 Ibid., 38 and 138.

9 Arnold Hauser, *The Social History of Art: Vol. 4, Naturalism, Impressionism, the Film Age* (London: Routledge, 1993), 169.

10 Richard Shiff presents an interesting analysis of the relationship among impressionism, naturalism, and symbolism. See *Cézanne and the End of Impressionism* (Chicago: University of Chicago Press, 1984), 7–8.

11 Jean Moréas, "Le symbolisme," *Le Figaro, supplément littéraire*, September 18, 1886.

12 Christian Krohg, *Kampen for tilværelsen* (Oslo: Gyldendal, 1954), 28. Original: "Allerede impresjonismen forla det kunstneriske mål fra den hittil tilbedte døde natur over til den menneskelige ånd, idet impresjonistene erklærte at det ikke var gjenstandene som var interessante, men måten på hvilken kunstneren oppfattet dem. Forsåvidt står altså symbolismen, når den legger hovedvekten på det åndelige, som en videre utvikling og nær beslektet med impresjonismen."

13 Øivind Storm Bjerke, *Edvard Munch and Harald Sohlberg: Landscapes of the Mind* (New York: National Academy of Design, 1995), 87.

14 B. W. Wells, "Zola and Literary Naturalism," *Sewanee Review* 1, no. 4 (1893): 386.

15 Evert Sprinchorn, "The Transition from Naturalism to Symbolism in the Theatre from 1880 to 1900," *Art Journal* 45, no. 2 (1985): 118–19.

16 Frits Thaulow, *I Kamp og i Fest* (Copenhagen: Gyldendalske, 1908), 145.

17 Ferdinand Brunetière, "La philosophie de Schopenhauer et les conséquences du pessimisme," *Revue des deux mondes* 60 (1890): 210–21. Brunetière had written about naturalist fiction many times, for instance, *Nouvelles questions de critique* (Paris: Calmann-Lévy, 1890); *Essais sur la littérature contemporaine* (Paris: Calmann-Lévy, 1900); *Discours de combat* (Paris: Perrin, 1904); and *Le roman naturaliste* (Paris: Calmann-Lévy, 1910).

18 Georg Brandes, "Arthur Schopenhauer (1788–1860)," *Ude og Hjemme* 7 (1884): 634–36.

19 The French antipositivist philosopher Elme-Marie Caro wrote a book about nineteenth-century pessimism, giving Schopenhaur a whole chapter. See Elme-Marie Caro, *Le pessimisme au XIXe siècle* (Paris: Hachette, 1880).

20 Joris-Karl Huysmans, *Against Nature*, trans. Margaret Mauldon (Oxford: Oxford University Press, 2009), 146.

21 Ibid., 185.

22 Paul Bourget, "Brev fra Paris: Et Overblik over den franske Literatur i Aaret 1884," *Tilskueren* 2 (1885): 73.

23 Hippolyte Taine, *On Intelligence*, vol. 2, trans. T. D. Haye (New York: Henry Holt, 1875),

120. Italics mine. Original: "Mais la folie est toujours à la porte de l'esprit, comme la maladie est toujours à la porte du corps; car la combinaison normale n'est qu'une réussite; elle n'aboutit et ne se renouvelle que par la défaite continue des forces contraires. Or, celles-ci subsistent toujours; un accident peut leur donner la prépondérance; il s'en faut de peu qu'elles ne la prennent; une légère altération dans la proportion des affinités élémentaires et dans la direction du travail formateur amènerait une dégénérescence." Hippolyte Taine, *De l'intelligence*, vol. 2 (Paris: Hachette, 1870), 207.

24 Guillermo Ferrero, "Er vi syge?" *Samtiden* 4 (1893): 362. Originally published in *La revue des revues*. This is a translation of the Norwegian version: "Renan og Taine er kanske de to værste pessimister, jeg kjender. . . . Taine, som skildrer de hæsligste former af den menneskelige grusomhed uden at blinke, som om han beskrev udviklingsstadierne i en krystallisation eller metamorfoserne i en plantes liv."

25 Émile Faguet, *A Literary History of France* (London: T. Fisher Unwin, 1907), 605. For more on Faguet's presentation of Taine's "pessimism," see Émile Faguet, *Politiques et moralistes du dix-neuvième siècle (troisième série)* (Paris: Société Française d'Imprimerie et de Librairie, 1903), 310–14.

26 Lorentz Dietrichson, *Betegner den moderne Naturalisme i Poesien et Fremskridt eller et Forfald?* (Kristiania: Studentersamfundet, 1882), 21.

27 Lorentz Dietrichson, *Norges kunsts historie i det nittende århundre* (Oslo: Messel, 1991), 168.

28 Dietrichson, *Betegner den moderne Naturalisme*, 22. Original: "Den moderne Naturalisme har med Iver stillet sig under Pessimismens Faner og lider selv under dennes Sygdom: den er jo sin Tids Barn saavelsom dens Fører."

29 Claudius Wilkens, "Moderne Naturalisme," *Tilskueren* 5 (1888): 493. Original: "En minutiøs, stereoskopisk spejlklar Gengivelse af Hverdagslivet."

30 Ibid., 495. Original: "Overalt indaande vi Positivismens Aand."

31 Ibid., 505. Original: "Naturalisterne [er] Vrangsidens Digtere."

32 Ibid., 506. Original: "En Generation bliver til en Degeneration."

33 Ibid., 507. Original: "Nedarvingen af de fineste aandelige Træk lade sig ikke konstatere: de kan kun gættes, føles."

34 Claudius Wilkens, *Æsthetik i Omrids: Med særlight Hensyn til Moderne Æsthetik* (Copenhagen: Gyldendalske, 1888), 231–32.

35 Émile Zola, *The Experimental Novel and Other Essays*, trans. Belle M. Sherman (New York: Haskell, 1964), 127. Original text: Émile Zola, *Le roman expérimental* (Paris: Charpentier, 1880), 127.

36 Wilkens, "Moderne Naturalisme," 510.

37 Ibid., 512. Original: "Den franske Romantik bar Naturalismen i sit Skød."

38 Ibid., 513. Original: "Pessimismen vil da forvandles til en modificered Optimisme."

39 Georg Brandes, *Friedrich Nietzsche*, trans. A. G. Chater (London: William Heinemann, 1914), 3. Original: "I det nærværende Tysklands Literatur synes Friedrich Nietzsche mig at være den interessanteste Skribent. Skøndt selv i sit Fædreland lidet kendt er han en Aand af betydelig Rang, som tilfulde fortjæner at studeres, at drøftes, at bekæmpes og at meddele Stemning og sætte Tanker i Bevægelse." Georg Brandes, "Aristokratisk Radikalisme: En Afhandling om Friedrich Nietzsche," *Tilskueren* 6 (August 1889): 38. For more on Brandes and Nietzsche, see Bertil Nolin, *Den gode Europén: Studier i Georg Brandes' idéutveckling 1871–1893* (Uppsala: Svenska Bokförlaget/Norstedts, 1965), 150–82; and Steen Klitgård Povlsen, "Nietzsche in Denmark," in *European and Nordic Modernisms*, ed. Mats Jansson, Jakob Lothe, and Hannu Riikonen (Norwich: Norvik Press, 2004), 163–76.

40 Arne Garborg, "Friedrich Nietzsche af Ola Hansson," *Samtiden* 1 (1890): 395.

41 Téodor de Wyzewa, "Nietsche i Frankrige," *Samtiden* 3 (1892): 10.

42 Hippolyte Taine, *Life and Letters of H. Taine, 1870–1892*, trans. E. Sparvel-Bayly (London: Archibald Constable, 1908), 262. Original: "Je recommanderais particulièrement aux philosophes votre premier morceau sur les philosophes et sur la philosophie; mais les historiens et les critiques feront aussi leur butin de quantité d'idées neuves." Hippolyte Taine, *Sa vie et sa correspondance*, vol. 4 (Paris: Hachette, 1907), 220.

43 For more on this, see Émile Faguet, *On Reading Nietzsche*, trans. George Raffalovich (New York: Moffat, Yard, 1918), 73.

44 Wyzewa, "Nietsche i Frankrige," 15.

45 Faguet, *On Reading Nietzsche*, 78. Original in Émile Faguet, *En lisant Nietzsche* (Paris: Société Française d'Imprimerie et de Librairie, 1904), 96.

46 Brandes, *Friedrich Nietzsche*, 62.

47 Friedrich Nietzsche, "Saalunde talte Zarathustra," trans. Sophus Michaëlis, *Ny Jord* (1889): 262–80. One could that same year also read a translation of Paul Bourget's text on Charles Baudelaire, Paul Bourget, "Charles Baudelaire," trans. Vald. K., *Ny Jord* (1889): 238–56.

48 Ola Hansson, *Friedrich Nietzsche: Hans Personlighed og hans System*, trans. Arne Garborg (Christiania: Cammermeyers, 1890). See also Ola Hansson, *Materialismen i Skönlitteraturen* (Stockholm: Albert Bonnier, 1892).

49 Hellen Lindgren, *Vittra Stormän: Kritiker och Porträtt* (Stockholm: Carl Deleen, 1894), 45 and 46.

50 See, for example, ibid., 57.

51 Ibid., 64. Original: "Nutidsmänniskan erfar också behofvet att ur denna borgerliga tillvaros stillasittande komma til något, som är mindre skenlif och mera driftlif. En längtan efter fara och ofrid har kommit, som är obetvinglig. Man flockas kring allt, som väcker de starka passionerna. . . . Det är omedvten Nietzsche-moral bland hvardagsmänniskorna, som ger sig till känna."

52 Arne Garborg expresses this new feeling in a wonderful way in a series of articles called "Lidt spiritisme," published in *Samtiden* in 1893.

53 Valdemar Vedel, "Om Nydannelse i Tidens Aandsliv," *Tilskueren* 9 (1892): 282. Vedel wrote: "Det gælder da om at vise, at Livet og Menneskene ikke ere saadanne, som moderne Romanforfattere og Populærfilosoffer — Darwinske, Taineske, Zolaske Eftersnakkere og Karikaturer — søger at bilde os ind, at altsaa al deres Pukken paa Sandhed og nøgen uhildet Livsskildringer er ganske ubeføjet."

54 Christian Krohg, "Impresjonistene," in *Christian Krohg 1852–1925* (Åmot i Modum: Stiftelsen Modums Blaafarveværk, 1993), 70–76.

55 Øystein Sjåstad, *Christian Krohg: Fra Paris til Kristiania* (Oslo: Labyrinth, 2012), 26–29.

56 Zola, *The Experimental Novel*, 19.

57 Arne Garborg, G. V. Lyng, and Henrik Jæger, eds., *Betegner den moderne naturalisme i poesien et fremskridt ellet et forfald?* (Kristiania: Studentersamfundet, 1882), 2. Original: "Det er Darwin, der har stemplet århundredets ånd."

58 Gerhard Gran, "Emile Zola," *Nyt Tidsskrift* 2 (1883): 296–97.

59 Jens Peter Jacobsen and Vilhelm Møller, *Darwin: Hans liv og hans lære* (Copenhagen: Gyldendalske, 1893), 19.

60 Georg Brandes, *Main Currents in Nineteenth Century Literature,* vol. 1 (New York: Macmillan, 1906), 177.

61 Georg Brandes, *Den Franske Æsthetik i Vore Dage: En Afhandling om H. Taine* (Copenhagen: Gyldendalske, 1870), 180. Original: "Til de gamle Theorier om Vanernes, Climaternes

og Ernæringens Indflydelse føier han [Darwin] Principet om den naturlige Udvælgelse, der bevarer og ophober alle de gunstige Variationer, sikrer deres Bestaaen gjennem Egenskabernes Arvelighed og saaledes sikrer dem den endelige Seir i Kampen for livet."

62 He writes about this in a letter to Otto Borchsenius on February 20, 1887. Quoted in Elias Bredsdorff, *Den store nordiske krig om seksualmoralen* (Oslo: Gyldendal, 1973), 189.

63 My argumentation here is built on Marsha Morton, "'Impulses and Desires': Klinger's Darwinism in Nature and Society," *Nineteenth-Century Art Worldwide* 2, no. 2 (2003): 1–30. http://www.19thc-artworldwide.org/index.php/spring03/223-excavating-greece-classicism-between-empire-and-nation-in-nineteenth-century-europe. Accessed September 5, 2011. For the close relationship between Krohg and Klinger, see Marit Lange, "Max Klinger og Norge," *Kunst og kultur* 80, no. 1 (1997): 2–40.

64 Hans Jæger, "Vor literatur: Albertine og naturalismen," in *Bohem mot Borger: Et utvalg fra Hans Jægers og Christian Krohgs "Impressionisten,"* ed. Anne Siri Bryhni (Oslo: Universitetsforlaget, 1971), 69. Original: "Albertine — hvem er hun? — et blegt ansigt skimtet i halvmørke og forsvundet. Hvor har du set det Krohg? du har jo aldrig været dernede. Hvad kjender *du* til livet som leves nede i de mørke schakter her lige under vore fødder, hvor elendigheden bor og menneskene færdes omkring mellem hverandre, ulykkelige og længtende op imod sol og luft — hvad kjender *du* til det? du har jo aldrig vært dernede."

65 Ibid., 70.

66 Ibid., 71.

67 Ibid., 74. Original: "Det du nu skal til at male, det har du set. Du har staat dernede paa hjørnet af Karljohan og Skippergaden og set denne queu af forsultne kjærringer og unger, der alle som en strækker de magre begjærlige arme i vejret, idet døren aabnes og brøduddelingen begynder. Du har staat der grebet af dette syn og svoret ved dig selv, at *det* billede vilde du stille frem for offentligheden for slig at som *du* var grebet af det, slig skulde hele almenheden bli det."

68 Quoted in Morton, "Impulses and Desires," 14.

69 Kirk Varnedoe, "Christian Krohg and Edvard Munch," *Arts Magazine* 53, no. 8 (1979): 91.

70 Ibid., 91–92.

71 Dietrichson, *Norges kunsts historie*, 168.

72 "Chr. Krohg: Kampen for Tilværelsen," *Aftenposten*, May 10, 1889.

73 Irgens Hansen, "Krohgs Maleri," *Verdens Gang*, May 8, 1889. Original: "Christian Krohg er naad længer end nogensinde før."

74 Julius Lange, "Norsk, svensk, dansk Figurmaleri: Indtryk og Overvejelser," *Tilskueren* 9 (1892): 252. Original: "Billedets Behandling er bred, energisk og djærv, og der er ypperlig følte Udtryk i disse Figurer: den lille Pige, der er trængt aller bagest ud i Flokken, staar som et Billede af resignert og inderlig Forventning; Drengen ved hendes Side med den usunde Ansigtsfarve og det graadige Blik fantaserer om varmt Hvedebrød, saa at hans Tænder løbe i Vand, og vil kaste sig som en Ulv over Byttet, naar hans Tur kommer; Konerne række Hænderne i Vejret og sende bedende, sultne Blikke til den Gudinde Ceres, som uddeler sine Gaver. Det er Sultens Inderlighed, den Inderlighed, som kommer fra Maven. Den er hverken saa skøn eller saa dyb som den der stammer fra Hjærtet; ti om end den gamle Odysseus har Ret i, at intet er saa uforskammet som Maven, saa kan dens Krav dog tilfredsstilles fra Dag til Dag, medens Hjærtets kan vokse og vokse like op i det uendelige. Men Sultens Inderlighed har — Gud bedre det! — en vældig stor Plads i det virkelige Liv; og vil Kunsten for Alvor trænge ned til de Kræfter, som røre sig i Nutidens

Samfundsliv, saa vil den ufejlbarlig ogsaa faa Øje paa Sulten, den store stygge Grib med de glødende Øjne og de hvasse Kløer."

75 Émile Zola, *Thérèse Raquin*, trans. L. W. Tancock (Harmondsworth: Penguin, 1968), 20.

76 Ibid.

EPILOGUE

1 Christian Krohg, *Kampen for tilværelsen* (Oslo: Gyldendal, 1954), 12. Original: "Bastien-Lepage malte hver fold og hver rynke i huden, det var likesom man kunne ta og føle på hver eneste form, selv den aller minste, *især* den aller minste."

2 Ibid., 13. Original: "Og når Zola skal skildre en aftenstemning over Paris, så gir han seg til å nevne hvert hus og hvert kirketårn, og skal han fortelle om lukten i hallene, så nevner han hver eneste slags lukt, han dissekerer lukten."

3 Ibid. Original: "Men så kom Manet—den franske maler Manet."

4 Ibid., 14. Original: "*Manet* ville jo det samme som realistene, han ville være med å skildre tiden, men det var ham bevisst, da han forsto at det var ikke nok å gjøre naturen efter, og det kunne ikke nytte å forsøke på å *lage* nature, man matte først lære å se på den, og våge å se på den med sitt eget øye og med tidens øye, og så male det man hadde sett så friskt som mulig og således at hvert penselstrøk bar preget av det *mål* man hadde, og at en av de *vesentlige ting var å stanse*—ikke å male mer enn man så, man måtte ikke lete efter noe."

5 Ibid. Original: "Det gjelder å male ikke så meget som mulig, men så lite som mulig."

6 Henrik Jæger, *Illustreret Norsk Litteraturhistorie*, vol. 2 (Kristiania: Hjalmar Bigler, 1896), 803.

7 Eugène Véron, *Æsthetics*, trans. W. H. Armstrong (London: Chapman and Hall, 1879), 360–61. For original text, see Eugène Véron, *L'esthétique* (Paris: Vrin, 2007), 392.

8 Johan Vibe, *Nogle Bemærkninger i Anledning af Naturalismen* (Kristiania: Mallings, 1884), 56–59.

9 Quoted in Carl G. Laurin, *Nordisk Konst: Danmark och Norges konst från 1880 till 1925* (Stockholm: P. A. Norstedt, 1925), 228–29. Original: "Jeg forsøgte først efterligne Bastien-Lepage, dernæst Impressionisterne. Jeg ville endelig være med paa det radikale Program."

10 Carl Gustaf Estlander, *Naturalismen enligt Zola* (Helsinki: J. C. Frenckell, 1891), 1. Original: "Då det nu tyckes afgjordt att naturalismens tid är ute . . . är det på tiden att börja undersöka hva som kan hafva varit dess uppgift vid konstens och konstlärans utveckling."

11 Lilian R. Furst and Peter N. Skrine, *Naturalism* (London: Methuen, 1971), 70.

12 Raymond Williams, *Drama from Ibsen to Brecht* (London: Chatto and Windus, 1971), 332.

13 Quoted in ibid., 332–33.

14 Ibid., 334.

15 Ibid., 338–39.

16 Lorentz Dietrichson, *Fra Kunstens Verden: Foredrag og Studier* (Copenhagen: Gyldendal, 1885), 193–94. For discussions of naturalism and photography, see Gabriel P. Weisberg, David Jackson, and Willa Z. Silverman, eds., *Illusion of Reality: Naturalist Painting, Photography, Theatre and Cinema, 1875–1918* (Amsterdam: Van Gogh Museum, 2010).

17 For more on this, see Richard Thomson, *Art of the Actual: Naturalism and Style in Early Third Republic France, 1880–1900* (New Haven, CT: Yale University Press, 2012), 118–25.

18 Georg Nordensvan, *De Bildande Konsternas Historia under 19: De Århundadet* (Stockholm: Hugo Gerber, 1900), 298. Original: "Men kameran gaf abstrakta verklighetsbilder och aldrig ett personligt intryck, och det är först den personliga uppfatningen, som gör en

naturafbildning till et konstverk. Redan Taine hade i sin Philosophie de l'art betonat, att konstnärens uppgift vid naturstudiet är att gifva ett föremåls 'caractère essentiel' och att han för att framhålla denna bestämmande karaktär äger att förbise eller utesluta sådana bisaker, som kunna skymma bort den. Fotografien har bidragit till att skärpa blicken för just det, som kameran *ej* kan återgifva i sin korrekta och själlösa verklighetstolkning. Fotografien medtager kritiklöst och tanklöst allt utan att skilja på hufvudsak och bisak, konstnären däremot *väljer*, ser naturen genom sitt temperament."

19 Claudius Wilkens, *Æsthetik i Omrids: Med særlight Hensyn til Moderne Æsthetik* (Copenhagen: Gyldendalske, 1888), 125. Original: "Men dette Realitetens Princip maa ikke forstaas saaledes, at Kunstneren blot skal være en Fotograf, der kopierer Virkeligheden, eller et kopierende Temperament, der kun spejler les documents humains i sin Sjæl. Den Zolaske Sætning, at en Digtning er et Stykke af Virkeligheden, spejlet i et Temperament, er, som hans eget Exempel viser, ikke rigtigt eller uklar."

20 For an insightful article on naturalism and photography, see Ville Lukkarinen, "The Naturalness of Naturalism Reconsidered," *Konsthistorisk tidsskrift / Journal of Art History* 65, no. 1 (1996): 51–59.

21 Peter Henry Emerson, *Naturalistic Photography for Students of the Art* (London: Sampson Low, Marston, Searle and Rivington, 1890), 91.

22 Andreas Aubert, *Dagbladet*, November 9, 1890.

23 For more on this, see Oscar Thue, *Christian Krohg* (Oslo: Aschehoug, 1997), 300–303; Trond E. Aslaksby, "Christian Krohg and Photography: Some Observations and Reflections," in *Christian Krohg: Bilder som griper/Picures That Captivate*, ed. Vibeke Waallann Hansen, Erik Mørstad, Birgitte Sauge, and Marianne Yvenes (Oslo: Nasjonalmuseet for Kunst, Arkitektur og Design, 2012), 219–27. For a study of Krohg's art after 1900, see Øystein Sjåstad, *Christian Krohg: Fra Paris til Kristiania* (Oslo: Labyrinth, 2012).

Bibliography

About, Edmond. *L'homme à l'oreille cassée*. Paris: Hachette, 1899.

Alexis, Paul. *Émile Zola: Notes d'un ami*. Paris: Charpentier, 1882.

Allen, Julie K. *Icons of Danish Modernity: Georg Brandes and Asta Nielsen*. Seattle: University of Washington Press, 2012.

Alsvik, Otlu. "Skribenten Christian Krohg." *Kunst og Kultur* 36 (1953): 39–52.

Armstrong, Carol. *Manet Manette*. New Haven, CT: Yale University Press, 2002.

Aubert, Andreas. "I Anledning af Christian Krohgs store Komposition: Fra Politilægens Ventværelse." *Dagbladet*, March 22, 1887.

———. "Breve fra Parisersalonen." *Aftenposten*, May 7, 1884.

———. "Chr. Krohgs Udstilling." *Dagbladet*, February 10, 1889.

———. "Før 'Salonens' Aabning." *Aftenposten*, March 27, 1884.

———. "Høstudstillingen II." *Dagbladet*, October 2, 1887.

———. "Krohgudstillingen." *Dagbladet*, February 9, 1890.

———. "Manet: Et Bidrag til Sujetets og Koloritens Historie i den nyere Tid." *Tilskueren* 5 (1888): 670–89.

———. "Vor egen Kunst paa Kjøbenhavnerudstillingen II." *Dagbladet*, June 17, 1888.

Austin, Lloyd James. "Mallarmé and the Visual Arts." In *French 19th Century Painting and Literature*, edited by Ulrich Finke. Manchester: Manchester University Press, 1972.

Baguley, David. *Naturalist Fiction: The Entropic Vision*. Cambridge: Cambridge University Press, 2005.

Bal, Mieke. *Narratology: Introduction to the Theory of Narrative*. Toronto: University of Toronto Press, 1997.

Balzac, Honoré de. *Oeuvres complètes de H. de Balzac*. Vol. 1. Paris: Michel Levy, 1875.

———. *Splendeurs et misères des courtisans*. Vol. 1. Paris: Potter, 1845.

Bang, Herman. *Realisme og Realister: Portrætstudier og Aforismer*. Copenhagen: Gyldendals Uglebøger, 1966.

Barrett, Brian Dudley. *Artists on the Edge: The Rise of Coastal Artists' Colonies, 1880–1920*. Amsterdam: Amsterdam University Press, 2010.

Barthes, Roland. *The Rustle of Language*. Translated by Richard Howard. Berkeley: University of California Press, 1989.

———. *S/Z*. Translated by Richard Miller. Oxford: Blackwell, 2000.

Barzellotti, Giacomo. *La Philosophie de H. Taine*. Translated by Auguste Dietrich. Paris: Félix Alcan, 1900.

Baudelaire, Charles. *Art in Paris 1845–1862: Salons and Other Exhibitions*. Translated by Jonathan Mayne. London: Phaidon, 1965.

———. *L'art romantique*. Paris: Louis Conard, 1925.
———. *The Painter of Modern Life and Other Essays*. Translated by Jonathan Mayne. London: Phaidon, 2003.
Bénédite, Léonce. "Alfred-Philippe Roll." *Art et décoration* 24 (July–Dec. 1908): 69–78.
Berg, Knut. "Naturalisme og nyromantikk 1870–1900." In *Norges malerkunst*, vol. 1, edited by Knut Berg. Oslo: Gyldendal, 2000.
Berg, Leo. *Der Naturalismus*. Munich: Verlag der Münchner Handelsdruckerei & Verlagsanstalt M. Poessl, 1892.
Berg, William J. *The Visual Novel: Emile Zola and the Art of His Times*. University Park: Pennsylvania State University Press, 1992.
Bergh, Richard. "Det fornødne." *Kunstbladet* 1, nos. 17–18 (1888): 213.
———. *Om Konst och Annat*. Stockholm: Albert Bonniers Förlag, 1908.
Bergson, Henri. *The Creative Mind: An Introduction to Metaphysics*. Translated by Mabelle L. Andison. Mineola, NY: Dover, 2007.
Berman, Patricia G. *In Another Light: Danish Painting in the Nineteenth Century*. London: Thames and Hudson, 2013.
Bernard, Claude. *An Introduction to the Study of Experimental Medicine*. Translated by Henry Copley Greene. New York: Macmillan, 1927.
———. *Leçons sur les phénomènes de la vie*. Vol. 1. Paris: Baillière, 1885.
———. *Principes de medicine expérimentale*. Paris: Presses Universitaires de France, 1947.
Bernardini, Léonie. *La littérature scandinave*. Paris: Plon, 1894.
Bernheimer, Charles. *Figures of Ill Repute: Representing Prostitution in Nineteenth-Century France*. Cambridge, MA: Harvard University Press, 1989.
Bertall, Charles-Albert Arnoux. "Impressionism in France." *American Art Review* 1, no. 1 (1879): 33–34.
Beuchat, Charles. *Histoire du naturalisme français*. 2 vols. Paris: Corrêa, 1949.
Beyer, Edvard, F. J. Billeskov Jansen, Hakon Stangerup, and P. H. Traustedt, eds. *Verdens Litteraturhistorie*. Vol. 9, *Naturalismen (1860–1890)*. Oslo: Cappelen, 1978.
Bigeon, Maurice. *Les révoltés scandinaves*. Paris: L. Grasilier, 1894.
Bigot, Charles. "L'esthétique naturaliste." *Revue des deux mondes* 35 (Sept. 1, 1879): 415–32.
Bjerke, Øivind Storm. *Edvard Munch and Harald Sohlberg: Landscapes of the Mind*. New York: National Academy of Design, 1995.
———. "Style and Technique as Strategic Devices used by the 'Middle Generation' 1882–86." In *Munch Becoming "Munch": Artistic Strategies 1880–1892*, edited by Ingebjørg Ydstie and Mai Britt Guleng. Oslo: Munch Museum/Labyrinth, 2008.
Bjørnson, Bjørn. *Bare ungdom*. Oslo: Aschehoug, 1934.
Boas, George, ed. *Courbet and the Naturalistic Movement*. Baltimore, MD: Johns Hopkins Press, 1938.
Bondevik, Hilde, and Knut Stene-Johansen. *Sykdom som litteratur*. Oslo: Unipub, 2011.
Bonnier, Eva. *Pariserbref*. Stockholm: Klara, 1999.
Bourget, Paul. "Brev fra Paris: Et Overblik over den franske Literatur i Aaret 1884." Translated by Carl Michelsen. *Tilskueren* 2 (1885): 56–74.
———. "Charles Baudelaire." Translated by Vald K. *Ny Jord* (1889): 238–56.
Boutroux, Émile. *Science et religion dans la philosophie contemporaine*. Paris: Flammarion, 1919.
Bowler, Peter J. *Evolution: The History of an Idea*. Berkeley: University of California Press, 2009.
Brandes, Georg. "Aabent Brev til Christian Krohg." *Politiken*, December 27, 1886.
———. "Aristokratisk Radikalisme: En Afhandling om Friedrich Nietzsche." *Tilskueren* 6 (August 1889): 565–613.

———. "Arthur Schopenhauer (1788–1860)." *Ude og Hjemme* 7 (1884): 634–36.
———. "Et Besøg i Holland." *Tilskueren* (August 1892): 577–96.
———. *Dualismen i vor nyeste Philosophie*. Copenhagen: Gyldendalske, 1866.
———. *Den Franske Æsthetik i Vore Dage: En Afhandling om H. Taine*. Copenhagen: Gyldendalske, 1870.
———. *Friedrich Nietzsche*. Translated by A. G. Chater. London: William Heinemann, 1914.
———. *Hovedstrømninger i det 19de Aarhundredes Litteratur: Emigrantlitteraturen*. Copenhagen: Gyldendalske, 1872. Translated as *Main Currents in Nineteenth Century Literature*. Vol. 1 (New York: Macmillan, 1906).
———. *Levned: Et Tiaar*. Copenhagen: Gyldendalske, 1907.
———. *Levned: Snevringer og Horizonter*. Copenhagen: Gyldendalske, 1908.
———. "Literære Studier II: Emile Zola som Kritiker." *Dagbladet*, August 23, 1879.
———. "Literære Studier III: Naturalisme i Frankrige." *Dagbladet*, August 30, 1879.
———. *Reminiscences of My Childhood and Youth*. New York: Duffield, 1906.
———. *Samlede Skrifter*. Vol. 7. Copenhagen: Gyldendalske, 1901.
———. *Udenlandske Egne og Personligheder*. Copenhagen: Gyldendalske, 1893.
———. "Virkeligheden og Temperamentet hos Emile Zola." *Tilskueren* (September 1887): 657–78.
Bredsdorff, Elias. *Den store nordiske krig om seksualmoralen*. Oslo: Gyldendal, 1973.
Brenna, Arne. "Albertine igjen." *Kunst og Kultur* 63, no. 1 (1980): 63.
Brinton, Christian. "Introduction." In *Scandinavian Art Illustrated*, edited by Carl Laurin, Emil Hannover, and Jens Thiis. New York: American-Scandinavian Foundation, 1922.
Brooks, Peter. *Body Work: Objects of Desire in Modern Narrative*. Cambridge, MA: Harvard University Press, 1993.
Broude, Norma. "Edgar Degas and French Feminism, ca. 1880: 'The Young Spartans,' the Brothel Monotypes, and the Bathers Revisited." *Art Bulletin* 70, no. 4 (1988): 640–59.
———, ed. *World Impressionism: The International Movement, 1860–1920*. New York: Harry N. Abrams, 1990.
Brown, Frederick. "Zola and Manet: 1866." *Hudson Review* 41, no. 1 (1988): 71–92.
Brunetière, Ferdinand. *Brunetière's Essays in French Literature*. Translated by D. Nichol Smith. London: T. Fisher Unwin, 1898.
———. *Discours de combat*. Paris: Perrin, 1904.
———. *Essais sur la littérature contemporaine*. Paris: Calmann-Lévy, 1900.
———. *L'évolution des genres dans l'histoire de la littérature*. Paris: Hachette, 1890.
———. "The Experimental Novel." Translated by Janice Best. In *Critical Essays on Emile Zola*, edited by David Baguley. Boston: G. K. Hall., 1986.
———. *Nouvelles questions de critique*. Paris: Calmann-Lévy, 1890.
———. "La philosophie de Schopenhauer et les conséquences du pessimisme." *Revue des deux mondes* 60 (1890): 210–21.
———. *Le roman naturaliste*. Paris: Calmann-Lévy, 1910.
Brunius, August. "Norsk Kolorisme: Fra Jubilæumsutstillingen." *Morgenbladet*, October 11, 1914.
Brunon-Ernst, Anne, ed. *Beyond Foucault: New Perspectives on Bentham's Panopticon*. Farnham: Ashgate, 2012.
Bryhni, Anne Siri, ed. *Bohem mot Borger: Et utvalg fra Hans Jægers og Christian Krohgs "Impressionisten."* Oslo: Universitetsforlaget, 1971.
Bryson, Norman. *Word and Image: French Painting of the Ancien Régime*. Cambridge: Cambridge University Press, 1981.

Bürger, William [Théophile Thoré]. "Van der Meer de Delft." *Gazette des Beaux-Arts* 21 (1866): 297–330, 458–79, 542–75.
Bynum, W. F. *Science and the Practice of Medicine in the Nineteenth Century*. Cambridge: Cambridge University Press, 1994.
Callen, Anthea. *The Spectacular Body: Science, Method and Meaning in the Work of Degas*. New Haven, CT: Yale University Press, 1995.
Canguilhem, Georges. *The Normal and the Pathological*. Translated by Carolyn R. Fawcett. New York: Zone Books, 2007.
———. *A Vital Rationalist*. Translated by Arthur Goldhammer. New York: Zone Books, 1994.
Caro, Elme-Marie. *Le pessimisme au XIXe siècle*. Paris: Hachette, 1880.
Cartwright, Julia. "J. Bastien-Lepage." In *The Portfolio: Monographs on Artistic Subjects*, edited by P. G. Hamerton. London: Seeley and Macmillan, 1894.
Cassirer, Ernst. *The Problem of Knowledge: Philosophy, Science, and History since Hegel*. Translated by William H. Woglom and Charles W. Hendel. New Haven, CT: Yale University Press, 1969.
Castagnary, Jules-Antoine. *Salons (1857–1870)*. Vol. 1. Paris: Charpentier, 1892.
Catalogue illustré du Salon de 1902. Paris: Baschet, 1902.
Chadwick, Owen. *The Secularization of the European Mind in the 19th Century*. Cambridge: Cambridge University Press, 2000.
Challons-Lipton, Siulolovao. *The Scandinavian Pupils of the Atelier Bonnat, 1867–1894*. Lewiston: Edwin Mellen, 2001.
Charlton, D. G. *Positivist Thought in France during the Second Empire 1852–1870*. Oxford: Clarendon, 1959.
"Chr. Krohg: Kampen for Tilværelsen." *Aftenposten*, May 10, 1889.
Christensen, Charlotte. "Max Klinger und Georg Brandes." In *Max Klinger: ". . . Der moderne Künstler schlechthin,"* edited by Richard Hüttel and Peter Schmidt. Berlin: Deutscher Kunstverlag, 2010.
Chu, Petra ten-Doesschate. "Nineteenth-Century Visitors to the Frans Hals Museum." In *The Documented Image: Visions in Art History*, edited by Gabriel P. Weisberg and Laurinda S. Dixon. New York: Syracuse University Press, 1987.
Clark, T. J. *Image of the People: Gustave Courbet and the 1848 Revolution*. London: Thames and Hudson, 1988.
———. *The Painting of Modern Life: Paris in the Art of Manet and His Followers*. London: Thames and Hudson, 2003.
Clayson, Hollis. "*Avant-Garde* and *Pompier* Images of 19th Century French Prostitution: The Matter of Modernism, Modernity and Social Ideology." In *Modernism and Modernity: The Vancouver Conference Papers*, edited by Benjamin H. D. Buchloh, Serge Guilbaut, and David H. Solkin. Halifax: Press of the Nova Scotia College of Art and Design, 2004.
———. *Painted Love: Prostitution in French Art of the Impressionist Era*. New Haven, CT: Yale University Press, 1991.
Coffin, Judith G. "Consumption, Production, and Gender: The Sewing Machine in Nineteenth-Century France." In *Gender and Class in Modern Europe*, edited by Laura L. Frader and Sonya O. Rose. Ithaca, NY: Cornell University Press, 1996.
———. "Credit, Consumption, and Images of Women's Desires: Selling the Sewing Machine in Late Nineteenth-Century France." *French Historical Studies* 18, no. 3 (1994): 749–83.
———. *The Politics of Women's Work: The Paris Garment Trades 1750–1915*. Princeton, NJ: Princeton University Press, 1996.

———. "Social Science Meets Sweated Labor: Reinterpreting Women's Work in Late Nineteenth-Century France." *Journal of Modern History* 63, no. 2 (1991): 230–70.
Cohen, Margaret, and Christopher Prendergast, eds. *Spectacles of Realism: Gender, Body, Genre.* Minneapolis: University of Minnesota Press, 1995.
Collin, Christen. *Kunsten og Moralen: Bidrag til kritik af realismens digtere og kritikere.* Copenhagen: Gyldendalske, 1894.
Comte, Auguste. *Cours de philosophie positive.* Vol. 4. Paris: Baillère, 1869.
———. *Introduction to Positive Philosophy.* Edited by Frederick Ferré. Indianapolis: Hackett, 1988.
———. *The Positive Philosophy of Auguste Comte.* Vol. 1. London: John Chapman, 1853.
Conti, Fiorenzo, and Silvana Irrera Conti. "On Science and Literature: A Lesson from the Bernard-Zola Case." *BioScience* 53, no. 9 (2003): 865–69.
Cooper, Grace Rogers. *The Invention of the Sewing Machine.* Washington, DC: Smithsonian Institution Press, 1968.
Corbin, Alain. "Présentation." In Alexandre Parent-Duchâtelet, *La prostitution à Paris au XIXe siècle*, 7–58. Paris: Seuil, 1981.
———. *Women for Hire: Prostitution and Sexuality in France after 1850.* Translated by Alan Sheridan. Cambridge, MA: Harvard University Press, 1990.
Cordulack, Shelley Wood. *Edvard Munch and the Physiology of Symbolism.* Madison, WI: Fairleigh Dickinson University Press, 2002.
Courbet, Gustave. *Letters of Gustave Courbet.* Translated by Petra ten-Doesschate Chu. Chicago: University of Chicago Press, 1992.
———. "Statement on Realism." In *Art in Theory 1815–1900: An Anthology of Changing Ideas*, edited by Charles Harrison, Paul Wood, and Jason Gaiger. Oxford: Blackwell, 2003.
Cox, Kenyon. "Antoine Vollon: A Painter's Painter." *Manhattan Magazine* 2 (1883): 557–61.
Crane, Diana. *Fashion and Its Social Agendas: Class, Gender, and Identity in Clothing.* Chicago: University of Chicago Press, 2000.
Crastre, Fr. *Bastien-Lepage.* Translated by Frederic Taber Cooper. New York: Frederick A. Stokes, 1914.
Croce, Benedetto. *Æsthetic as Science of Expression and General Linguistic.* Translated by Douglas Ainslie. London: Macmillan, 1922.
Daston, Lorraine, and Peter Galison. *Objectivity.* New York: Zone Books, 2010.
David-Sauvageot, A. *Le réalisme et le naturalisme dans la littérature et dans l'art.* Paris: Calmann Lévy, 1889.
da Vinci, Leonardo. *Leonardo on Painting.* Translated by Martin Kemp and Margaret Walker. New Haven, CT: Yale University Press, 2001.
Dawkins, Heather. *The Nude in French Art and Culture 1870–1910.* Cambridge: Cambridge University Press, 2002.
Debord, Guy. *Society of the Spectacle.* Detroit: Black and Red, 2010.
Demetz, Peter. "Defenses of Dutch Painting and the Theory of Realism." *Comparative Literature* 15, no. 2 (1963): 97–115.
Deri, Max. *Naturalismus, Idealismus, Expressionismus.* Leipzig: E. A. Seeman, 1920.
Desprez, Louis. *L'évolution naturaliste.* Paris: Tresse, 1884.
Dewhurst, Wynford. *Impressionist Painting: Its Genesis and Development.* London: Georges Newnes, 1904.
Dietrichson, Lorentz. *Betegner den moderne Naturalisme i Poesien et Fremskridt eller et Forfald?* Kristiania: Studentersamfundet, 1882.

———. *Fra Kunstens Verden: Foredrag og Studier*. Copenhagen: Gyldendal, 1885.
———. *Norges kunsts historie i det nittende århundre*. Oslo: Messel, 1991.
———. *Svundne Tider af en Forfatters Livserindringer*. Vol. 4. Christiania: Cappelen, 1917.
Draper, John Williams. *The Conflict between Religion and Science*. New York: Appleton, 1875.
D'Souza, Aruna, and Tom McDonough, eds. *The Invisible* Flâneuse*? Gender, Public Space, and Visual Culture in Nineteenth-Century Paris*. Manchester: Manchester University Press, 2008.
Dubos, René, and Jean Dubos. *The White Plague: Tuberculosis, Man, and Society*. New Brunswick, NJ: Rutgers University Press, 1996.
Dumas, F.-G. *Catalogue illustré du Salon*. Paris: L. Baschet, 1882.
Duranty, Edmond. *La nouvelle peinture à propos du groupe d'artistes qui expose dans les galeries Durand-Ruel*. Paris: E. Dentu, 1876.
———. "Suède. Norvège. Danemark. Russie." In *L'art moderne à l'exposition de 1878*, edited by Louis Gonse. Paris: A. Quantin, 1879.
Eagleton, Terry. *Marxism and Literary Criticism*. Berkeley: University of California Press, 1976.
Edelfelt, Albert. *Ur Albert Edelfelts Brev: Liv och Arbete*. Stockholm: Almqvist & Wiksells Förlag, 1926.
———. *Ur Albert Edelfelts Pariserbrev till sin Mor*. Stockholm: Albert Bonnier, 1917.
Elmgaard, Bertel. "Norsk Bohêmlitteratur." *Tilskueren* (April 1887): 318–32.
Emerson, Peter Henry. *Naturalistic Photography for Students of the Art*. London: Sampson Low, Marston, Searle and Rivington, 1890.
Énault, Louis. *Paris-Salon: Triennal 1883*. Paris: E. Bernard, 1883.
Estlander, Carl Gustaf. *Naturalismen enligt Zola*. Helsinki: J. C. Frenckell, 1891.
Evans, David Owen. *Social Romanticism in France 1830–1848*. Oxford: Clarendon, 1951.
Explication des ouvrages de peinture, sculpture, architecture, gravure et lithographie. Paris: E. Bernard, 1884.
Exposition Universelle des Beaux-Arts 1885, catalogue général, première partie: Belgique—Autriche—Espagne—France—Hollande—Norvège—Suisse. Anvers: J.-E. Buschmann, 1885.
Facos, Michelle. *Nationalism and the Nordic Imagination: Swedish Art of the 1890s*. Berkeley: University of California Press, 1998.
———. "Richard Bergh: Natural Science and National Art in Sweden." *Interdisciplinary Science Reviews* 35, no. 1 (2010): 39–50.
Faguet, Émile. *En lisant Nietzsche*. Paris: Société Française d'Imprimerie et de Librairie, 1904. Translated by George Raffalovich as *On Reading Nietzsche* (New York: Moffat, Yard, 1918).
———. *A Literary History of France*. London: T. Fisher Unwin, 1907.
———. *Politiques et moralistes du dix-neuvième siècle (troisième série)*. Paris: Société Française d'Imprimerie et de Librairie, 1903.
Feir, Charles de. *Guide de Salon de Paris 1882*. Paris: Au Bureau du Moniteur des Arts, 1882.
Ferrero, Guillermo. "Er vi syge?" *Samtiden* 4 (1893): 361–67.
Filon, Augustin. *The Modern French Drama: Seven Essays*. Translated by Janet E. Hogarth. London: Chapman and Hall, 1898.
Finke, Ulrich, ed. *French 19th Century Painting and Literature*. Manchester: Manchester University Press, 1972.
Fischer, Ernst. *The Necessity of Art*. Translated by Anna Bostock. London: Verso, 2010.
Flint, Austin. *A Treatise on the Principles and Practice of Medicine*. Philadelphia: Henry C. Lea, 1873.
Fosli, Halvor. *Kristianiabohemen*. Oslo: Samlaget, 1997.

Foucault, Michel. *The Birth of the Clinic: An Archeology of Medical Perception*. Translated by A. M. Sheridan Smith. New York: Vintage, 1994.
———. *Discipline and Punish: The Birth of the Prison*. Translated by Alan Sheridan. London: Penguin, 1991.
———. *The History of Sexuality: An Introduction*. Translated by Robert Hurley. New York: Vintage, 1990.
———. *The Order of Things*. London: Routledge, 2005.
———. *Speech Begins after Death*. Translated by Robert Bononno. Minneapolis: University of Minnesota Press, 2013.
Franklin, Charles Kendall. *What Nature Is: An Outline of Scientific Naturalism*. Boston: Sherman, French, 1911.
Fried, Michael. *Absorption and Theatricality: Painting and Beholder in the Age of Diderot*. Chicago: University of Chicago Press, 1988.
———. "Caillebotte's Impressionism." *Representations* 66 (1999): 1–51.
Fromentin, Eugène. *The Masters of Past Time, or Criticism on the Old Flemish and Dutch Painters*. New York: E. P. Dutton, 1913.
Frothingham, O. B. "The Morally Objectionable in Literature." *North American Review* 135, no. 311 (1882): 323–38.
Furst, Lilian R., and Peter N. Skrine. *Naturalism*. London: Methuen, 1971.
Gage, John. *A Decade of English Naturalism: 1810–1820*. Norwich: Norwich Castle Museum, 1969.
Gallagher, Catherine, and Thomas Laqueur, eds. *The Making of the Modern Body: Sexuality and Society in the Nineteenth Century*. Berkeley: University of California Press, 1987.
Garborg, Arne. "Friedrich Nietzsche af Ola Hansson." *Samtiden* 1 (1890): 386–95.
———. "Hr. Statsraad Dr. Blix." *Dagbladet*, December 22, 1886.
———. "Lidt spiritisme." *Samtiden* 4 (1893): 1–7.
Garborg, Arne, G. V. Lyng, and Henrik Jæger, eds. *Betegner den moderne naturalisme i poesien et fremskridt eller et forfald?* Kristiania: Studentersamfundet, 1882.
Gastine, L. "Salon de 1882." *La presse*, May 22, 1882.
Gauguin, Pola. *Christian Krohg*. Oslo: Gyldendal, 1932.
———. "Torvet 8." *Kunst og Kultur* (1947): 65–84.
Gauthier, E. Paul. "Zola on Naturalism in Art and History." *Modern Language Notes* 70, no. 7 (1955): 514–17.
Gibbs, Jean Beverly. "Impressionism as a Literary Movement." *Modern Language Journal* 36, no. 4 (1952): 175–83.
Goncourt, Edmond de. *Chérie*. Paris: Charpentier, 1884.
Goncourt, Edmond de, and Jules de Goncourt. *Germinie Lacerteux*. Paris: Charpentier, 1875.
———. *Journal des Goncourt: Mémoires de la vie littéraire*. Vol. 2, *1862–1865*. Paris: Charpentier, 1887.
———. *Journal des Goncourt: Mémoires de la vie littéraire*. Vol. 3, *1866–1870*. Paris: Charpentier, 1888.
———. *Manette Salomon*. Paris: Gallimard, 1996.
———. *Pages from the Goncourt Journals*. Translated by Robert Baldick. New York: New York Review of Books, 2007.
Goodsell, Willystine. *The Conflict of Naturalism and Humanism*. New York: Teachers College, Columbia University, 1910.
Gran, Gerhard. *Alexander L. Kielland og Hans Samtid*. Stavanger: Dreyer, 1992.

———. "Emile Zola." *Nyt Tidsskrft* 2 (1883): 296–318.
———. *Henrik Ibsen: Liv og Verker*. Vol. 2. Kristiania: Aschehoug, 1918.
———. *Norsk Aandsliv i Hundrede Aar*. Kristiania: Aschehoug, 1919.
———. "Taine og hans Kunstphilosophi." *Ny Illustreret Tidende*, April 18, 1880.
Grande, Jan Groven. "Veien, Sannheten og Livet: Norske medisineres vitenskapelige moderniseringsarbeid ca. 1840–1880." PhD diss., Norwegian University of Science and Technology, 2004.
Guérard, Albert. *Literature and Society*. New York: Cooper Square, 1970.
Gunnarsson, Torsten, and Hans Henrik Brummer. *Impressionism and the North: Late 19th Century French Avant-Garde Art and the Art in the Nordic Countries 1870–1920*. Stockholm: Nationalmuseum, 2002.
Guthmüller, Marie. "Procédés empiriques et savoir esthétique: Hippolyte Taine, fondateur de la critique scientifique de la psychologie expérimentale." In *Vers la science de l'art: L'ésthetique scientifique en France 1857–1937*, edited by Jacquelin Lichtenstein, Carole Maigné, and Arnauld Pierre. Paris: Presses de l'université Paris-Sorbonne, 2013.
Hamel, Maurice. "Danemark. Suède. Norvège. Finlande. Russie. Sussie." In *Exposition universelle de 1889: Les beaux-arts et les arts décoratifs*, edited by Louis Gonse and Alfred de Lostalot. Paris: Journal de Temps, 1889.
———. "La peinture du Nord." *Gazette des Beaux-Arts* 38 (1888): 388–404.
———. *The Salons of 1902*. Translated by Paul Villars. Paris: Goupil, 1902.
Hamerton, Philip Gilbert. *Thoughts about Art*. Boston: Roberts Brothers, 1871.
Hamm, Christine. "'Sjælemalerier': Amalie Skram leser Albertine." *Edda* 106, no. 3 (2006): 254–68.
Hamon, Philippe. *Expositions: Literature and Architecture in Nineteenth-Century France*. Berkeley: University of California Press, 1992.
Hannover, Emil. *Erindringer fra Barndom og Ungdom*. Copenhagen: Foreningen for Boghaandværk, 1966.
———. "Nogle Billeder paa den franske Udstilling." *Tilskueren* 5 (1888): 561–75.
———. "Nogle Indtryk fra Foraarsudstillingen paa Charlottenborg." *Tilskueren* 4 (May 1887): 365–89.
Hansen, Irgens. "Krohgs Maleri." *Verdens Gang*, May 8, 1889.
Hansen, Vibeke Waallann, Erik Mørstad, Birgitte Sauge, and Marianne Yvenes, eds. *Christian Krohg: Bilder som griper / Picures That Captivate*. Oslo: Nasjonalmuseet for Kunst, Arkitektur og Design, 2012.
Hansson, Ola. *Friedrich Nietzsche: Hans Personlighed og hans System*. Translated by Arne Garborg. Christiania: Cammermeyer, 1890.
———. *Materialismen i Skönlitteraturen*. Stockholm: Albert Bonnier, 1892.
———. *Tolke og Seere: Kritiske Essays*. Kristiania: Aschehoug, 1893.
Hansson, Olaf. "Krohgs og Werenskiolds Maleriudstilling." *Dagbladet*, March 22, 1885.
Harsin, Jill. *Policing Prostitution in Nineteenth-Century Paris*. Princeton, NJ: Princeton University Press, 1985.
Haugen, Trond. "Litterære forstyrrelser 4." *Vinduet* 66, no. 4 (2012): 32–39.
Hauser, Arnold. *The Social History of Art*. Vol. 4, *Naturalism, Impressionism, the Film Age*. London: Routledge, 1993.
Havard, Henry. *Histoire de la peinture hollandaise*. Paris: A. Quantin, 1882.
Hayek, F. A. *The Counter-Revolution of Science: Studies in the Abuse of Reason*. New York: Free Press, 1955.
Heiberg, Gunnar. "Fra Kunstudstillingen i København." *Dagbladet*, July 27, 1883.

Hemmings, F. W. J. "Zola, Manet, and the Impressionists (1875–80)." *PMLA* 73, no. 4 (1958): 407–17.
Hertel, Christiane. *Vermeer: Reception and Interpretation*. Cambridge: Cambridge University Press, 1996.
Heyerdahl, Hans. "Prostitutionen." *Verdens Gang*, December 11, 1886.
Hoel, Aud Sissel. *Maktens bilder*. Trondheim: Norsk Rettsmuseum, 2007.
Hooper, Lucy H. "The Paris Salon of 1878." *Art Journal* 4 (1878): 254–55.
Horn, David G. "This Norm Which Is Not One: Reading the Female Body in Lombroso's Anthropology." In *Deviant Bodies: Critical Perspectives in Science and Popular Culture*, edited by Jennifer Terry and Jacqueline Urla. Bloomington: Indiana University Press, 1995.
Horn, Pierre L., and Mary Beth Pringle, eds. *The Image of the Prostitute in Modern Literature*. New York: Frederick Ungar, 1984.
Hugo, Victor. *William Shakespeare*. Translated by Melville B. Anderson. Chicago: McClurg, 1891.
Hunter, Mary. "'Effroyable réalisme': Wax, Femininity, and the Madness of Realist Fantasies." *RACAR* 33, nos. 1–2 (2008): 43–58.
Huysmans, Joris-Karl. *Against Nature*. Translated by Margaret Mauldon. Oxford: Oxford University Press, 2009.
———. *Écrits sur l'art*. Paris: Flammarion, 2008.
———. *Marthe: The Story of a Whore*. Translated by Brendan King. Sawtry: Dedalus, 2006.
Høffding, Harald. "Om Realisme i Videnskab og Tro." *Tilskueren* 1 (1884): 20–32.
Høifødt, Frank. "The Kristiania Bohemia Reflected in the Art of the Young Edvard Munch." In *Edvard Munch: An Anthology*, edited by Erik Mørstad. Oslo: Unipub/Oslo Academic Press, 2006.
Illich, Ivan. *Limits to Medicine*. London: Marion Boyars, 1995.
Ipsen, Alfred. *Georg Brandes: En Bog om Ret og Uret*. Copenhagen: Olaf O. Barfod, 1902.
Irigaray, Luce. *Speculum of the Other Woman*. Translated by Gillian C. Gill. Ithaca, NY: Cornell University Press, 1986.
Iskin, Ruth E. *Modern Women and Parisian Consumer Culture in Impressionist Painting*. Cambridge: Cambridge University Press, 2007.
Iversen, Irene. "Blikk, Speil, Begjær: To impresjonistiske kvinneportrett." *Skrift: Skriftserie for litteraturvitenskap ved Universitetet i Oslo* 15 (1995): 34–54.
———. "Kjønnet sprengjer det moderne." *Syn og Segn* 3 (1997): 195–208.
Jackson, David, ed. *Nordic Art: The Modern Breakthrough 1860–1920*. Munich: Hirmer, 2012.
Jacob, François. *The Logic of Life: A History of Heredity*. Translated by Betty E. Spillmann. New York: Pantheon Books, 1973.
Jacobsen, Jens Peter, and Vilhelm Møller. *Darwin: Hans liv og hans lære*. Copenhagen: Gyldendalske, 1893.
Jameson, Fredric. *The Political Unconscious: Narrative as a Socially Symbolic Art*. Ithaca, NY: Cornell University Press, 1982.
Jansson, Mats, Jakob Lothe, and Hannu Riikonen, eds. *European and Nordic Modernisms*. Norwich: Norvik Press, 2004.
Jay, Martin. "In the Empire of the Gaze: Foucault and the Denigration of Vision in Twentieth-Century French Thought." In *Foucault: A Critical Reader*, edited by David Couzens Hoy. Oxford: Blackwell, 1996.
Jensen, Mette Bøgh. *At male sit privatliv: Skagensmalernes selviscenesættelse*. Skagen: Skagens Museum, 2005.
Johansen, Annette, and Mette Bøgh Jensen, eds. *Christian Krohg og Skagen*. Skagen: Skagens Museum, 2004.

Johnsen, Rosenkrantz. "Krohgs Maleri 'Albertine.'" *Dagbladet*, March 17, 1887.
Jowell, Frances Suzman. "Thoré-Bürger and the Revival of Frans Hals." *Art Bulletin* 56, no. 1 (1974): 101–17.
Jæger, Hans. *Fra Kristiania-Bohemen*. 2 vols. Oslo: De norske Bokklubbene, 1997.
Jæger, Henrik. "Christian Krohg og hans Emner." *Christiania Intelligentssedler (Dagens Nyheder)*, March 26, 1885.
———. *Illustreret Norsk Litteraturhistorie*. Vol. 2. Kristiania: Hjalmar Bigler, 1896.
———. *Kristiania og Kristianienserne*. Kristiania: F. Beyer, 1890.
Jæger, Herman. *Taine: En Tænkerprofil*. Kristiania: Aschehoug, 1917.
Kahn, Sholom J. *Science and Aesthetic Judgment: A Study in Taine's Critical Method*. New York: Columbia University Press, 1953.
Kern, Stephen. *Eyes of Love: The Gaze in English and French Paintings and Novels 1840–1900*. London: Reaktion Books, 1996.
Kimball, M. Douglas. "Emile Zola and French Impressionism." *Bulletin of the Rocky Mountain Modern Language Association* 23, no. 2 (1969): 51–57.
Koefoed, Holger. *Malernes Oslo: 1880- til 1980-årene*. Oslo: Aschehoug, 1988.
Koehler, S. R. "Wilhelm Leibl." *American Art Review* 1, no. 11 (1880): 477–80.
Kristensen, Sven Møller. *Georg Brandes: Kritikeren, liberalisten, humanisten*. Copenhagen: Gyldendal, 1980.
Kroeber, A. L. *Anthropology: Culture Patterns and Processes*. New York: Harbinger, 1963.
Krog, Gina. "Albertine." *Dagbladet*, December 24, 1886.
Krohg, Christian. *Albertine*. Oslo: Bokklubben, 1995.
———. "Havets land: 1910." In *Christian Krohg og Skagen*, edited by Annette Johansen and Mette Bøgh Jensen. Skagen: Skagens Museum, 2004.
———. "Impresjonistene." In *Christian Krohg 1852–1925*. Åmot i Modum: Stiftelsen Modums Blaafarveværk, 1993.
———. *Kampen for tilværelsen*. Oslo: Gyldendal, 1954.
———. *I Smaa Dagsreiser til og fra Paris*. Kristiania: Aschehoug, 1897.
———. "Syttende Maj 1887." *Impressionisten* 5 (1887): 1–3.
Kronen, Torleiv. *De store årene: Fransk innflytelse på norsk åndsliv 1880–1900*. Oslo: Dreyer, 1982.
La Berge, Ann, and Mordechai Feingold. *French Medical Culture in the Nineteenth Century*. Amsterdam: Rodopi, 1994.
Lacambre, Geneviève. "Toward an Emerging Definition of Naturalism in French Nineteenth-Century Painting." In *The European Realist Tradition*, edited by Gabriel P. Weisberg. Bloomington: Indiana University Press, 1982.
Lafanestre, Georges. "Af Indberetningen fra den international Jury for Klasse 1 og 2 (Maleri og Tegninger)." In *Beretninger om Norges Deltagelse i Verdensudstillingen i Paris 1889*. Christiania: Fabritius, 1891.
Lange, Julius. *Bastien Lepage og andre Afhandlinger*. Copenhagen: P. G. Philipsen, 1889.
———. *Om Kunstværdi: To Foredrag*. Copenhagen: G. E. C. Gad, 1876.
———. "Norsk, svensk, dansk Figurmaleri: Indtryk og Overvejelser." *Tilskueren* 9 (1892): 241–72.
———. *Udvalgte Skrifter*. Vol. 2. Edited by Georg Brandes and P. Købke. Copenhagen: Det Nordiske Forlag, 1901.
———. *Vor Kunst og Udlandets: Et Foredrag*. Copenhagen: P. G. Philipsen, 1879.
Lange, Marit. "Max Klinger og Norge." *Kunst og kultur* 80, no. 1 (1997): 2–40.
Langeland, Nils Rune. *Siste ord: Høgsterett i norsk historie 1814–1965*. Vol. 1. Oslo: Cappelen, 2005.
Langås, Unni. *Kroppens betydning i norsk litteratur 1800–1900*. Bergen: Fagbokforlaget, 2004.

Lathers, Marie. *Bodies of Art: French Literary Realism and the Artist's Model*. Lincoln: University of Nebraska Press, 2001.
Laurin, Carl G. *Nordisk Konst: Danmark och Norges konst från 1880 till 1925*. Stockholm: P. A. Norstedt, 1925.
———. *Stamfränder*. Stockholm: P. A. Norstedt, 1925.
Laurin, Carl G., Emil Hannover, and Jens Thiis, eds. *Scandinavian Art Illustrated*. New York: American-Scandinavian Foundation, 1922.
Lemaître, Jules. *Les contemporains*. Vol. 6. Paris: Lecène, Oudien, 1896.
Lemoine, Serge, ed. *Jules Bastien-Lepage (1848–1884)*. Paris: Musée d'Orsay and Nicolas Chaudun, 2007.
Leroi, Paul. "Salon de 1882." *L' art: Revue hebdomadaire illustrée* 29, no. 2 (1882): 152–54.
Lervik, Åse Hjort, ed. *Gjennom kvinneøyne*. Tromsø: Universitetsforlaget, 1980.
Levine, George. *Darwin and the Novelists: Patterns of Science in Victorian Fiction*. Cambridge, MA: Harvard University Press, 1988.
Lichtenstein, Jacqueline. "Préface." In Eugène Véron, *L'esthétique*, 7–19. Paris: Vrin, 2007.
Lindgren, Hellen. *Emile Zola*. Stockholm: Wahlström & Widstrand, 1898.
———. *Vittra Stormän: Kritiker og Porträtt*. Stockholm: Carl Deleen, 1894.
Lipton, Eunice. *Looking into Degas: Uneasy Images of Women and Modern Life*. Berkeley: University of California Press, 1988.
Lombardo, Patrizia. "Hippolyte Taine between Art and Science." *Yale French Studies* 77 (1990): 117–33.
Lombroso, Cesare, and Guglielmo Ferrero. *Criminal Woman, the Prostitute, and the Normal Woman*. Translated by Nicole Hahn Rafter and Mary Gibson. Durham, NC: Duke University Press, 2004.
Lucie-Smith, Edward, and Celestine Dars. *Work and Struggle: The Painter as Witness 1870–1914*. New York: Paddington, 1977.
Lukács, Georg. *Studies in European Realism*. Translated by Edith Bone. New York: Howard Fertig, 2002.
Lukkarinen, Ville. "The Naturalness of Naturalism Reconsidered." *Konsthistorisk tidsskrift / Journal of Art History* 65, no. 1 (1996): 51–59.
Macherey, Pierre. *A Theory of Literary Production*. Translated by Geoffrey Wall. London: Routledge, 2006.
Madsen, Karl. *Billedkunsten*. Copenhagen: Frem, 1901.
———. "Foraarsudstillingen 1887." *Politiken*, April 22, 1887.
———. "I Holland." *Tilskueren* 9 (1892): 887–919.
———. "Michael Ancher." *Tilskueren* 3 (1886): 210–30.
———. "Van der Meer fra Delft." *Tilskueren* 1 (1884): 970–78.
Malmanger, Magne. "'Impressionismen' og *Impressionisten*: Chr. Krohg og det moderne gjennombrudd i 1880-årene." In *Christian Krohg*, edited by Oscar Thue, 31–49. Oslo: Nasjonalgalleriet, 1987.
———. "Norsk kunstdebatt ved modernismens terskel: Fra 'erindringens kunst' til 'det dekorative.'" *Kunst og Kulturs Serie* 1 (1985): 2–45.
Mancoff, Debra N. *Fashion in Impressionist Paris*. London: Merrell, 2012.
Marlais, Michael. *Conservative Echoes in* Fin-de-Siècle *Parisian Art Criticism*. University Park: Pennsylvania State University Press, 1992.
Marshall, David. *The Surprising Effects of Sympathy: Marivaux, Diderot, Rousseau, and Mary Shelley*. Chicago: University of Chicago Press, 1988.

Marx, Karl. *Capital.* Vol. 1. Translated by Ben Fowkes. London: Penguin, 1990.
Maupassant, Guy de. *Alien Hearts.* Translated by Richard Howard. New York: New York Review of Books, 2009.
———. *Bel-Ami.* Paris: Louis Conard, 1910. Translated by Douglas Parmée as *Bel-Ami* (London: Penguin, 2012).
———. *Fort comme la mort.* Paris: Louis Conard, 1908.
———. *Pierre and Jean.* Translated by Leonard Tancock. London: Penguin, 1979.
Mednick, Thor J. "Danish Internationalism: Peder Severin Krøyer in Copenhagen and Paris." *Nineteenth Century Art Worldwide* 10, no. 1 (2011): n.p.
Merz, John Theodore. *A History of European Thought in the Nineteenth Century.* Edinburgh: William Blackwood, 1896.
Messel, Nils. *Tekster om norsk kunst og kunsthistorie.* Oslo: Labyrinth, 2013.
Michel, André. "Af *Journal des Débats*, 27de August 1889." In *Beretninger om Norges Deltagelse i Verdensudstillingen i Paris 1889.* Christiania: W. C. Fabritius, 1891.
Mitterand, Henri. *Le Paris de Zola.* Paris: Hazan, 2008.
"Modern French Painting." *Art Critic* 1, no. 2 (1894): 26–30.
Moi, Toril. *Henrik Ibsen and the Birth of Modernism: Art, Theater, Philosophy.* Oxford: Oxford University Press, 2008.
Moore, Olin H. "The Literary Methods of the Goncourts." *PMLA* 31, no. 1 (1916): 43–64.
Morawski, Stefan. "The Problem of Value and Criteria in Taine's Aesthetics." *Journal of Aesthetics and Art Criticism* 21, no. 4 (1963): 407–21.
Moréas, Jean. "Le symbolisme." *Le Figaro, supplément littéraire,* September 18, 1886.
Morehead, Allison. "Creative Pathologies: French Experimental Psychology and Symbolist Avant-Gardes, 1889–1900." PhD diss., University of Chicago, 2007.
Moritzen, Julius. *Georg Brandes in Life and Letters.* Newark: D. S. Colyer, 1922.
Morris, George S. "The Philosophy of Art." *Journal of Speculative Philosophy* 10, no. 1 (1876): 1–16.
Morton, Marsha. "'Impulses and Desires': Klinger's Darwinism in Nature and Society." *Nineteenth Century Art Worldwide* 2, no. 2 (2003): 1–30.
Müller-Wille, Steffan, and Hans-Jörg Rheinberger, eds. *Heredity Produced: At the Crossroads of Biology, Politics, and Culture, 1500–1870.* Cambridge: MIT Press, 2007.
Mulvey, Laura. *Visual and Other Pleasures.* Bloomington: Indiana University Press, 1989.
Munro, Thomas. *Evolution in the Arts and Other Theories of Culture History.* Cleveland: Cleveland Museum of Art, 1963.
———. "Meanings of 'Naturalism' in Philosophy and Aesthetics." *Journal of Aesthetics and Art Criticism* 19, no. 2 (1960): 133–37.
Mørstad, Erik. "Christian Krohgs kunstteori i 1880-årene." *Kunst og Kultur* 74, no. 2 (1991): 69–107.
———. "Krohg and Brandes: Friendship and Professional Dialogue." In *Christian Krohg: Bilder som griper / Pictures That Captivate,* edited by Vibeke Waallaann Hansen, Erik Mørstad, Birgitte Sauge, and Marianne Yvenes, 189–201. Oslo: Nasjonalmuseet for Kunst, Arkitcktur og Design, 2012.
Nielsen, Ragna. "Albertine." *Dagbladet,* December 24, 1886.
Nielsen, Yngvar. *Christiania og Omegn: Illustreret Haandbog for Reisende.* Christiania: Grønneberg/Cammermeyer, 1894.
Nietzsche, Friedrich. *Beyond Good and Evil.* Translated by R. J. Hollingdale. London: Penguin, 2003.

———. "Saalunde talte Zarathustra." Translated by Sophus Michaëlis. *Ny Jord* (1889): 262–80.
Nochlin, Linda. *Courbet*. London: Thames and Hudson, 2007.
———. *Realism*. London: Penguin, 1990.
———. *Representing Women*. London: Thames and Hudson, 1999.
Noël, Benoît, and Jean Hournon. *Parisiana: La capitale des peintres au XIXème siècle*. Paris: Presses Franciliennes, 2006.
Nolin, Bertil. *Den Gode Europén: Studier i Georg Brandes' idéutveckling 1871–1893*. Uppsala: Svenska Bogförlaget/Norstedts, 1965.
Nordau, Max. "Bjornson's Paris Days." *Bookman* 32, no. 1 (1910): 63–67.
———. *Degeneration*. Lincoln: University of Nebraska Press, 1993.
Nordensvan, Georg. "Bastien-Lepage: Till hans tafla: Ett kärlekspar." *Ny Illustrerad Tidning* 4, no. 41 (1883): 360–61.
———. *De Bildande Konsternas Historia under 19: De Århundradet*. Stockholm: Hugo Gerber, 1900.
———. "Franskt Måleri och Tyskt: Några Anmärkningar." *Nordisk Tidsskrift för Vetenskap, Konst och Industri* 9 (1886): 532–46.
O'Dowd, Michael J., and Elliot E. Phillip. *The History of Obstetrics and Gynaecology*. New York: Parthenon, 1994.
Ohlsen, Nils. "Christian Krohg's Student Years in Berlin." In *Christian Krohg: Bilder som griper / Pictures That Captivate*, edited by Vibeke Waallaann Hansen, Erik Mørstad, Birgitte Sauge, and Marianne Yvenes. Oslo: Nasjonalmuseet for Kunst, Arkitektur og Design, 2012.
Olmsted, J. M. D., and E. Harris Olmsted. *Claude Bernard and the Experimental Method in Medicine*. New York: Henry Schuman, 1952.
Olson, Richard G. *Science and Scientism in Nineteenth-Century Europe*. Urbana: University of Illinois Press, 2008.
Oxfeldt, Elisabeth. *Nordic Orientalism: Paris and the Cosmopolitan Imagination 1800–1900*. Copenhagen: Museum Tusculanum Press, 2005.
Parent-Duchâtelet, Alexandre. *La prostitution à Paris au XIXe siècle*. Paris: Seuil, 1981.
———. *De la prostitution dans la ville de Paris*. Paris: Ballière, 1857.
Parker, Rozsika. *The Subversive Stitch: Embroidery and the Making of the Feminine*. London: I. B. Tauris, 2010.
Parr, T. "Determinismens konsekventser for moral og religion." *Samtiden* 4 (1893): 369–81.
Patterson, J. G. *A Zola Dictionary*. London: Routledge, 1912.
Pearson, Karl. *The Grammar of Science*. London: Adam and Charles Black, 1900.
Perry, Ralph Barton. *Present Philosophical Tendencies*. New York: Longmans, Green, 1912.
Perry, Thomas Sergeant. "Science and the Imagination." *North American Review* 137, no. 320 (1883): 49–56.
Peters, Wilhelm. *Hvad jeg saa og hvem jeg mødte: Erindinger fra et kunstnerliv*. Kristiania: Gyldendalske, 1914.
Petersen, Emil. "Franske Naturforskere ved Slutningen af det 18de Aarhundrede, III: Cuvier." *Tilskueren* 1 (1884): 708–26.
Peterssen, Eilif. "Christian Krohg og Antwerpenerudstillinge." *Aftenposten*, September 3, 1885.
Pietschker, Carl. *Carl Gussow und der Naturalismus in Deutschland*. Berlin: Mitscher & Röstell, 1898.
Pitt, Alan. "The Irrationalist Liberalism of Hippolyte Taine." *Historical Journal* 41, no. 4 (1998): 1035–53.

Plahter, L. E. "Christian Krohgs 'Albertine i Politilegens Venteværelse': En røntgenundersøkelse." *Kunst og Kultur* (1978): 107–27.
Poincaré, Henri. *The Foundations of Science.* Translated by George Bruce Halstad. Cambridge: Cambridge University Press, 2015.
Pollock, Griselda. "Feminism/Foucault—Surveillance/Sexuality." In *Visual Culture: Images and Interpretations*, edited by Norman Bryson, Michael Ann Holly, and Keith Moxey. Hanover, NH: Wesleyan University Press, 1994.
———. *Vision and Difference: Femininity, Feminism and the Histories of Art.* London: Routledge, 2000.
Ponsonailhe, Charles. *Les artistes scandinaves à Paris.* Paris: Grande Revue/Nilson, 1889.
Popple, Simon. "Photography, Crime and Social Control." *Early Popular Visual Culture* 3, no. 1 (2005): 95–106.
Poulsen, Hanne Kolind, Peter Nørgaard Larsen, and Hans Dam Christensen, eds. *Viljen til det menneskelige: Tekster omkring Julius Lange.* Copenhagen: Museum Tusculanum, 1999.
Poulsson, Vidar. *Frits Thaulow: En internasjonal maler.* Oslo: Labyrinth, 2006.
Pratt, James Bissett. *Naturalism.* New Haven, CT: Yale University Press, 1939.
"The Rafaëlli Exhibition." *Art Amateur*, June 1, 1884.
Raffaëlli, Jean-François. *Catalogue illustré des oeuvres de Jean-François Raffaëlli.* Paris, 1884.
Rajchman, John. "Foucault's Art of Seeing." *October* 44 (1988): 88–117.
Reed, Arden. *Manet, Flaubert, and the Emergence of Modernism.* Cambridge: Cambridge University Press, 2003.
Reff, Theodore. "Degas and the Literature of His Time I." *Burlington Magazine* 112, no. 810 (1970): 586–89.
Renan, Ernest. *L'avenir de la science—pensées de 1848.* Paris: Calmann-Levy, 1890.
Robinson, Marian S. "Zola and Monet: The Poetry of the Railway." *Journal of Modern Literature* 10, no. 1 (1983): 55–70.
Rod, Édouard. "Zola og moralen." *Samtiden* 2 (1892): 148–60.
Rosenberg, Adolf. *Geschichte der Modernen Kunst.* Vol. 3. Leipzig: Verlag von Fr. Wilh. Grunow, 1889.
Rosenblum, Robert. "Fernand Pelez, or The Other Side of the Post-Impressionist Coin." In *Art, the Ape of Nature: Studies in Honor of H. W. Janson*, edited by Moshe Barasch and Lucy Freeman. New York: Harry N. Abrams, 1981.
Rubin, James Henry. *Realism and Social Vision in Courbet and Proudhon.* Princeton, NJ: Princeton University Press, 1980.
Röhrl, Boris. *Kunsttheorie des Naturalismus und Realismus: Historiche Entwicklung, Terminologie und Definitionen.* Hildesheim: Georg Olms, 2003.
Röstorp, Vibeke. *Le mythe du retour: Les artistes scandinaves en France de 1889 à 1908.* Stockholm: Stockholm Universitets Förlag, 2013.
Saabye, Marianne. "Krøyer and Bastien-Lepage." In *Krøyer: An International Perspective.* Skagen: Skagens Museum, 2011.
Sainte-Beuve, C.-A. *Causeries du Lundi.* Vol. 13. Paris: Garnier, n.d.
"Salon de 1882." *Courrier de l'art*, June 15, 1882.
"Salon de 1882." *Paris moderne: Revue littéraire et artistique* 1 (1881–82): 1–8. Reprinted in *Paris moderne: Revue littéraire et artistique* 2 (1882–83): 101–8.
Savile, Anthony. "Naturalism and the Aesthetic." *British Journal of Aesthetics* 40, no. 1 (2000): 46–63.
Schiøtz, Aina. *Folkets helse—landets styrke 1850–2003.* Oslo: Universitetsforlaget, 2003.

———. “Prostitusjonen i Kristiania ca. 1870–1890: En sosialhistorisk undersøkelse.” Master’s thesis, University of Oslo, 1977.
Schmoll gen. Eisenwerth, Adolf J. *Epochengrenzen und Kontinuität: Studien zur Kunstgeschichte.* Munich: Prestel, 1985.
Schwartz, Walter. *Malere ved Staffeliet.* Copenhagen: Gyldendalske, 1941.
Sekula, Allan. “The Body and the Archive.” *October* 39 (1986): 3–64.
Sellars, Roy Wood. *Evolutionary Naturalism.* Chicago: Open Court, 1922.
Seys, Pascale. *Hippolyte Taine et l’avènement du naturalisme: Un intellectuel sous le Second Empire.* Paris: L’Harmattan, 1999.
Sheon, Aaron. “Parisian Social Statistics: Gavarni, ‘Le Diable à Paris,’ and Early Realism.” *Art Journal* 44, no. 2 (1984): 139–48.
Shideler, Ross. *Questioning the Father: From Darwin to Zola, Ibsen, Strindberg, and Hardy.* Stanford, CA: Stanford University Press, 1999.
Shiff, Richard. *Cézanne and the End of Impressionism.* Chicago: University of Chicago Press, 1984.
Sjåstad, Øystein. “Absorbert og teatralt i Christian Krohgs og Edvard Munchs kunst.” *Kunst og Kultur* 93, no. 3 (2010): 172–79.
———. “Blikkene i politilegens venteværelse.” *Kunst og Kultur* 95, no. 3 (2012): 153–63.
———. *Christian Krohg: Fra Paris til Kristiania.* Oslo: Labyrinth, 2012.
———. “Christian Krohgs maleklatt: *Tache* som motiv i modernismen.” *Kunst og Kultur* 92, no. 3 (2009): 174–83.
Skram, Amalie. *Samlede verker.* Vol. 7. Oslo: Gyldendal, 1993.
Skredsvig, Christian. *Dager og netter blandt kunstnere.* Oslo: Andresen og Butenschøn, 2010.
Skålevåg, Svein Atle. “Kjønnsforbrytelser: Sedelighet, seksualitet og strafferett 1880–1930.” *Tidsskrift for kjønnsforskning* 33, nos. 1–2 (2009): 7–27.
Sprinchorn, Evert. “Ibsen and the Immoralists.” *Comparative Literature Studies* 9, no. 1 (1972): 58–79.
———. “The Transition from Naturalism to Symbolism in the Theatre from 1880 to 1900.” *Art Journal* 45, no. 2 (1985): 113–19.
St-Cère, Jacques [Armand Rosenthal]. “La polygamie en Scandinavie.” *Le Figaro*, January 11, 1888.
Stoeckius, Alfred. “Naturalism in the Recent German Drama.” PhD diss., Columbia University, 1903.
Strindberg, August. *August Strindbergs Samlade Verk.* Vol. 27. Stockholm: Almqvist & Wiksell, 1984.
Strömbom, Sixten. *Konstnärsförbundets historia.* Vol. 1. Stockholm: Bonnier, 1945.
“Svar til Christian Krohg.” *Kunstbladet* 1, no. 15 (1888): 184–87.
Sørensen, Øystein. *1880-årene: Ti år som rystet Norge.* Oslo: Universitetsforlaget, 1984.
Taine, Hippolyte. *Histoire de la littérature anglaise.* Vol. 1. Paris: Hachette, 1863. Translated by H. Van Laun as *History of English Literature* (New York: American Book Exchange, 1880).
———. *De l’idéal dans l’art.* Paris: Baillière, 1867. Translated by J. Durand as *The Ideal in Art* (New York: Henry Holt, 1874).
———. *De l’intelligence.* Vol. 2. Paris: Hachette, 1870. Translated by T. D. Haye as *On Intelligence*, vol. 2 (New York: Henry Holt, 1875).
———. *Les philosophes classiques de XIXe siècle en France.* Paris: Hachette, 1905.
———. *Philosophie de l’art.* Vol. 1. Paris: Hachette, 1895. The first part translated by John Durand as *The Philosophy of Art* (New York: Holt and Williams, 1873).

———. *Philosophie de l'art dans les Pays-Bas*. Paris: Germer Baillière, 1869. Translated by J. Durand as *The Philosophy of Art: Art in the Netherlands* (New York: Leypoldt and Holt, 1871).

———. *Sa vie et sa correspondance*. Vol. 2, *1853–1870*. Paris: Hachette, 1904. Translated by R. L. Devonshire as *Life and Letters of H. Taine, 1853–1870* (Westminster: Archibald Constable, 1904).

———. *Sa vie et sa correspondance*. Vol. 4, *1876–1893*. Paris: Hachette, 1907. Partially translated by E. Sparvel-Bayly as *Life and Letters of H. Taine, 1870–1892* (London: Archibald Constable, 1908).

Taxil, Léo. *La prostitution contemporaine*. Paris: Librairie Populaire, 1884.

Thaulow, Alexandra. *Mens Frits Thaulow Malte*. Oslo: Gyldendal, 1929.

Thaulow, Frits. *I Kamp og i Fest*. Kristiania: Gyldendalske, 1908.

Theuriet, André. *Jules Bastien-Lepage and His Art: A Memoir*. London: T. Fisher Unwin and Macmillan, 1892.

Thiis, Jens. *Norske malere og billedhuggere*. Bergen: John Griegs Forlag, 1904.

Thomson, Richard. *Art of the Actual: Naturalism and Style in Early Third Republic France, 1880–1900*. New Haven, CT: Yale University Press, 2012.

Thue, Oscar. "Fra Albertine-striden." *Samtiden* 65 (1956): 662–70.

———. *Christian Krohg*. Oslo: Aschehoug, 1997.

———. "Christian Krohgs sosiale tendenskunst." Magister Degree diss., University of Oslo, 1955.

T.J. [pseud.]. "Exposition Universelle des Beaux-Arts d'Anvers." *Courrier de l'art* 5 (1885): 359–61.

Todts, Herwig, Dorine Cardyn-Oomen, and Nathalie Monteyne, eds. *Tranches de vie: Le naturalisme en Europe 1875–1915*. Antwerp: Musée Royale des Beaux-Arts d'Anvers and Ludion, 1996.

Turner, Bryan S. *The Body and Society: Explorations in Social Theory*. London: Sage, 1996.

Uitert, Evert van. "Vincent van Gogh and Paul Gauguin in Competition: Vincent's Original Contribution." *Simiolus: Netherlands Quarterly for the History of Art* 11, no. 2 (1980): 81–106.

Usselmann, Henri. "Complexité et importance des contacts des peintres nordiques avec l'impressionnisme." PhD diss., University of Gothenburg, 1979.

Ustvedt, Øystein. "The Story of a Masterpiece." In *Edvard Munch: Det syke barn / The Sick Child*, edited by Øystein Ustvedt and Trond E. Aslaksby. Oslo: Nasjonalmuseet for Kunst, Arkitektur og Design, 2009.

Varnedoe, Kirk. "Christian Krohg and Edvard Munch." *Arts Magazine* 53, no. 8 (1979): 88–95.

———. *Gustave Caillebotte*. New Haven, CT: Yale University Press, 2000.

———. *Northern Light: Realism and Symbolism in Scandinavian Painting 1880–1920*. New York: Brooklyn Museum, 1982.

Vedel, Valdemar. "Émile Zola." *Tilskueren* 3 (1886): 528–48.

———. "Om Nydannelse i Tidens Aandsliv." *Tilskueren* 9 (1892): 273–91.

Véron, Eugène. *L'esthétique*. Paris: Vrin, 2007. Translated by W. H. Armstrong as *Æsthetics* (London: Chapman and Hall, 1879).

Vibe, Johan. *Nogle Bemærkninger i Anledning af Naturalismen*. Kristiania: Malling, 1884.

Virtanen, Reino. *Claude Bernard and His Place in the History of Ideas*. Lincoln: University of Nebraska Press, 1960.

Vollard, Ambroise. "Cezanne and Zola." *Soil* 1, no. 1 (1916): 13–14.

Voss, Knud. *Skagensmalerne*. Oslo: Grøndahl og Dreyer, 1996.

Walker, Philip. "The Mirror, the Window, and the Eye in Zola's Fiction." *Yale French Studies* 42 (1969): 52–67.
Walkowitz, Judith R. *Prostitution and Victorian Society: Women, Class, and the State.* Cambridge: Cambridge University Press, 1989.
Waller, John. "'The Illusion of an Explanation': The Concept of Hereditary Disease, 1770–1870." *Journal of the History of Medicine and Allied Sciences* 57, no. 4 (2002): 410–48.
Weingarden, Lauren S. "Imaging and Imagining the French Peasant: Gustave Courbet and Rural *Physiologies.*" *Nineteenth Century Art Worldwide* 12, no. 1 (2013): n.p.
Weinstein, Leo. *Hippolyte Taine.* New York: Twayne, 1972.
Weisberg, Gabriel P. *Beyond Impressionism: The Naturalist Impulse.* New York: Harry N. Abrams, 1992.
———. *The Realist Tradition: French Painting and Drawing 1830–1900.* Cleveland: Cleveland Museum of Art and Indiana University Press, 1980.
———. "The Traditional Realism of François Bonvin." *Bulletin of the Cleveland Museum of Art* 65, no. 9 (1978): 281–98.
Weisberg, Gabriel P., David Jackson, and Willa Z. Silverman, eds. *Illusion of Reality: Naturalist Painting, Photography, Theatre and Cinema, 1875–1918.* Amsterdam: Van Gogh Museum, 2010.
Wellek, René. "Hippolyte Taine's Literary Theory and Criticism." *Criticism* 1, no. 1 (1959): 1–18.
Wells, B. W. "Zola and Literary Naturalism." *Sewanee Review* 1, no. 4 (1893): 385–401.
Werenskiold, Erik. "Christian Krohg." *Samtiden* 36 (1925): 529–33.
———. *Kunst—Kamp—Kultur.* Kristiania: Cammermeyer, 1917.
Wiarda, Rein. *Taine et la Hollande.* Paris: Droz, 1938.
Wichstrøm, Anne. "Det intime portrettet: Christian Krohgs portrett av Oda Engelhart, 1888." *En face* 1 (2003): 28–35.
———. *Kvinneliv, Kunstnerliv: Kvinnelige malere i Norge før 1900.* Oslo: Gyldendal, 2000.
Wilkens, Claudius. "Moderne Naturalisme." *Tilskueren* 5 (1888): 490–515.
———. *Æsthetik i Omrids: Med særlight Hensyn til Moderne Æsthetik.* Copenhagen: Gyldendalske, 1888.
Williams, Henry Smith. *A History of Science.* Vol. 4. New York: Harper, 1904.
Williams, Raymond. *Drama from Ibsen to Brecht.* London: Chatto and Windus, 1971.
———. *Keywords: A Vocabulary of Culture and Society.* London: Fontana, 1990.
———. "A Lecture on Realism." *Afterall Journal* 5 (Spring/Summer, 2002).
———. *The Long Revolution.* London: Chatto and Windus, 1961.
———. *Politics of Modernism.* London: Verso, 2007.
Wolfenstein, Martha. "The Social Background of Taine's Philosophy of Art." *Journal of the History of Ideas* 5, no. 3 (1944): 332–58.
Wolff, Janet. "The Invisible *Flâneuse*: Women and the Literature of Modernity." *Theory, Culture & Society* 2, no. 3 (1985): 37–46.
Wyzewa, Téodor de. "Nietsche i Frankrige." *Samtiden* 3 (1892): 10–22.
Young, Marnin. "Heroic Indolence: Realism and the Politics of Time in Raffaëlli's *Absinth Drinkers.*" *Art Bulletin* 90, no. 2 (2008): 235–59.
———. "The Motionless Look of a Painting: Jules Bastien-Lepage, *Les Foins*, and the End of Realism." *Art History* 37, no. 1 (2014): 38–67.
———. *Realism in the Age of Impressionism: Painting and Politics of Time.* New Haven, CT: Yale University Press, 2015.

Zola, Émile. *The Beast in Man.* Translated by R. G. Goodyear and P. J. R. Wright. London: Neil Mentor, 1975.
———. *The Belly of Paris.* Translated by Brian Nelson. Oxford: Oxford University Press, 2009.
———. *Le docteur Pascal.* Paris: Charpentier, 1893.
———. *Écrits sur l'art.* Paris: Gallimard, 1991.
———. *The Fortune of the Rougons.* Translated by Brian Nelson. Oxford: Oxford University Press, 2012.
———. "From Naturalism in the Theatre." Translated by Albert Bermel. In *The Theory of the Modern Stage*, edited by Eric Bentley. London: Penguin, 1992.
———. *The Kill.* Translated by Arthur Goldhammer. New York: Modern Library, 2005.
———. *Ladies' Delight.* Translated by April Fitzlyon. London: Oneworld Classics, 2008.
———. *Nana.* Paris: Charpentier, 1893. Translated by George Holden as *Nana* (London: Penguin, 1972).
———. *Le roman expérimental.* Paris: Charpentier, 1880. Translated by Belle M. Sherman as *The Experimental Novel and Other Essays* (New York: Haskell, 1964).
———. *Thérèse Raquin.* Translated by L. W. Tancock. Harmondsworth: Penguin, 1968.
"Øjebliksfotografier." *Dagbladet*, March 24, 1885.
Østby, Leif. *Fra Naturalisme til Nyromantikk.* Oslo: Gyldendal, 1934.

Index

Page references followed by italicized *fig.* indicate illustrations or material contained in their captions. Color plates are indicated by a bold **pl.**